The Burry
Gwendreath Valley Railway
and its Antecedent Canals
Volume Two: The Railway and Dock

by
R.W. Miller

THE OAKWOOD PRESS

© Oakwood Press & R.W. Miller 2009

British Library Cataloguing in Publication Data
A Record for this book is available from the British Library
ISBN 978 0 85361 685 6

Typeset by Oakwood Graphics.
Repro by PKmediaworks, Cranborne, Dorset.
Printed by Cambrian Printers, Aberystwyth, Ceredigion.

Title page: The seal of the BP&GV Railway Company 1866.   *Author*

Front cover: A loaded coal train for Burry Port approaching Craiglon bridge on 15th June, 1983 hauled by three locomotives, class '03s' Nos. 03141, 03145 and 03152. This was a common practice at that time.   *Tom Heavyside*

Rear cover, top: A coal train from Cwmmawr nearing Kidwelly Junction hauled by a '1600' class pannier tank in August 1965, just two months before the end of steam working over the line. The River Gwendraeth Fawr is in the left foreground.   *R.E. Bowen*

Rear cover, bottom: A '1600' class 0-6-0PT and brake van relax between duties outside the Burry Port engine shed on 16th July, 1965. The shed had ceased to be used from March 1962.   *R.E. Bowen*

Published by The Oakwood Press (Usk), P.O. Box 13, Usk, Mon., NP15 1YS.
E-mail: sales@oakwoodpress.co.uk
Website: www.oakwoodpress.co.uk

Contents

Introduction 5

Chapter One   Converting Canal To Railway, 1865-1869 7

Chapter Two   The Struggle To Survive, 1870-1896 33

Chapter Three   Prosperity At Last, 1897-1908 59

Chapter Four   The Light Railway Years, 1909-1921 76

Chapter Five   Burry Port Dock & Harbour, 1832-1940 109

Chapter Six   Up and Down the Line 143

Chapter Seven   The Industrial Connections 187

Chapter Eight   Motive Power...225

Chapter Nine   Carriages, Wagons and Train Services........................280

Chapter Ten   From Grouping to the End, 1922-1998 307

Appendix One   Half-Yearly Dividends, 1899-1922 334

Appendix Two   Principal Shareholdings, 1st July, 1922 335

Appendix Three   Chairmen, Directors and Officers 1866-1922..............336

Appendix Four   Log of Journey 1951 338

Appendix Five   Trials with Locomotive *Mountaineer*,

                  20th June, 1870...339

Appendix Six   Working Collieries in 1884, 1896, 1909 and 1923 340

                  Sources and Bibliography 341

                  Index...343

No. 7 *Pembrey* on the 6.00 pm from Burry Port has just exchanged tokens with the signalman at the Dock Junction box and is coasting (hence the drifting smoke) into the reverse curves under bridges 1 and 2.   *LCGB Ken Nunn Collection 2209*

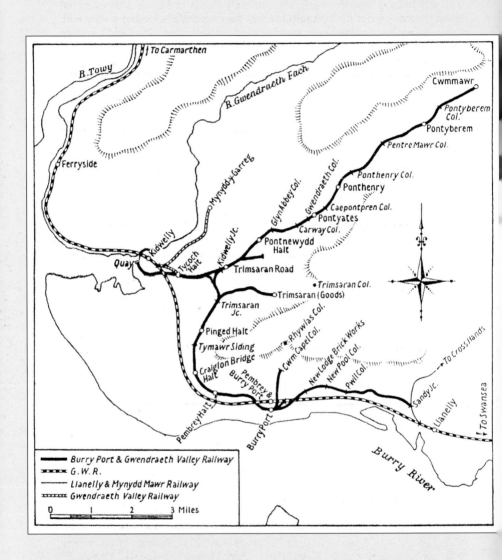

Introduction

It was Raymond Bowen who proposed to divide this book into two volumes, the first devoted to the canals and early tramroads and this second part dealing with the railway and the dock. His untimely death in March 2000 occurred when his manuscript for Volume One was nearing completion but a start with Volume Two had not then been made. Fortunately his close friend and associate Martin Connop Price was able to step into the breach and complete the first part to enable its publication the following year.

Somehow it seemed natural to assume that Martin would carry on and produce Volume Two, even though Ray had not completed all the research required. Accordingly, Martin set about collecting more material and undertaking further research of his own before he reluctantly had to give up the project due to the pressure of his many other commitments. The result is that when I came to take over the reins I found that, whilst no text had been written, an enormous amount of the preparatory work had been done for me. Ray's widow Sylvia freely allowed all of his notes and papers, including those concerned with the canals, to be passed to me and Martin similarly unloaded a vast amount of material that he had accumulated.

As a result the amount of research I have undertaken myself is much smaller than would otherwise have been required. Of course the words are all mine, as is the selection of what to include and what to omit. One problem, which concerns all authors writing in English about times past is how to present Welsh place names. I have elected to use the Anglicised spellings that were current to the period being discussed, the more correct British forms being restricted to the treatment of more recent events. To use other than the old spellings would make it more difficult for researchers to align the text with then current newspaper accounts, maps, timetables and the like.

For background information I have found John A. Nicholson's four volume history of *Pembrey & Burry Port* invaluable. Book One *Aspects of their History* and Book Two *A Historical Miscellany* were published by Llanelli Borough Council in 1993-94, whilst Book Three *Further Historical Glimpses* and Book Four *Some Historical Events & Recollections* were produced by Carmarthenshire County Council in 1996 and 1994. However, I would particularly like to thank the staffs of the Public Record Office (now the National Archives), Kew; the Library at the National Railway Museum, York; the County Record Office (now Archives), Carmarthen, the Llanelli Public Library, the records of the Industrial Locomotive Society, of which I am a long time member, and the Locomotive Club of Great Britain for the use of photographs from the Ken Nunn Collection.

Individuals, of whom a few have unfortunately not survived to see publication, but whom I would particularly like to thank are Richard M. Casserley for his photographs and those of his late father Henry C. Casserley, Alun & Marina Clement of Harbour House, Burry Port (the former General Manager's home), Brian and Lorna Cripps of Burry Port, Emlyn Davies, whose wife was brought up in Burry Port, Glyn Davies, Richard J. Doran, V. Emmanuel, Michael Hale and Tom Heavyside who all supplied photographs and information, Hermas Nicholas, formerly Deputy Chief Inspector of Mines and a native of the Gwendraeth Valley, Terry Powell, Mrs Thelma Rees of Ponthenri who travelled a great deal on the train in her younger days, the late

Richard C. Riley, Richard Rowlands of Llanelli who, as a boy, travelled daily by train in the Gwendraeth Valley to and from school, Richard Oldfield, John Ryan and John Sykes whom I count as personal friends of long standing, Stuart Thomas of Ferryside, Chairman of the Gwendraeth Valley Railway Society and whose grandfather started with the Locomotive Department of the Burry Port & Gwendreath Valley Railway (BP&GV) in 1916, progressing to driver, and Donald Williams the Pontyberem historian who has in 2007 been awarded his BA at the age of 83.

In addition I would like to thank all those not named but who have helped Martin Connop Price and Raymond E. Bowen in the past. Martin himself has given every encouragement and gently but consistently prodded me along towards completion. Finally, whilst my interpretations of events may be somewhat different from that originally envisaged by Raymond, I do trust that the result of all this tremendous help has combined to produce a worthy monument to Ray's lifetime interest, without which this task would never have been started.

R.W. Miller
February 2009

The terminus at Cwmmawr on 8th July, 1950 with No. 1609 waiting to leave with a train of two bogie carriages.   *C.H.A. Townley*

Chapter One

Converting Canal to Railway,
1865-1869

There are two Gwendraeth Rivers and thus two Gwendraeth Valleys, the Gwendraeth Fach or Little Gwendraeth and the Gwendraeth Fawr or Big Gwendraeth; it is the latter that really concerns us. This river has its source at Llyn Llech Owain just 1½ miles north of Cross Hands and flows south-westward to reach tidal waters south of Kidwelly (now Cydweli). The valley is not deep and steep-sided like the typical Glamorganshire valleys, but is much shallower and more gentle, and soon broadens out as the coast gets nearer. The Little Gwendraeth runs largely parallel to its neighbour, keeping about two to three miles distant to the north before turning south to flow through Cydweli and join the estuary of the Gwendraeth Fawr and onwards into Carmarthen Bay. It is here, especially on the south side of the estuary at low tide, that the dramatic expanse of shimmering white sands is to be seen. Indeed, Gwendraeth translates into English as white sands or white shore.

The Kidwelly & Llanelly canal which, as detailed in Volume One had in 1865 at last taken the decision to convert itself into a railway, traversed the valley from Cwmmawr along the south side of the Gwendraeth Fawr River (as most of the coal pits lay on this flank) then crossed over to the north side near Glyn Abbey and ended up at Kymer's Quay on the tidal estuary of the Gwendraeth Fach about ¾ mile west of the town of Kidwelly. Due to the silting of the estuary, the quay and thus the lower portion of the canal became little used; instead from a junction near Tycoch the main canal struck off to the south, back over the Gwendraeth Fawr and, keeping to the eastern edge of the Pinged Marshes, arrived at the harbour of Burry Port - a distance of about 12¾ miles from Cwmmawr.

This harbour had opened in 1832 on a section of the foreshore to the east of Pembrey known as Tywyn Bach, and was at first called Pembrey New Harbour. At that time there was hardly even a hamlet at this spot, just a few scattered houses to the south of the village of Achddu and to the east of Pembrey. The name Burry Port was adopted three years later; an Act of 1835 (5 William IV, cap. 11) allowed the New Pembrey Harbour Company to change its name to the Burry Port Company. The Burry River is the wide estuary of the Loughor River and separates Carmarthenshire in the north from the Gower Peninsula to the south. The estuary gets its name from the strong tidal currents and in English means wild water (bur = wild and wy = water). In 1961 the local Urban District Council decided that a Welsh version of the name Burry Port was required and settled on Porth Tywyn, a nice mixture of the pre- and post-1835 versions. Incidentally, the area known as Tywyn Mawr is further to the north-west beyond the airfield, on the south side of the Gwendraeth estuary. On the stretch of coastline between Tywyn Mawr (Big Marsh) and Tywyn Bach (Little Marsh) lies the Cefn Sidan Sands, on which many a ship has been stranded and, in earlier years, cruelly plundered.

Burry Port in the 19th century was part of the Parish of Pembrey, which also included the districts of Pwll and Trimsaran. The name Pembrey (formerly

Commercial postcard view of Burry Port *circa* 1912 with the outer harbour clearly visible in the centre, the Pembrey Copper Works chimney on the left and that of the Ashburnham Tinplate Works on the right.   *R.E. Bowen Collection*

A postcard published about 1906 by Charlie Snook, the local newsagent and photographer, with the Dockmaster's Office (the former reading room) on the left, then continuing right after the mast can be seen the lighthouse (in the distance), the Coastguard station, the Harbour View Hotel, the coastguard's houses (three-storey, with the six chimney stacks) and finally on the extreme right the BP&GV Harbour Offices.   *Brian Cripps Collection*

Coastguard Station and Harbour Offices, Burry Port.

Penbré) approximates in English to little end of the hill (from pen = head or end of the hill and bre = promontory or little hill). The population of the whole Parish was 1,528 in 1811, 2,850 in 1841 (then with only about 350 in Burry Port), 4,145 in 1861 (about 1,550 in Burry Port) and 5,590 in 1881 At this latter date the total included 712 for Pwll, 783 in Trimsaran, 1,109 in Pembrey itself and 2,986 in Burry Port so that this new town had by then grown to almost three times the size of its parent village - Pembrey. Of the 2,986 population some 2,097 (70 per cent) had been born in the Parish, 819 in other parts of Wales and only 70 outside Wales. The rapid rise in the population was accompanied by a similar increase in the number of houses. It is interesting to note that the Burry Port, Pembrey & Gwendraeth Valleys Building Society was founded in 1875 and that after six years it had 52 members and assets of £2,987.

There were 618 occupied houses in 1881 and in the majority Welsh was the first language. In the 1891 census, when 3,479 were living in Burry Port (6,444 in the entire parish), the language spoken by all except infants was recorded, showing that less than half of the population could then speak English, the actual totals and percentages being:

Welsh only	1,755	52·8%
English only	430	12·9%
Both languages	1,139	34·3%

Of these 3,479 including the infants, some 2,521 were born in the parish, 765 elsewhere in Wales, 168 in England, 19 in Scotland, four in Ireland and one each in France and Denmark. These figures exclude the masters and crews of the five ships moored on the night of the census in Burry Port Dock. The 1901 population of Pembrey (including Burry Port) was 7,513 and in 1961 it had risen to 8,013 (5,938 just in Burry Port). The (civil) Parish Council of Burry Port was created in 1894 and became an Urban District in 1899, being absorbed into the enlarged Borough of Llanelli (spelt Llanelly prior to 1966) in 1974. It was not until 1951 that Burry Port became a separate ecclesiastical parish. The old village of Pembrey, prior to 1974, was in the Llanelly Rural District and thus separated politically from Burry Port after 1894.

The Great Western Railway (GWR) had promoted the semi-independent South Wales Railway in 1844 to build a broad gauge (7 ft 0¼ in.) line along the coast through Burry Port. The first locomotive reached Pembrey from Swansea on 21st August, 1852 and the line from Landore to Carmarthen opened for traffic on 11th October, 1852, being leased to and worked by the GWR from the outset; full amalgamation followed on 1st August, 1863. From Landore as far as Pembrey it was double track and then single on to Carmarthen, this section being doubled in February 1853. The Pembrey station was actually in Burry Port, precisely where it remains to this day, but the first intention had been to site it by Cliff Cottage, just west of the Ashburnham Road bridge and much nearer to Pembrey where the original Plant's level crossing stood (Henry Plant was still the crossing keeper in April 1861; the present road bridge is known as Challenor's bridge after a later crossing keeper). The GWR station was renamed Pembrey and Burry Port on 1st February, 1887. By this time the line had been converted to standard gauge. The last broad gauge trains ran in the evening of

One of the five iron tub-boats from the canal which can be seen at low tide at the base of the east breakwater, believed originally to have belonged to the Carway Coal Company.   *R.E. Bowen*

Several sections of the canal were retained in the dock area at Burry Port for use as storage reservoirs. The last portion is seen in this April 1970 view looking east with the locomotive sheds in the distant centre and the stacks of the Carmarthen Bay power station on the right.
R.E. Bowen

Saturday 11th May, 1872. The up line (to Swansea) was converted first and, after engines and stock for the first up trains had been sent west during the night, passenger trains were able to use the single line in both directions on 13th May, 1872; standard gauge goods trains only commencing on the following day, 14th May, 1872, after the down line had been converted.

The full name of the canal company that terminated in Burry Port was the Kidwelly and Llanelly Canal and Tramroad Company, being authorized on 20th June, 1812 (52 Geo. III, cap. 173). Two tramroads (or plateways, believed to be 4 ft 2 in. gauge) were operated with horses by the canal company from Burry Port; one northwards to Cwmcapel and the other eastwards along the old shore line to Sandy where it joined the Stradey Estate tramroad from Cille Colliery to the Carmarthenshire Dock in Llanelly (now Llanelli). A stormy high tide in 1846 breached the line at the Sandy end and was not repaired, so from this time the line from Burry Port terminated at the colliery and brickworks at Pwll. There were also two short branch canals which were extended by tramroads to the collieries at Trimsaran and Carway. These two tramroads were owned by the collieries although that to Carway had originally been built under the aegis of Kymer's canal (*see Volume One*).

The main line of the canal up the Gwendraeth Fawr Valley reached Ponthenry with the aid of three locks having a total rise of just 22 feet (plus a two feet rise at Ty Mawr on the Burry Port section). The continuation to Cwmmawr incorporated inclined planes, the first at Ponthenry with a rise of 57 feet over a length of 750 feet, the second at Capel Ifan (Pontyberem) which rose 56 feet over a 420 feet length, whilst the third at Hiraun Isaf (about a mile from the Cwmmawr terminus) was the biggest and had a rise of 84 feet over an approximate length of 900 feet. The gradients, which would have a particular relevance when the canal was converted to a railway, respectively work out at 1 in 13, 1 in 7½ and 1 in 10¾. By 1865 the top portion of the canal above this last incline seems no longer to have conveyed any traffic, although still required as a water course. Instead, a tramroad was laid along the towpath. Raymond E. Bowen discusses this fully in Volume One.

The canal was not completed until 1837, well into the railway age, and at first the company resisted any attempt to modernise by changing itself into a railway. When the broad gauge main line of seven feet (plus a ¼ in.) of the South Wales Railway was opened as far as Carmarthen in 1852 it crossed the tramroads to Pwll and Cwm Capel on the level, and twice spanned the canal near Pembrey and outside Kidwelly with low bridges. Another broad gauge line, the Carmarthan & Cardigan Railway (C&CR), was formed in 1854 and soon developed ambitious plans which, never receiving sufficient capital, were only partially completed.

One scheme was for a line north-eastwards from Kidwelly up the Gwendraeth Fach Valley to a junction near Llanddarog with another projected line from Carmarthen to the Llanelly Railway's Mountain branch. The powers for these lapsed but in 1864 a Bill was presented to build two branches on the broad or mixed gauge from the GWR at Kidwelly. One, known as the 'Lime Line', went via Mynydd-y-Garreg as far as Limestone Hill, Velindre (near Crwbin) in the Fach Valley; the other, known as the 'Coal Line' ran east to cross

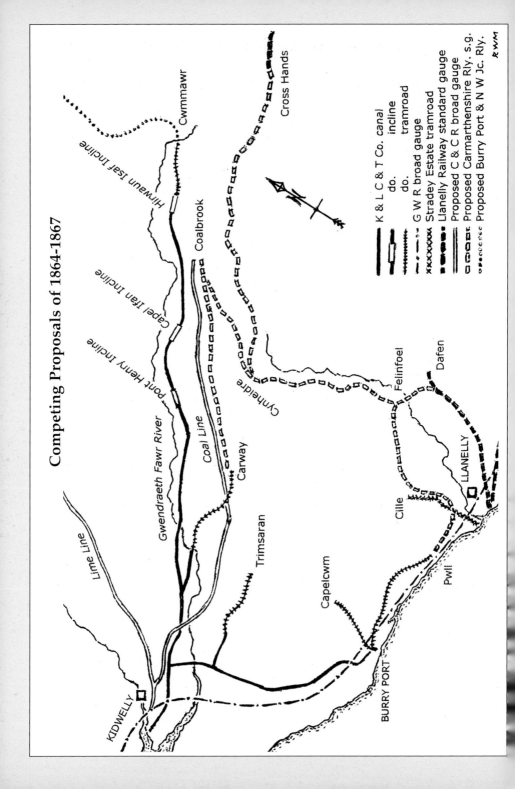

Competing Proposals of 1864-1867

Legend:
- K & L C & T Co. canal
- do. incline
- do. tramroad
- G W R broad gauge
- Stradey Estate tramroad
- Llanelly Railway standard gauge
- Proposed C & C R broad gauge
- Proposed Carmarthenshire Rly. s.g.
- Proposed Burry Port & N W Jc. Rly.

Places:
Cross Hands
Cwmmawr
Hirwaun Isaf incline
Coalbrook
Capel Ifan incline
Pont Henry incline
Gwendraeth Fawr River
Coal Line
Cynheidre
Felinfoel
Dafen
Carway
Lime Line
Trimsaran
Cille
LLANELLY
Pwll
Capelcwm
BURRY PORT
KIDWELLY

R WM

the canal and the river Gwendraeth Fawr near Spudders bridge (Pont Spwdwr) and then curve north-eastwards via the Carway Colliery up the Fawr Valley to Coalbrook (to the south-east of Pontyberem). It might be mentioned that the secretary of the C&CR, Owen Bowen, was the founder in 1858 of the Carway & Duffryn Steam Coal Co. Ltd and was their Company Secretary; he leased the limestone workings at Mynydd-y-Garreg as well.

The 'Coal Line' was thrown out due to the strong opposition of the Kidwelly & Llanelly Canal Company and landowner Lord Dynevor but the 'Lime Line' was approved by the C&CR Act passed on 28th April, 1864 and construction started the following Spring. Undeterred, application was again made to Parliament for the 'Coal Line' and this time met with success, being authorized by the C&CR (Kidwelly Extension) Act of 29th June, 1865. Yet by 1866 the C&CR was hopelessly insolvent and, as as part of the financial solution, the two Kidwelly branches, one up each valley, were transferred to a new company: the Gwendraeth Valleys Railway (GVR), authorized by Act of 30th July, 1866. This new concern duly completed a short length of the 'Lime Line' to Mynydd-y-Garreg and this opened to broad gauge traffic in 1868. Of the 'Coal Line' only some of the formation of the first 500 yards was built and subsequently abandoned. The complex early history of these lines is fully explained in *The Gwendraeth Valleys Railway: Kidwelly to Mynydd-y-Garreg* by M.R.C. Price (Oakwood Press, 1997).

Naturally, this proposed incursion into what was regarded as its own territory considerably alarmed the Kidwelly & Llanelly Canal & Tramroad Company. At the same time it was having to ward off an attack on the other flank. The Carmarthenshire Railway was authorized by an Act of 1864 to convert the four feet (more accurately 4 ft 2 in.) gauge Carmarthenshire Tramroad from Llanelly to Cross Hands - opened in 1804 and now largely abandoned - to the standard gauge and construct a branch from Cynheidre down the hillside to Coalbrook (Pontyberem) and, with a reversal, on to the Carway Colliery.

At last the canal company was panicked into taking some action. Advertisements were placed calling on shareholders to attend an Extraordinary Meeting and the belated decision was taken to apply to Parliament to approve the conversion of its own canals and tramroads into a railway. This was done and the Act (28 & 29 Vict. cap. 218) was signed on 5th July, 1865. The canal company was to change its name to The Kidwelly & Burry Port Railway Company (K&BPR) with powers to absorb the Kymer's canal (which it managed) and to, 'fill up, stop up, and discontinue the Use or Maintenance of all or any Part of the Canals … as may be required'.

In all 18½ miles of new railways were authorized:

1. From the inner harbour at Burry Port to a junction with the Mountain Branch of the Llanelly Railway in the Parish of Llanarthney.
2. From No. 1 in the Parish of Llanon to Cross Hands Colliery.
3. From No. 1 to the Kidwelly Quay at the end of the canal of the Company.
4. From No. 1 near the Aqueduct [over the Gwendraeth Fawr River] and terminating at the shipping stage where the branch canal joins the site of the old Trimsaran Tramway.
5. From No. 1 near Morpha [Morfa] Bach and terminating at the shipping stage where the branch canal joins the railway leading to Carway Colliery.

Three years were allowed for completion and the capital was to be £120,000 in shares and £18,000 in loans. Of the shares £72,400 represented the old canal company property and £47,600 was allowed for the new works. Note that there was no provision in the Act to convert the two tramroads from Burry Port to Cwm Capel and Pwll. The canal property was grossly over-valued at £72,400 and this payment was to become the company's millstone for the next 34 years.

The Directors of the new company in 1866 were all English industrial financiers. G.H. Charles Cancellor of 7 Tokenhouse Yard, EC was Chairman and the others were Christopher Robert Pemberton of Newton, Cambridge, Lt-Gen. George Alexander Malcolm CB of 67 Sloane Street, SW (he also resided at Gwendraeth House in Burry Port from 1870 to 1888), Wadham Locke Sutton of Great Berkhampstead, Herts, and solicitor George F.P. Sutton of 80 Coleman Street, EC. This latter address was additionally the office address of the Secretary as well as being the railway's head office. The Company Secretary was John James Russell (born in Richmond, Surrey in 1827), appointed in February 1864 as Secretary of both the Kidwelly & Llanelly Canal & Tramroad Co. and the Burry Port Co. (the owner of the dock) with a combined salary of £200 per annum, whilst the Superintendent and Harbourmaster in Burry Port was Captain John Paisley Luckraft RN (born in Cornwall in 1803 and whom we first met in Volume One), appointed by the Burry Port Co. on 23rd March, 1864. His salary was £300 pa plus the use of the house next to the harbour office. He is reputed to have served on HMS *Bellerophon*, launched in 1824 and a member of the Black Sea fleet during the 1854 war with Russia. Other officers soon to be appointed included Sutton & Ommanney as solicitors, John Vaughan & William Taylor as auditors and, perhaps most influential of all, Shelford & Robinson of 7 Westminster Chambers, Victoria Street, SW as engineers.

William Shelford (Sir William from 1904) was born at Lavenham, Sussex in 1834 and died in 1905. The partnership with Henry Robinson (Professor Henry from 1902) dated from 1865. It was Robinson, born in London in 1837 and died in 1915, who seems to have been the more involved with the infant BP&GV railway and it is he who made the detailed survey of the planned route. Most of the Directors, and many of the shareholders, were common to both the new railway and the existing Burry Port company so it was not surprising that the two companies quickly agreed that their positions would be greatly strengthened by amalgamation. A further Act (29 Vict. cap. 5) was obtained on 30th April, 1866 vesting the Burry Port Co. in the K&BPR and changing the name of the enlarged undertaking to the Burry Port & Gwendreath Valley Railway, the harbour company's share and loan capital of £85,000 being added to that of the K&BPR.

Not for the first time the English legislators showed a complete lack of respect for Welsh spelling. The 1766 Kymer's Canal Act had used the spelling Gwendreath and it was repeated in the 1865 Kidwelly & Burry Port Railway Act. The mistake does not seem to have been noticed for almost two years; it was on 13th March, 1868 that the Company Secretary wrote from his London office to Captain Luckraft that,

> I was given to understand, when I pointed out that the word 'Gwendraeth' was spelt incorrectly, that it was too late to alter it, but I will refer the question to the Solicitor when I see him.

It is believed that it was Luckraft who was largely responsible for the initial drafting of the 1866 Act. It still seems extraordinary that it was deemed too late to alter the spelling in the 60 days remaining before the new Bill going through Parliament, which was applying for an extension of time to 1st August, 1871 to complete the works, was passed. This Act (31-32 Vict. cap. 1) received the Royal Assent on 29th May, 1868 and thus perpetuated the wrongly spelt name of the company as The Burry Port & Gwendreath Valley Railway. Despite further Acts obtained by the Railway in 1871, 1872, 1874, 1877, 1890 and 1891 it was never subsequently changed; presumably it was thought to be of little importance. The raising of further capital was also authorized in the 1868 Act; £18,000 by the issue of 5 per cent first preferential shares and the issue of mortgages also totalling £18,000 bearing an interest rate of 6 per cent per annum.

Company Secretary John Russell attempted to explain the financial position in a letter to the Reverend R. Lawson, the Rector of Upton on Severn, dated 25th November, 1868:

> The Company's total debenture issue could be £33,000, but at present the total to be raised is £18,000. This sum with the preference shares will complete the line the whole length of the late canal from which a gross revenue of £5,000 and upwards was collected. The £18,000 debenture or mortgage (after a £10,000 £5 per cent mortgage the only debt of the Company) is the first charge on the profits of the undertaking, and as no canal ever gave way to a railway without considerably increased profits, the debenture property of the Company may be looked upon as of the best description, for without an increase, there would be ample to pay the interest on them.

Quite what the Reverend Lawson thought of this reply is not known but he was suitably impressed to invest no less than £1,000 in this little railway with the big but incorrectly spelt name. However, Russell proved to be a poor prophet when he said that even without an increase there would be ample to pay the interest out of the company's profits.

Another potential shareholder had been told to hold on to his money because it was alleged that one part of the canal would never be cleared of water. Russell obtained specific assurance from the Engineer that the allegation was false in order to make the investor think again. Russell also had to deal with claims made against the new railway, such as that of a man who derived toll income from the use of the canal and believed he would suffer loss in the event of its closure.

An assistant engineer named Douglas got his representative W.D. Llewellyn to claim compensation on 29th April, 1868 following his dismissal. This eventually reached Board level and their decision was conveyed to Llewellyn by Russell on 15th August by first quoting the report given to the Directors by Robinson the Engineer:

> I deny most peremptorily that his services were at all such as he describes them. All the work he did was under distinct instructions from me and fall very far short of what he enumerates ... of course I engaged him on behalf of the Company but he has no reason to suppose, and therefore no right to assert that it was after consulting the Company, and the engagement was not at a year's salary, but a weekly wage of £3. [Russell added that because he was dismissed after the expiration of a fortnight's notice the] Directors decline to entertain your claim for compensation.

In addition John Russell had to devote time and energy to the feverish concerns felt by his Directors about any rival schemes which could be considered hostile. One nervous worry was that the Gwendraeth Valleys Railway might and could re-commence work on their planned 'Coal Line' to Carway at any time. The following passage extracted from a letter sent from Russell to Luckraft on 14th March, 1868 shows the anxiety felt, even to gossip:

> Mr Holden (Contractor for the Gwendraeth Valleys Railway) has raised £15,000 and is going to commence at once the construction of a line 4½ miles in length to some place unknown, supposed to be to complete the 'Lime Line' - or do you suppose to Carway? Have you heard anything about it? He is to be the Chairman of the Company.

Like so much gossip it was not entirely correct and well out of date! Howard A. Holden had been at work for much of 1865 (for the broad gauge Carmarthan & Cardigan Railway, not the GVR) but was given formal notice of the termination of his contract on 7th October, 1865 and no further work on the 'Coal Line' was ever attempted. The company of which he was to be Chairman was the Kidwelly Railway, Lime and Colliery Co., formed in September 1869 and dissolved (after only a very few shares were taken up) in July 1870.

More tangible was the proposal put forward in the Autumn of 1867 by the standard gauge Llanelly Railway for a connection to be made with the Pwll tramroad of the BP&GV. The idea was that the Carmarthenshire Railway scheme of 1864 should be resurrected in modified form by extending the Llanelly Railway's Dafen (St Davids) branch to Felin Foel and from there continue over the closed Carmarthenshire Tramroad to Cross Hands; there was to be a branch from Felin Foel to Sandy and then over the abandoned BP&GV tramroad route to Pwll. There was no mention of that other controversial branch from Cynheidre to Carway.

Accordingly, Richard Glascodine (the Secretary of the Llanelly Co.) approached John Russell to discuss the possibility of there being a connection between the two companies at Pwll. This was reported to the BP&GV Board who decided that, 'it would be valuable to have a direct connection with the Stradey Estate Railway before joining the Llanelly Railway at or near the station at Llanelly'.

Clearly a junction at Pwll was not going to be entertained, but one at Sandy (sometimes called Sandygate) was a different matter. Negotiations ensued and various terms and conditions were put forward for discussion and, in November 1867, it seemed that agreement was getting close. However, when C.W. Mansel Lewis, the owner of the Stradey Estate, was brought into the picture, he was not at all enthusiastic. Perhaps he was worried that the proposals could have an inverse impact on the traffic and profitability of his own line. Again Russell confided in Captain Luckraft:

> The Llanelly junction rather hangs fire. Mr. Lewis and the Llanelly directors have not yet come to terms, but I hope soon to hear of a satisfactory arrangement. Until the Llanelly Company have settled their part of the business with Mr. Lewis the Company cannot move more in the matter than it has done and that has been so far so good.

If Russell sounded slightly optimistic that agreement would eventually be reached then he was mistaken. After some delay the negotiations fizzled out and the proposal was quietly dropped. It was to be many years later before the old tramroad route to Cross Hands was at last to be largely used by a new Company, the Llanelly & Mynydd Mawr Railway, which opened to traffic in July 1881. Meanwhile, by the Autumn of 1868, work on building the BP&GV main line was at last under way.

A payment of £4,576 9s. 11d. was made on 30th September, 1868 for a supply of sleepers. Then in the six months period ending 31st December, 1868 £2,000 was received for sleepers sold to the contractor with a further £500 for sleepers sold to the contractor during the following half-year. There seems no obvious explanation for the contractor paying the railway for sleepers needed for its construction; perhaps they were required for another purpose or was there some sort of contra account involved?

The Directors' half-yearly Report to the Shareholders for the six months ending on 31st December, 1868 states that since the last ordinary meeting (meaning 30th June although the meeting was held on 26th August, 1868) 'a contract has been entered into with a highly respectable contractor' to build the 10 miles 60 chains from Burry Port to Pontyberem, together with the branch of about ½ mile to join the Carway Railway, the whole to cost about £33,000 (an average of just under £3,000 per mile). The report continues:

... he has made very considerable progress, and it is believed that the Railway will be opened for public traffic early in April next. Had it not been for the extraordinary wet season, the works would have been completed some time before that period.

The accompanying accounts reveal that three miles owned by the company had been constructed; further that up to the year end the contractor had received £13,030 and between then and 18th February, 1869 another £6,530 had been paid to him. The contractor takes the £18,000 preference shares in payment of the remainder of his contract.

The figures in the company's cash books add up to slightly different amounts with £13,791 13s. 4d. being shown as paid out up to 31st December, 1868 with an additional £6,566 13s. 4d. by 28th February, 1869. The differences are not great but do show that accountancy practices as early as the 1860s had found it was possible to make two and two equal five when the occasion suited them. The figure of £3,000 per mile is, however, a very low amount for the construction of a standard gauge railway. For comparison the single track Newtown & Machynlleth Railway, admittedly built to passenger standards with intermediate stations and involving somewhat heavier earthworks, cost around £10,000 per mile to build in 1859-63.

Captain John Luckraft, the Superintendent and Harbourmaster, before coming to Burry Port had previously been at Havant, Portsmouth and Raymond E. Bowen (author of Volume One) was of the opinion that it was no coincidence that the contractor to be appointed should be Frederick Furniss of Langstone, Havant and York Buildings, Westminster. As the relevant Board Minutes for this period have not survived it is difficult to be certain, but it would appear that competitive tenders were not requested by the Board. The *Llanelly Guardian* for 1st July, 1869, referring to events the previous year, reported that:

> General Malcolm, Mr Sutton, Mr Cancellor and others, with Mr Furniss, banded together determined if possible to carry out the undertaking. Mr Robinson CE was at once requested to make a survey and report.

Nine months earlier the *Carmarthen Journal* for 25th September, 1868 had said much the same:

> Strenuous efforts were made by General Malcolm, Mr Sutton and other Directors which resulted in a complete survey of the undertaking by Mr Henry Robinson CE, a gentleman of considerable practice in railway work. He was accompanied by Mr Fred Furniss, the celebrated contractor and financier, who on receiving the Engineer's report unhesitatingly declared his willingness to make the line, and advanced the whole of the money upon certain conditions, amongst which was included a mortgage upon the property of the old company.

Could it possibly be that Furniss was deliberately 'head-hunted' because of his willingness to be paid in preference shares, or was it simply that he was recommended by Captain Luckraft?

Frederick Furniss was born in Ashford (near Bakewell) in Derbyshire in 1825 and was a cousin of George (who spelt his name Furness), also a railway contractor. After assisting in the building of the West Somerset Railway in 1859-62, Frederick contracted in his own name in 1863 to construct the Hayling Railway in Hampshire. The first portion, from Havant to Langstone, had opened in January 1865 and the line was completed to South Hayling on 17th July, 1867. In addition he was working the trains for the railway company using his own locomotives and carriages, which he continued to do until 31st December, 1871. From 1865 he was busy building the main drainage system for Portsmouth and Southsea, later also for Peterborough. In addition he had been involved with three local railway lines in Essex - all to the east of Colchester - where he had in 1865 replaced William Munro, the original contractor, who left in acrimonious circumstances. Furniss duly completed the Wivenhoe & Brightlingsea Railway on 18th April, 1866 followed by the Tendring Hundred Railway (Wivenhoe to Walton) on 17th May, 1867. However, he was less successful tackling the Mistley, Thorpe & Walton Railway as he was forced to give up the contract soon after when the money ran out leaving the line (from Mistley to Thorpe) unfinished. It never was completed, the railway company being dissolved in 1869 with Furniss being owed £12,000, although a portion of that was recouped from the sale of materials.

The contract to build the BP&GV was dated 9th July, 1868 and contained a clause which stipulated, 'the works shall be completed within eight months after the water is let out of the canals which is to be not later than 15th August, 1868'.

Before then the contractor was to use the canal free of charge for the distribution of his materials and clearly agreement must have been reached with Furniss some time before this date, despite what the report of 31st December, 1868 said to the shareholders. There were to be stage payments to

Furniss on the first day of every month, commencing on 1st September, 1868 and he was:

> ... to be paid at his option in debentures for five or seven years or in debenture stocks of the Company or mortgage bearing interest at the rate of 6% per annum from 1st August 1868 and preference shares of the Company bearing interest at 6% per annum from 1st August 1868 in the proportion of six parts of the amount so certified in debentures or debenture stock or mortgage and five parts in preference shares but the amount of debentures or debenture stock or mortgage to be issued under this provision shall not exceed £18,000 and preference stock not to exceed £15,000. The £18,000 debentures or debenture stock (to be secured by a mortgage if desired) shall forever have priority over the £15,000.

Perhaps the Reverend Lawson of Upton on Severn would like that also to be explained to him! It was further agreed that Captain Luckraft should give three weeks' notice to traders of the canal closure; this was duly given on 22nd July. In the event the canal was actually kept open a week longer, until 22nd August, 1868. Despite this, some water must have been retained in the canal for another month to enable a ceremony (detailed below) to be enacted. In addition the following letter from Russell was sent to Sutton & Ommanney, the company solicitors, on 7th September, 1868:

> On 19th August last the Directors passed the following resolution 'that the necessary steps be taken for selling the boats purchased from the Carway Coal Company as a security for tolls due to the Company in accordance with the agreement'. Will you be good enough as soon as the canal is closed (which will be shortly) to carry out this desire of the Board with the least possible delay.

The BP&GV had been holding on to these boats for over 12 months, since 29th May, 1867, so whilst there was still water available these flat-bottomed iron tub-boats are said to have been brought down to Burry Port and there lifted out whilst it was decided what to do with them. A suggestion that they could be turned into water tanks was rejected. and it would seem that the auction sale of them did not take place until late in 1870; I have not been able to discover if any were sold. I doubt if there were many purchasers forthcoming for boats on a closed canal! Subsequently five (could this be all of them?) were used as part of the defence works at the base of the East Breakwater (east side) at the harbour entrance. The unpaid tolls due to the BP&GV amounted to £429 6s. 4d. and the boats are believed to have cost about £80 each to build.

As iterated in Volume One, Monday 21st September, 1868 was the day set aside for the 'Cutting of the First Sod' ceremony to take place. As a precursor to this event, just after 1.30 pm to the cheers of the vast multitude, Mrs G.F. Stone (assisted by Capt. Luckraft) gracefully drew down the handle to allow the very dirty waters to rush out and clear the canal for the last time. Only then was Mrs Sutton allowed to cut the very first sod with her polished spade, place it in her polished wheelbarrow and in a polished workmanlike manner wheel it for about 30 yards before overturning it. She was followed by Mrs Onslow, Mrs Roderick, Miss Josephine Briggs, Miss Emma Briggs, Miss Rees of Kilymaenllwydd (Pwll) and lastly by General Malcolm, all performing the same duty. They then all returned to the Neptune Hotel for a sumptuous *dejeuner* under the Presidency of General Malcolm, supported by Colonels Stepney and Onslow and Mr Sutton (Vice-Chairman).

Miss Bertha Rees, then aged 18, was tragically to die of tuberculosis the following July; she was the youngest daughter of John Hughes Rees JP and her elder brother Mansel was a local solicitor; three older sisters all died in 1855, two by drowning off Pwll sands and the other of scarlatina. Tragedy also surrounded the two Briggs' sisters, the daughters of Captain Luckcraft's predecessor as Superintendent of Docks and Canals. This was Thomas Briggs, who came from Solihull, and drowned in his Burry Port harbour in 1863 age 52. Emily, his widow and the sisters' mother, lived for only three months after the ceremony, dying in December 1868 aged only 52. Mrs Sutton was the wife of a Director and partner of the company solicitors. Mrs Stone was the wife of colliery proprietor Robert Stone of Trimsaran. The Stepneys, as mentioned in Volume One, were members of a powerful Llanelly entrepreneurial family and owned the Stradey Estate at Sandy. The Onslows, Douglas and Caroline, were both born in Ireland; he was a JP for Carmarthenshire and manager of the Lead Works and New Lodge Colliery for the Burry Port Smelting Co. Ltd of which Astley Thompson of Glyn Abbey (related by marriage) was a Director. This leaves us with only Mrs Roderick not identified; she was probably the wife of Captain Thomas Roderick, Principal Customs Officer at Burry Port, two of whose daughters (Mary Ann and Fanny) had married the Parkes brothers (Alexander and Henry of Birmingham), industrial chemists at the Pembrey Copper Works. Another possibility, although thought to be less likely, is that she was the wife of William Roderick who was Manager of the Llanelly branch of the South Wales District (later the London & Provincial) Bank, with whom the BP&GV had an account, and also a shareholder in the BP&GV.

The Neptune Hotel, which features in the background of many of the photographs taken of the BP&GV station in Burry Port and which still stands, was, 'erected for the accommodation of merchants, masters of vessels and others frequenting the harbour' by the Burry Port company and formally opened on 13th October, 1842. The first licensee was William McKiernon, who also happened to be the Manager and Engineer of the Harbour company, operator of the stone quarry at Cwmcapel and, as detailed in Volume One, had earlier been one of the contractors employed in building the South Wales Railway besides building many houses in the town. He was still in charge of the *Neptune* on 7th April, 1861, but 10 years later William Gwynne was 'mine host'.

Of course, having now closed the canal, it was essential to complete at least part of the railway as quickly as possible as the traders (mostly colliery proprietors, many of them also shareholders in the new railway) would naturally be suffering financially all the while that decent transport was denied them. The first monthly payment (£5,708 6s. 8d.) was made to Frederick Furniss for work done (as certified by the Resident Engineer - A.D. Williams) on 31st October, 1868 so construction had evidently started by early October.

Furniss was clearly anxious that he would receive his monthly shareholding promptly as Russell told him on 26th November, 1868 that, 'If I Receive the Certificate from the Engineer on the 1st or 2nd proximo I will have the shares ready for you on the 4th'.

Then on 2nd December Russell wrote to A.D. Williams,

I beg to acknowledge the receipt of work done and materials purchased during the month ended 30 Novr. I conclude I shall receive your report as to the progress of the works before the Board day which is on the 4th.

Clearly Russell believed in making sure reports were produced on time. It was not only Furniss that received payment in shares; on 7th January, 1869 Russell wrote to Henry Robinson, the Engineer, 'I have forty £10 preference shares ready for you, when it is convenient for you to call for them'.

Judging by the amounts paid there was not a lot of work completed in November, or during March 1869, whilst February was only a little better. The completion forecast for April 1869 came and went. The wet winter caused considerable flooding over the low-lying part of the route, which hampered progress. There was also the failure of the supplier of rails to deliver on time. An agreement had been reached with Robert Dunkin of Llanelly but when it emerged that not a single rail could be rolled in the specified period, the contract was cancelled in May. Over two years later Dunkin was still demanding compensation and the dispute was only ended when he accepted seven second-preference shares in the BP&GV in lieu.

On 2nd December, 1868 the Secretary was writing to Captain Luckraft to inform him that the Board was instructing him,

... to dispose of the iron lying about the incline(s). Mr. Waddle is a purchaser [and] as the Company owe him an account it would [could] be set off but he must pay for what he buys and receive a cheque from [for] the like amount from the Company.

This is not the John Waddell later connected with the Llanelly & Mynydd Mawr Railway as he did not appear on the scene until 1879 (in 1868 he was building the Cleland and Midcalder line of the Caledonian Railway and had just started the Bathgate to Coatbridge section of the North British Railway). No, this was John Robert Waddle, engineer and iron founder, of Salamanca Road, Llanelly. The iron would be the old rails, chairs and rollers on the inclines and a payment of £516 16s. 2d. received on 31st December, 1870 would appear to be for this old iron.

The contractor did not have any exceptionally heavy engineering works to contend with. As far as possible the track was laid on the tow-path but there were some places where this was not possible. At sharp bends in the canal the curve was eased by the track crossing over to the non tow-path side and back again. Sometimes the marshy ground required large quantities of copper slag to be tipped for a firm foundation and in a few places it was necessary to use fascines (long fagotts) in just the same way that Stephenson had over Chat Moss. Under bridges it was decided to use the canal bed in most places, but permission was obtained from the County and Local Boards to substitute level crossings for bridges in five places. Most of the bridges were of timber or iron construction on stone abutments and these were raised by between two and five feet, the beams being jacked up so that the abutments could be raised by using old materials wherever possible.

One of the two locomotives built by Henry Hughes & Co. of Loughborough, the *Lizzie*, used on the construction of the line. *LGRP 18208*

The reverse curves under the GWR main line at bridge 2, looking towards Cwmmawr, on 16th July, 1951. The fields in the background were to be covered with housing during the next few years. *R.J. Doran*

When it came to the stone arch bridges and the Great Western Railway girder bridge at Gorse (later altered to Gors) it was required to lower the old bed of the canal and underpin the abutments before laying the track. Even so the distance from rail level to the underside of the arch was only 11 ft 9 in. and the line at these low points was to suffer in wet seasons from serious flooding problems for the rest of its life. This particularly applied to the GWR, Stanley's and the Pembrey Village bridges. The two canal crossings of the Gwendraeth Fawr River consisted of iron troughs laid over masonry arches (six at Morfa Mawr near Llandyry and a single arch at Pontnewydd, near Glyn Abbey); these had the troughs filled with rubble up to the new trackbed level.

Where the line had to be lowered under the bridges it required short but stiff gradients of up to 1 in 50 down at one side and up the other. The two locks near Ynis Fawr, between Pontnewydd and Pontyates, necessitated short rises at 1 in 68 and 1 in 86 respectively going up the valley. Apart from these the new line was virtually level to just beyond Pontyates but then there was a rise at 1 in 256, steepening to 1 in 110 to replace the third lock. At Ponthenry the upper part of the first incline was dug away to form a cutting so that the new track was laid on a gradient of 1 in 56 at the bottom, 1 in 50 in the middle and 1 in 45 at the top. After this it is level until the Capel Ivan incline is reached. Here the new line took a completely fresh course nearer to the river in order to ease the grade but nevertheless there is still a long pull at 1 in 63, steepening to 1 in 53 and through a deep cutting before rejoining the canal towpath at the incline top at Pontyberem. This cutting was through coal measures and rock and required blasting; some of the material and that from the Ponthenry cutting being suitable for ballast.

At Pontyberem the line passed 'through Mr Watney's colliery (Pontyberem South) with which it will be connected by sidings and the usual screens with tips and shoots' according to the *Carmarthen Journal* of 25th July, 1869, which also says of Pontyates that,

... a siding has been made to enable the coal from Mr Evan's colliery (Glan Gwendraeth) together with the fire bricks ... and coal from Mr Everett's (Ynyshafren) and the Ffoy collieries to be placed on the line. Probably it will be found necessary to have a branch line up the Ynyshafren Valley ... It is contemplated to extend the present line to the two collieries of Dr Norton at Cross Hands and the colliery of Mr B Jones of Groscoch. This line will pass the colliery of the Reverend Parry Thomas of Cwmmawr.

It was to be some time before Cwmmawr was reached and the line was never extended as far as Cross Hands.

The contractor had the use of two new locomotives supplied by Henry Hughes & Co. of Loughborough in 1868. Both were 0-4-0ST (four-wheeled saddle tank) engines with outside cylinders. One, named *Lizzie* (Henry Robinson's fiancée was Elizabeth) was quite small with 12 in. by 20 in. cylinders and 2 ft 9 in. wheels; the other was called *Gwendraeth* and was a more powerful engine with 3 ft 9 in. wheels. It is not certain who owned these two locomotives at first, the contractor or the BP&GV Railway Co., before they came into the company's possession after Furniss had finished his work in 1869. Unfortunately the company's Minute Books (of the Directors' meetings) of this

After a period of wet weather it was not difficult to imagine how the canal might have looked where the line dipped under a bridge, as here at bridge 3 looking east in August 1980.

R.E. Bowen

Looking west from the same bridge in August 1980.   *R.E. Bowen*

time, which might have provided the answer, have not survived and it is not clear from the company's Cash Books who was paid (*further details are given in Chapter Eight*). However, it does seem that the two locomotives were ordered by Robinson, and not by Furniss. Furthermore, on 18th January, 1869 the Secretary had written to Captain Luckraft calling on him to attend the next Board Meeting to discuss traffic arrangements, to discuss the '*hire of locomotives* and the laying of branches [*sic*] to Star Colliery, Trimsaran'. Whilst this probably refers to the two existing locomotives being hired to Furniss, there is a possibility that it could mean that the hire of additional locomotives was going to be discussed. The question as to whether the company should work the traffic or it should be put out to contract also needed to be decided. Apparently Sutton and Pemberton were in favour of them working the line themselves whilst General Malcolm felt it should be contracted out. Note that Furniss was using locomotives he both owned and hired on his contemporary Hayling Railway contract in Hampshire.

The amounts paid for the two BP&GV locomotives, as revealed in the company's Cash Books, call for comment. Some £700 was paid for one, presumably *Lizzie*, but this amount does seem on the low side for a new 12 inch-cylindered engine so perhaps she was indeed second-hand and sold by Furniss after he had finished with her. The payment for the other locomotive, presumably *Gwendraeth*, amounted to £1,050, about the expected price for a slightly larger version, suggesting that this engine will have been purchased new.

The track was very lightly laid with flat-bottomed rails weighing 50 to 60 pounds to the yard and spiked directly to the wooden sleepers. The Directors and the Secretary were still predicting an early completion. On 9th April, 1869 John Russell wrote to Captain Luckraft that the line will be opened in the middle of next month and 'I am to write to the traders to tell of it'. A few days later, on 16th April, he wrote to H. Robinson Esq. of 7 Westminster Chambers informing him that, 'you are authorised by [the] Directors to inform Mr. Furniss that the Company will not avail themselves of the power of his plant if the work be completed by 1st June, 1869'.

In other words, he should clear all his plant by that date. Eventually, the official opening of the railway was fixed for Wednesday 23rd June. Both the *Llanelly Mercury* of 24th June and the *Llanelly Guardian* for 1st July, 1869 state that the BP&GV was opened for mineral traffic on 23rd June, but it would appear that it was chiefly a ceremonial opening that took place that day. A full report appeared in the *Carmarthen Journal* for Friday 25th June, 1869, but differed in some important respects from the previous day's edition of the *Llanelly Mercury*:

> About half past one o'clock a train consisting of a dozen open trucks conveyed a party of about 1250 ladies and gentlemen along the new line and on its way ... the populace cheered lustily.

reported the *Journal*. An average of 104 persons per wagon would pale into insignificance the overcrowding in that infamous Calcutta cell of 1756! The *Mercury* perhaps was nearer the correct figure in quoting 'about 200 of the elite'

At bridge 4 the line 'tunnelled' under Stanley's Tram Road from his collieries to the old Pembrey Harbour. Water was taken by the engines here in earlier days. Looking east, September 1964.

R.E. Bowen

Another reminder on the line of its former life as a canal could be seen in Pembrey Village at bridge 5 with flooding of the track and towrope marks in the nearside stonework, the original tow path side. Burry Port is to the right, 27th August, 1988. *M.R.C. Price*

but goes on to say that this elite was accommodated in carriages to view the line. Any such carriages would have had to be hired from another railway and, as the GWR through Burry Port was then broad gauge, any such a hiring seems most unlikely. The 'carriages' used clearly were open and suitable also for the conveyance of coal!

A luncheon was held in a marquee at Pontyberem according to the *Mercury*, but the *Journal* begs to differ. This account has two trucks laden with coal from the Revd D. Thomas's colliery being attached to the train when it reached Pontyberem and brought down to Burry Port where, on arrival, a magnificent champagne luncheon was partaken at the invitation of the Directors in a large marquee in front of the Neptune Hotel, with sweet music throughout the repast performed by the Band of the Llanelly Rifle Volunteers. An item in the company's cash books shows a payment of £210 9s. 0d. to 'Morris, Sundries for Opening'. At just over one pound per head, if indeed there were about 200 of the elite in attendance, this would allow for quite a reasonable quality of champagne to be served. The *Journal* adds that a little later in the evening a coal train from Glan Gwendraeth Colliery (at Pontyates) put in an appearance to the great delight of the inhabitants. Perhaps both versions are correct; by the time they got back to Burry Port it would have been well into the afternoon and rather late for lunch, but not too late for plenty of toasts and speeches. As the *Journal* reporter comments, 'in fact Burry Port was quite *en fête* on Wednesday'.

Some gleanings from the ensuing oratory reveal many interesting snippets of information. After the usual formal toasts to the Queen, the Prince and Princess of Wales, the Army (including General Malcolm), the Navy (including Captain Luckraft) and the Volunteers (including Captain Roderick), it was time to hear Charles Cancellor the Chairman refer to the good work, the arduous duties, which had been performed by the Engineers - Mr Shelford and Mr Robinson - and he mentioned financial difficulties. He said those who were on the experimental trip would agree it was a great success and would hope that passenger traffic would [soon] open. General Malcolm proposed the toast to the Engineers. Mr Robinson replied,

I will not go into the difficulties we have had to meet in some parts of the line or the bottom of the canal which was so soft that it was with the greatest possible difficulty we could overcome the impediment with stakes and other things after the manner of the great George Stephenson.

Christopher Pemberton the Vice-Chairman was next to his feet with,

Some eight or ten months ago a man came to us utterly unknown to us. He said he was prepared to make our line, a man who has by his honest and generous confidence, not only in us as a Company, but in his own judgement and the capability of completing the Gwendraeth Valley railway he came forward in an hour of great need. He told us he was prepared with his own money to assist us in this great undertaking. Gentlemen, I need not tell you that I am referring to Mr. Furniss ... we have determined since we came down here to go a short distance further. We have decided to carry the line two miles further on.

The view from bridge 8, the Craiglon bridge as the line, built on the old tow path, turns to the north. The remnants of the canal are to the right of the track and on the left the last houses of Pembrey are left behind as open country is reached. 1964. *R.E. Bowen*

At Ty Mawr, looking north, in 1964 with an extended Lock Cottage on the right. The canal (and the lock) were between the cottage and the track. *R.E. Bowen*

(clearly referring to the extension to Cwmmawr). He then proposed a toast to Mr Furniss.

Mr Furniss was enthusiastically cheered on rising, but one can detect the first notes of bitterness in his reply. He referred to Mr. A. Williams the Resident Engineer and to other members of the staff - Messrs A. Ford, G. Lock, C.C. Mumbery and Wing.

> These gentlemen have worked unsparingly on this difficult undertaking, and have four or five nights a week being up contending with the elements and other hardships. I have personally superintended this work, not usual with me in similar undertakings, and I just say I have found the ablest support from the Assistant Engineer Mr. Williams ... and was chiefly led in to the work by the promise of local assistance. This I did not get ... we have brought down 110 tons of coal with one engine ... although I ought particularly to have received local support I never had a shilling's worth, but now that you have the line made, I hope that you will assist on making it remunerative.

If this speech was made before the arrival of that evening's coal train from Glan Gwendraeth Colliery, does this mean that a trial loaded coal train of 110 tons had previously run?

In proposing the health of the landowners, Christopher Pemberton mentioned that the cost of the line had been but £3,000 per mile ... because 'there being a shallow canal previously at not much profit they had been able to purchase the land it occupied at a comparatively small sum'. Another Director, George Sutton, proposed the health of the traders, of which there was a large body present, and Mr Astley Thompson replied on their behalf. Thompson, whose company was the Lead and Silver Works of the Burry Port Smelting Co. Ltd, also the New Lodge Colliery, was born in Cheetham Hill. Manchester in 1837 and lived at Glyn Abbey. From 1869 he is reputed to have travelled on the train every working day between Pontnewydd and Burry Port until 1877, presumably in the guard's van.

Quite what Frederick Furniss, the contractor, meant when he said he had never had a shilling's worth of local support can only be supposed. Perhaps he had been unable to sell any of his newly acquired shares. He was to become increasingly bitter and angry as the true economic picture was revealed and no dividends were forthcoming. He had undoubtedly been given to understand that the line had only to be completed and a torrent of coal would flow down to the sea. Alas, gentle flowed the Gwendraeth Fawr!

In a magazine article about the BP&GV in 1909 the statement is made that, 'the first mineral train was brought down the new line, amidst much local rejoicing, in July 1869'.

The article acknowledges the valuable assistance of Mr Henry Court CE, who had been appointed Assistant Engineer to the BP&GV in 1870 and might have been expected to know what was the correct version. This statement has been repeated many subsequent times. After the ceremonial opening there is a possibility that the railway was not quite finished and was forced to close for a couple of weeks or so, but curiously no payment was made to the contractor for any work done in July so it is more likely that perhaps flooding of the line caused a temporary delay, if indeed there was one. There is little doubt that mineral traffic, however small, was worked over the main line on 23rd June, 1869, and that this should be treated as the opening date of the railway between Burry Port and Pontyberem, and the conversion from canal to railway had at last been effected. Both the late Raymond E. Bowen and John A. Nicholson (the Pembrey and Burry Port historian) quoted 23rd June as the opening date. Incidentally, the Revd D. Thomas's colliery was at Cwmmawr so the coal from there was evidently transhipped into the standard gauge wagons at Pontyberem before being attached to that ceremonial first train.

The total amount paid to the contractor up to the end of June 1869 was £31,917 according to the entries in the BP&GV Cash Books and with the other known costs of £2,077 net for sleepers (£4,577 less £2,500 worth sold), £154 paid to Stevens and Son (this would be for the rudimentary signalling in use in the early days) and £210 sundries for opening, less the £517 received for the disposal of the old iron, a grand total of £33,841 is reached. This averages £3,148 per mile for the 10¾ miles opened as far as Pontyberem, but unless the payments to Furniss included the costs of rails he had purchased (which is unlikely) then a further allowance has to be made for these rails. There is no specific entry showing a payment for track but one large item not so far included is for £2,488 paid on 30th June, 1869 to 'Law, refs S & O' which does not have any obvious meaning to me (it is not legal charges) but might be for rails and would raise the average up to £3,379, rather more than the claim that the line had been constructed for £3,000 per mile.

At Ponthenry at the top of the 1 in 45 bank, looking towards Burry Port, June 1972. The Incline Hotel, upper right, was named after the canal incline and not that of the railway. Note the change in grade just beyond bridge 15.   *R.E. Bowen*

Conveniently forgotten when quoting costs is the £72,400 paid to the canal company, which for the 15½ miles to be converted to railway amounted to an additional £4,671 per mile (of course, the harbour and dock estate were also included so this last figure is an exaggeration). The actual monthly stage payments made to Furniss were as follows (note that 6s. 8d. is one-third of a pound):

	£	s.	d.		£	s.	d.
31st October, 1868	5,708	6	8	31st March, 1869	1,558	6	8
30th November, 1868	1,375	0	0	30th April, 1869	2,685	6	8
31st December, 1868	6,708	6	8	31st May, 1869	4,483	6	8
31st January, 1869	3,508	6	8	30th June, 1869	2,858	6	8
28th February, 1869	2,058	6	8				

All these costs were taken out of the capital account of the railway. Other expenses, such as salaries and wages, came out of revenue, of which there was some (such as rents) even after the canal closure and before the railway opened. Another capital cost obviously not included in the construction figures is the £3,520 9s. 5d. required for the purchase of Exchequer Bills lodged as Parliamentary Deposit in the Court of Chancery. The cost of land purchase was not a large item as much was already BP&GV property due to the absorption of the old canals and harbour; the amount newly acquired cost a total of £970. A contemporary report says that Lord Ashburmham, Lord Dynevor, Earl Cawdor, Col Pemberton's Trustees, Astley Thompson, Lewis Morris, Richard Jennings, G.H. Rees, Col Stepney, Revd Parry Thomas and others had conceded the extra land required by the company on favourable terms.

Other capital costs needing to be included were those of the services of engineers and surveyors (£122) and legal fees (£220). There was also the provision of locomotives and rolling stock. The first two engines, together with a third added early in 1870, cost £3,572; the amount spent on rolling stock is not known but nearly all the coal to be carried over the line would be in wagons provided by the collieries and not by the railway. Even so it was quite clear that the balance of capital amounting to £47,600 was never going to be sufficient even for the reduced mileage of 15½ miles completed or under construction, hence the need to raise additional capital and further loans, some of it authorized by a Board of Trade Certificate granted under the Railway Companies Powers Act, 1864. By the end of 1869 the addition of £29,600 second preference 5 per cent share had raised the total shareholding to £183,000 plus a further £33,000 in loans.

Details of the revenue receipts are given in the audited accounts for the half-year ended 31st December, 1868, remembering that there had been no earnings from the canal since 21st September. Despite this £1,620 had been taken for tolls and dues, with a further £917 outstanding, whilst rents amounted to £160 plus £146 still to be paid. The balance sheet also shows £1,111 owing for 'sundry outstanding accounts', which seems rather a lot for sundries. Out of this revenue £1,151 had been paid during the half-year in expenses. These included £212 10s. 0d. in salaries for the Secretary and Harbour Master, £431 in other wages, £77 in legal costs, rates and taxes, £70 in unspecified commission (possibly in arranging loans and mortgages, or the sale of stocks), £50 for the Directors' travelling expenses and £4 4s. 0d. auditors' fee. This was all some six months before the railway had opened to traffic.

Another old canal bridge is the one at Glyn Abbey, seen in October 2004 with the track under water. Cwmmawr is to the left. *Author*

Approaching Pontyberem the line passes under Cook's bridge, named after an English soldier sent to quell the Rebecca Riots shortly before the canal was built. The site of the mileage siding, lifted *circa* 1940, was on the left. Looking towards Cwm Mawr, 19th August, 1964. *M.R.C. Price*

Chapter Two

The Struggle to Survive, 1870-1896

The main line from the harbour at Burry Port to Pontyberem was up and running by 23rd June, 1869 but no attempt had been made to open the Carway branch at this time, presumably because the colliery company was in financial difficulties and no traffic was expected. Similarly the 1¼ mile Trimsaran branch had not been completed; the Engineer had been ordered on 16th April, 1869, 'to lay down the railway on the extent of the Trimsaran branch canal to form a junction with the existing line to the Star Colliery'. Nevertheless it was not until June 1872 that it was reported that the branch to connect with the newly-formed Trimsaran Coal, Iron & Steel Co. Ltd was opened to traffic. Thomas Cadman re-opened the Carway Colliery in 1871 (it became the Carway Anthracite Colliery Co.) and an agreement was made on 21st September, 1870 for the construction of this 1⅜ mile-long branch but some preparatory work would appear to have already been undertaken; on 30th June, 1870 £800 was paid for materials for the Carway branch. It seems to have opened about the end of the year.

Clearly the completion of the BP&GV main line encouraged the starting of new and the re-opening of old collieries. Pentremawr Colliery was established in 1870 followed by Capel Ifan Colliery the following year; both had sidings connections to the BP&GV between Ponthenry and Pontyberem. Another pit opened in this period was Pumpquart, south of Pontyates, and during 1872-74 the nearby Ffoy and Plasbach Collieries both commenced production. Unfortunately, other collieries closed down including Glan Gwendraeth in 1870, Pontyates in 1872, Ynishafren in 1873, Carway in 1874 and Gwendraeth Slants in 1878. The frequent and multiple failures of the pits and slants in the Gwendraeth Fawr Valley was to haunt the BP&GV for the next 30 years; new companies would be formed and re-openings would bring expectancy only for hopes to again be dashed by yet another closure. Chapter Seven records the histories and changing ownerships of the individual collieries.

Meanwhile work continued on completing the main line beyond Pontyberem for a further mile to just short of the foot of the Hirwaen Isaf incline at Groes-faen, a mile before reaching Cwmmawr. Here a private branch struck off to the west for almost a half-mile to the Dynant Colliery. Commencing on 31st August, 1869 further payments were made to the contractor (Furniss) amounting to £7,175, the last being on 31st March, 1870 which suggests that this section had been completed by this date; an event that does not appear to have been chronicled in the local press. A report of a locomotive trial on 20th June, 1870 has the engine working 11½ miles up the line (well past Pontyberem) and it clearly had been opened by 14th August, 1878 when a cargo of coal was shipped from Dynant Colliery. Other payments during this period include £161 to F. Furniss for materials; £94 to Maybury, also for materials, believed to be sleepers; £152 2s. 11d. to Burt & Co, also for sleepers. This latter includes 17s. 11d. for dock dues paid on 31st August, 1870 so the delivery evidently arrived by ship.

Bridge 3, now the Furnace Road, also originally carried a tram road down to Pembrey Old Harbour. October 1975, looking west. *R.E. Bowen*

The Quarry bridge, No. 7, was built by the railway to replace a swing bridge over the canal to give access to the Carreg Llwyd Quarry and Brickworks. October 1975, looking north. *R.E. Bowen*

Whilst Frederick Furniss is believed to have built this extension to Groes-faen (on the same terms as his main contract), he appears to have had nothing to do with the Carway and Trimsaran branches; these were both built by direct labour. Commencing on 31st January, 1870 there are regular payments on Capital Account shown as for 'Railway Construction' or 'Wages, Railway Construction' continuing until the end of 1870 and totalling £2,021 up to then. Unfortunately the Cash Book for the period beginning in January 1871 has not survived so that the total amount spent on the Trimsaran branch is not known.

After leaving the BP&GV, Furniss went in 1872 to Somerset to build the Minehead Railway (Minehead to Watchet), completed in 1874, was involved with installing a street tramway system in Great Yarmouth (for which he was not fully paid) then returned to Hampshire where he obtained the contract to build the line from Portsmouth Town station to the Harbour for the London, Brighton & South Coast and London & South Western Joint Railways. Authorized in 1873, the line was completed and opened on 2nd October, 1876. Just prior to this, Furniss filed for liquidation by arrangement with his creditors, with assets of £30,000 and debts totalling £35,000. Afterwards Furniss was employed as Agent for Lucas & Aird, the contractors of the Hull & Barnsley Railway, becoming permanent way superintendent for that railway when it opened. At this time he lived in Drax, near Selby in Yorkshire, and died there in 1891 at the age of 66; his estate was valued at only £85.

Mason and Elkington Ltd, the copper works owners, had taken delivery of their first standard gauge shunting locomotive as early as August 1862. At this date there were no other standard gauge lines in the district so the engine must have been limited to shunting within the works and bringing copper ore from the dockside. They acquired the Pool (later known as Pwll) Colliery in 1865 and set about converting the old canal tramroad from Pool to Burry Port into a standard gauge railway. This was evidently still being done on 2nd April, 1867 when there is a reference to the progress being made on the line to Pool Colliery. The Cwm Capel tramroad was also converted to standard gauge by Mason and Elkington a few years later, in 1876. An agreement was signed between the BP&GV and Mason & Elkington Ltd on 26th February, 1876 allowing the firm to work its own traffic over the Cwm Capel branch as well as the Pool line, providing both were maintained well enough for such traffic. Their own traffic to and from the Gwscwm and Craiglon Collieries in Pembrey was also worked; in exchange the BP&GV was allowed the free use of Mason's stage and steam crane on the East Dock if not in use for unloading copper ore.

Until early in 1870 there were only two small locomotives available to work all the traffic. The railway was then offered the chance to test one of the new Fairlie patent double-boiler articulated engines on the line. This was the *Pioneer* (renamed *Mountaineer*), built in December 1869 and only the fourth such locomotive constructed to the designs of Robert Fairlie. The trials were so successful that the BP&GV readily agreed to purchase her for £1,822; she had proved capable of taking trains twice as long as those handled by the other engines in a trial during February 1870. She replaced the smallest locomotive.

On 20th June, 1870 Fairlie brought a delegation of engineers to Burry Port to observe the new engine at work, they having also been taken to see the similar

The Fairlie patent locomotive *Pioneer* was built for a Swedish railway in 1869, but instead was sold to the BP&GV early in 1870, proving capable of taking twice the loads of the existing engine.
Author's Collection

The same engine was immediately renamed *Mountaineer* on the BP&GV and is seen nearly 20 years later, possibly with silica sand wagons at Kidwelly Junction.   *Author's Collection*

locomotives on the Festiniog and the Brecon & Merthyr railways. A lovely story that circulated afterwards had the driver of *Mountaineer* being dismissed the day before the delegation arrived, the fireman being promoted to driver in his place and one of the dock workers being hastily drafted in to stoke the locomotive. Due to his inexperience it is said that as well as the engine having steaming problems, the delegation were unfortunately engulfed in much thick black smoke! A planned second run had to be cancelled because, notwithstanding the remonstrance of Mr Fairlie, the unfortunate stoker was continually poking the fire and broke two fire bars. However the man did learn and better steaming was achieved on five further trips although one was spoiled because the inexperienced driver could not prevent the engine from slipping to a stand on the bank (*see Appendix Five*).

A further Act of Parliament was obtained on 18th July, 1872 (35 & 36 Vict. cap. 106) allowing the raising of additional capital to pay for new works, mostly connected with the Burry Port Dock and Harbour and to purchase another locomotive, but also to complete Railway No. 3 - the branch to Kymer's Quay at Kidwelly. The additional capital consisted of £97,000 third preference 5 per cent shares (of which only £2,220 were taken up), £18,000 loans (£17,850 was actually borrowed) plus a further £32,000 of loans which could only be made when all the Authorized shares were sold (they never were).

There was however enough raised for the remaining 2¼ mile-long section of Kymer's canal, to the Quay at Kidwelly, to be converted to a railway using direct labour during this period, and this opened for traffic in June 1873 bringing the total mileage in use up to 16½. The neighbouring Gwendraeth Valleys Railway had re-opened in 1872 as a standard gauge line from a junction with the Great Western Railway at Kidwelly to Mynedd-y-Garreg. A short branch, only ¼ mile long, was rebuilt in 1873 to standard gauge by the GVR to Tycoch where a junction, opened in September 1873, was made with the BP&GV Quay line. This GVR branch had originally been constructed in 1866 as a broad gauge line to a wharf on the canal, but had become disused from August 1868 with the closure of the canal. This new junction enabled traffic to and from the west to be exchanged with the GWR but as most of the BP&GV's through traffic was eastwards, to Llanelly or Swansea, the BP&GV preferred to route all such goods via Burry Port, whether east or west bound.

Due to the silting in the Gwendraeth estuary, Kymer's little Quay at Kidwelly could only take small ships and the BP&GV found it needed to work the branch by only a couple of trains a week. This did not suit the GVR which wanted at least a daily connection at Tycoch Junction and complained bitterly to the BP&GV. No improvement was effected and relations between the two railways deteriorated so badly that the BP&GV threatened to remove the junction. This prompted the GVR to seek legal redress and in 1875 they went to the Railway Commissioners for a ruling under the Regulation of Railways Act of 1873; the Commissioners ruled in favour of the GVR and required the BP&GV to operate at least a daily connection.

As a result there followed a period of much closer working relations between the two lines and this led to the BP&GV agreeing to work all the traffic over the GVR with a minimum of one train per day. This was duly formalised on 30th

The railway purchased a larger and more powerful Fairlie patent locomotive, the *Victoria*, in 1873, carried on 12 instead of eight wheels.

Emlyn Davies Collection

November, 1876, the BP&GV paying the GVR a proportion of the receipts. The BP&GV also had to furnish a statement of all westbound through traffic, whether by Tycoch or Burry Port. The GVR's only locomotive was taken into the stock of the BP&GV at a cost of £1,000.

To supervise all this new construction performed by direct labour, the BP&GV in 1870 engaged Henry Court as Resident Engineer and assistant to Luckraft. Aged 21 and born in Camberwell, he was the son of the Chief Clerk at the National Debt Office and had been working in the Engineering Department of the Post Office, having previously been articled to H.H. Fulton. Court left in 1878 but returned to the BP&GV in 1889 after the death of Luckraft to become Chief Engineer. Luckraft also had assistance from George Redford, age 33 from Surrey, appointed traffic manager in 1869.

There were also changes in the Board room. Charles Cancellor resigned in 1872 and General Malcolm became Chairman; prior to this he was described as Managing Director. George Alexander Malcolm, unusually for one of the BP&GV Directors both then and later, resided locally at Gwendraeth House (later part of the Royal British Legion Club) although he also had a London address. He took a keen interest in local affairs, for example donating 27 volumes of journals and magazines to the Working Men's Club & Institute when it was formed in 1876. Following the replacement of Sutton & Ommanney as the company's solicitors by the Llanelly firm of Johnston & Stead, both the Suttons resigned as Directors whilst Francis Alexander Pemberton replaced his brother Christopher, all these changes taking place before the end of 1876. There was also one other new Director, Sir Harcourt Johnstone Bt MP of Hackness Hall, York. He left in 1884 when Francis Cancellor, a London stockbroker and son of Charles, joined the Board.

Three further changes took place during the late 1880s; General Malcolm left through ill health in 1887 (he died in June 1888) followed by Francis Pemberton who resigned on 21st September, 1888. Francis Cancellor became Chairman and new arrivals were solicitor Francis Ommanney, John Clarke Crossthwaite McCaul in 1888 and Bertram the 5th Earl of Ashburnham in 1889; Cancellor immediately stepped aside to allow the 49-year-old Lord Ashburnham to become Chairman. Curiously the 4th Earl, who died in June 1878, only rarely visited the area and apart from purchasing some original shares, showed little interest in Burry Port affairs. In contrast the 5th Earl came down frequently, was a JP for Carmarthenshire, and became immersed in local affairs as well as the railway and port. Raymond E. Bowen provides more details about the Ashburnham family in Volume One on pp. 179-181.

Also during the second half of 1887 William Taylor resigned and Roderick Mackay was now joined by William Barclay Peat of 3 Lothbury (next to the Bank of England) as the company's auditors. Before all this took place there had been a severe financial blow which was to plunge the BP&GV even further into debt. On 17th July, 1880 the West of England Bank Company failed, and among the companies it brought down in its wake was the Pontyberem Colliery Co., one of the BP&GV's most important customers. The result was that shareholders were informed that the receipts for that year would not be enough to allow for the payment of any interest due on the loans. The debenture holders

Achddu Mill, on the Cwm Capel branch which can be seen in the foreground. Picture taken before the development of Achddu Colliery in 1905. Burry Port is to the right. The water wheel was taken away as scrap metal at the beginning of World War II.   *Author's Collection*

Another view on the Cwm Capel branch, this time with Burry Port to the left. This is Pemberton crossing with the Colby Road (A484) with the Pemberton Arms Hotel on the right.
Brian Cripps Collection

accordingly referred the company to the Court of Chancery who, on 29th July 1881, placed the running of the company in the hands of a Receiver. The latter appointment, fortunately for the BP&GV, was John Russell, the company's Secretary. He now took over the management of the railway from the Directors, running the affairs from 3 Great Winchester Street, Westminster, part of the offices of Sutton and Ommanney the Solicitors, having moved there from 80 Coleman Street.

The BP&GV was by no means unique in suffering such an indignity. Following the financial crisis of 11th May, 1866 such illustrious names as the Great Eastern, London Brighton & South Coast, London Chatham & Dover and the North British railways had all failed to pay any dividends or interest and were forced into receivership, not recovering until the 1870s. It was to take the BP&GV a long time to recover. The lead and silver works operated by the Burry Port Smelting Co. on the east side of the docks failed in 1877 and never re-opened. Following Pontyberem other anthracite pits were struggling to keep going: Ffoy Colliery was abandoned in 1880 followed by Plasbach in 1884, Pumpquart in 1885, Carway in 1887 and Dynant Colliery in 1889. Plasbach restarted in 1886, closed in 1892, re-opened in 1893 and was again abandoned in 1896 - activities not designed to inspire confidence in the industry. The track was lifted from the BP&GV's portion of the Carway branch early in 1887 when Owen Bowen was the lessee of the colliery. Bowen's solicitors then demanded that the track be relaid but this was rigorously rejected as the BP&GV had no faith in the pit being re-opened by Bowen (it was not until 1898 that it was eventually restarted and the track reinstated). Raymond E. Bowen, no relation of Owen Bowen, was of the opinion that the opportunity was taken to lift the track to provide spare materials for other sections of the BP&GV; however, much of it was too poor for further use.

Meanwhile the BP&GV continued its largely uneventful existence, transporting coal down to Burry Port where some was shipped in the dock, a little was used by the local industries and most of the rest was forwarded over the Great Western to Llanelly or Swansea. Occasionally some event would be brought to the attention of its readership by the local newspapers, especially if there was an injury because of an accident.

One such occurred early in February 1887 when two little boys aged seven and nine were seriously injured whilst playing around with moving trucks on the Pwll branch of the BP&GV near Burry Port. Each of the boys received severe leg injuries which unfortunately left them crippled. The son of Mr Jones, a commercial traveller of Parymina Road, sustained severe injuries in his right leg and the son of Mr Rees, landlord of the Pemberton Arms, received a crushed right foot. This latter inn was right next to where the Cwmcapel branch crossed the Colby Road (the present A484) on the level, so the boy should have had plenty of warning of the danger of moving wagons. It would seem that Mr Jones wrote to the head office of the railway asking for financial help, pleading poverty, as on 5th April Russell wrote the following to Mitchell:

I have this day rec'd the enclosed calling my attention to the very sad accident that happened to the boy Jones & requesting assistance.

Would you call on the writer, the boy's father, & tell him how deeply I regret that it was found necessary to remove the poor boy's foot, & altho' I am satisfied that no blame whatever can be attached to the Co'y or to any servant of the Co'y & that the boy alone was to blame I feel it will meet with the approval of the Co'y to take the memorial into consideration with a view to seeing to what extent the relief he seeks can be met, & therefore I will, acting on my convictions, determine how far I may be able, for the Co'y, to assist, when I have gone into the matter with you, & this I will do on my next visit which will be in about a fortnight's time.

Is this Jones a collier? - I do not quite take in all he says in his memorial, but no doubt it is a sad affair for him as well as for the boy.

Do not lead him to expect he will get a large amount, for that he will not get, but he must not be allowed to sell his furniture to meet the bills incidental to the accident.

It would seem that Jones persisted with his claim, for Russell adds on 14th May in another letter,

I cannot approve of some of the items and think it an injudicious appeal. The Doctors fee, the Chemist, Butchers and Nurse I would have settled .... The worst of it is that the man will now never be satisfied, but always feel aggrieved as he will not get all he asks for. Certainly not his loss of employment which he puts down at £15, how many days this represents he does not say, but it is such claims that make one feel rather vexed and blunts the sympathy one naturally feels.

I have not been able to trace what, if any, *ex gratia* payment was eventually made. More serious was the involvement of a locomotive on the dock lines at Burry Port resulting in the death of Lewis Reynolds on 5th March, 1887. He was the 66-year-old watchman at the copper works. Of course, the Board of Trade was informed (as was required under Section 6 of the Regulation of Railways Act of 1871) and they clearly had requested further details for on 2nd May, 1887 Russell wrote to the Assistant Secretary at the Railway Department:

Sir,
    With reference to your letter of the 27th ult'o I beg leave to enclose the depositions of the engine driver and stoker of the Co'ys engine 'GWENDRAETH' representing the facts of the case from their point of view, also a copy of the *Llanelly & County Guardian* of the 10th March in which a report will be found of the evidence taken at the inquest held at the White Lion Inn, Burry Port on the 7th of March resulting in a verdict of accidental death.

John Russell, Receiver & Secretary

There seem to have only been a few accidents on the BP&GV resulting in the death of a railwayman. One such occurred on the evening of 12th July, 1887 when Thomas Williams, the driver of the locomotive shunting the coal tips at the docks, for some unclear reason left his engine which struck him down and killed him. He had been with the company about four years and previous to being put in charge of the engine had been a stoker for 15 months. At the inquest held the following day a verdict of accidental death was returned.

The Cwmcapel branch was worked by the Pembrey Copper Works (Elliott's Metal Co. Ltd, previously Mason & Elkington until 1884) using one of their own locomotives. The line left the copper works and headed north, crossing or connecting with various other BP&GV tracks, then crossed the GWR main line on the level followed by a public crossing over a street. An eight-year-old boy, the son of John Griffiths, was killed on this crossing at about 1 pm on 27th September, 1892. The following details are taken from the report of the inquest held two days later at the 'Hope & Anchor'. The engine involved was the *Norah* hauling 10 (presumably empty) wagons back to the Cwmcapel Colliery. Besides the driver there were three others on the footplate, the works' accountant, the guard and a youth who always went off the engine at the GWR crossing and went ahead to check the road was clear. This day there were a lot of children on the crossing. The driver said he was doing about three miles per hour, then put on steam on clearing the crossing only to bring the train to a stop because of a lot of shouting. The body of the boy was lying across the rails behind the last wagon. Accidental death was again the verdict, the Foreman suggesting that the Jurers' fees should be handed to the father.

In the 1870s the London & North Western Railway (LNWR), like the GWR one of the largest railway companies in Britain, was extending its Central Wales line from Craven Arms into Carmarthenshire, having reached Llandovery in 1868. The line from there to Llandilo was built by the Vale of Towy Railway, opened in 1858 and leased to the Llanelly Railway, which was re-leased to the Llanelly (later GWR) and LNWR jointly from 1867. The Llanelly obtained an Act for a railway from Llandilo to Carmarthen in 1861 which opened in 1864 and over which the LNWR were granted running powers in 1867. Due to financial difficulties this last line became the independent Central Wales and Carmarthen Junction Railway in 1873, being worked by the LNWR and later absorbed by them in 1891. Through LNWR carriages were operated to Pembroke Dock via the Pembroke & Tenby Railway from 1869 and clearly through goods traffic also. An LNWR route to the south of Ireland was one objective.

A link between the LNWR and the BP&GV was first proposed in 1872 but it took three years before the Bill for the Burry Port and North-western Junction Railway, surveyed by Henry Court, was deposited in Parliament on 30th November, 1875 and received the Royal Assent on 27th June, 1876 (39 and 40 Vict. cap. 73) The Act was to build a line just short of six miles in length (5 m. 79.4 chains) from Cwmmawr (which the BP&GV had yet to reach) to a junction at Llanarthy 9.5 chains west of the platform end. The route included a tunnel 534 yards long just north of Porthyrhyd and the maximum gradient was 1 in 47. The capital allowed was £78,000 plus £26,000 in loans, the first Directors were named as John Kemp, Jacomb Hood, Astley Thompson and Alexander Josiah Patrick Wise, and five years were allowed for completion with powers for either the LNWR or the BP&GV (or both jointly) to work the line.

An Amendment Act was obtained on 3rd June, 1881 allowing for an alteration in the route near Porthyrhyd to avoid the tunnel and a branch railway to be built from the Llanelly & Mynydd Mawr Railway (LMMR) at Cwm Blawd down the hillside at 1 in 50 to join the original route from Cwmmawr at Drefach. A four-arch viaduct over the Gwendraeth Fawr was planned. There seemed to be little interest from the investing public, despite further Acts of 1884 and 1887 allowing more time for completion. The BP&GV was only an interested spectator, but from 1881 could have no official connection with the proposal, and the LMMR was likewise not interested. However, rumours abounded that the LNWR would themselves build the line and take over either the BP&GV or the LMMR, or both. The *Llanelly & County Guardian* on 20th January, 1887 stated that the LNWR was negotiating for the purchase of the BP&GV and also Pembrey Old Dock. Certainly the LNWR must have considered making some sort of move judging by the following story.

This concerned the visit of two LNWR officials to the BP&GV offices in Burry Port on 4th and 5th July and again on 2nd September, 1887, evidently to gain statistics respecting the trade in the Gwendraeth Valley, and Russell was aghast to hear that they had been freely given information from the company's books. Writing to Edward Evans on 9th September he remarks,

> … it was rather a cool thing to do on the part of these officials and … to allow our books to be overhauled in that off hand way was an error of judgment and should not have been allowed … a more cool proceeding I cannot conceive … what would the London and North Western authorities say if you went to Swansea to overhaul their books?

It would seem that the cool officials were not suitably impressed and the LNWR made no effort to either make a bid or back the proposed link. With no one else showing any interest it was not surprising that an Act was obtained on 12th August, 1889 (52 & 53 Vict. cap. 153) for the abandonment of the Burry Port & North-western Junction Railway and the possibility of hearing the distinctive sound from the exhaust of an LNWR locomotive in the Gwendraeth Valley was lost forever.

During the long period that the company was in Chancery, 1881 to 1898, Secretary John Russell was also Receiver and Manager. As briefly mentioned in Chapter One, John James Russell was born in Richmond, Surrey in 1827 and was appointed as Secretary of both the Kidwelly & Llanelly Canal & Tramroad Co. and the Burry Port Co. in February 1864, having previously enjoyed a civil service background. His salary was raised to £200 per annum on 7th June, 1872, then two years later there was a further increase to £300 annually. In 1881 he and his family (he had three daughters and two sons) lived at The Lodge, Halliford on Thames, Shepperton where he could afford to employ five live-in servants.

His world was completely transformed in 1881. From a relatively sheltered position, taking instructions from a Board of Directors answerable to the shareholders, Russell was now pitched into having to make all decisions on his own, subject only to severe monetary considerations. He had become an industrialist and an employer and was operating a business designed to serve other businesses. Not only had he to keep his operation up and running, he had to try and make sufficient profit to pay off all the debts. He had constantly to argue with the colliery owners over the rates to be charged for the carrying and shipping of their coal, remembering that they were all well represented by the Directors and shareholders of the railway. He would have no guidance other than from Court Officials who would repeatedly refuse to let him spend any more money than the amount earned. He revealed his feelings to the landowner Henry Williams Pemberton (to whom he addressed his letter of 5th May, 1887 by 'My dear Pemberton' instead of the usual 'Dear Sir') when seeking his approval to the lifting of the track on the Carway branch, writing, 'the fact is, I stand alone, and have so stood so long, without so far as I know the approval of the shareholders'.

Russell was continually having to explain to new shareholders (who might have inherited their holdings) why there were no dividends and no one would buy the shares. A typical letter, sent to solicitors in Norwich on 13th June, 1887 says,

> I have not yet found anyone willing to purchase the five original shares held by the Executors of the late Mrs Tate ... I think no one would buy them with the idea of their paying interest ... but simply for the votes they would represent. What would the Executors be prepared to accept?

Despite the lack of finance, Russell devoted much of his energy towards the completion of two projects which he believed would change the company's fortunes for the better. One was to complete the West Dock at Burry Port so that larger ships than those able to use the East Dock would not in future have to be diverted to Llanelly or Swansea with consequent loss of earnings; the other was to complete the main line to Cwmmawr and connect with the collieries at that end of the valley and thus increase the traffic carried over the line.

Using direct labour diverted from other duties at slack periods, the West Dock was finally put in a state to receive its first ship at the beginning of September 1888 although the vessels were little larger than those already using the East Dock. Direct labour could also be used on the construction of the final extension to Cwmmawr but purchasing the permanent way materials was another matter. The date when the main line was finally completed to Cwmmawr is frequently quoted as 'by the end of 1869' but that clearly is wrong. Less often it is shown as June 1886 but always without mentioning the source of the information. Raymond Bowen was unable to confirm the exact date, despite a thorough search of the local newspapers. Cwmmawr gets a listing in the fifth edition of Oliver & Airey's *Hand-book of Stations* published in June 1877, which suggests it had been reached by then, but this would seem to have been an error. The 1880 edition of the 1:2,500 scale Ordnance Survey map, which quotes a survey date of 1878-79, shows no track beyond Groes-faen and the branch to Dynant Colliery, nor any indication of any track on the old canal incline. The Revd D. Parry Thomas had died and his trustees had put the Cwmmawr Colliery up for sale in May 1873, which suggests that the colliery might have closed by then and thus the incentive to complete the BP&GV to this point was not very strong. The mine seems to have re-opened in a small way by 1880. Closyryn Slant was established by Anthony & Harris in 1884, as was Glynhebog Slant which was started by George Herring, the owner of Coalbrook or Pontyberem Slants. Also wanting a rail connection was the Cwmparc Silica Brick Co. of Swansea.

These latter three concerns were all persuaded by Russell that the best way for them to be connected was to loan cash to the BP&GV for the purchase of materials. With the additional incentive of special rebates on coal traffic until the loans were repaid, agreement was reached at a meeting at Burry Port held on 27th February, 1886. This allowed work on the extension to proceed over the next few months so that the June 1886 date for completion can be considered as quite likely, even though the source is not known. In a letter written by Russell on 28th January, 1887 reference is made to the portion of line lately constructed beyond Pontyberem, 'the Company has extended the line at a heavy outlay' and in another letter the following day to Cecil Bull of the Pontyberem Colliery Co. concerning the new traffic from Glynhebog (which Russell spells Glendebog) …

> … being charges for services rendered and traffic carried over … the portion of line lately constructed beyond Pontyberem … that charge is 2*d*. per ton … when the debt of construction is paid off the Coy might then fairly be asked to reconsider the charge and extend the through rate to the collieries between Pontyberem and Cwm Mawr but not till then.

Clearly the line to Cwmmawr was in use by the end of January 1887 and, with the lack of other evidence, June 1886 can be accepted as the probable completion date. Even though direct labour was used, it was only possible to slightly improve the gradient of the old canal tram road incline, which was 1 in 10¾. The new extension now included a section as steep as 1 in 14.

In charge of day to day affairs at Burry Port was Captain John Luckraft, Superintendent, Harbourmaster and Engineer, being assisted in the latter capacity by Henry Court (who as previously mentioned left in 1878), and helped in other respects by John Mitchell. A 38-year-old Scot who came to Burry Port from Lambeth, Mitchell was appointed traffic manager (replacing George Redford) and Clerk of Works 27th August, 1873; he also covered the duties of Harbourmaster during the long illness of Luckraft from 1883 to 1887. Captain Luckraft died on Wednesday afternoon on 24th August, 1887 age 85. Due to his impaired health and failing eyesight (he was nearly blind at the end) he was allowed to retain his position but had been on a reduced salary of £200 per annum since January 1883. According to a Board minute of 26th August, 1887 following the death of Luckraft, Russell had reported to the Chancery Court's solicitors that he would himself take up the position of Harbourmaster without pay and attend the Llanelly Harbour & Burry Navigation Commissioners meetings when required, also he would appoint John Mitchell as Deputy Harbourmaster and increase his salary by £26 per annum and give him the use of the house on the harbour as from 23rd August, 1887 formerly occupied by Luckraft. At that time Mitchell was living at Brynmore Villa on Carway Terrace in Burry Port.

In a letter to Mitchell written on 9th July, 1887 Russell says,

> I have applied to the Burry Navigation Commissioners to be allowed to nominate you to act as Deputy for Captn Luckraft but the answer is as much to say that cannot be, I will wait a little longer and see what had better be done.

and it was not until the following year that the Commissioners accepted Mitchell's position as Deputy Harbourmaster.

Towards the end of Capt Luckraft's life his niece Fanny Pearne (also from Cornwall) moved into Harbour House to look after him. After Luckraft's death Russell wanted the house vacating for John Mitchell to move in, but Miss Pearne did not go easily. On 28th October Russell was asking Mitchell 'Could you find out from Miss Pearne what she wishes to do as she cannot leave the furniture in the house'.

She had been offered the house formerly occupied by the Trimsaran Co. as offices at a very low rent indeed, but had declined; she was also told she could shelter the furniture there pro tem. Then on 29th November Russell wrote to her in Burry Port (so she evidently had found somewhere locally to stay) saying:

I spoke to Mr Mitchell about the garden tools ... you told me belonged to you and we collected all we could find ... I have no hesitation in saying that Mr Mitchell has a bona fide belief that he bought them and everything else in the garden. [During the course of a long letter Russell added:] Do not encourage the bitterly hostile feelings you have against Mr and Mrs Mitchell so completely apparently to engross your whole thoughts and do not please again make before me, or any one else, such slanderous accusations as you did yesterday about Mr Mitchell.

Anyway, to try and end the recriminations, Russell sent Miss Pearne 10 shillings to cover the cost of the missing syringe and bill hook which could not be found. He was most surprised to receive the following telegram on 2nd December, 1887:

NO PART PAYMENTS CAN BE ACCEPTED BY MISS FANNY PEARNE UNTIL ALL THE GOODS BELONGING TO THE LATE CAPTAIN LUCKRAFT ARE FAIRLY GIVEN UP BY MR MITCHELL.

Evidently it was quickly sorted out as just three days later she was told, 'You can cash the cheque and I hope this business is now settled to your satisfaction'.

Russell was keen every Christmas to send a little extra money to all the office staff at Burry Port, even when there was hardly any to spare. In December 1886 and again in 1887 the amounts were £8 8s. 0d. to John Mitchell, £5 5s. 0d. to Edward Evans (accounts clerk), £2 10s. 0d. to John Lear (weighing clerk) and £2 2s. 0d. to George Hancock (assistant clerk). Captain Luckraft does not appear to have been in receipt of any such a gift, although since January 1883 he was doing far less work because of his ill health, Mitchell having taken over many of his duties. Always there was a nice seasonal letter to Mitchell, as on 24th December, 1886,

Acting on the old proverb 'Twice over you give if you give quickly' I had the pleasure in the name of the Co.y to acknowledge your special services in my letter of the 23rd June. The enclosed cheque for £8 8/- is a Xmas gift from the Coy, not for any special service but as a mark of confidence & good will. Allow me to wish you and Mrs Mitchell a happy Xmas. P.S. I enclose cheque for pay.

He was also not above asking for the odd favour. In his letter to Mitchell on 30th March, 1887 he remarks that

... with respect to the work you were good enough to have put in hand for me and for which I paid 6s. 9d. I did not intend to trouble you about it but let a carpenter have it as a private job to be done after hours. As it was however done in the shop ... the usual percentage as payment to the Company should have been added.

It would seem that the 'black economy' goes back many years.

Russell was not the only one to appreciate the good work that Mitchell performed for the BP&GV. Mrs Malcolm, the Chairman's wife who died in 1887, left £50 each to Mitchell and to Edward Evans (the Accountant) in her will. Then, in a letter to Miss Catherine Malcolm, the General's sister, on 28th December, 1886 Russell says, 'Glad you gave Mr Mitchell the screen he made for Mrs Malcolm, it was I think the right thing to do and he was much pleased'.

After receiving an anonymous letter on 20th August, 1887 which referred to his men attending to 'other peoples cows and hay', Russell was informed by Mitchell that he owned six trucks (presumably horse-drawn and evidently used for carting around the docks). Clearly upset, he reminded Mitchell that, 'it was a point with the Board, when there was a Board, that no one in the pay of the Company should be allowed to have ... any chattel on the harbour property'.

Because of this principle all the machinery and odd things about the docks, which the Harbourmaster once claimed, had been purchased from him for £208 17s. 1d. on 21st January, 1876 after which all items in theory should have belonged to the BP&GV. Russell continued,

The principle the Board acted on ... must be maintained. I do not like to take the initiative in the matter, it would come better from you, knowing as you now do ... the principle I am bound to keep before me if I have to decide a question of management

Russell was writing almost daily, sometimes twice a day, to Mitchell and occasionally he would let his feelings surface, as on 30th July, 1887 when he revealed,

I feel depressed about the business although telling you this will not mend matters ... It is also to a certain extent a relief to me to tell you for the responsibility is heavy on me, not having any Directors to consult and share it with me.

Clearly Russell had built up a special relationship with Mitchell. Working from his office in Westminster (3 Great Winchester Street) or from his home in Halliford on Thames, John Mitchell was his representative on the spot and Russell relied heavily on him to see that his wishes were carried out, yet the expenditure kept down to the very basic minimum.

Reminders were continually being sent to Harbour Office on the need for economy. On 28th June, 1887 Mitchell was told by Russell that, 'I am still extremely anxious about the business and fear that it will be absolutely necessary to discharge or put on half time every man you can possibly spare'. Then on 20th April, 1888, after seeing the coal bill for the locomotives total 70 tons for March, Mitchell was asked 'whether you cannot do the traffic with one loco 'till trade to some extent returns?', evidently forgetting that the Agreement with the GVR virtually precluded this. On 20th October he told Mitchell:

I am in great want of money, at the present time I believe I have only £20 at the London & Provincial Bank. If Mr Chivers has not paid ... get the enclosed ... instruction to (the Solicitors) ... for the amount owing ... £59-15-7. I think you must press Mr. Young to pay for the repairs to his loco ... Mr Baile has owed £2-19-6 since the end of May.

Normally staunchly loyal in defending his employees' actions, there could be occasions when Russell was unable to offer an excuse, as when writing on 15th December, 1887 to the Court of Chancery to explain why it was necessary to pay now for goods supplied as long ago as between 12th July, 1871 and 11th August 1885, that,

> The late Harbour Master is to blame in the matter, as he every half-year was asked for all outstanding accounts and he never mentioned to me one word about these castings &c he had himself ordered.

On the other hand Russell showed understanding (perhaps it was the Christmas spirit) when writing to Mitchell on 23rd December, 1887, 'it is unfortunate that the first two cases, you have on your own responsibility exercised your discretion, both have turned out to the disadvantage of the Coy I don't blame you for it at all'.

In an earlier letter to Mitchell, on 1st February, 1887, Russell notes that the youth Archer had been sent by Capt. Luckraft to collect outstanding accounts in Llanelly. Although not approving, 'at least he did collect', observed Russell. This was followed by an instruction to Capt. Luckraft sent on 18th February that in future only Edward Evans and his assistant (J. George Hancock) would be allowed to handle cash.

Edward Evans, born in Carmarthen in 1850, had joined the company in the early 1870s to look after the accounts; he lived locally at Penybanc on Elkington Road and married a local girl. His son John, born in Burry Port in 1879 and who later was also to work for the BP&GV, was still living in the same house in 1938. Edward's young assistant in 1887 - George Hancock - was then aged 18 and lived in the Coastguard Station where his father John was a Coastguard officer, virtually next door to the Harbour Office where George worked. Although George was born in Amlwch in Anglesey, the Hancocks were an English family with his father coming from Frome and his mother from Rye. Eldest brother William (born Winchelsea) was an engine fitter in the BP&GV workshops just around the corner; another brother Harry was a clerk with the rival Great Western. When Evans retired in 1912, George Hancock took his place as the BP&GV Accountant. Henry Court returned to the BP&GV as Chief Engineer in 1889 following the death of Luckraft; William Shelford continued to act as Consulting Engineer whenever required.

By the late 1880s John Waddell and Sons, the major shareholders in the Llanelly & Mynydd Mawr Railway, were becoming more and more frustrated by the actions of the Llanelly Harbour Commissioners (it is of interest to note that John Russell became a Commissioner in August 1889). The gap between the BP&GV at Pwll and the LMMR at Sandy along the route of the one time tramroad amounted to only 1¾ miles, so a link between the two railways could quite easily be constructed, although bringing up to standard the rest of the line to take the extra traffic would involve a total cost around £3,750. Also a way leave would have to be negotiated to cross the Stradey Estate Railway of Mansell Lewis, which ran alongside the LMMR on its western side. The Board directed the Secretary on 28th February, 1889 to meet George Waddell and see if he would co-operate in helping to bring about a junction.

A train on the Sandy branch worked by the Hughes' locomotive *Gwendraeth* about 1898, looking towards Llanelly. The Pwll Colliery chimney is on the extreme right.   *H. Court*

The track gang at work on the Sandy branch near Pwll, about 1898, looking towards Llanelly. This is probably the same gang as that seen in the background of the previous picture.

H. Court

George Waddell would not commit himself to Russell but clearly afterwards gave the matter some consideration as he next formed a Syndicate (who else was involved is not known) that made an approach to the BP&GV in December 1889 to purchase the company outright for £96,000. It would seem that the possibility of shipping Great Mountain coal from Burry Port instead of Llanelly was the main attraction. The Directors discussed the offer on 20th December and agreed that a letter of the same date, signed by the Secretary, should be sent to all the share and debenture holders giving full details of the proposals and endorsing them with the statement that, 'the Directors, who after due consideration, accepted them as worthy of favourable attention from all parties interested' and a suitable form giving assent or dissent was enclosed for return. The letter mentioned that on 1st August last the arrears of interest due to debenture bondholders was £7,930 10s. and to debenture stockholders was £7,947 10s. with no chance of any payment 'within a reasonable time' and no hope of any dividend 'for many years'. It was proposed to pay the full amount for all the loans amounting to £60,850. Ordinary shareholders would receive £4 for each £100 share, third preference shareholders would receive a quarter of their original value, Second Preference one half the value and first preference holders two-thirds of their investment. Also £1,600 would go to the estate of the late General Malcolm to repay that debt, leaving a balance of £779 to pay the costs and expenses.

Although mentioned at the shareholders' meeting on 28th February, 1890 and briefly discussed at the Directors meeting that same day when Francis Ommanney said he had been assured by Mr Stead (the solicitor) that the whole scheme would be submitted to Counsel, this interesting offer was not discussed again at Board level and the response was insufficiently encouraging to call for the promised Special General Meeting.

Nevertheless the BP&GV Board decided to press ahead with the Pwll to Sandy link, obtaining an Act on 28th July, 1891 (54 & 55 Vict. cap. 171) for its construction, and another three years later for an extension of time when no work had started. It was eventually to be completed, using direct labour, as will be revealed in Chapter Three.

At a previous Shareholders meeting on 31st August, 1888 one of those present, A.G. Thomas, accused John Mitchell of having bought no rails at the Carway Colliery sale as he claimed and that the rails he subsequently sold to Mr Young (could this be Alexander Young of Kidwelly?) were taken from the company's store and from the smith's shop at Burry Port. Russell believed that Thomas seemed to have completely misunderstood what had happened - it was explained that Mitchell actually purchased all the iron left in the Carway yard *after* the sale and this included rails dug up from under accumulated rubbish. Russell concluded, 'I am satisfied by careful investigation that the allegations he (Thomas) made cannot be sustained and that so far as the Company is concerned the matter is at an end'. Nevertheless Mitchell was advised to see his solicitor.

Undeterred, Thomas continued his attack, making fresh accusations. This time he wrote to Lord Ashburnham who brought it up for discussion at the Directors' meeting on 25th February, 1889. Thomas insisted that a considerable quantity of the company's materials had been disposed of and the proceeds pocketed by the company's servants (although he added this did not include Russell). The solicitor - Mr Stead - explained the steps he had taken and laid before the Board the depositions on oath of the men in a position to speak about the facts of the case. In Stead's opinion Mr Russell was completely justified in holding that the charges brought were not worthy of belief and he had written to Mr Thomas' solicitor to that effect. He had since heard that Thomas had applied to shareholders, debenture stock and bond holders for their co-operation in bringing the management of the company before the Court of Chancery. The Board resolved that the enquiry made by the Receiver and Solicitor had been searching and proper.

Thomas retaliated, stating he had collected more evidence which he then passed on to Lord Ashburnham. At the meeting on 25th November, 1890 the Board handed the papers to Stead who was instructed to investigate thoroughly. A special Board meeting was held on 8th June, 1891 just to discuss this issue and it was decided to send to Mitchell a verbatim copy of the evidence and ask him to answer the charges. We now move forward to 31st March, 1892, forty-three months after Thomas had first made his accusations. Lord Ashburnham this time said he had received Mitchell's defence against the charges, and as far as he was able to judge it was one man's word against another. Nevertheless the Board decided that Mitchell should resign and requested the Secretary to inform him of their decision.

One can't help feeling that John Mitchell was badly served. He does not appear to have been given the chance to question any of Thomas's witnesses or allowed to be present to state his case against what would seem to be a personal and vindictive vendetta. Mitchell was 57 and would also lose the use of Harbour House; he had joined the Company on 27th August, 1873 - so much for 19 years' service. There is no mention in any of the surviving records that any form of compensation was ever paid to him for loss of office. What Russell thought is not recorded but he must have been bitterly disappointed with the Board's decision which would mean that he would lose his staunchest ally, his able lieutenant and his main provider of the information so vital to him in judging exactly what could be achieved.

The Directors made several attempts to reduce the capital and the loan interest of the company as a means of improving the finances, but even though some schemes were acceptable to the shareholders, they were usually blocked by the bond and debenture holders and thus unacceptable to the Court of Chancery. One difficulty was the decision of the Court that the capital of the preferred debenture bonds (£16,500) had to be paid off before any of the remaining debentures (£34,350) could have either the interest or the principal dealt with. Finally an agreed scheme of arrangement was filed with the Court on 28th November, 1890 and became effective (enrolled) on the following 24th February. The Authorized capital previously allowed for £280,000 in shares to be issued together with £93,000 in loans, totalling £373,000; however the amounts received by the company were actually £185,220 in shares (of which 5 per cent preference shares amounted to £49,820) and £60,850 in five and six per cent loans and debentures. Under this new scheme the Authorized share and loan capital was reduced to a more manageable £150,000 (£59,650 in shares), of which the actual amounts issued were:

Ordinary shares @ £10 each	£25,350
5% Preference shares @ £10 each	33,120
4% Debenture bonds	50,000
4% Debenture stock	40,350
	£148,820

Two of the new preference shares would be issued for every three of the old preference shares. Note the reduction of the interest rate on the loans to 4 per cent; in addition all the arrears of interest were wiped out. With an improvement in trading results it was at last possible to start paying some of the interest due on the loans; the Board thus felt sufficiently confident to apply in June 1895 to the Court of Chancery for their discharge. This was granted from 5th July and the Directors agreed that John Russell, although no longer Receiver, should continue to act as Manager. He received no salary as Receiver but had been awarded a well-earned pay rise as Secretary to £400 per year from the beginning of 1891.

There was now sufficient confidence to order a new locomotive, which was badly needed, from Peckett & Sons of Bristol which was received just before the end of 1891. The Court of Chancery was petitioned to allow payment to be made out of revenue, the terms being a first payment of £385 and 12 quarterly payments of £105. It had been intended that £350 received for a strip of land sold in December 1891 would go towards the deposit; instead it was retained by the solicitors to offset what was owed to them and was never received by the BP&GV! The deposit was paid in January but unfortunately the engine, named *Dyvatty*, soon developed faults so that when the final instalment was made on 17th September, 1895 the BP&GV felt justified in deducting £55 from that payment. A second-hand locomotive was also purchased towards the end of 1894 which received the name *Cwmmawr*, so the company were now much better equipped to handle any increase in traffic.

John Mitchell resigned in 1892 and was replaced as Deputy Harbourmaster by Edward Russell in 1894 (acting from 1892), who had evidently been working for his father; there are several letters sent by the office of the Receiver and signed by Edward on behalf of John Russell. It is believed that Edward moved into Harbour House although the new lease was signed, on 23rd May, 1893, by his father (who lived at The Lodge, Halliford on Thames, Shepperton). Edward John Henderson Russell, born Shepperton, Middlesex in 1870 so only a youthful 24, was on 14th March, 1894 appointed traffic manager as well as his other duties.

There were also changes in the Boardroom; McCaul resigned in June 1891 through ill health followed by Cancellor in March 1892. They were replaced by Charles Henry Ommanney age 40, the solicitor, of the Old Rectory, Little Berkhampstead and William Armine Bevan the founder of the Ashburnham Tinplate Works. Then in March 1894 William Joseph Buckley JP of Penyfai, Llanelly joined the Board, increasing the number of Directors to five, but did not stay long as he resigned on 28th January, 1895 with William Sproston Caine MP,

JP, age 52 and an Old Birkonian of 42 Grosvenor Road, SW, taking his place. Caine (1842-1903) was Liberal MP for Bradford but later lost his seat, being duly re-elected as the Member for Camborne in 1900.

At the General meeting of Proprietors on 3rd December, 1895 the Directors were voted a collective annual salary of £600; however, due to the financial position it was to be many years before anything approaching that amount was taken. Later that same day at the Directors' meeting the Board decided that Johnson and Stead of Llanelly were no longer to be employed as solicitors because the explanation they gave for not handing over the money due to the BP&GV (mostly from the late General Malcolm's estate) was deemed unsatisfactory; this had been withheld against payment of costs which were being disputed. Instead Sutton, Ommanney and Rendall of Great Winchester Street, City of London, Solicitors to the Crown Agents for the Colonies, were appointed and immediately instructed to take action to recover the monies claimed. It was not until 11th August, 1896 that a compromise settlement was agreed. The new firm had for many years been used as Parliamentary solicitors and part of their offices was occupied by John Russell as his and the Railway's head office. At this period W.I. Stilwell and W. Barclay Peat were the company's auditors. With the appointment of the new solicitors, both Francis and Charles Ommanney agreed, 'to place their seats on the Board at the Disposal of the Directors'. They were replaced on 3rd March, 1896 by William J. Buckley (for the second time) and Thomas P. Whittaker. On 7th July the appointment of Whittaker as a Director was cancelled when it became clear that he had no intention of qualifying by purchasing the requisite number of shares.

In the meantime the company was again struggling to pay the interest on its borrowings and, on the application to the Court of Chancery by a disgruntled debenture holder, Mr Justice Sterling again on 6th February, 1896 appointed John Russell as Receiver and Manager of the railway.

There are instances, including several with photographic evidence, of passengers being conveyed in trains of open coal wagons over the BP&GV. These were not daily affairs, but excursions which operated from time to time, one example being on Saturday 30th June, 1883 with the train from Pontyberem arriving at Burry Port just after 10.00 am, after which the passengers (miners and their families) were reported as 'seeming to enjoy their holiday and change of air'. Other occasions were on Whit Mondays 1887 and 1888. On 2nd July, 1895 the Directors duly considered the submission of the,

Pontyberem Collieries Company to be allowed the use of the line, and to have a locomotive placed at their disposal on Saturday 6th instant … the object of the application is to give the colliers, their wives, and children, a holiday by the sea side.

The locomotive placed at their disposal was the *Dyvatty*, the colliery providing its own open wagons for the excursionists. Other special trains were operated in connection with the eisteddfodau held in the grounds of Glyn Abbey.

As already mentioned, Astley Thompson, who lived at Glyn Abbey, is reputed to have travelled by train every working day from Pontnewydd to his office at the Pembrey Lead & Silver Works, Burry Port until his company failed in 1877. Presumably he travelled in the guard's brake van. The company later (in 1903) admitted to the Board of Trade to the practice of enabling 'parties' to be carried in the brake vans. General Malcolm, when Chairman, used to have a seat fixed to the front of the *Mountaineer* locomotive whenever he inspected the line.

However, there were other occasions when something rather better than open trucks, brake vans or even a seat on the engine might be required. One early report of passenger travel concerned a special working in February 1876 from Burry Port to Pontyberem just for the conveyance of buyers to attend the sale of plant and other assets at Coalbrook Colliery; the iron lots were bought by William Roberts of the Burry Port Foundry. As the GWR line through Pembrey had been converted to standard gauge in 1872, there would have been no physical difficulty to the BP&GV hiring one or more passenger coaches for this and other special reasons; possibly this is what occurred.

Clearly it was impractical to use open coal wagons regularly for passengers. For such use they had to be specially cleaned out and fitted with some sort of seating, which meant taking them away from the traffic for which they were designed. Exactly when a regular service of workmen's trains for colliers began is not known, and neither is the type of vehicle used at first. From the second half of 1885 until the six months ending on 31st December, 1896 the BP&GV was using some six or seven more vehicles classified as covered goods wagons than would be expected for a railway of this size. It is just possible that they might have been used instead of open wagons for the colliers' trains, perhaps with an open doorway like those in use for miners on the neighbouring Mynydd Mawr line. The time when the stock of these vans was suddenly reduced from 10 to three without obvious reason (December 1896) was also about the time that the first two bogie workmen's coaches made their initial appearance.

An excursion train for Burry Port loading at Pontyates, possibly in 1883. No fares were charged, the train being paid for by the colliery company.   *LGRP 18185*

A return excursion from Burry Port to Pontyberem on 6th July, 1895. The train has stopped at Stanley's Bridge so that the locomotve *Dynatty* can take water.
Emlyn Davies Collection

It would be imagined that the use of open wagons to convey passengers, whether colliers or excursionists, might have ceased with the introduction of these workmen's carriages, but this is not certain. Not until their meeting on 6th March, 1900 did the Directors decide that the Manager should refuse to run these excursion trains in future 'having regard to difficulties that might arise with the Board of Trade'. Yet only three years later little regard seems to have been given for just such a difficulty that definitely did arise.

The introduction of these two workmen's carriages was performed in a most unusual manner, evidently due to the Receiver refusing to sanction the expenditure required. I have been unable to establish the exact date that the two coaches appeared on the line but it was sometime between February 1896 and December 1898, both inclusive (secondary sources quote 1898). If the Directors discussed the matter (and surely they must have done) they did not record anything about it in the Minutes. It may be relevant to mention that George Herring, the Chairman of the Pontyberem Collieries Co. Ltd, became a Director of the BP&GV from 26th March, 1897.

It was two other colliery companies in particular, Pentremawr and Ponthenry, that had been urging the BP&GV to provide proper carriages for workmen and, with the refusal of the Receiver to allow them to be bought direct, the collieries were approached to see if they would agree to finance the purchase. A deal was worked out, what nowadays could be described as a sponsorship. The two bogie carriages, costing £350 delivered to Burry Port, were duly built by the Ashbury Railway Carriage & Iron Co., Manchester and two collieries (believed to be Pontyberem and either Pentremawr or Ponthenry) bought one each for use on the BP&GV, with the understanding that the railway could later purchase them at cost price.

The carriages had a body length of 46 ft 2 in., with matchboard sides and end doors, mounted on a composite (teak and iron) frame. Internally there was a single saloon with a central seat running lengthwise down the centre of the coach (room for about 54 seated miners) and they were complete with brakes and lamps. As each coach was supposed to have provided accommodation for up to 100 men a good many of the colliers must have had to stand at busy times. Those colliers using the workmen's service had one shilling per week deducted from their pay by the colliery companies, so the BP&GV did not collect any fares or issue any tickets. They did, however, make a weekly charge of £2 10s. 0d. to each of the collieries for operating the trains. The BP&GV sought to get the colliery companies to sign a form of indemnity against loss and expenses, 'in consequence of any accident to your coach or any of its inmates while running over or being in our system', but was met with a strong refusal on the grounds that the collieries had no control over the state of the railway line or the behaviour of the railway company's servants. In the meantime any thoughts about trying to operate a full passenger service were still way in the future. The first priority was to bring about a final and lasting release of the company from Chancery.

Interchange sidings were developed with the GWR at Burry Port when the broad gauge lines were converted to standard in 1872 and lasted until 1984 when rail traffic on the dock estate finally ceased. Looking east towards the houses on Glanmore Terrace, summer 1982.

Emlyn Davies

A passenger train for Burry Port, hauled by 0-6-0PT No. 1607, passes Kidwelly Junction on 16th July, 1951. The line to Tycoch and Kidwelly curves away to the right and follows the line of the power cable poles.

R.J. Doran

Chapter Three

Prosperity at Last,
1897-1908

The vacancy on the Board which had been caused by the cancellation on 7th July, 1896 of Thomas Whittaker's appointment, due to his failure to purchase the minimum qualification of £500 worth of stock (*see Chapter Two*), was filled on 30th October by George Herring of 1 Hamilton Place (near Hyde Park Corner) and Bridge House, Maidenhead, a 63-year-old Londoner who was the Chairman and major shareholder in the Pontyberem and Pentremawr Colliery companies which included the Capel Ifan, Coalbrook and Glynhebog pits; later he also became Chairman of the City of London Electric Lighting Company Ltd, the Electric & General Investment Co. Ltd, and the Municipal Trust Co. Ltd as well as two gold mining concerns in Mysore. He was to become an important influence in the turn-around of the railway's fortunes. From March 1897 the Board meetings were held at either 2 Adelaide Place, London Bridge or at Burry Port Harbour Office where a room was refurbished to become a Board room. Then from August the shareholders' meetings and all the London Board meetings were henceforth held at 1 Great Winchester Street, EC at the offices of the Pontyberem Colliery Co. Ltd (Mr Herring's office).

The reason was that there had been yet another fall-out with the solicitors. At their meeting on 30th June, 1897 the Directors minuted that due to the increasing costs of litigation over cases in dispute it was resolved that Sutton, Ommanney and Rendall were no longer employed and that Seaton Frank Taylor of 5 Grays Inn Square be appointed solicitor. Taylor, aged 52, lived in Bromley but had been born in Bengal. It would seem that some preparative work had been going on behind the scenes as on 19th October Taylor produced a draft of a new Scheme of Arrangement with the Creditors which the Board approved; unfortunately this had to be withdrawn as not all the shareholders at that time were won over.

Nevertheless work on completing the line from Pwll to Sandy was now going ahead, using direct labour under the supervision of Henry Court the Chief Engineer. In May 1898 George Herring agreed to advance a loan of £2,000 to purchase the track and materials required, and in October a new drawbridge over the entrance to the West Dock at Burry Port was completed by Fred R. Willcocks the mechanical engineer. This allowed wagons after discharge to be taken across to the sidings on the south side. Other improvements on the dock estate made at this time included a new weighbridge and grid-iron sidings, Willcocks being presented with a bonus of £50 in November 1898 for all his good work.

Meanwhile a fresh attempt to develop a new financial package acceptable to the share and debenture holders was made; this was filed in the Chancery Division of the High Court on 7th April, 1898 and received the approval of the shareholders at an Extraordinary General Meeting held on 13th May. Finally this was enrolled by the Court on 29th July, 1898, Russell being discharged from that date as Receiver, and the company were now authorized to increase their

A loaded coal train for Burry Port passes between the houses of Pembrey, hauled by class '03' locomotives Nos. 03141, 03145 and 03152, on 15th June, 1983.   *Tom Heavyside*

loan capital by the issue of £19,650 of 4 per cent debenture stock and £30,000 of 4 per cent debenture bonds, plus a further £50,000 of these bonds to be applied in paying off the whole of the existing debenture bond debt of the same amount. On 30th August Russell was instructed to pay the half-year interest now due on the existing debenture bonds, with the aid of a further loan of £2,000 from George Herring.

By 24th October, 1897 it was reported that most of the new debenture bonds had now been taken up and they were able to repay the £4,000 loan (plus interest) to Herring. At the end of that month the Directors decided that £11,758 of the new debenture stock should be issued to the debenture stockholders in payment of their arrears of interest. It would seem that the bulk of the remaining stock was not issued, as much as £7,392 worth on 27th August, 1901 when it was decided to offer the balance to existing debenture and stock holders at 75 per cent of their face value. Even so they were not all issued until August 1904, £5,501 of stock going to George Herring.

W. Sproston Caine resigned his seat on the Board in July 1898, the last meeting he attended being in May, and Major Thomas Edward Milborne Swinnerton Pilkington of Chevet Park, Wakefield age 40 was invited to take his place on 4th August. He had served in South Africa and Egypt during 1880 to 1884, became a Baronet in 1901 and a Lieutenant-Colonel in 1903; he was a fellow Director with Herring of the Pontyberem Collieries Co. Ltd.

The receipts for the six months to 30th June, 1898 indicated that at last the company could have turned the corner and might even have made a profit. They were the highest half-year takings achieved so far in the history of the Railway. Compared with the same period the previous year, the figures were:

Half-year to	June 1897			June 1898		
	£	s.	d.	£	s.	d.
Railway receipts	3,630	15	2	5,301	12	1
Dock receipts	1,709	11	3	2,357	12	1
Miscellaneous	275	1	0	252	15	11
Totals	5,615	7	5	7,911	8	1

whilst the average receipts for the eight previous half-years (to December 1897) amounted to £6,461. The tonnage (mostly coal) being carried by the railway was also increasing, being 156,477 for the second half of 1897. This compares with an average of 129,967 tons for the six half-years from 1894 to 1896. It was agreed that the Directors' remuneration, as from the beginning of 1898, should be £300 for the year in total, with £50 to the Chairman and £25 to each other Director; the balance of the £300 being divided in proportion to the attendances at meetings. The actual amounts paid for 1898 were calculated as:

	£	s.	d.
Lord Ashburnham	97	14	6
George Herring	88	12	6
William J. Buckley	40	18	6
W. Sproston Caine	15	18	0
Maj. Thos. Pilkington	56	16	6
Total	300	0	0

Arthur and Emma Morgan outside Harbour House about 1910. The company's offices were next door, on the left, whilst the workshops were behind. *Alun Clement*

A modern view of Harbour House with the former offices on the left, 18th July, 2006. *Author*

John James Russell, Secretary, Manager and Harbourmaster, died on 22nd December, 1898 aged 66. He had been due to retire at the end of that year and was going to be made a Director by the grateful Board. His son Edward seems to have left about the same time, possibly even before the death of his father, and his departure seems to have been anticipated. The position of traffic manager had been advertised in the *Daily Telegraph, Railway News* and *Herapath*, the Board were informed on 2nd January, 1899, and several applications had been received. The Directors decided that Mr Garswood of Newport should be approached. There must have been a swift reappraisal as only nine days later the Directors were interviewing Arthur Morgan for the position of General Manager; clearly the death of Russell had caused the rethinking. Also on 2nd January Seaton F. Taylor was appointed as the new Secretary (as well as Solicitor) at a salary of £150 per annum, the company to have the use of his offices and staff at 5 Grays Inn Square for Board meetings as well as for all secretarial work. The first Directors' meeting at the new venue took place on 1st February, 1899 .

Arthur Morgan was appointed General Manager, Harbourmaster and Dock Superintendent as from 25th February, 1899 at a salary of £300 per annum plus the use of Harbour House rent free. Born in Risca in 1860, so aged only 39, he started his career as a booking clerk on the local Monmouthshire Railway which in 1880 became a part of the GWR. He rose to become station master at Abersychan and Talywain on the GW and LNW Joint line; then next took up the position of Station and Dock Superintendent at Briton Ferry for the GWR before coming to Burry Port.

Following the unexpected death of John Russell on 22nd December, 1898 his widow Ada had joined their son Edward at Harbour House, Burry Port. Edward is believed to have soon left but Ada remained *in situ*, the lease being automatically transferred to her having originally been signed by her late husband. When the new Manager, Arthur Morgan, was appointed on 25th February, 1899 he was told he would, 'be invited to occupy the local Manager's house free of rent' but Ada Russell, who was not entitled to any pension from the railway, decided that the surrender of her lease would be negotiable. After some manoeuvring, she eventually settled for £500 and surrendered the lease and vacated the house on 31st October. She was not exactly destitute, as John Russell's estate was valued at £4,524 10s. 1d., whether or not this £500 payment was included in the estate is not known. At last, after a wait of more than eight months, Arthur and Emma Morgan and their four children, Mary (11), Eira (9), Trevor (7) and Robert (3) were able to move in. It was agreed on 21st October, 1901 that a porch could be added to the front of the house and by then Kate Pearn, a 19-year-old from Swansea, was living in the house employed as a domestic servant. Next door at the Harbour Office a local lady, Mrs Anne Martin (40), was engaged as the office cleaner.

Earlier in 1901 we find a previous occupant of the Manager's house, John Mitchell who had resigned in 1892, and his wife living in Deptford where he is a Manager for a builder and contractor. He had married 21-year-old Georgiana Mary White at St Martin's, London in 1859 and they lived in Lambeth before coming to Burry Port in 1873; she at least retained her links with the Pembrey area as is confirmed by this comment of August 1903 which mentions that,

... among the numerous visitors last week we notice Mrs. Mitchell, wife of John Mitchell, late Traffic Manager of the Burry Port Docks and Railway. Mrs. Mitchell was the guest of Mr. and Mrs. Thomas Griffiths JP.

It might be added that there were many visitors at that time as the annual National Eisteddfod was held that year in Llanelly.

For some reason the work on completing the line from Pwll to Sandy and a junction with the Mynydd Mawr line was only proceeding slowly. The Directors informed Henry Court that his services would not be required after 31st January, 1899 and promoted the mechanical engineer - Fred R. Willcocks - to Engineer with a salary increase from £177 14s. to £192 0s. per year, back dated to the 1st January. I have not been able to trace when Willcocks first joined the BP&GV but it was after 5th April, 1891 and before 1st May, 1895. On 13th February, 1899 he was given instructions to finish off the Pwll line extension, the fences etc. to enable the railway to get through to the works at Llanelly. On 13th April Mr Willcocks' report on the Pwll line was deferred for further discussion until the Directors visited Burry Port. This occurred on 1st May but no details are revealed and the construction of this line is not referred to again at any subsequent Board meeting. It is clear the line opened sometime during April 1899 but the exact day is not known.

The company's Accountant at Burry Port - Edward Evans - received his salary increase from £180 to £200 per annum from 1st April, 1899. Then on 14th June Fred Willcocks proposed to hire a draughtsman at about £2 per week to get out the plans of the proposed new hydraulic house on the dock estate, to which the Directors agreed. Other new appointments made about this time included a yard and traffic inspector plus a store and time keeper, it being agreed on 21st March, 1899 to fill these new positions. The inspector was Charles Herbert Owen, age 30, from Bedwellty, Monmouthshire (although both his parents were English - from Bath and Bristol). On the same date it was also said that three employees *should* be retired on a pension of 8s. per week as being no longer able to work. They were locomotive driver David Bowen, age 61, with the company since 1870 and on 36s. per week; David Lloyd the Dockmaster age 73 and on 30s. per week plus a uniform and a house; William Morris the oldest of the three at 74 who had started with the canal company in 1854 and was earning 24s. weekly as a pattern maker and carpenter. None of the three enjoyed any length of retirement; Morris died the following day and Lloyd and Bowen both died in June 1899, the families of all three being each awarded £2 towards their funeral expenses. David Rees was the new Dockmaster, appointed on 1st May and his weekly wage was increased to 35s. but he had to pay one shilling rent for the house and his uniform was reduced to just a cap! He did not stay long, being replaced by Captain William Davies (age 57) of Llanelly in April 1900. Also joining the company at this time was a local youth, William Richmond Harries born in Burry Port in 1885, as a docks clerk and believed to have taken over from John Lear who had retired. The latter, who had joined the company in 1873, enjoyed a long retirement in Burry Port until his death aged 86 on 18th February, 1919; his wife Agnes predeceased him in 1908 aged 74.

The crippling amount of capital having been greatly reduced to a manageable proportion and the lowering of the interest rate on the debentures from 5 and 6 to 4 per cent, together with the improved trading results, meant that by the

Summer of 1899 for the first time there could be enough profit made to allow the preference shareholders to at last receive some reward for their investment. For the six months ending 30th June, 1899 the Directors decided they could pay 2½ per cent on the preference shares; ordinary shareholders would have to wait another 12 months before they received any payment. For the second half of 1899 a further 5 per cent was paid on the preference shares, the average for the whole year being 3¾ per cent. The tonnage of goods (nearly all coal) originating on the railway amounted to 371,480 in 1899 (185,740 tons average per half-year).

Two new locomotives were purchased in 1900, the *Ashburnham* arriving in August at a cost of £1,575 and the *Pontyberem* in November for £1,400, the payments being on capital account financed by the sale of the new debenture stock. It was also decided that the five oldest locomotives should all be replaced out of revenue account over the next few years; the next new engine, the *Burry Port*, arriving in September 1901 at a cost of £1,400 less a £400 allowance for the old locomotive of the same name taken in part exchange. Also in 1901 the new power house on the dock estate was completed at a cost of £3,229 charged to capital. As well as hydraulic power for the machinery and capstans there was electrical power enabling the offices, workshops and (soon) the Neptune Hotel to be lit by electricity.

The workmen's service with the two colliery-owned carriages (*see Chapter Two*) introduced before the end of 1898 was operated by a train which left Burry Port at 4.45 am every morning and called at the Trimsaran Road bridge at Morfa to pick up those miners who had walked the 1½ miles from Kidwelly (now Cydweli). Evidently the track on the Kidwelly branch was then too poor to accommodate even a workmen's train. However, this branch was relaid with heavier rail as far as Tycoch Junction (with the Gwendraeth Valleys Railway) in 1899 and from then a service was operated from the Tycoch bridge (on the Pembrey Road), which is less than ½ mile from the centre of Kidwelly - and slightly nearer to the town than the Great Western station. The Fairlie locomotive *Victoria* is recalled operating this train, being remembered as the 'double puffer'.

As well as the daily service a weekly train every Thursday was put on to carry the colliers' wives to and from market (the one in Llanelly), at first using goods vans. No fare was extracted but the women had to pay a 6*d*. parcel charge for each parcel of shopping with which they returned home; it was remarkable how many wares could be packed into one large parcel! It would appear that anyone, including children, could avail themselves of this service and not just the wives. The opinion has been expressed that as the market was in Llanelly the train may have run through over the recently opened Pwll line to Sandy Gate rather than the passengers having to use the GWR from Pembrey station. Originally it would appear that ordinary goods vans (of which there were three on the line) plus a goods brake van (of which there were two) were used for these market trains. At their meeting on 21st March, 1899 the Directors minuted that:

... the Manager reported that great inconvenience & hindrance to traffic was caused on market days by the wives of colliers using the company's goods vans for travelling up & down the line & suggested that application should be made to the Pontyberem & other collieries for leave to use their coaches.

From 1900 the company set out to completely renew all the locomotive stock. The first new engine came from Chapman & Furneaux and was named *Ashburnham*.   *Author's Collection*

Several smaller engines were obtained from the Avonside Engine Co., including No. 2 *Pontyberem* in 1900. This engine became too small for requirements and was sold in 1914.

LPC 3108

and just six weeks after their March meeting the Directors decided on 1st May, 1899:

... that £2 10s. 0d. per week be charged to each colliery for a special train calling at each colliery daily, leaving Pontyberem at 4.45pm., also every Thursday one of the coaches ... [be used] ... to carry the colliery women to and from the market.

It would appear that this new charge was for an additional workmen's train now introduced in addition to the existing early-morning train.

It was only after the introduction of authorized passenger trains from 2nd August, 1909 (*see Chapter Four*) that the workmen's trains on the main line became regular service trains; however the Ponthenry and Pentremawr halts for the collieries were not shown in the public timetable, and only certain trains stopped there. The halt at Trimsaran Road became a regular stopping place. Additional halts were opened to serve other collieries at Trimsaran Junction and Carway Colliery Sidings (between Glyn Abbey and Pontyates). I have seen it suggested that this latter halt was first opened in 1898 but it would seem unlikely that the owners of the two coaches in use before 1909 would allow them to serve a rival establishment. More likely there was a halt established at the site of the later Pontnewydd (Glyn Abbey) station for miners who lived in the locality. Another halt was later opened to serve Glynhebog Colliery, probably when the passenger service was extended to Cwmmawr on 29th January, 1913. Workmen's trains continued to run to Tycoch on the Kidwelly branch but these were not shown in the public timetable.

It would be imagined that the use of open wagons to convey passengers, whether colliers or excursionists, might have ceased with the introduction of these workmen's carriages, but this is not certain. Not until their meeting on 6th March, 1900 did the Directors decide that the Manager should refuse to run these excursion trains in future, 'having regard to difficulties that might arise with the Board of Trade'. Yet only 3½ years later little regard seems to have been given for just such a difficulty that did then arise.

Again, on 20th July, 1903 Arthur Morgan, the Manager, was instructed that he was to refuse to run a train specially for the local regatta. The shoppers' specials every Thursday continued to run as before for the benefit of the colliers' wives; presumably these were not classed as excursions. Also it would appear that the 'passengers' were not always conveyed in the colliery coaches as later in 1903 the BP&GV did admit to the Board of Trade to the practice of allowing 'parties' to ride in the brake vans. No passenger duty was paid on carrying such 'parties' as the BP&GV strenuously denied they could be classed as passengers.

Requests from local representatives for an ordinary passenger train service along the Gwendraeth Valley were made at regular intervals in the early 1900s but it was clear that considerable expenditure would be required before the Board of Trade would be prepared to sanction such a service. However, the company continued to run its workmen's trains for the colliers using the two bogie carriages.

Fred R. Willcocks, the Engineer, resigned his position on 29th August, 1899; no reason is given in the Board Minutes. A Cornishman from Launceston, he was then aged 32; two years later he was living in Huddersfield still as a mechanical and civil engineer. He was soon replaced, Robert A. Carr being appointed on 11th September at a salary of £260 per annum after the Directors had considered several applicants. (perhaps if Willcocks had been offered such a salary he might have stayed). However, Carr did not last long and he tendered his resignation, finishing on 30th April, 1901, although he was retained as a consulting engineer for a few months to oversee two projects he had started. One was the building of the cofferdam to replace the West Dock gates, completed in May, and the other the building of a new locomotive by Chapman & Furneaux of Gateshead which was delivered in September. Mr Carr's fees were paid on 21st October, 1901.

On 10th April, 1901 the Directors instructed the Secretary to write to Mr Morgan regarding his proposal that Mr Eager be appointed as 'Foreman of the Engineer's Department' saying that the Board required a formal application with testimonials. Then on 13th June George Herring explained to his fellow Directors what had taken place in connection with Mr Eager's appointment, which the Board confirmed. Presumably Eager had taken over from 1st May.

John Eager was born in Newport (Mon.) in 1855 and was an apprentice engineer under Ald. John McConochie at the Bute Docks workshops in Cardiff, then transferring to the Taff Vale Railway as a fitter under Tom Hurry Riches. From 1882 he was a marine engineer on several steamships operating from Cardiff, then had charge of extensive repairs for the Channel Docks & Engineering Co. In 1897 he became Manager of the Glyncorrwg Engineering Works at Briton Ferry and Engineer and Locomotive Superintendent of the South Wales Mineral Railway. He and his wife Louisa with their three sons and three daughters moved into a new house - Cae Helyg on Elkington Road, Burry Port - and there were still members of the family living there in 1938.

Arthur Morgan, General Manager and Harbour Master 1899 to 1922.
GWR Magazine

John Eager, Engineer and Locomotive Superintendent 1901 to 1922.
GWR Magazine

Just before he resigned Robert Carr received a letter written on 23rd March, 1901 from a foreman named Dring who had been dismissed, asking for recompense to cover the cost of moving his family back to London. This was passed to the Board who authorized the Secretary to pay him a reasonable sum not exceeding £20. William Dring, 47, was the foreman mechanical and electrical engineer and it seems it was originally intended to replace him with Eager, before changing the latter's position to Engineer. Another change in the workforce that was deemed necessary was the decision on 27th August, 1901 to purchase an additional horse (name not recorded), whilst the retirement of one of the Auditors, W.J. Stillwell, on 30th September, 1902 needs to be recorded. He was replaced by Reginald B. Petre of the firm of W.B. Peate & Co. On 21st February, 1905 the Board agreed an increased fee for auditing the books of £21 per half-year, commencing with that for the period ending 31st December, 1904.

The continuing improvement in the company's annual figures enabled a dividend to be paid to ordinary shareholders for the first time ever during 1900, the average for the year being 3¾ per cent; this was in addition to the 5 per cent paid on preference shares. The following year was not quite so good, 3½ per cent on the preference shares but nothing to spare for the ordinary shares. However, 1902 was better with 2½ and 5 per cent respectively on ordinary and preference shares, and after this the company never looked back. A total of 395,159 tons of goods originated on the line, nearly all coal, being transported during 1903. The half-year average of 197,579 tons showed a healthy 52 per cent increase over the 129,967 mean figure for the 1894 to 1896 period. The receipts for the six-monthly periods to 30th June in 1902 and 1903 make an interesting comparison with those given earlier for 1897 and 1898:

Half-year to	June 1902			June 1903		
	£	s.	d.	£	s.	d.
Railway receipts	5,923	11	10	6,302	17	11
Dock receipts	2,547	16	6	2,693	1	1
Miscellaneous	292	9	7	263	2	4
Totals	8,763	17	5	9,259	1	4

The balance from the profit made after the end of June 1903 that was available for dividend was £1,366 9s. 10d. and this allowed 5 per cent to be paid to all shareholders for the third time with a surplus of £197 9s. 10d. being carried forward.

At the Directors' meeting on 17th December, 1903 the solicitor reported to the Board the offer to sell to the BP&GV the Gwendraeth Valleys Railway for £3,000, as proposed by Miss Threlfall representing the majority shareholders in the line. An agreement had been drafted (curiously spelling 'Gwendreath' as such for the names of both parties) showing the date of the sale as 1st July, 1905; the Secretary and other officers of the GVR were to be excluded from the take-over, which would need to be confirmed by an Act of Parliament to be obtained by the purchaser. The BP&GV Board decided it was worth trying to negotiate for a lower price. This was not the first time their smaller neighbour had been up for sale. Having been placed in receivership in 1892, the Receiver, George Williamson, was by 1898 ready to sell the GVR if a buyer could be found.

Accordingly an approach was made to the BP&GV and on 30th June, 1898 John Russell wrote to George Herring enclosing the correspondence he had had with Williamson. At that time the Kidwelly Tinplate Works was closed so the BP&GV was only prepared to buy the section from Tycoch Junction to the GVR's connection with the GWR at Kidwelly. To this Williamson would not agree.

On 18th January, 1904 their Solicitor informed the Board that Mr Williamson was not prepared to consider any offer under £3,000. Some further correspondence ensued, and it was discussed by the Board for the last time on 7th March, but no agreement was reached. Williamson's patience was rewarded for towards the end of that year (November/December) the GVR was sold to the Kidwelly Tinplate Co. Ltd for £3,000. The new owner ordered a locomotive in December and gave the BP&GV three months' notice that the agreement for the BP&GV to work the GVR, which had been in place since 1876, was being terminated. The BP&GV thus ceased to work the GVR from March 1904.

A collision between a light engine and a workmen's train at the Dock Junction was reported by Morgan on 3rd September, 1903 and his correspondence with the Board of Trade was discussed at the next Directors' meeting on 14th September. Nearly four years previously, on 28th November, 1899, the Secretary had written to the Board of Trade fully stating the terms on which the colliery coaches were run, so they were well aware of what was happening. The suggestion that they were astonished to hear about the practice as a result of the accident, as claimed by some writers, is clearly unfounded. However, the Board did write to the BP&GV on 23rd September,

I am to draw attention to the responsibility incurred by your Company in carrying persons in this manner without the proper safeguards adopted for passenger lines.

Note the careful use of the term 'persons' rather than passengers. As a result the BP&GV Director, George Herring, arranged a meeting in February 1904 with Mr Jeckyll of the Board of Trade, followed a couple of weeks later by Arthur Morgan having what he described as a 'satisfactory interview with Colonel Yorke' (the chief inspecting officer) to find what safeguards, if any, the Board of Trade considered desirable. Lt Col H.A. Yorke advised that his Board, 'could not recognise the practice of carrying outsiders and that if one should suffer a fatal accident a great deal would depend on the verdict of the jury'.

Despite this the BP&GV went ahead and purchased a small passenger carriage (seating 32) in December 1904, presumably for the colliers' wives and not for 'outsiders'.

It would seem that one of the safeguards suggested was an improvement to the signalling on the railway. The minutes taken at the Directors' meeting on 22nd October, 1906 include the following not very illuminating statement:

Re. new signalling system:
Mr Morgan produced plans - Matter adjourned.

and that is all. As nothing further appears on the subject, the plan seems to have been quietly dropped for the time being.

Arthur Morgan's salary was raised to £400 per year from the beginning of 1903, and John Eager had his pay increased by £20 annually from 1st September, 1905. There were also bonuses paid to each for Christmas 1905 - £25 to Morgan and £20 to Eager. Captain Davies had to retire from his position of Dockmaster at the end of 1905 due to illness, and he was replaced by Captain Morgan from the beginning of 1906. A decision taken by the Board on 22nd May, 1905 was that new overcoats would be provided to the goods guards, whilst on the same day they were told that three horses had been sold.

The receipts for the second half of 1905 amounted £10,620 9s. 11d. enabling a 6 per cent dividend to be paid on the ordinary shares for the year, instead of the 5 per cent paid in the two previous years. The interest paid on the preference shares remained constant at 5 per cent. The Directors also decided that they were due for a rise, up to 50 per cent more at £450 in total for the year, divided as previously. They decided against taking their full entitlement of £600 for the time being.

W.J. Buckley, one of the Directors, died on 19th January, 1905 and was replaced by John Leonard Matthews of Westcoign, Maidenhead, appointed on 21st February. Then Lord Ashburnham resigned as a Director on 30th May, 1905 and he was replaced as Chairman by George Herring; the vacancy on the Board being filled by the banker Henri Louis Bischoffsheim of Warren House, Stanmore and The Severals, Newmarket on 17th July. Curiously his eldest daughter, Ellen Odette, had in 1881 become the second wife of the Earl of Desart whose only child, Lady Kathleen, had married Major Thomas Pilkington in 1895 (now Lt Col Sir Thomas Pilkington, a fellow BP&GV Director). The Earl of Ashburnham had been Chairman for 16 years during which time he had overseen the complete reversal of the company's fortunes.

Of interest was the attendance of Professor Henry Robinson at the 78th half-yearly Meeting of the Proprietors held on 12th March, 1905 and who moved a vote of thanks for the Chairman and explained he had been the original Engineer of the line and had come that day to congratulate the Board and officials upon the very satisfactory progress made by the company. The good times meant increases in salaries for the principal officers. From 1st January, 1906 Seaton Taylor received £300 per year as Secretary and Arthur Morgan had his raised to £425; it was further increased to £450 per annum from 2nd September, 1907 and at the same time there was a £15 annual increase to the salary of Edward Evans. John Eager had his annual salary increased to £250 on 13th May, 1907 although this was still less than Carr was paid in 1899; he had received a cheque for £25 from the company on 24th September, 1906 on completion of the fitting of the new steel dock gates. Evans had been given a £10 bonus at the end of that year.

The improved financial situation enabled some reserves to be invested for use in the future. It was reported on 18th June, 1906 that £5,000 worth of 3 per cent Transvaal Government Stock had been purchased for £4,965 13s. 6d. One costly project under consideration was the realignment of the line between Pontyberem and Cwmmawr in order to ease the severe gradient. At their meeting on 13th May, 1907 the Directors looked at the alternative schemes prepared by John Eager. Then on 10th June, 1907 the Board decided they

Another small Avonside, probably No. 5 *Cwm Mawr* of 1904, is captured working an empty wagon train to Cwm Capel.   *Glyn Davies Collection*

An attempt in 1906 by Avonside to build a larger engine like *Ashburnham* resulted in this rather humpy looking No. 6 *Gwendraeth*, seen ready to depart with empty wagons from Burry Port on 15th May, 1919.   *LCGB Ken Nunn Collection 2211*

preferred the one bridge scheme and agreed they would ask the local Urban Council if they would be willing to contribute towards the cost of the bridge. There is no subsequent reference in the Board minutes for that year, but the increased calling at that time for a passenger service doubtless caused further discussion about this very necessary scheme to be postponed.

Between 1903 and 1907 the remaining five old locomotives were replaced by four new engines. The termination of the agreement to work the Gwendraeth Valleys Railway in March 1904 meant that one locomotive was no longer required. The new *Kidwelly* arrived in May 1903 at a cost of £1,600 less £275 allowance for the old engine of the same name. This was followed in March 1905 by the *Cwm Mawr* for £1,305 less £200 part exchange, the *Gwendraeth* in September 1906 at £1,730 less £90, and the *Pembrey* received in June 1907 costing £1,820 less a deduction of £200 for the *Dyvatty* (the old name was not perpetuated as the engine had given much trouble). In addition to these replacements, the old double puffer *Victoria* was sold for £200 for scrap in June 1903. The railway was now operating with seven locomotives of which none had been built before 1900.

There were also improvements in the equipment of the dock. The first of two new steel coal tips at the East Dock was used for the first time on 18th June, 1904, Morgan reporting on 28th March, 1905 that the second tip was now completed. These hoisted and then tipped a loaded coal wagon so that the contents went down a chute into the hold (or bunker) of a ship. The order was given on 18th November, 1903 to Jennett Walker & Co. of Leeds, but the tendered price (including two capstans) is not quoted in the Board minutes. £2,000 was paid on 25th April, 1904, another £700 on 20th May and a final £150 on 17th April, 1905 - all out of revenue - but I cannot be certain if any other payments are missing from the records consulted. These tips were followed by the fitting of the new dock gates (the old ones had been in use for over 70 years and were leaking badly) in August 1906, the cost being estimated at £1,936. The tips and the gates were operated by hydraulic power.

The company lost the services of their new Chairman with the untimely death of George Herring on 2nd November, 1906 (his estate was valued at no less than £1,371,152 18s. 8d.), Sir Thomas Pilkington taking over as Chairman. The new Director was the Hon. Sidney Cornwallis Peel of 2 Old Broad Street in the City of London whose appointment was confirmed on 22nd February, 1907. Born in 1870, the third son of Viscount Peel, he had served in South Africa with the Bedfords Yeomanry. Before agreeing to the appointment Peel told Seaton Taylor on 21st January that he was going to inspect the company's property at Burry Port before deciding whether to join the Board. Just over a year later came the death of Henri Bischoffsheim on 11th March, 1908; a merchant banker and close associate of Herring, he was born in 1829 in Amsterdam and became the principal investor in the BP&GV and a naturalised British subject. This gave the opportunity for another member of the Herring family to join the Board, William of 14 New Cavendish Street, Westminster being elected on 18th May, 1908.

The net revenue available for dividend amounted to £5,404 for the first half of 1908; for the six months to June 1909 it rose to £8,228. Dividends at this period remained constant at 5 per cent on preference shares, was no less than 10 per

The terminus at Cwmmawr was not opened to passengers until 1913. It had reverted to its former status by the time this later view was taken, showing it after closure to passengers in 1953.

R.E. Bowen

cent for ordinary shares in 1906, followed by 7½ per cent for both 1907 and 1908, then back to 10 per cent for the period to 30th June, 1909. No wonder Henry Robinson felt the need to congratulate everyone involved.

Undoubtedly the main reason for the remarkable change in the company's fortunes was the huge increase in the production (and thus the sales) of anthracite, from around 1,678,000 tons in 1895 to 4,032,000 tons in 1910, an increase of 140 per cent in just 15 years. The figures are for the total of anthracite sold, the proportion just for the Gwendraeth Valley alone being about 12 per cent. Much of it, well over 60 per cent, went for export, either through Burry Port, Llanelly or Swansea.

Local agitation for a regular passenger service in the Gwendraeth Valley was becoming more vocal by the Spring of 1907. A petition was received and discussed by the Directors at their meeting on 23rd April when it was agreed to ask both the Manager and the Engineer to report on the approximate cost that would be involved. The figure they came up with was that an outlay of around £8,500 would be required. The petition, together with 'further correspondence with Mr Harries including his letter of 7th May', was discussed by the Directors on 12th May, 1907. The Secretary was instructed to reply 'that the Directors regretted that they had no funds available for the alteration'. This Mr Harries may have been, or was a relative of, the Thomas Harries who was involved with the Pentremawr (or Capel Ifan) Colliery at Pontyberem from 1872 until 1890.

Just over 10 months later more petitions and resolutions passed at local meetings in the Gwendraeth Valley were received by the company and brought up at the Directors' meeting on 25th March, 1908, which was attended by Mr Yockney representing a local committee and,

> ... who further explained the wishes of the local residents for a passenger service, suggesting its adoption by this Company under the Light Railways Act. The matter was considered at length and Mr. Yockney was ultimately informed that in view of the cost involved and the limited population of the Gwendraeth Valley the Directors were not prepared to launch into the scheme without being satisfied that the capital outlay would be likely to be remunerative.

Poor Mr Yockney was evidently only being stalled as it would seem that the BP&GV was by now already making further inquiries about the cost involved in operating the line as a light railway, as suggested. On 7th April two of the Directors, Sir Thomas Pilkington (Chairman) and the Hon. Sidney Peel, together with Arthur Morgan, met a large number of residents of the Gwendraeth Valley at a meeting in Pontyberem and the cogent reasons that were advanced, together with the promise of patronage that would be forthcoming, left the company with little alternative but to proceed with making an application for a Light Railway Order.

Chapter Four

The Light Railway Years, 1909-1921

The first attempt to define the term 'light railway' had been made in the Regulation of Railways Act of 1868, Section 28 of which fixed the maximum axle load at 8 tons and the maximum speed at 25 mph for such lines. The Light Railways Act passed on 14th August, 1896 curiously made no attempt to define a light railway nor impose any operating conditions. Instead it made it easier for the authorization and construction of a light railway to go ahead, with the cost being considerably less than that for a main line railway, by enabling a light line to be built to certain relaxed standards. The Act allowed the formation of a Light Railway Commission which could grant a Light Railway Order and which authorized the building of a railway without the necessity of first obtaining an Act of Parliament. However, the Commissioners, whilst accepting an application, had also to receive the approval of the Board of Trade, who could impose whatever conditions they thought necessary, before an Order was granted. As the 1868 Act had never been repealed, such conditions usually included a 25 mph speed limit for a standard gauge line.

Although intended mainly to apply to new lines, there was provision in the 1896 Act, under Section 18, for a company to be granted an Order to work an existing railway, or a part of it, as a light railway. It is this section that would apply to any Order that might be granted to the BP&GV. In the 22 years following the 1896 Act (to 31st December, 1918) there were 687 applications for Light Railway Orders, including 124 amendments to existing Orders, proposing a total mileage of 5,052. Of this only 2,101 miles were confirmed by Orders being granted and only about 900 miles were eventually built. Of these 900 miles some 350 were actually for electric street tramways rather than railways. Nearly all of these were new or resurrected lines; there had been very little use of the Act to enable existing lines to be worked as a light railway other than on the BP&GV.

Just a month after Mr Yockney's appeal on 25th March to the Directors to consider the application of the Light Railways Act to the BP&GV, the Company Secretary - Seaton Taylor - reported on 27th April, 1908 to the Directors on his interviews with both the Light Railway Commissioners and the Board of Trade. The Directors then 'considered that with a view to ascertaining the probable cost an engineer of experience in similar applications should be consulted - Mr Peel undertook to make inquiries as to this'.

The Hon. Sidney Peel, a Director of the BP&GV, was also a Director of the National Bank of Egypt with which the railway had a deposit account. During World War I he became a Colonel and was awarded the DSO and also became an MP. He must have known the right persons to ask as he received some excellent advice. He evidently came up with the name of H.F. Stephens as an engineer of suitable experience quite quickly as only three weeks later, on 18th May, the Secretary was reporting to the Directors the results of his interview with Stephens.

Sidney Peel could not have made a better choice. Holman Fred Stephens (1869-1931) was born in Hammersmith and studied civil engineering at University College, then spent three years as a pupil of J.J. Hanbury, the locomotive superintendent of the Metropolitan Railway at its Neasden Workshops. In 1888-90 he was Resident Engineer during the building of the Cranbrook & Paddock Wood Railway. Between 1895 and 1900 he was an Acting Inspector at the Railway Department of the Board of Trade. He was Engineer in turn of the Rye & Camber Tramway (from 1894), Rother Valley Railway (1895), Sheppey Light Railway (1897), Hundred of Manhood & Selsey Tramway (1897), Cranbrook & Tenterden Light Railway (1898), Bere Alston & Calstock Light Railway (1904) and Shropshire & Montgomeryshire Light Railway (1907). In several instances after the opening of these lines Stephens stayed on as Manager and Locomotive Superintendent as well as continuing as Engineer.

Stephens thus had plenty of experience in building and seeing to completion small and light railways at low cost. Having worked at the Board of Trade for six years he knew exactly the minimum acceptable requirements and thus did not involve his employers with any unnecessary expenditure. He must have saved the BP&GV considerably more than the fee and expenses he charged. He was promoted to Lieutenant Colonel in the Corps of Royal Engineers in 1916, during the war, and is frequently referred to in railway writings as 'Colonel Stephens'; however, this was in the future and on the BP&GV he was always just plain 'Mister'. His middle name was Fred, not as commonly quoted Frederick, which was his father's name, and to close friends and family he was known as 'Holly'.

So it was that Mr Stephens was instructed to inspect the line, report on what would be required to make it suitable for passenger traffic between Burry Port and Pontyberem and on the Kidwelly branch, and prepare an estimate of the probable cost. His report was discussed on 15th June and it was agreed to invite him to attend the next Directors' meeting on 13th July, 1908, which he duly did. It was then decided that Messrs Stephens, Morgan and Taylor (the solicitor) should together attend the Board of Trade to ascertain their actual requirements regarding bridges, stations, rolling stock etc. On 28th September Seaton Taylor produced the drafts of the proposed application for the Light Railway Order and press notices, which were approved by the Directors, as were Stephens' revised estimates which amounted to £8,500 in total. It was on 26th October that the required alterations to the By-Laws were discussed and the following tenders for mechanical signalling were considered:

		£	s.	d.
Tyer & Co.	Carlisle	1,112	17	0
Saunders & Co.	91 York Road	1,470	0	0
Atkinson & Co.	Tothill Road	1,517	0	0
W.R. Sykes	Clapham	1,587	0	0

and it was decided to ask Morgan (the Manager) and Eager (the Engineer) for their comments. It was agreed to purchase 100 tons of 75 lb. flat-bottomed steel rails from Guest, Keen & Co. at £4 18s. 0d. per ton. Events were now moving quite quickly and some aspect or other concerning the proposed passenger workings was being discussed at every Directors' meeting, the minutes reading like a catalogue. The dates concerned and a summary of the main items recorded are:

23/11/1908   Mr Stephens' fee of £400 plus expenses agreed.
Proposed passenger fares discussed.
The Company's seal was affixed to the application to the Light Railway Commissioners.
Cheque for £50 payable to the Board of Trade signed to go with the application.

14/12/1908   Petition received from inhabitants of Cwmmawr to extend the Light Railway Order. [A similar petition, with 108 signatures, was received by the Light Railway Commissioners.]
Solicitor reported deposit of plans and draft Order and issuing of advertisements.
Secretary reported order given to Hudswell, Clarke & Co. for a new locomotive to cost £1,670.
Tender of Tyer & Co. to be accepted for mechanical signalling.
Mr Stephens to send particulars of the electrical staff signalling to be ordered from the Railway Signal Co.

4/1/1909   The Secretary of the Light Railway Commissioners requested the insertion of advertisements for objections but agreed to waive the need for a local inquiry.

4/2/1909   The Llanelly Urban District Council urged the extension of the Light Railway Order to the Llanelly branch.
Solicitor reported meeting the Commissioners on 2nd February to agree finally the terms of the draft Order.
Rowell & Co.'s tender and plans of the station buildings discussed, Stephens to be asked for his approval.

15/3/1909   Reported that the Commissioners had approved the Light Railway Order and submitted it to the Board of Trade.
Cheque for £600 signed for payment to Metropolitan Railway for 10 second-hand coaches [repairs to cost extra].
The GWR claimed a portion of land on which the Burry Port station was about to be built, the Solicitor to investigate.
Mr Morgan reported there were objections to the man (Burfoot) sent by Mr Stephens to do the signal wiring.

19/4/1909   Tyer & Co.'s tender had been increased in consequence of the extra signal work on the Kidwelly branch.
£3,000 on deposit to be transferred to current account to pay for the new locomotive and the Light Railway Order.

7/6/1909   Solicitor reported correspondence with the Board of Trade re. the Cheap Trains Service [*sic*].
Proof print of the book of the revised rules & regulations approved.

5/7/1909   The Light Railway Order was approved by the Board of Trade on 30th June.
The proposed extension to the 'engine house' was sanctioned.
Prints produced of the new By-Laws as approved by the Board of Trade, the Company's seal affixed to two copies to be sent to the Board as required by them.
The Directors decided to dispense with an opening Ceremony at the start of passenger services but Mr Morgan was to entertain the Press at a luncheon to cost about £5 and all employees were to be given an extra day's pay.

The dispute with the GWR over a plot of land at Burry Port to be settled by an exchange with a similar sized plot; Mr Morgan and Mr Reece to negotiate the details.

30/8/1909   Mr Morgan reported that 10,000 passengers had been carried since the opening [on 2nd August], also he had instructed Mr Stephens to perform the certain alterations that he and Mr Eager required [this was for an extra signal at Kidwelly Jn].

Green & Burrows of Liverpool's offer of £45 per annum for five years advertising contract for stations and coaches accepted.

Passenger insurance was to be effected with the Railway Passengers Assurance Co.

As a total of £3,963 4s. 5d. of cheques were signed today it was agreed to sell £2,500 worth of the £5,000 Transvaal Government Stock held by the Company.

It is obvious that there was every confidence that the Light Railway Order would be obtained without difficulty as considerable work had been done before the Order was finally approved on 30th June, 1909, only 33 days before the passenger service began. Not all details discussed by the Directors were minuted; there were written reports read at each meeting from Stephens, Morgan and Eager on the progress with the work required, but all that is recorded is that their 'reports were read'. There is no mention, for example, of the tickets to be ordered for passenger journeys (they were printed by Williamson & Co. of Ashton under Lyne), or of extra staff required. Arthur Morgan attended all but one of the meetings, with Holman Stephens and John Eager both present on 14th December, 1908. All were held as usual at the company's London Office at 5 Grays Inn Square.

The estimate for the cost of the engineering works required under the proposed Light Railway Order submitted to the Commissioners on 13th November, 1908 and signed by H.F. Stephens was:

		£	s.	d.
Main Line 11 miles 3 chains (Railway No. 1)				
Earthworks: cuttings 1,080 cu. yds				
embankments 1,080 cu. yds	est. cost 110		0	0
Bridges, public roads		50	0	0
Culverts and drains		50	0	0
Metalling of roads and level crossings		20	0	0
Permanent way, fencing and signalling		2,508	0	0
Land		nil		
Stations		1,575	0	0
Kidwelly branch 1 mile 20 chains (Railway No.2)				
Permanent way, fencing and signalling		180	0	0
Land		nil		
Station		50	0	0
Contingencies	15 per cent, say	682	0	0
	Total	5,225	0	0

From this it will be noticed that only the first 1¼ miles of the Kidwelly branch, as far as Tycoch, were to be included in the Light Railway Order, together with a small station costing only £50; just a short platform was to be provided at Tycoch by way of a station.

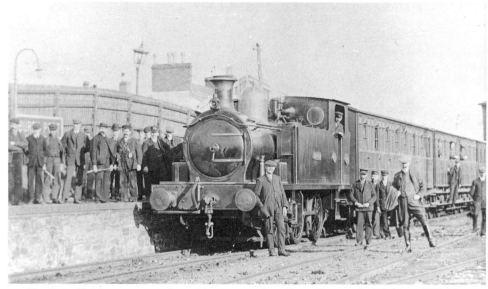

The first official passenger train waiting to start from Burry Port on 2nd August, 1909. The consulting engineer H.F. Stephens is standing on the right with his coat over his arm; John Eager is by the right buffer of the locomotive *Pioneer* which unfortunately had later to be substituted as an axle box ran 'hot'. *R.E. Bowen Collection*

On arrival at Pontyberem on 2nd August, 1909 everyone gets out whilst the engine runs round. *Brian Cripps Collection*

After running round at Pontyberem the engine, by now the substitute *Pembrey*, waits for the 'right away' for the first official return journey on 2nd August, 1909.   *LGRP 18209*

Setting off from Pontyberem with *Pembrey* on the first return passenger train on 2nd August, 1909. It looks as if the driver has asked the figure on the right if they are on the right road and has received the reply, 'Yes, straight on for Burry Port, you can't miss it'.   *Author's Collection*

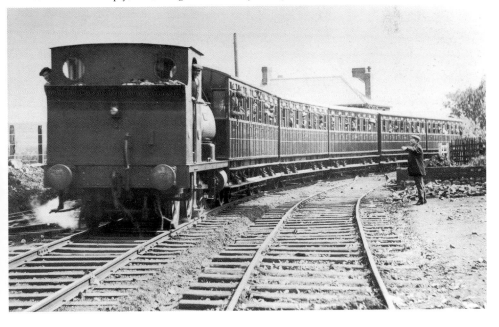

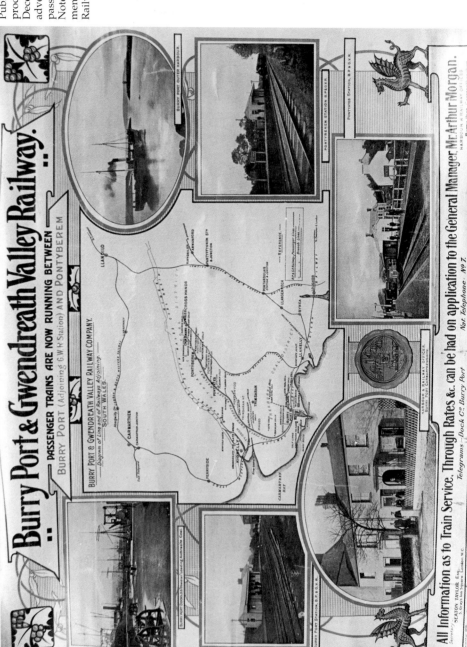

Publicity poster produced in December 1909 to advertise the new passenger service. Note there is no mention of a 'Light' Railway.

R.E. Bowen Collection

With regard to the extra signalling work required for the Kidwelly branch, previously mentioned, the following letter sent to the Board of Trade on 9th September, 1909 by Stephens from his office in Tonbridge will explain:

BURRY PORT AND GWENDREATH VALLEY RAILWAY
Sir,
Kidwelly Junction
The Company will be glad if permission will be given for the erection of an up stop signal as shown on the enclosed Diagram, worked from one of the Spare Levers at Kidwelly Junction Box, to enable trains to be taken on from Pont Yates under the 'Section clear but station blocked signal' during the time the Kidwelly Branch Junction is fouled for shunting purposes. The signal would be 250 yards on the Pont Yates side of the branch Junction.
     I am Sir,
          Your obedient Servant.
          (signed) H. F. Stephens

The Board of Trade replied on 24th September giving permission, 'provided that there is a view obtainable of the proposed new signal for at least a quarter of a mile'.

Note that at that period the direction of travel was 'up' from Pontyberem to Burry Port. It was changed to being 'up' to Cwmmawr and 'down' to Burry Port in 1913 (or late 1912).

At the Directors' meeting on 27th September, 1909 the company's seal was affixed to a Power of Attorney to De Zaete & Gorton, stockbrokers, for the sale of the remaining £2,500 of Transvaal Government Stock (which realised £2,421 5s. 0d.) and this allowed cheques to be signed for £1,534 12s. 7d. to Tyer & Co., £464 0s. 0d. to H.F. Stephens (the account he presented was for £464 0s. 1d. so he was actually short paid by one penny!) and £128 17s. 0d. to the solicitor for the balance of legal costs. At the next meeting, on 18th October, it was stated that the total expenditure on the Light Railway works to date amounted to £8,656 7s. 3d.; had the cost of entertaining the press to luncheon been included? All was not yet done, however, as Arthur Morgan reported that work had now started on the signalling alterations near Trimsaran Road required by the Board of Trade, whilst a letter from the Board was read asking whether their Inspector's requisitions had been complied with - the letter to be sent to Stephens for reply. It was not until 16th December that Stephens confirmed that he had now complied with all the requisitions and a cheque for £40 was made out to Tyer & Co. Ltd for their extra signalling work.

The above total, even without the additional £40, is rather more than the amount expended according to a further application made by the BP&GV on 30th May, 1911 for a new Order. The Commissioners were now told that the total spent as a result of the 1909 Order was £7,542 9s. 3d. of which £1,138 11s. 2d. was paid out of Revenue and the balance from the Reserve Funds. The difference amounts to some £1,154; have we another example of 'creative accounting' here or were the Commissioners deliberately being given false figures? The difference is about the amount that the nine carriages used only for the colliers cost, the other four coaches (five originally) obtained in 1909 being the ones used for the passenger service so their cost is included. It would seem

The new station at Burry Port after the addition of the toilet block on extreme left. Clearly a different style of architecture from that used by Stephens for the main station building. The two carriages nearest the camera are ex-LSWR and the two further away are Metropolitan.

R.E. Bowen Collection

This 'magnificent' signal box was built in 1909 at Dock Junction ready for the new passenger service. Although Tyer & Co. supplied the equipment it seems unlikely they were responsible for the cabin.

Author's Collection

that it had been decided that the provision of these extra carriages for the colliers' service was not as a result of the 1909 Light Railway Order.

This was not quite the end of everything concerned with getting a passenger service up and running as the BP&GV and GWR solicitors were taking their time in reaching agreement over the exchange of two small plots of land at Burry Port; finally, on 21st March, 1910, the Deed of Exchange was at last sealed and BP&GV passenger trains could now terminate in a station built entirely on its own land.

It is difficult to quantify the influence that H.F. Stephens had on the appearance of the line following the introduction of passenger working. Certainly the station buildings bore a strong resemblance to those built for the other Stephens-engineered railways. They were of simple, single-storey construction mostly with timber framing clad with zinc sheeting (popularly referred to as corrugated iron) plus decorative boarding at the gable ends, containing just a booking office, parcels office and a waiting room; the sheeted roof was extended over that part of the platform in front of the building. Ponthenry, which was different in that the walls were built of brick, was added much later, believed in 1919. All platform faces were of brick or stone, backfilled with colliery waste. Toilets were only added later. The order to build a new goods shed, opposite the Burry Port terminus, was placed with Rowell & Co. for £84 on 16th December, 1909.

The new passenger locomotive, No. 8 *Pioneer*, was quite different from the existing BP&GV saddle tanks, being a smartly-proportioned side tank like the engines built new for the other Stephens' railways. She was finished in a maroon livery (all the other BP&GV engines were green) and was received from the makers, Hudswell, Clarke & Co. of Leeds, in March 1909 at a cost of £1,670. The carriages were second-hand from the Metropolitan Railway but might not Stephens, who had once worked for that line, have suggested that some might be available and arranged an introduction?

Prior to the new signalling, the line had been worked on the staff and ticket system, with telegraph communication. The new signal boxes, which were little more than small huts, were provided at Dock Junction (¼ mile west of Burry Port station) with three levers of which one worked the points, Kidwelly Junction (4¾ miles) with 10 levers, and Pontyates (7¾ miles) which had eight levers. The frames were supplied by Tyer & Co. Ltd of Carlisle with the levers at 5½ inch centres and the trains from Dock Junction to Pontyberem were controlled by the electric train staff and block telegraph with instruments made by the Railway Signal Co. Ltd of Fazakerley, Liverpool. The signal boxes themselves would appear to have been built by a local firm, possibly by Rowell & Co. as part of their station buildings contract. The short section, just under a quarter of a mile, from the Burry Port terminal to the Dock Junction signal box was controlled by a wooden train staff whilst the Kidwelly branch was operated by 'one engine in steam' regulations with a hexagonal staff.

All the turnouts were provided with what were known as economical point locks, just the one lever working both the point movement and the locking. Whilst this would not have been allowed on a main line (a separate lever being required for facing point locks) it was tolerated on a light railway with the slow speeds prevailing. Similarly the BP&GV was permitted to do without any distant signals on the line, and only one level crossing (at Pontyates) was provided with gates; even that was hand-worked and hand-locked. Other level crossings, except those in the dock area at Burry Port, were protected by cattle grids, referred to in one contemporary report as an 'imported American idea'. Pontyberem (11 miles) at the terminus of the passenger working had a ground frame with five levers. There were a further 17 single-lever ground frames on the main line plus four on the Kidwelly branch. Stations were situated at Burry Port (a single 350 ft-long platform), at Pontyates with two platforms each 250 ft and a passing loop, and at Pontyberem which had a loop but only one 250 ft platform. There were halts at Pembrey village, Pinged, Trimsaran Road, Pontnewydd and Ponthenry, also at Tycoch on the Kidwelly branch, and all were provided with name boards, lighting and a platform three feet above rail level, but no waiting shelter.

The track included some older 65 lb. rail as well as the new 75 lb. per yard flat-bottom rail, fastenings were ¾ inch fang bolts to wooden sleepers of 10 inch by 5 inch section, 9 feet long, laid in slag and ashes ballast. Pontyates was the only place where one passenger train could pass another passenger train, but there were a number of places (including Pontyberem) were one could cross a goods train, or two goods workings could pass. Coal trains could also be 'locked in' at colliery sidings, using the electric train staff, allowing another train to continue along the single line. The overall speed limit was 25 mph but reduced at certain places such as 5 mph over Pontyates crossing and 10 mph at all other level crossings.

A party of Journalists from Llanelly and Carmarthen were taken for a trip over the line by Arthur Morgan on Monday 26th July (was this when they were entertained for luncheon? Perhaps there were no more than a dozen or so of them, at the most, so the cost of about £5 is not unreasonable) and it would seem that the original intention was to start the passenger service on 31st July, the *Llanelly and County Guardian* commenting on Thursday 29th July, 1909 that 'the line will be opened to the public on and after Saturday next'. In the event it was after, not on, with passenger trains starting on the Bank Holiday Monday, 2nd August. This is confirmed by *Bradshaw's Manual* which says 'the line was equipped for passenger service in 1909, and the first passenger train was run on 2nd August. The initial service, as detailed in Chapter Nine, comprised four down (to Pontyberem) and three up trains on weekdays, with five each way on Saturdays.

Mention was made earlier that no toilet facilities were provided at first; the party of journalists may have remarked unkindly on their absence because on 16th December, 1909 the Directors approved the expenditure of £52 3s. 3d. on lavatories. How many stations were thus provided for in 1910 is not stated but they were definitely not in the luxurious class! Pembrey was later provided with a waiting shelter.

During 1910, the first full year of the new service, 110,447 ordinary passengers were carried, not including colliers or workmen. Such a statistic is calculated by counting a single ticket as one whilst a return is valued at two. The amount of coal and other goods carried and originating on the system in 1911 totalled 550,409 tons, and had more than doubled in just 15 years. The profitability of the company remained unaffected by the new passenger service, the continued excellent results allowing a 10 per cent dividend to be paid to the ordinary shareholders in 1909, and the same in both 1910 and 1911; the dividend on preference shares also remained steady at 5 per cent. A map of the system, mounted on linen and on rollers by Sefton Praed & Co., was approved on 16th December, 1909 when it was decided to send one to all shareholders having 10 or more shares. Arthur Morgan was paid an increased salary of £550 per annum on 1st January, 1909 whilst John Eager received a bonus of £25 and had his salary raised to £270 on 1st September, 1909. Edward Evans was awarded a £10 bonus on 18th October, 1909. The Directors also decided to take their full entitlement of £600, divided among them as previously, from the beginning of 1910. There were further salary increases to £600 for Morgan, and of £300 to Eager, awarded from 1st April, 1911.

The following year Leonard Matthews died, in September or October 1912, and the Rt Hon. Alexander, the 8th Earl of Dunmore (1871-1962), of Thornhill, Weybridge, was invited to become a Director, being elected on 15th January, 1913. As Captain the Hon. Alexander E. Murray he had served in India in 1895-98, seeing action with the Guides Cavalry during the Frontier War in Afghanistan and was awarded the Victoria Cross, medal and clasp in 1898; then he served with the 16th Lancers in South Africa 1899-1900. He was to see further action as a Major in World War I. Lord Ashburnham, the 5th Earl, former Chairman and a prominent landowner around Burry Port and Pembrey, died on 15th January, 1913 aged 72. His only son had died in infancy so he was succeeded by his younger brother, Thomas who became the 6th and last Earl, and who died in 1924 without an heir; he was a Canadian resident and seldom visited Britain. Then in 1915, on 7th June, former Director and solicitor Charles Ommanney died aged 63.

During August 1912 a delay in finalising the accounts for the half-year to 30th June was reported, due to the illness of Edward Evans, then aged 62. A clerk from the Auditors' office (W.B. Peat & Co., which was now at 11 Ironmonger Lane in the City) was sent to Burry Port to assist. Evans retired at the end of the month and was awarded an annual pension of £75. In his place John George Hancock (known as George) was promoted to Accountant from 1st September at a salary of £180 per annum, raised to £200 after 12 months and to £220 from 1st July, 1915. Hancock, born in Amlwch, Anglesey in 1868, had been with the company since at least 1888, probably since leaving school. Edward Evans of Penybanc, Burry Port, died on 4th February, 1918; his widow Ann died in 1930 age 90.

The engagement of an extra draughtsman for the Engineer's office was agreed on 14th February, 1910, followed on 11th February, 1913 by the engagement of a junior clerk at 20s. per week A new appointment was of an official named Henderson to shipping canvasser as from July 1911 for a fee of £100 for a half-year; he was succeeded by F. John Evans, a local shipping broker, from July 1914. Raymond Taylor became Assistant Secretary from the beginning of 1913 at a salary of £50 per year. An additional locomotive fitter was also engaged at this time at 33s. weekly whilst ganger Thomas Williams

Two of the new side tank locomotives with one of the older saddle tanks outside the engine sheds at Burry Port about 1915. *Left to right, Pioneer, Burry Port* and probably No. 2.
Author's Collection

Two more engines outside the sheds on 15th May, 1919; Avonside saddle tank *Kidwelly* and Hudswell side tank No. 13.   *LCGB Ken Nunn Collection 2210*

was promoted to be permanent way inspector from 5th February, 1913 for which he was paid an extra 5s. per week. Ganger Davies was retired in November 1913 with a weekly pension of 5s. Another appointment made for the first time in February 1913 was of a telegraph lineman at 24s. per week with a remit to attend to the electric train staff instruments, telephones and to assist with the electric lighting. Previously it is understood that there was an agreement with the GWR to hire their lineman at Llanelly for any work required, the BP&GV agreeing to be liable if there was any accident to the man. Of course, with brand new equipment there should not have been much maintenance needed at first.

Besides the new passenger locomotive, further new engines were purchased for the anthracite trains, being similar in style to *Pioneer* but larger, and were without names. They also were built by Hudswell, Clarke & Co. of Leeds, No. 9 in November 1909 for £1,750, No. 10 in December 1910 at a cost of £1,695, and No. 11 which arrived in January 1913 priced at £1,810. The hire of a steam roller for use on the roads around the Dock estate was agreed on 14th February, 1910. An enlargement of the engine shed at Burry Port was urgently required but, having discussed the estimate and plans on 15th November, 1909, the go-ahead by the Board was not finally given until 13th September, 1910. Before that, on 27th May, 1910, the order was given to Brawn Thomas & Co. for new shed doors and repairs to the ventilators and existing roof costing £119. A further extension was soon needed and John Eager was told on 15th May, 1912 to obtain estimates. In August a tender for £322 5s. was approved but it was decided to wait until the following year before work would begin. The delay would seem to have been because a shed, which it was thought could have been suitable, was coming up for sale in April 1913 at the copper works; there is no evidence that this purchase was ever made.

The Directors were informed on 21st July, 1910 that the locomotive belonging to Thomas Evans (the owner of Gwscwm Colliery) had on 30th June damaged the Jolly bridge, the cost of repairs being estimated at £23; Mr Evans subsequently agreed to pay £15. This bridge is No. 6 at 1 mile 44½ chains west of Burry Port and is named after the local hostelry 'The Jolly Sailor'. Whilst it could be expected that Evans' engine might work over BP&GV metals to Burry Port, it is not known what was it doing operating almost a mile further west beyond the Gwscwm Siding. A possibility is that it was going to or from the Craiglon Colliery, that connection being only a further 27½ chains past the Jolly bridge.

An interesting example of the relationship between local neighbours is revealed by the decision of the BP&GV Board to send a cheque for five guineas on 13th September, 1910 to the fund for the widow of the late Mr Williams, the GWR station master at Pembrey and Burry Port. Relationships between railwaymen and management on the other hand could be strained at times and the railway trade unions had grown considerably in strength. The BP&GV, being quite a small railway, had to go along with the decisions of the larger companies (such as the GWR) when it came to hours and conditions of work as well as pay. In 1907 the unions got the larger railways to agree an arbitration scheme but the BP&GV rejected it as quite unnecessary. On 7th January, 1908 Arthur Morgan explained the position to the Board of Trade thus:

The handsome lines of the Hudswell, Clarke side tanks are seen to good effect in this broadside view of No. 12 outside the engine shed about 1920.   *J. Harper*

Avonside saddle tank *Kidwelly* has presumably been marshalling empty Metropolitan carriages at Burry Port as she is not fitted with the vacuum brake so would not have been allowed to work a passenger train.   *R.E. Bowen Collection*

... in view of the amicable relations which have long existed, and still exist, between this Company and its Employees, it is not considered that any object would be gained by adopting the scheme for conciliation and arbitration.

It was on 18th September, 1911 that the Directors were told about the men's deputation with demands for increased pay. At that time it was decided to wait and see what the GWR and other big companies intended to do. At the year end the BP&GV made an offer to the men which was acceptable to the Amalgamated Society of Railway Servants (ASRS) and was confirmed at the Directors' meeting on 15th January, 1912. An example of the 'amicable relations' then existing was revealed by this appreciative letter sent on 7th January by Robert Collins, Secretary of the Burry Port branch of the Union:

On behalf of your employees, I respectfully beg to inform you that we have decided unanimously to accept the terms submitted to us by you for consideration. Moreover, I may add that we feel extremely grateful to you for your kindness and generosity. You can rely upon us doing our utmost to discharge all duties entrusted to us with reliability and satisfaction to our superiors and all concerned. Again thanking you heartily on behalf of the men.

However, on 11th June, 1912 the Board of Trade was writing to the BP&GV about a new scheme agreed with the Unions for a suitable number of permanent Conciliation Boards to be established on each railway. Morgan replied pointing out they were a very small company and,

I understand there are several Companies similarly situated who have not thought it necessary to form Conciliation Boards, and as there are no grievances or outstanding disputes unsettled between us, I hope it will not be necessary to incur needless expense ... I am living amongst the men and they see me daily, and I have always listened to their demands and received deputations whenever they have asked me to.

The Board of Trade passed on this reply on 19th June to the Burry Port branch of the ASRS which Robert Collins in turn dispatched to his headquarters to deal with. Thus the General Secretary of the Union, J.E. Williams, on 28th June wrote to the Board of Trade that,

I would point out that Clause 9 of the scheme definitively lays it down that a suitable number of Conciliation Boards shall be established on each Railway, and in view of the fact that the employees of this Railway Company have expressed a desire to have Conciliation Boards formed, I shall be glad if you will make such representations to the Company as will result in Boards being established.

Unfortunately for the Union, Clause 9 (I think they meant 19) did not apply to a railway that had not adopted the scheme, and there were no powers to force the company to adopt the scheme. Accordingly the Union were told,

... that the question as to whether the Scheme should be adopted on the B. P. & G. V. Railway was one for agreement between the Company concerned and their employees in regard to which the Board was not prepared to intervene.

A year later the Directors dealt with further demands and decided on 30th July, 1913 that they would confirm the terms conceded by Mr Morgan as to 'overtime, platelayers, gangers and fitters'; subject to this the rates of wages to stand as agreed in January 1912. Still there were more demands, this time for increases for all grades and on 12th November, 1913 Morgan reported on the increases which had been provisionally agreed. This the Directors approved and they congratulated Mr. Morgan on the terms settled.

Arthur Morgan had had his salary increased to £650 per year from January 1913, and 12 months later John Eager received his more modest increase to £320. The Directors never valued the services of their Engineer as highly as their Manager. On 3rd March, 1914, on hearing that Pearson & Co. had gone into liquidation, it was decided to award a new contract for clothing to Smith & Sons of Derby, and on the same date a bonus of £10 was presented to George Hancock.

Back in December 1908, when the company first received a petition from the inhabitants of Cwmmawr calling for a passenger service, it was estimated the cost of doing so would be £4,000. Even without introducing passengers it was realised that the very steep gradients beyond Pontyberem, as much as 1 in 14 and 1 in 15, would need to be eased to cope with the increasing mineral traffic. The success of the passenger trains to Pontyberem made the Directors think again about extending the service.

Although the decision was yet to be taken, it was agreed on 18th April, 1910 that negotiations could begin for the purchase of the additional land required for a station at Cwmmawr. On 22nd November it was arranged to purchase a strip of land from Mr Morgan Jones and a small frontage piece from Mr Treharne for £160 and £30 respectively, payment being made on 23rd May, 1911. On 21st May, 1910 H.F. Stephens had been asked to survey and report generally on the proposal; his report was considered on 13th September when the Directors decided they would need to visit the area before coming to any conclusion. Stephens' estimate included in his report amounted to £2,850 including a second platform at Pontyberem, a new station at Cwmmawr, much of the fencing to be renewed and new signalling; it did not include the cost of land, permanent way or the electric train staff.

A letter from Stephens about the necessary diversion of the line to ease the gradients was discussed by the Directors on 24th January, 1911 and his further report awaited. This was sent on 20th February together with plans and sections, and two days later he was asked to furnish a detailed estimate, which he did on 10th March. It was discussed by the Directors three days later when Arthur Morgan was asked to ascertain the terms the collieries required to supply the fill from their waste tips, also for Stephens to get out the cost of his alternative loop scheme. Decisions were now left to a sub-committee of Sir Thomas Pilkington and Leonard Matthews to act in association with Stephens and were not referred to the monthly Board meetings. Incidentally, Pilkington had been appointed High Sheriff for York in 1911-12.

With only the full Board minutes available from this period the date the actual decision was taken on the route and the application for a Light Railway Order is not known. The next discussion on the subject minuted by the

Directors was not until 27th April when the solicitor produced a draft of the proposed application; the final revision was approved on 23rd May and the Company seal was duly attached, the application being forwarded to the Commissioners on 30th May, 1911 together with a cheque for £50 payable to the Board of Trade. The estimate by Stephens for the cost of the engineering works, which formed part of the application, reveals the following costings:

Length of line 1 mile 47 chains:			£	s.	d.
Earthworks: cuttings	44,152 cu. yds				
embankments	41,151 cu. yds	Cost	2,270	6	0
Accommodation bridges			90	0	0
Culverts and drains			70	0	0
Mettalling of roads and level crossings			50	0	0
Permanent way, fencing and signalling			1,011	0	0
Stations			660	0	0
Land, 1 acre, 3 roods, 2 perches			100	0	0
Contingencies	15 per cent, say		592	14	0
	Total		4,844	0	0

Why an extra 3,001 cubic yards needed to be extracted from the cuttings is not explained and no provision appears to have been made for tipping this extra material. Stephens in his previous estimates had allowed 6d. per cubic yard for the purchase of colliery waste to provide additional fill yet now he appears to have quoted for a surplus rather than the need to purchase more. Why was only £100 shown as the cost of the land required, when £190 had been paid just a week earlier? Also, the 15 per cent for contingencies seems to have been calculated on a figure some £300 less than the total estimate. One wonders if anyone at the Commissioners or the Board of Trade bothered to check these figures. The price quoted for stations included a second platform 272 ft long at Pontyberem as well as the terminus at Cwmmawr with its single 300 ft platform.

Holman F. Stephens' fee of 150 guineas plus expenses was confirmed on 20th June, 1911. Then on 18th September the Directors were informed that the Light Railway Commissioners had agreed the application and it had been passed to the Board of Trade for their approval; further, on 24th October, they heard that the Light Railway Order had been confirmed on 4th October, 1911. One interesting clause relating to trespass (not in the 1909 Order), inserted because there had been a long history of local people using the line as a footpath, followed the form used in Section 4 of the Shropshire and Montgomeryshire Light Railway (Amendment) Order 1910, and Section 87 of the East Kent Light Railway Order 1911, both railways associated with Holman Stephens.

Work now started in earnest at building a new line alongside the existing one but using a less steep gradient. Stephens had advised that in his opinion the Board of Trade would not sanction the line for passengers if the grade was any steeper than 1 in 40, so that was the incline of the new line. The construction was being carried out by direct labour; on 27th November it was reported that 25 men were now employed on the works, and the number would be increased in the Spring. A late decision, not included in the estimates, was to build a cottage at Cwmmawr and £50 was agreed with Morgan Jones on 21st February, 1912 to purchase from him an additional plot of land (£53 10s. 10d. was actually paid including vendor's costs).

So work continued throughout the year on the new alignment using what men could be spared from other duties; remarkably without any serious interruption to the existing traffic. The decision was taken on 19th November, 1912 to purchase three former London & South Western Railway six-wheel carriages, converted to four wheels only, at a cost of £91 each. At the same time arrangements were concluded with the New Dynant Anthracite Colliery Ltd for the supply of water and electricity to the Cwmmawr station. With the works virtually complete and ready for inspection the company's seal was affixed on 15th January, 1913 to an undertaking required by the Board of Trade that the extension would be worked by the electric staff and block telegraph.

On 18th January Stephens had reported that he was finishing his work and gave great praise to Mr Eager 'the excellent Resident Engineer who has carried out my wishes'. Earlier Stephens had been somewhat critical of John Eager due to slow progress but this would seem to be mainly because the work was carried out by direct labour; Stephens clearly would have preferred to have used a contractor. Mr Stephens' expenses to date amounted to £211 2s. 8d. (this is in addition to his previously agreed fee).

Lt Colonel E. Druitt reported on 17th January the details of his inspection. Some connections with siding points still had to be completed and he required a safety rail round the back of the Pontyberem and Glynhebog Collieries' Sidings lever frame. When these were done he could recommend the Board of Trade to sanction the use of the line for passenger traffic. The line opened to passenger services without any special ceremony on 29th January, 1913.

Col Druitt's report quotes the length of the new single line as 1 mile 51.75 chains, the track and ballast as in the 1909 inspection except the flat-bottom steel rails were of 75 lb. and 80 lb. per yard weight. The sharpest curve was of 9 chains radius and the steepest gradient 1 in 40 for a length of 45.6 chains. The new embankment was 31.5 chains in length with a maximum height of 30 feet. There was one overbridge and one underbridge; two parish roads and one private road were crossed on the level with the usual cattle guards but no gates. A speed of 10 miles per hour would be allowed over them. A ground frame at Cwmmawr to work the signals etc. had five levers, another near by had two levers to control both the loop and one end of the New Dynant Colliery Siding; the further end had a single-lever frame. A two-lever frame worked the Pontyberem Colliery and Glynhebog Colliery Sidings. All these ground frames were released by the electric train staff for the Pontyberem to Cwmmawr section.

Pontyberem was now a crossing place for two passenger trains and had a signal box with 13 levers (three spare). At Pontyberem goods yard there was a single-lever frame for the siding connection. The Pentremawr Colliery connection had been moved 7 chains nearer Burry Port and a second connection had been laid at 9 miles 43 chains from Burry Port, both controlled by single-lever frames. A new siding connection for Caepontbren Colliery, worked by a single-lever frame, had been laid. All these ground lever frames were controlled by the electric train staff for the Pontyates to Pontyberem section.

The new signals and lever frames were supplied by the Railway Signal Company. The very basic layout provided at the terminus at Cwmmawr (a run-round loop alongside the platform line and just the one siding behind the platform) proved inadequate right from the start of the new services. Only 13 days later, on 11th February, 1913, additional facilities were authorized including a carriage siding and another siding for coal and miscellaneous traffic, plus a shunting spur (i.e. neck) so that the main line was not blocked. To build these a further strip of land, 600 ft long by 15 ft wide, had to be purchased from Mr Jenkins. Then on 21st January, 1914 it was found necessary to order the lengthening of the platform at a cost of around £50.

The availability of ready printed tickets was a normal adjunct to running passenger trains. The original supply of tickets in 1909 was printed by A. Williamson & Co. of Ashton under Lyne, Lancashire. Those issued at stations were the standard 2¼ by 1¼ inch Edmondson pasteboard tickets and all were third class only; on singles the company title was shown in full in sans-serif upper case style as 'BURRY PORT & GWENDRAETH VALLEY RLY.' (note the spelling of Gwendraeth) whilst on returns the initials 'B. P. & G. V. RY.' appeared on each coupon. All the remaining print on the tickets was with serif type. Conditions appeared in three lines on singles and a shortened version occupying two lines was shown on returns; backs were blank. The printer's imprint appeared in small lettering along the bottom edge. The return halves of return tickets had a large skeletal 'R' overprint in serif style. All numerals (the ticket number) contained four digits, as in 0027. Single coupon tickets had the numerals at the right end with just the two-coupon returns having numerals repeated at both ends. As a result booking clerks were able to stamp the date on the fronts of single tickets instead of the backs.

As examples of the fares charged, it was 5d. single from Burry Port to Trimsaran Road and 6d. from the latter to Pontyberem, or 11d. for the full journey. Ordinary returns were exactly double but there were market returns at a slight reduction such as 1s. 6d. (instead of 1s. 10d.) for the full journey. All returns were for the day of issue only; child tickets were half price and privilege tickets (for staff) were a quarter fare. Ordinary tickets were either green or buff, with returns usually having half one colour and half the other. Most other tickets exhibited a variety of colours, or coloured bands, as was quite normal for pre-Grouping railways. As well as being sold at the stations on the line, tickets could be purchased from a single-storey wooden office on the corner by the harbour offices.

Colliers were issued with weekly tickets, printed in single coupon style in the standard size, at vastly reduced fares. Pontyates to Capel Ifan Colliery was 9d. for the week, whilst Burry Port to either Gwendraeth Colliery or to Pontyberem Colliery was only 1s. 6d. In addition to the Edmondson pattern tickets there were also punch (tramway) type soft card tickets for use of the guard to issue to passengers boarding at the halts. These, printed in the normal upright style of tramway and omnibus tickets, had all the stations and halts (including Tycoch) down each side so that the guard could punch or nip the destination station. The fare was shown on the face by a large overprint such as 2D, 5½D, or 1/2 as required, usually in red. There was also a tramway type dog, bicycle or

BURRY PORT & GWENDRAETH VALLEY RLY.
This Ticket is issued subject to the Regulations
and Conditions stated in the Company's Time
Tables and Bills.

BURRY PORT
TO
TRIMSARAN ROAD
THIRD CLASS FARE 5d.
Williamson, Ticket Printer, Ashton-u-Lyne

6.6.11.   3499

B. P. & G. V. RY.
Issued subject to Coy's
Bye-laws & Regulations
Privilege Ticket
BURRY PORT
TO
PONTYBEREM
Third Class
Available day of
issue only.
Williamson, Ticket Printer, Ashton-u-Lyne

0688

B. P. & G. V. RY.
Issued subject to Coy's
Bye-laws & Regulations
Privilege Ticket
PONTYBEREM
TO
BURRY PORT
Fare 6d
Available day of
issue only

0688

A 2864

DOWN   UP
BURRY   PONTY-
PORT   BEREM
PEMBREY   PONT-
             HENRY
PINGED   PONT-
             YATES
TYCOCH   PONT-
TRIM-   NEWYDD
SARANRD   TRIM-
PONT-   SARANRD
NEWYDD   TYCOCH
PONT-   PINGED
YATES
PONT-   PEMBREY
HENRY   BURRY
PONTY-   PORT
BEREM
Williamson, Printer, Ashton

BURRY PORT & GWENDRAETH VALLEY RLY.
This Ticket is issued subject to the Regulations and
Conditions stated in Company's Time Tables, Bills
and Notices.

B. P. & G. V. RY.
Issued subject to Coy's
Bye-laws & Regulations
Burry Port
TO
TRIMSARAN RD.
Third Class.
Available day of
issue only.

4200

Burry Port & Gwendraeth Valley Rly.
COLLIER'S WEEKLY TICKET
REVISED FARE 4/6
Available in Colliers' Coaches for One Journey
each way daily, between
**BURRY PORT, PEMBREY, PINGED,
TYCOCH & CWMMAWR**
During Week Ending. -2 SEP '22
NOT TRANSFERABLE.

794   794

B. P. & G. V. RY.
Issued subject to Coy's Bye-laws & Regulations
Cwmmawr   Cwmmawr
TO
PINGED
10d   THIRD CLASS. 10d
Available day of issue only.
Pinged   Pinged

248   248

B. P. & G. V. RY.
Issued subject to Coy's
Bye-laws & Regulations
DAY TRIP.
Ponthenry
TO
BURRY PORT
Fare 1/2
Available day of
issue only.

777

B. P. & G. V. RY.
Issued subject to Coy's Bye-laws & Regulations
Pontyates   Pontyates
TO
BURRY PORT
1/2 Third Class Revised Fare 1/2
Available day of issue only.
Burry Port   Burry Port

4140   4140

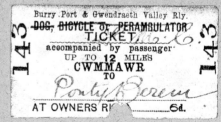

Burry Port & Gwendraeth Valley Rly.
**DOG, BICYCLE or PERAMBULATOR
TICKET**
accompanied by passenger
UP TO 12 MILES
CWMMAWR
TO
Pontyberem
AT OWNERS RISK   6d.

143   143

perambulator ticket at owner's risk with the fare overprint but omitting any named stations (so evidently available for the whole line); it is not known if there was an Edmondson card equivalent. Note that the ticket did not state that the item had to be accompanied by the passenger, as was usual.

A market return ticket from Pontyates to Burry Port numbered 0000, so the first one to be issued, has survived which is dated 29th July, 1909, which is the Thursday before the official Bank Holiday Monday opening. Might this ticket have been (perhaps deliberately) wrongly dated, used during staff training prior to opening, or is it possible that some passengers were actually carried on the date of the ticket? I don't suppose we shall ever know.

After the passenger service was extended to Cwmmawr on 29th January, 1913, the tramway type tickets for issue by the guard continued to be printed by A. Williamson & Co., but Tycoch was now omitted from the list of stations, Pontnewydd had become Glyn Abbey and, of course, Cwmmawr had been added. A curiosity was that in the title the spelling was now altered to 'GWENDREATH'. All the other (Edmondson card) tickets were provided by a new printer, having all the appearance of having been made by Waterlow & Sons although I have not been able to confirm this. Three digit ticket numbers now omitted the initial '0' prefix and the company title was now shown in serif type using only initials on the singles as well as the returns. The latter had the skeletal 'ℝ' overprinted in sans-serif style on the return halves whilst singles had the shortened conditions contained in a single line. The destination station was now shown in upper case sans-serif style but all other lettering had serifs. Miniature repeats were now shown on both the left and the right of the singles which suggests they could be cut in half and used as two child singles. Numerals were now repeated at both ends of all tickets, including singles, so that they were all dated on their backs on being issued.

Some of the new (presumed) Waterlow printings appeared well before the 1913 extension date. Examples are known of such printings for a return from Pontnewydd dated 26th January, 1911 and a single from Trimsaran Road issued on 18th February, 1911. It is thought that these were the first printings for tickets from these two stations; none being provided among the original stock from Williamson in 1909. The new collier's weekly tickets were similar to the earlier prints except that the title, given in full as before, was in serif style with lower case type, and the spelling was 'Gwendreath'. There was also a workmen's weekly ticket which cost rather more than that for colliers, for example three shillings from Burry Port to Pontyates and return for the six days; such workmen presumably had the use of upholstered seating. There was also now an Edmondson card ticket for a dog, bicycle or perambulator accompanied by the passenger.

The dating presses used in the booking offices used two initials only for the month, followed by the number for the date in the month (without an 0 prefix if it was less than 10) and the last two numerals of the year - for example 'SE 9 09'. However there are many surviving examples where the date had been applied by a hand-held rubber stamp with the day first, three letters for the month and the year shown in four digits as '-9 AUG 1910'.

On 1st January, 1917 there was a wartime 50 per cent increase in all fares and to distinguish new printings from existing ticket stocks the words 'Actual Fare'

Ponthenry soon after the building of the brick station building in 1919. Note the original platform still intact on the right. Looking towards Burry Port.   *R.E. Bowen Collection*

Pontyates looking towards Burry Port. This and the next photograph both look as if they were taken about the time of opening in 1909.   *R.E. Bowen Collection*

were printed in front of the cost so that the booking clerk knew he did not need to alter the printed amount. There was a further increase on 6th August, 1920, fares now rising to 75 per cent above the pre-war rate, and all subsequent ticket printings showed the words 'Revised Fare' on the front. From 1922 onwards standard GWR post-Grouping tickets were used and some for through bookings from BP&GV to GWR stations are known. Such through tickets may not have been pre-printed prior to 1922; the audited statistics sent to the Board of Trade for 1913 stated that all passengers carried on the BP&GV that year originated on the system.

As early as April 1911 an additional passing place near Craiglon bridge was called for to break up the long (over 4½ miles) single-line section from Dock Junction to Kidwelly Junction. It was clear by 1913 that it urgently needed to be done and on 11th February it was agreed to go ahead at an estimated cost if £160. The proposal for a loop at Ty Mawr controlled by eight levers (one spare) was submitted to the Board of Trade on 27th June which was approved. Nothing happened for nine months until a revised scheme was submitted on 12th March, 1914 and accepted six days later. Then on 22nd April, 1914 the tender of Tyer & Co. for £202 18s. 4d. was confirmed for the work. The installation was inspected in July 1914 by Lt Col Druitt, his report being dated 22nd July. The signal box had nine levers of which two were spare; there were no distant signals. Two passenger trains could not be passed, only one with a goods train or two goods trains. There was provision to switch the box out at quiet periods, it being expected to be in use for about 10 hours daily.

Despite the heavy expenditure during 1912 it was still possible to pay 6½ per cent that year on the ordinary shares, the amount had returned to 10 per cent for 1913 and dropped to 7 per cent for 1914; throughout the interest paid on the preference shares remained steady at 5 per cent. Arthur Morgan, in his annual report to the Directors on 15th January, 1914, said that the passenger receipts for the Cwmmawr extension had fallen short of expectations but with more houses being built in the valley the receipts should increase in the future. The receipts from passengers, workmen, mails and parcels amounted to £4,080 in 1912, and to £6,492 in 1913, but perhaps not all the increase was due to the new extension. The actual number of passengers carried in 1913 was 150,776 plus 39 season ticket holders and 29,417 workmen. For 1915 the number of ordinary passengers showed a modest increase to 158,024. Dividends that year had returned to 10 per cent on ordinary shares and remained at 5 per cent on preference shares.

Regarding the tonnage of goods and minerals carried, which was nearly all coal, the figures were 603,270 in 1912 and 699,416 (89.9 per cent was coal) in 1913. Around 17 per cent of the total (or 18½ per cent of just the coal) was shipped through the Burry Port Dock, some 100,500 tons in 1912 and 116,500 tons in 1913. With the outbreak of war in August 1914 there was a considerable reduction in the amounts shipped, down to 32,971 tons in 1916 and 30,380 tons in 1918.

The number of miles worked by the locomotives during 1913 amounted to 118,534, an average of 10,236 per engine (No. 12 had arrived towards the end of May 1913). A total of 36,955 miles was run on passenger trains, 51,096 on goods, 27,727 in shunting and 2,756 miles as light or assisting engines. The locomotive

Probably taken on the same day, Pontyates looking to Pontyberem. Note the GWR wagons loaded with pit props standing on the New Caepontbren Colliery siding.   *R.E. Bowen Collection*

Another view of Pontyates looking towards Pontyberem, definitely taken in 1909. It has the look of this being the official first return passenger train that is approaching.   *R.E. Bowen Collection*

running costs for the year 1913 were £5,862 plus a further £3,329 spent on maintenance, an average of £794 per engine. Turning to the financial results for 1913 the total gross revenue from the railway, dock and rents was £37,557 and the total expenditure £25,307, resulting in a profit of £12,250. Of this £5,600 was paid out in interest on loans and debentures, whilst £4,191 was distributed to shareholders. Clearly 1913 was a very good year.

The locomotive No. 12, just mentioned, cost £2,075, and was followed by another costing £2,197 from the same maker - Hudswell, Clarke & Co. - at the beginning of May 1914 which became No. 2. This was because the previous engine with this number, *Pontyberem*, was sold for £225 as being now too small.

The railway had been placed under Government control, through the Railway Executive Committee (REC), on the outbreak of hostilities. The war greatly affected the meetings of the Board; that planned for 5th August, 1914 (the day after war was declared) had to be cancelled owing to the Directors' military duties on mobilisation. The war service of Colonel the Hon. Sidney Peel and Major the Earl of Dunmore has previously been mentioned and clearly they had to miss many meetings. Indeed full Board meetings were infrequent and mostly were replaced by Committee meetings with just the Chairman and Secretary plus usually Arthur Morgan (or John Eager, or both) attending. The death of William Herring on 8th December, 1916 enabled Colonel Atherton Edward Jenkins of Wherwell Priory, Andover to be appointed in his place; aged 57 and thus no longer an active soldier, he was able to attend regularly. He had been born in Paddington in August 1859 and took his seat on 17th April, 1917, which was the first Board meeting to be held since 2nd February, 1916. Then in May 1917 Lt Col Sir Thomas Pilkington (nearly 21 months older than Jenkins) was ordered to France so the Committee meetings once more resumed, now chaired by Jenkins. At the same time Peel was seeing action in France where he was awarded the Distinguished Service Order in 1917, a medal also bestowed on Lord Dunmore (who was wounded in the action) in 1917 to add to his Victoria Cross.

Of course it was not just the Directors that served in France; many railwaymen answered the call to arms. John Eager was authorized to increase pay by 1s. 2d. per hour on 15th June, 1915 when he complained of the difficulty in replacing the men enlisting from the workshop. The Railway Executive Committee arranged from 1st January, 1915 for funds to pay a war bonus of 3s. per week to low paid railwaymen and 2s. to those earning 30s. or more per week. This was increased in October to 4s. per week to all railwaymen, further increased to 15s. 4d. from September 1917 and to 30s. weekly 12 months later, reflecting the high inflation rate later in the war. For Taylor, Eager and Hancock the war bonus was raised to £40 per annum from September 1917. For ordinary railwaymen the weekly bonus eventually reached 33s. by the end of 1918. There were annual salary increases of £100 to Secretary Taylor from July 1915, to Manager Morgan of £50 (to £700) and Engineer Eager of £20 (to £340) in May 1916, and of £30 to Accountant Hancock (to £250) in September. In April 1916 it was agreed to raise the Auditors' fees from 40 to 50 guineas per year.

The Plasbach Colliery at Pontyates was re-opened in 1913 by the newly-formed Gwendraeth Anthracite Collieries Ltd and by 1917 over 100 men were

A 1909 view of Pontyberem with a train arriving at the single platform. The station staff seem more interested in the photographer than the approaching train.   *R.E. Bowen Collection*

An Ernest T. Bush postcard of about 1912 taken at Burry Port terminus. The engine looks like *Pembrey* and could that be the photographer's friend Charlie Snook standing nearest to the camera?   *R.E. Bowen Collection*

employed here. New sidings were laid down and additional signalling was installed in 1916 requiring 10 levers to operate. The eight-lever frame in Pontyates signal box was altered to one of 14 (so four were spare for future use) and the Railway Department at the Board of Trade was advised on 15th February, 1916 that the new layout was ready for inspection; Colonel Druitt it was who gave his approval.

The company's offices at 5 Grays Inn Square were damaged by bombs dropped during a Zeppelin (German airship) attack on London. On 12th July, 1916 Seaton Taylor reported that the net cost of the repairs over the amount received from the insurers was £50 17s. 0d. and he proposed to share this loss with the company. This was agreed and he was handed a cheque for £25 8s. 6d. in consequence.

It was not just the offices, or the railwaymen, that were affected by the war. On 26th February, 1915 the Board had agreed that another locomotive was required and instructed the Secretary to obtain tenders. Eighteen days later Hudswell, Clarke's quotation for £2,225 was discussed and, before placing the order, it was agreed to ask if some reduction in price could be made. It is not known if any reduction was achieved, but due to wartime shortages the new engine was a long time being built. On 15th December the manufacturer was being pressed to complete the engine on order when it was reported that they were scarcely doing anything to it as they were under Government control; it was pointed out to Hudswell's that the Minister of Munitions had previously agreed for the work to be proceeded with. Then on 2nd February Morgan proposed that Hudswell, Clarke be offered the £1,100 first payment immediately the locomotive was delivered (presumably as an additional enticement). On 6th March, 1916 the Secretary reported to his Directors that the engine (the maker's No. 1164) had at last been completed on 24th February but was immediately requisitioned by the Ministry of Munitions for war service and sent to the Royal Artillery Experimental Station, Shoeburyness (where she became No. 8). However Hudswell, Clarke & Co had promised to supply another identical locomotive in three to four months' time.

The replacement, duly completed later that year, was Hudswell, Clarke No. 1222, but just as it was ready to be dispatched to Burry Port on 20th October, 1916 it was also commandeered, this time by the War Office, and taken to Richborough Sidings, Sandwich, Kent. Again, a further replacement was promised as soon as possible. Understandably the BP&GV Directors made furious representations to the Government, quoting their Priority Classification and their Ministry of Munitions Permit. The War Office relented and agreed to accept the second replacement, when it was built, instead. Just over a month later, the new engine was released and finally came to Burry Port on 25th November, 1916 and received the number 13. Unfortunately, due to inflation, the cost had risen to £3,008. The second replacement, works No. 1288 and built to the order of the BP&GV, was completed on 31st August, 1917 and delivered to the Inland Waterways & Docks depôt at Chepstow. Just to complete the story, the original engine requisitioned in February 1916 was eventually released from war service and purchased by the BP&GV in May 1920.

It was much later in the war that the Directors, on 17th May, 1918, considered a letter written the previous day by Arthur Morgan containing a proposal regarding his motor car. This was referred to Colonel Jenkins to settle with Mr Morgan when he next went to Burry Port. At the following meeting on 19th June Col Jenkins reported on his visit and especially mentioned that the trespassing was now getting most serious (see the following paragraph) and also that he recommended that they agreed to 'Mr Morgan's request re. licence of motor car'; this was confirmed. There is no suggestion that the BP&GV had paid for the motor, but presumably they had just decided to pay the annual road fund licence.

Mention has earlier been made that the 1911 Light Railway Order included a clause relating to trespassing; this being contained in Section 10 and provided that, 'any person who shall trespass upon any of the lines of the railway or of the railway of 1909 shall on conviction be liable to a penalty not exceeding Forty shillings'.

The usual cast-metal warning notices required were duly erected. Despite this the public continued to defy the warnings and walk along the line as before. Most of the trespassers were colliers walking between Pontyberem and Glynhebog Colliery, the number varying from 100 up to 250 each way daily. The company decided to take action and on 3th April, 1916 yard inspector Charles Owen took the names of a representative six trespassers (David John, David Davies, Daniel Price, William Rees, Oliver Thomas and John Finnemore) and advised them they would be facing prosecution.

The Magistrates heard the case in the Court of Summary Jurisdiction at Llanelly on 10th May, 4th July and 30th August. The defendants claimed there existed a right of way which had been used daily for more than 40 years and produced many witnesses who confirmed that (in the words of one) 'it was a free road for every one to go' and had been used without cessation or interruption until the present proceedings were instituted. The Magistrates decided that 'the right claimed was not impossible in law' and dismissed the case. Application was then made to the High Court, King's Bench Division, to overturn the ruling but, just as in a previous trespass case (*see Chapter Five*), the Divisional Court in December 1916 upheld the decision of the Justices although they did agree to give leave to appeal to the Court of Appeal. The Committee Meeting on 16th January, 1917 listened to their solicitor reporting on Counsel's opinion and as a result it was agreed to withdraw the appeal that had been tabled.

The question was discussed again by the Directors on 27th February, 1920 when they heard about a Scottish case which had gone to their Appeal Court (the Court of Sessions) where it was held that it was in the public interest, due to the danger involved, for a trespasser on the line to be liable to a penalty, and on these grounds it might be possible for the BP&GV to obtain an injunction from the High Court. This would be cheaper than again going to the Appeal Court but, despite this, no further action seems to have been contemplated and the trespassing continued without any more interruption.

Traffic continued to grow after the war. Goods originating on the system during 1919 amounted to 589,455 tons, of which 563,429 were coal, rising to

663,099 (636,328 coal) tons in 1920 when 289,371 tons were shipped through Burry Port Dock. For the same two years the number of ordinary passengers (excluding colliers and workmen) amounted to 187,377 (1919) and 190,972 (1920). Dividends remained remarkably steady at 5 per cent for preference shareholders and 10 per cent on the ordinary shares for every year from 1916 to 1920 inclusively, due in part to the Government guaranteeing the pre-war net income in exchange for Government traffic being carried free of charge. The Board had no difficulty in persuading shareholders to agree new annual fees from 1st January, 1918 of £250 for the Chairman and £200 for each of the other three Directors. Col the Hon. Sidney Peel DSO was elected the MP for Uxbridge in 1918.

A circular from the Railway Executive Committee dated 12th October, 1918 increased the war bonus of salaried staff (Arthur Morgan excluded) to £78 per annum from 20th September. In addition, from the end of that month, George Hancock was awarded a £25 annual increase to his salary. The eight-hour day was agreed with railwaymen from 1st February, 1919; whilst the hours worked were not necessarily reduced it did mean that overtime rates were paid once the eight hours were exceeded. A national railwaymen's strike was begun on 27th September, 1919 and settled by the Government on 5th October, one result being a further increase in the war bonus by 5s. to 38s. weekly plus a single payment of £1.

Further annual increases for the senior staff were approved on 17th May, 1920, of £70 to Morgan, £66½ to Eager and £60 to Hancock. Seaton Taylor retired as Secretary at the end of 1919 and was awarded an annual pension of £100. The new Secretary, appointed on 1st January, 1920, was Walter John Wenham (45), an Eastbourne solicitor, his salary being £300 per annum. Seaton Taylor continued to act as the company solicitor. A new position, that of H.J. Smith to be locomotive inspector, was made at the same time, his wage being £5 5s. 0d. per week. Also in 1920 it was agreed to increase the Auditors' fees to £75 per annum.

The Ministry of Transport Act was passed on 13th April, 1919, Sir Eric Geddes being the first Minister and the Railway Department of the Board of Trade was passed to the new Ministry. This was seen as a prelude to what became known as the Grouping. Although the Railway Executive Committee ceased to exist from the end of 1919, the Government still exercised control (until 15th August, 1921) through the new Ministry. In June 1920 Geddes revealed that the Government had rejected nationalisation and soon after announced that they were thinking of reorganizing the railways into seven regional groups.

The bill for the new Railways Act was published on 11th May, 1921; after much debate four groups were eventually agreed and the Act received the Royal Assent on 19th August, 1921. It established a Railway Amalgamation Tribunal to oversee the groupings, which had to come into effect no later than 1st July, 1923. As early as 9th August, 1920 Wenham, the new Secretary, revealed he had been to see the Ministry of Transport who advised that as the BP&GV was a Light Railway it was not to be taken over unless the GWR could make out a strong case and offer fair terms which would need to receive Ministry approval. Arthur Morgan's report of 6th October, 1921 would suggest

Looking the other way at Burry Port about 1912 with a Hudswell, Clarke tank attached to the train. On the right is a Trimsaran coal wagon.   *R.E. Bowen Collection*

The new passenger terminus at Cwmmawr with two of the ex-Metropolian Railway 8-wheelers in the siding, about 1920.   *Alan Ellis Collection*

that the GWR had already made overtures about taking over the BP&GV and four days later the GWR was asked to submit their scheme of absorption.

The Burry Port Council were worried that, if taken over by the GWR, the port would be allowed to decline and instructed Lewis Phillips (the Clerk to the Council) to ask the Ministry to clarify the position. They replied 'that the utilisation of the port facilities was a matter for consideration with the local trading and transport communities'. Three local Councillors plus Lewis Phillips accordingly went to see Felix Pole and E. Lowther of the GWR at Paddington on 27th October, 1921 to voice their anxieties; could the GWR assure them that Burry Port would continue to ship a fair share of the coal exports of the Gwendraeth Valley? Mr Pole, the GWR General Manager, replied,

> ... that there was no reason to anticipate any injury to the trade and interests of Burry Port as the result of the amalgamation ... the question of the amount of coal sent for shipment at Burry Port rested very largely with the colliery owners who shipped at the port which best suited their business.

and he added that any future development of the docks depended on an improvement in the present difficult financial situation. The deputation announced they were well satisfied with the explanation and assurances given.

The Government had eventually agreed to compensate the railways for losses incurred when subject to war-time control, under the Regulation of Forces Act of 1871. Payments to the BP&GV of £3,138 and £4,367 were agreed in May and June 1920. Further payments were made under the provisions of the Railways Act of August 1921, section 12 (1) (a), £6,454 being agreed in November and £8,850 in April 1922. Cynics had intimated that these payments were to soften the railways' opposition to the Grouping scheme.

Pontyberem station on 31st July, 1958 showing the second platform (*on right*) brought into use in 1913 when the passenger service was extended to Cwmmawr.   *Michael Hale*

The traffic results for 1921, the last full year of the company's existence, were marred by the 12 week national strike in the coal industry, so were well down compared with 1920. Goods traffic originating on the system amounted to 439,112 tons, of which 420,932 tons were coal (1920 figures were 663,099 and 636,328 respectively). A total of 116,970 ordinary passengers (190,972 in 1920) were carried, not including colliers and workmen. Receipts for 1921 amounted to £95,711 and the expenditure was £78,369, resulting in a gross profit of £17,342. This was still sufficient to pay a dividend of 10 per cent on the ordinary shares and 5 per cent on the preference shares, the same as for the previous six years. For the half-year to 30th June, 1922 just 3 per cent and 2½ per cent dividends were paid on the ordinary and preference shares.

At the next Directors' meeting on 21st November it was agreed to give the GWR Accountants permission to interview the BP&GV Accountant and Auditors. Following this the GWR submitted an offer which was discussed in detail by the Board on 13th February, 1922; also attending were Arthur Morgan, George Hancock (Accountant) and Reginald Petre (Auditor). Interestingly as Walter Wenham was absent through illness, 77-year-old Seaton Taylor acted as Secretary at this meeting. The terms to be offered to the shareholders were all agreed in principle and it was clear that the BP&GV was about to lose its independence by being absorbed by the GWR. Twenty-five years earlier and the Directors would have welcomed even the most derisory of offers; now they were in a position to demand a generous award.

A free pass was awarded annually to H.F. Stephens. This is the 1922 issue, which shows that by then Stephens was Lieutenant-Colonel.

Chapter Five

Burry Port Dock & Harbour, 1832-1940

Actually the title to this chapter could have read 'Docks' as for a short period from 1888 there existed both an East Dock (the original) and a West Dock; the latter reverting to its former use as a scouring reservoir in 1900 after little use by shipping. So for most of its existence as a port Burry Port just had the one small wet dock together with a larger and tidal outer harbour.

In February 1831 *The Cambrian* newspaper announced that the new harbour was to be partially opened. This would seem to have been premature as it was over a year later, in April 1832, that Certification was presented to the Court of Sessions for Carmarthenshire that the harbour was at last able to receive shipping. Later that year, as the harbour wall settled, several sections collapsed and had to be rebuilt. After a further three years even the walls of the reservoir had started to collapse. As a result it was not until 1836 that the ceremonial opening of the harbour finally took place. Despite these difficulties shipping was using the harbour; the *Ninus* of about 300 tons, of Scarborough, was loaded with anthracite from the Ynyshafren Colliery early in 1836 and a list of 16 ships using the port during 1837 is given in Volume One (p.154).

A plan of April 1832 showed the two early tram roads, from Pwll and from Cwm Capel, combining (and thus of the same gauge, which is believed to have been 4 ft 2 in.) to the north of the harbour and serving the western pier which had two loading 'jetties'. A lighthouse, 30 ft high, was erected early in 1838 at the end of the West Pier. In much later years the white light flashed every five seconds and could be seen from 15 miles distant.

As detailed in Volume One, the canal reached Burry Port in 1838. The original scouring reservoir, immediately to the north of the harbour, was altered to become a wet dock (later the East Dock) with lock gates whilst a new scouring reservoir (known locally as Pownd Clai) was built to the west. The canal was extended round the north of the dock and then down the east side. The dock measured 392 ft long, 153 ft wide and had an entrance width of 45 ft. With a depth of water over the cill of 22 ft at high spring tides (but only about 14 ft at neap tides) this allowed ships of up to 700 tons burthen to be accommodated. The main works seem to have been completed in 1841 but it was not until 1843 that the new dock became fully operational. The Neptune Hotel, built for the use of visiting captains and mariners, opened in October 1842.

It had been intended to develop the scouring reservoir as a dock (the West Dock) and it was provided with gates at the entrance of the same size as those at the East Dock. They were unused for nearly 50 years, there being sluices to allow the reservoir water out to scour the outer harbour at regular intervals.

Ignoring the evidence, when the GWR became the new owner of the dock from 1922 it clearly accepted the April 1832 date for the opening by claiming the Burry Port Dock was now the oldest on the system, just beating the Llanelly Railway's New Dock of 1833-34 into second place.

A plan dated 5th December, 1844, drawn for the conveyance of 131 acres of land from Lord Cawdor to the Burry Port Dock Company, depicts two tips on

A paddle tug is seen towing a two-masted sailing ship out of the East Dock in this pre-1888 view.
R.E. Bowen Collection

A screw tug in 1909 is taking a three-masted barque out of the East Dock.
R.E. Bowen Collection

the east wall of the dock and another on the north wall, also two further tips on the north-east side of the outer harbour. All the tips are served by tram roads. The network of lines was soon to be increased by the building of the copper works, started in March 1849, on the east side of the harbour; the first charge of ore was smelted on 10th November, 1849.

The plan also shows buildings on the site of the harbour offices on the west side of the outer harbour. These offices, which still stand, have all the appearance of dating back to at least the 1850s so those shown on the 1844 plan are likely to be the ones still existing. They were built as a three-house terrace with the harbour office in the centre and the home of the Dock (and Canal) Superintendent and Harbourmaster - Harbour House - on the right. By 1842 and again in March 1851 William McKiernon (aged 44 in 1851), the licensee of the Neptune Hotel, was describing himself as Superintendent so was possibly the original holder of the office. Ten years later, on 7th April, 1861, the Superintendent was Thomas Briggs, age 50 and born in Solihull, Warwickshire; he had been appointed by about 1854. As mentioned in Chapter One, he tragically drowned in his own dock on 15th March, 1863.

His eventual replacement was the redoubtable Captain John Paisley Luckraft, whom we first came across in Volume One (p.175). A 60-year-old Cornishman, he came to Burry Port from Havant, near Portsmouth, and also acted as the company's Engineer, being appointed Superintendent and Harbourmaster on 23rd March, 1864. Just 12 months later, under questioning by the House of Lords Select Committee, he revealed he was a Royal Navy Captain, the Canal Superintendent, the Docks Superintendent, a nautical surveyor, a land surveyor and a contractor. His name is sometimes spelt Luckcraft, both versions being used in local newspaper reports. However, the shorter form is used by Russell in all his letters to him, by his niece and on the 1881 Census return. He is reputed to have served with HMS *Bellarophon* (launched in 1824) as part of the Black Sea Fleet during the war with Russia in 1854.

William McKiernon was also quite a character; he had built the inner harbour and supplied much of the stone used from his quarry at Cwm Capel, was a builder responsible for many of the houses in Burry Port and, as we shall see shortly, a purchaser of wrecks on the Cefn Sidan Sands (such purchases being made at the auctions held at his Neptune Hotel). He was a Shropshire lad, having been born in St Martins near Oswestry in 1807. Raymond E. Bowen in Volume One describes him as 'a new star in the firmament. As a little known engineer/contractor he was to prove himself a remarkable man who moulded himself into the life and times of the town and dock of Burry Port'. Local historian John A. Nicholson refers to him as 'a very competent and versatile marine and civil engineer'.

On the 1881 Census, at the age of 74, he describes himself as a retired civil engineer living with his daughter Elizabeth and her husband Richard Williams, also from Shropshire (Ellesmere) and one time architect and surveyor but now the Post Master in Burry Port. McKiernon is also reputed to have built a section of the sea wall for the South Wales Railway between Llanelly and Burry Port.

Work on the construction of the broad gauge South Wales main line (to be worked by the GWR) along the coastline through Burry Port started in 1851 and the first trains commenced running on 11th October, 1852. The deposited plan of the railway as authorized by Parliament in 1845 showed a branch line from the main line curving round to the west side of the dock. The junction, facing towards Swansea, was just about the point where the Cwm Capel tramroad (curiously not shown on the plan) crossed the main line. The other tramroad, that from Pwll, was shown but served only two tipping points on the eastern quay of the dock, according to this plan.

This broad gauge branch appears never to have been built, and is not listed by MacDermot. Raymond E. Bowen believed that no broad gauge tracks were ever built on the dock estate or into the copper works. However, another Burry Port historian - W.D. Hall Jenkins - stated that after the BP&GV had opened in 1869 some of the lines on the dockside were of mixed gauge with three rails. The source of this information would appear to be an anonymous article in the magazine *The Locomotive* for 15th November, 1909 which stated:

> Improvements at Burry Port were authorised in 1872, the oversea [*sic*] trade at that time being principally conducted by sailing vessels, a large trade being done with St. Malo and other ports in Brittany. Most of the sidings at the docks were laid with a third rail to accommodate the G. W. broad gauge stock, and transfer stages had to be erected.

Personally, I suggest it is most unlikely that broad gauge wagons ever found their way onto the dock estate. The BP&GV Railway Act of 1872 (35-36 Vict. cap 126) did give authority to add a third rail to the dock lines and this does suggest that no third rail had been put down before then. However, in 1870 the BP&GV also did build a loading bank (transfer stage) alongside a broad gauge siding on the south side of the GWR line between the two tramroad crossings. Coal could then be hand shovelled from the standard gauge wagons on the bank into the GWR wagons alongside but at a lower level. Whether this applied in the reverse direction is not known; the BP&GV at this time (June 1870) was buying locomotive coal from Broad Oak Colliery, which is at Loughor and will thus have arrived in broad gauge wagons. A trial of the locomotive *Mountaineer* on 20th July, 1870 (*see Appendices*) involved climbing a short (about 75 yards) gradient of 1 in 32.18 at Burry Port. The only place this could be is the ramp up to this loading bank; a rise at this grade for such a length would indicate that the bank was about 7 feet above the broad gauge tracks. This arrangement only lasted until the last broad gauge trains through Burry Port ran on 11th May, 1872. The speed and efficiency with which the change of gauge was effected would suggest it had been carefully planned well in advance and there would be little point in providing mixed gauge tracks to the dock for such a *known* short period.

The BP&GV tracks constructed late in 1868 were not the first railway, as distinct from tramroad, lines laid in the dock estate. In August 1862 the copper works of Mason & Elkington had taken delivery of a new standard gauge shunting locomotive, so evidently lines within the works and to the east side of the dock were established about then, a steam crane to unload the copper ore being positioned on the quayside at an early date (before 1876). The tramroad to Pool Colliery was being converted to standard gauge during March and April 1867 after the copper works had acquired the colliery in 1865. By mid-1870 the standard gauge tracks extended to all the tips and shipping points around the dock and harbour.

Coal exports had finally ended from Pembrey (Old) Harbour in 1863 due to the expansion of Burry Port, much of which had taken place between 1851 and 1861. What is clear is that by the time the BP&GV Railway came to Burry Port in 1869 the dock and harbour were busy enough despite all the exports up to that time having to arrive by canal or tramroad. An attempt to use statistics from the 10-yearly census returns for the period from 1841 to 1881 to show the growth of the port has produced rather mixed results. Using the four occupations of coastguard, mariner, pilot and dock worker the general increase is as expected up to 1881 except for those calling themselves dock workers:

	1841	1851	1861	1871	1881
Coastguards	-	-	6	8	9
Mariners	2	7	24	25	47
Pilots	2	9	8	7	25
Dock workers	-	9	37	8	-

Perhaps job descriptions were changing by 1871; for example there were 13 ship coal trimmers and an engine driver on a steam dredge listed as occupations for the first time in 1881 as well as an engine driver, a second officer and five stokers on steam tugs, two other marine engine drivers, a shipwright, a captain in the merchant service, two dock labourers and finally a steward on board a gentleman's yacht! This latter would be the schooner *Dream* of 41 tons burthen, registered at the Port of Llanelly on 3rd July, 1865 under the ownership of Howard Elkington (1836-99), one of the brothers owning the copper works; the yacht was normally moored in Burry Port.

The Elkington family are known to have operated two steam paddle sloops at Burry Port, evidently purchased second-hand if the certificate dates quoted are when they were obtained, The earlier boat was the *Pilot* of 90 tons burthen built 1857 in South Shields, for which the certificate was issued on 9th November, 1868. The other was the *Hero* of 96 tons built 1864 in Northumberston, certificate issued on 2nd June, 1873. Both had to be registered at Llanelly because Burry Port was not a port of registration.

The Burry Port Smelting Co. Ltd, through its subsidiaries the Burry Port Steamship Co. Ltd and Thompson, Wise & Co. (all quoted 20 St Helens Place, Bishopsgate, London as their address), operated two ships which were both called *Udea*, the name of both the wife and daughter of director Astley Thompson of Glyn Abbey, High Sheriff of Carmarthenshire. One was a steam screw ketch of 146 tons built 1873 at Wallsend on Tyne and registered in 1873. The other vessel, of 87 tons, was also registered in 1873 and had the number 60770; as they both had the same name presumably one replaced the other. The Thompson companies were declared bankrupt in July 1877 so what happened to these ships is not known. Note that Thompson, Wise & Co. also operated Pontyberem South and the New Lodge collieries.

It would seem from the census returns that the Coastguard station, which was built on BP&GV land immediately south of and abutting the harbour offices, was established sometime between 1851 and 1861. I have not been able to discover the date the Custom House was erected; it was on the pier between the lock entrances to the East and West Docks and was shown on the Ordnance Survey map surveyed in 1878-79, so was evidently in use by then.

These returns can also be used to reveal a snapshot of the vessels in the harbour on census day, or more accurately overnight. Only one ship is listed for 2nd April, 1871, the *Falcon* with a crew of five, all from Dublin. Five ships were in port on 3rd April, 1881, two - the brig *Coila A* with a crew of eight and another boat with a name that looks like *Tweed Ba* also having a crew of eight - both had their masters and many of the seamen from Whitstable or that area of Kent. The other ships were the *Tiger* with a crew of four from Gloucester, the *Mary Turtle* with the Master and two others from Bridgwater and a local seaman from Ferryside, plus a schooner called *D.W. Pickering* which had the skipper and one of the other three seamen from Connah's Quay in Flintshire. Also in 1881 a vessel named *Rose Emma* was berthed at Milford Haven which may have come from Burry Port as the master - John James - and one of the crew gave Burry Port as their birthplace, the other three crew members coming from Llanelly.

No attempt was made to complete the West Dock and the entrance lock gates remained firmly closed. A fixed timber bridge was put across the entrance and at some date soon after 1878 this had been strengthened to allow a railway track over and take the weight of a locomotive. By this means wagons, after being emptied at the tips on the west side of the East Dock, were worked back along the south side of the scouring reservoir for return to the collieries.

During the long period (1881 to 1898) that the company was in Chancery, John Russell - the Receiver and Manager - became convinced that opening the West Dock to (larger) shipping was what was needed to change the company's fortunes. Much bigger than the East Dock, it was believed that boats of up to 8,000 tons burthen could be encouraged and far fewer exports would have to be sent to Llanelly and Swansea for shipping. Writing to the solicitors to the Chancery Court, Russell confided 'I firmly believe that the advent of the first large vessel chartered for Burry Port will prove the commencement of working at a profit'. And in a letter to Miss Catherine Wellesly Malcolm, the Chairman's sister, on 10th August, 1887 he confirmed, 'I firmly believe as soon as the Company puts the colliery owners in a position to compete with those who ship at Llanelly and Swansea, a profit will be made'.

John Mitchell, as Clerk of Works (appointed in 1873) was encouraged to spare what men he could to build quayside walls, starting on the east side and then working along the north face. The men were mostly coal trimmers diverted whenever there was no ship waiting for loading or discharging. But with no money to spare progress was extremely slow. Typical was the letter sent by Russell to Mitchell on 20th January, 1887 which includes, 'I am glad you are satisfied about the progress made at the walling of the West Dock … I am badly in want of money so put off having the masons as long as you can'.

On 5th May the same year it was said that 500 yards of stone were still required to finish the pitching on the north side of the dock. Eight days later it was announced that the 150 ft landing stage on the east side of the reservoir was now complete.

The fixed timber bridge over the West Dock entrance would have to be replaced by a swing bridge if ships were going to use it. Even using their own labour, money was still required for materials, both for a new bridge and for tackle to open the gates. On 14th June, 1887 Russell wrote a begging letter to Hopgood, Foster & Dawson, the solicitors to the Chancery Court, asking 'for assistance out of funds in the hands of the Court to carry out what I consider a very important work'.

The amount requested was £368 19s. 4d. and Russell stressed this was for materials only. It appears to have been too much for the Court to sanction. Later that month Mitchell managed to open the gates for the first time for nearly 50 years; a great deal of work was still required to get them ready for regular use, and this continued whenever possible. Some of the work, including laying new stone and concrete in the cill, could only take place at low tide. On 15th July an order for materials to make the connecting lines to the new stage was placed with D.M. Davies & Co. of Newport (Mon). This was made up of:

		£	s.	d.		£	s.	d.
12 tons of steel rails	@	3	16	8	=	46	0	0
Creosoted sleepers	@		2	9	=	31	12	6
10 cwt of fastenings	@		9	0	=	4	10	0
Total						82	2	6

which expenditure this time was duly sanctioned by the court officials.

At the beginning of 1888 the long job of putting the gates into repair was finally finished, the total cost to date being given as £296 17s. 4d. for materials and £256 0s. 0d. for labour. There still remained much walling, pitching and ballasting to be done, and the fixed bridge to be moved. Finally, on 1st September, 1888 the West Dock was used by a ship for the very first time, the timber bridge having just been removed. There was no sign of sufficient funds being made available for a new bridge, so the dock railway system had to manage without one. Ironically larger ships were not attracted to the new dock as they were unable to turn in the small area that had been dredged. It would have taken considerable capital to have deepened the whole area of the dock, so it was never finished on the southern 'side' which was left undisturbed in its virgin state. Thus the ships of moderate size using the new dock could just as easily have continued to use the old East Dock; indeed most of them did.

Sixteen days after the first ship used the new dock it had to be closed when it was realised that the landing stage had shifted by about 18 inches at the bottom and was out of perpendicular. Mitchell had to have piles driven in to stop the wall by the stage from settling before the stage could be rebuilt. It was not until 8th January, 1889 that a ship again was able to berth in the West Dock.

The wooden coal tip at the new dock would appear to be of the same design as the three serving the East Dock. Each consisted of two gallows or hoisting frames. That next to the dock edge was for raising and lowering the shute; behind was a movable gallows which could be adjusted to suit the length of the railway truck, lifting it at the non-door end so that the coal was tipped through the end door onto the shute. Local wagons usually had fixings for attaching the gallows chains to the solebars for hoisting.

The depth of water over the lock cills of both docks of 22 feet at high spring tides enabled laden ships drawing 20 feet or less to use the docks, but at neap tides there was considerably less water. On 5th October, 1887 the Agent of the Pontyberem Colliery reported difficulties with the *Ellida* of 520 tons register and 'if she cannot leave this morning may be delayed 10 or 12 days'. That very same day a slightly exasperated Russell wrote to the colliery company,

Looking across the East Dock from the south-west corner in the days of sail, pre-1904.
R.E. Bowen Collection

The East Dock from the south-east corner with plenty of steam visible in this pre-1904 view.
Note the short open wagon with its end door ajar lettered 'B.P.& G.V.'   *Author's Collection*

... we have repeatedly loaded S. Ships with 800 to 900 tons of coal in one night and the ship has left on the next tide to its arrival ... if you will ascertain how much she draws loaded you can by reference to our tide tables ascertain the value of your agent's conjecture, anyhow I cannot control the wind and waves.

The *Ellida* seems to have left the dock all right that morning, after all. It later turned out that she was a converted old 'man o' war' drawing 17 feet of water.

John Russell, writing to the solicitors - Johnson & Stead of Llanelli - on 15th June, 1887 about some slow paying accounts, mentions that the Harbour Master had allowed the steamship *Fawn* to leave the dock on several occasions during 1885 after loading with tinplate without the Llanelly & Liverpool Steam Ship Co. first paying the dues. The same company had also not paid dues on 10 occasions before their vessels had left the dock loaded between 2nd April, 1887 and 4th June, 1887, amounting to £88 18s. 7d. of which £37 6s. 2d. had since been paid. Would you (the solicitors) call at their offices in Llanelly and request them 'to pay the balance now owing at once'.

A further letter sent by Russell to the solicitors on Tuesday 13th September, 1887 mentions another steamship operated by the Llanelly & Liverpool concern, and one can almost hear the chuckle in Russell's voice in saying 'after all the efforts to despatch the *Llanelly* from here last Friday she stuck on a sandbank at the entrance to Llanelly harbour and there she lays still'.

Details of another bill, for which the same shipping firm was again behind with payment, were sent to the solicitors on 14th December, 1887 and show the sort of charges being made for dockwork (a cheque was duly dispatched by hand to the solicitors four days later):

SS *Propero*					*Nov. 16. '87*		
					£	s.	d.
Dues	Harbour Dues on	266 tons @ 2d.	=		2	4	4
	Discharged	225 tons @ 1d.	=		0	18	9
	Stemming				0	2	6
Crane charges	Discharging	225 tons @ 4d.	=		3	15	0
	Nightwork				0	10	0
	Tin loaded	63¹⁴⁄₂₀ tons @ 4d.	=		0	16	0
Total					8	6	7

Note the flat charge for night work, although one wonders what sort of illumination was available. Was it possible that steamships in 1887 were equipped with a dynamo and electric lighting? As can be seen the dues charged were not all straightforward. For example, for every vessel entering the port with cargo less than the registered tonnage, and discharging all or part of such cargo and then loading outwards, the charge was 2d. per ton register and 1d. per ton on the cargo discharged but nothing on that loaded outwards. For every vessel entering the port with cargo and not unloading but loading outwards, the charge was two pence per ton register. For copper ore unloading there was a straight charge of three pence per ton ship to works.

Responsible for checking and recording correctly all such tonnages at the harbour office was John Lear, a Devonian born in 1832 who came to the company in 1873 as the weighing clerk. Evidently he had previously worked for the

Admiralty (his daughter Mary, who was totally deaf, was born in Devonport in 1865) as on 17th July, 1889 we find Russell writing to Lord Ashburnham for a testimonial to support Lear's application for an Admiralty pension, adding, 'I can say this, a more trustworthy man is not in the Company's service, at all times quiet, sober and industrious; he has given great satisfaction'.

Regarding the provision of lighting in those pre-electric days, some oil lamps had been put in place around the dockside. Russell wrote to Mitchell on Saturday 23rd July, 1887 to say he had ordered a replacement 50 candle power lamp and burner from Defries of Holborn Viaduct, complete with spider holdfast, for delivery on Monday, adding,

> ... let the old lamp be repaired and put into store with its burner ... I saw a very good wall lamp that would do well against the Custom House ... I will consult you about ordering one or two more.

Needless to say there was a follow up letter on 30th July:

> I called to know why the lamp had not been sent as promised on Monday last; plenty of excuses of course, but it was sent, I was told, on Thursday.

Then on 8th April, 1889 Mitchell was told 'On Thursday without fail Messrs Defries have promised to send down a 62 candle power lamp' which was followed by a telegram on 17th April to Defries, 'LAMP PROMISED LAST THURSDAY NOT YET COME. WHY?'

That same month, July 1887, a complaint was received from the Trimsaran Colliery that the 21 ton smack *John & Elizabeth* had wanted to enter the East Dock after loading with 30 tons of coal in the outer harbour, but another ship had been allowed to enter first. They were informed that the basket stage wanted was occupied by another ship, and other methods of loading (by the tip or a wagon being lifted by the steam crane) were offered but refused so she had to wait her turn. There was also a complaint that the charges on ballast had been increased. Not so was the answer, but in May last the ballast taken out of the *John & Elizabeth* was weighed and found to be 15 tons and not the 12 tons they had declared, so they were now being charged the correct amount.

At the Board meeting held on 25th November, 1890 it was reported that loading and trimming by the company had ceased the previous day and the shippers were having to conduct it themselves. There appears to have been a strike by the trimmers and as there is no further report it is presumed it was all over very quickly. It could take a lot more time if the professional trimmers were not employed, as quoted in a letter from Russell to Cecil Bull of the Pontyberem Colliery Co. Russell explained that the coaster *Arc* belonging to Messrs Sully was loaded with 126 tons of coal on 26th March, 1888 and trimmed (by agreement) by the crew which took them 2¾ hours, more than twice as long as it would have taken the company's trimmers.

Rather more information (than in 1881) can be gleaned from the 1891 census when there were five ships and their crews berthed for the night of 5th April in the Burry Port Dock. One was a steam ship, the others all sail. The details of the four sailing ships are:

Norma, port of registration Vannes (France), 107 tons, called at Falmouth on 28th March with a crew of five (all French).

Bergthorail, port of registration Skien (Norway), 173 tons, arrived at Burry Port on 4th April with a crew of six (Norwegians, Swedes and Danes).

Elizabeth Drew, port of registration Plymouth, No. 65145, tonnage not given, arrived at Burry Port on 3rd April with a crew of five (all from Cornwall).

Caroline, port of registration Bideford, No. 13873, 49 tons, arrived at Burry Port on 3rd April with a crew of three (all from Appledore).

The steamship was the *Harrington,* port of registration Whitehaven, No. 94031, 120 tons, which arrived at Burry Port on 4th April, 1891 with a crew of eight of whom three were Welsh and speaking Welsh only, one was Welsh and spoke English, two were Scots, one Irish and one English. Also on board was the Captain's Welsh wife who was bi-lingual. It is worth noting that the steamship, with two engineers and a stoker, required rather more crew members than did sailing ships of equal size.

Steamships were now becoming much more common. At the company's half-yearly meeting held on 7th March, 1893, shareholders were told that 23 steamships had arrived in the port during January 1893 besides the usual number of sailing ships. Clearly this was more than usual or it would not have deserved comment. Unfortunately, the usual number of ships arriving in a month is not given; I would imagine at this period it would be somewhere between 30 and 40. The shareholders were also informed that during this month over 8,000 tons of minerals were landed or shipped, which included larger than usual imports of iron ore (for Trimsaran) and copper ore.

Eleven years later, in 1904, the average number of ships of all types using the dock worked out at 33½ per month. However, as sail gradually gave way to steam, it was not the number of ships that was increasing, it was their size and thus the tonnage they could handle. The average amount (mostly coal) loaded on each ship using the port during 1904 was 323 tons; this had risen to 649 tons in 1922 (by which time there can hardly have been very much sail left using the dock) and 10 years later - in 1932 - the average loading amounted to 779 tons.

When the tinplate works was established in 1890 on the south-west side of the West Dock it was mostly built on land (five acres) leased from Lord Ashburnham, but two acres were leased from the BP&GV over which a rail connection was put in place before the year end. The connection crossed the road leading to the BP&GV workshops, the harbour offices and the coastguard station, as well as the west pier. There was also a rail connection into the workshops which crossed the road. The BP&GV considered this to be its private road, part of the dock estate. However, the road also led to the Harbour View Hotel which was situated just behind the coastguard station, and also afforded a route to the shore.

The hotel was originally called the Lord Nelson but had been renamed Harbour View by 1861. It was owned by Captain George Bowser (1828-1911), grandson of the George Bowser (1778-1835) the local colliery owner who is frequently referred to in Volume One and was one of the main instigators in the establishment of a harbour at Burry Port. In 1893 Captain Bowser found that his use of the road was being challenged by the BP&GV and the company duly accused him of trespassing on their land following several months of abuse and

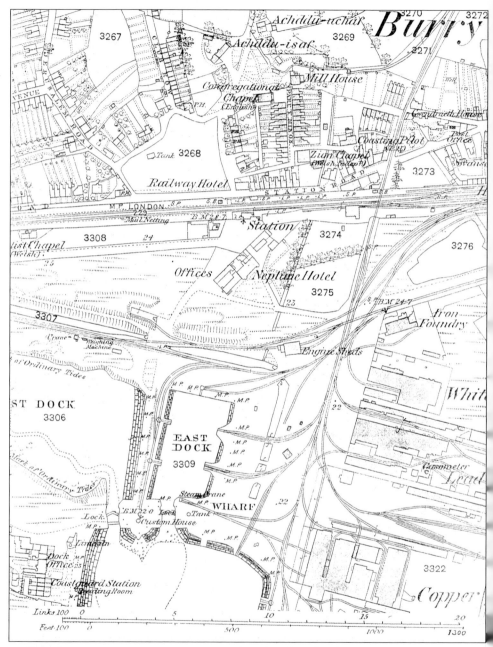

Burry Port.   *Reproduced from the 25", 1880 Ordnance Survey Map*

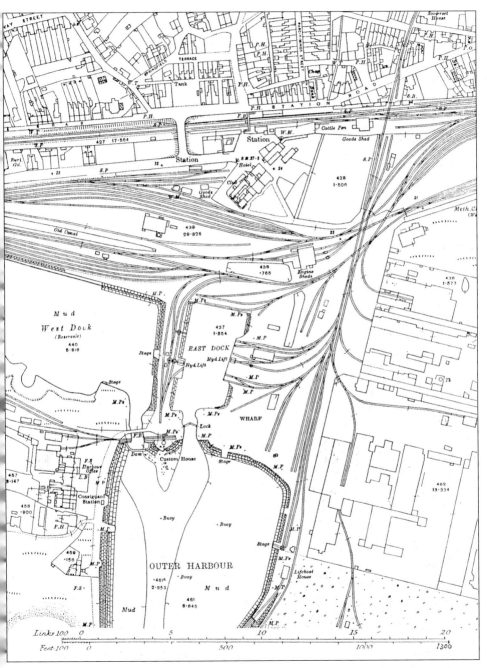

Burry Port.   *Reproduced from the 25", 1915 Ordnance Survey Map*

Looking north-east from the West Dock entrance with one steam and several sailing ships in the East Dock, plus the locomotive *Mountaineer*, on the occasion of the opening of the West Dock on 1st September, 1888.
Emlyn Davies Collection

A view taken from an upstairs window at the Harbour Office showing the West Dock in use with steam at the wooden coal tip on the left and a two-masted sailing ship in the centre. On the right both steam and sail can be seen in the East Dock. The wagon in the foreground carrying pit props is of GWR design but the two vans could belong to the BP&GV.
Emlyn Davies Collection

threats from both sides culminating with Bowser refusing to pay the shilling he owed for the easement (or licence) for that year.

The position was discussed by the Board (with Lord Ashburnham in the chair) at their meeting on 15th June, 1893. The Secretary reported that the Bowser family had up to then been paying one shilling per year for the easement for 30 years (actually since 1859, the licence being first granted on 10th May, 1859), but paid no toll on any goods carted to the hotel. Under the powers conferred on the company no cart was allowed over the road to remove goods or cargo without payment, and that no one except Mr Bowser disputed this right. The plan of the area was inspected and the correspondence between Bowser and the Secretary was read. It was decided to instruct the solicitor to look into the matter.

There was no further discussion at Board level as the dispute was deemed sufficiently serious to warrant the attention of the Receiver John Russell (who just happened to also be the Company Secretary) and he in turn involved the solicitors to the Receiver (not the company), Hopgoods and Dawson. They advised that the shilling annual payment gave acknowledgement for the easement and if no acknowledgement of trespass be insisted on then the power to levy toll for the use of the road would be lost. Acting on their instructions Russell gave notice to Capt. Bowser on 16th December, 1893 that the footway and road would be closed against him a month from the date of this notice.

Accordingly one month later Bowser found that a padlocked gate and fence had been thrown across the road and, furthermore, on the rail crossing into the workshops a locomotive and wagons had been deliberately parked. Capt. Bowser got his men to remove the lock and a portion of the fence and, bypassing the locomotive and trucks by crossing the land on the side of the West Dock, was able to carry on using the access to his hotel.

As a result the Receiver applied to Mr Justice Stirling to commit Capt. Bowser for contempt of court, an action that was rigorously resisted. The Receiver in the name of the company was instead given leave to bring an action in the next Carmarthenshire Assizes for trespass. This was done, together with an application for an injunction to prevent Bowser from using the road, believing the legality of the issue was entirely in their favour. It would seem that it was not expected that George Bowser would fight back or that they were about to embark on a disastrous episode in public relations, all for the sake of one shilling per year. Not for the first (or the last) time opinion was to side on what was perceived as the little man up against the bullying big corporate body.

The hearing took place on 7th, 8th and 9th June, 1894 in Carmarthen before Mr Justice Kennedy. The company claimed it was a private road, that there had been gates across it for 39 years, that Bowser had been paying 1s. per annum for more than 30 years, and that carts using the road had paid wharfage during that period. Witnesses called by the BP&GV included Edward Evans, John Russell, George Hancock and D. Griffiths the Dock Manager.

Captain Bowser countered by claiming the road had been used for more than 65 years, beginning by carrying salt and coal to and from his family's early commercial enterprises (grandfather George had established a salt works before 1830 on a site next to the future hotel), that bathing machines had for 50 years been taken along the road to the sands, and that for over 50 years groceries and general

Above: One of the west-side wooden coal tips at the East Dock photographed in 1904 just before being replaced by a new steel tip. Carway and Pentrmawr wagons are evident plus (*on left*) one lettered 'H&HE SMART - KIDWELLY'.

R.E. Bowen Collection

Right: The first of the two new steel tips is used for the first time on 18th June, 1904 watched by Arthur Morgan standing in the centre, Dockmaster Capt. Davies with white-topped cap on right and, between them leaning back, is John Eager. The wagon is lettered 'SAMUEL THOMAS - BROADOAK COLLIERY - LOUGHOR'.

R.E. Bowen Collection

supplies had been delivered to his hotel. Indeed it was the only way he could get to and from his premises except by balloon. He produced a plan of 1834, published by the Burry Port company itself, clearly showing a public roadway, also an 1844 land conveyance document and various Acts of Parliament favourable to his claims, including the Enclosure Act of 1830. He then went on to call 17 elderly (many were over 80) male witnesses of whom one was a surveyor and another a land agent and surveyor and who all confirmed that in their lifetime the road had been used as claimed by the Captain, without let, interference or hindrance.

The jury, after a retirement of but 30 minutes, agreed that it was a public road before 1836. The Judge explained that the law was that 'once a public high way, always a public high way', and accordingly gave judgement to the defendant with costs. The victorious Captain returned on that Saturday evening, 9th June, 1894, by GWR train to Pembrey station where he was,

> ... met by an enthusiastic crowd of people and received a most flattering ovation on all hands. He was borne through the streets on the shoulders of a few of the most demonstrative and conducted to his home amid ringing cheers.

The newspaper report suggested that a fund be created to reimburse Bowser for all his expenses, adding that the 'public have never received with more abounding satisfaction the decision of a jury at Assize'. Riding high on this popular support, Bowser put his name forward, and was duly elected, to serve on the local Parish Council, telling the electors that they were,

> ... aware of my action in breaking the chains of tyranny over the right-of-way question, and the blessing I conferred upon my fellow ratepayers in fighting the case. The poor have the benefit of the stand I then took, and now those who go for cockles and mussels to the beach have not anything to pay.

Popular rhetoric indeed.

Clearly the Directors, at their next Board meeting held only four days later on 13th June, 1894, were completely taken aback by the court's decision, the phrase that their evidence 'went for nothing' appearing in the minutes. Any further consideration was adjourned, and wisely seems never to have been brought up again. As an aside, it may be mentioned that George Bowser's daughter Mathilde (known as Tilly), who was aged 11 at this time, also later became a popular local personality. She was appointed headmistress at the Pinged Board School on 13th September, 1915, transferring to the Copperworks Infants' School on 1st October, 1918 and only retired shortly before World War II; she died on 3rd September, 1971 aged 98. The school closed at the end of 1992 and is now used by the local Scouts, Guides, etc. One former pupil was Raymond E. Bowen who remembered well being taught by Miss Bowser in 1933-35.

Tilly's father had not quite such a long life; he was 83 when he died on 18th October, 1911. The Harbour View Hotel was replaced by a new building nearer to the harbour edge (and next to the present Yacht Club) in October 1896; the old building became Sandhurst House. The new hotel remained a feature of dockside life for very many years; it did not become a private dwelling until 1971. The road to the hotel was not the only thoroughfare on the dock estate used by the public.

There was a road where the Cwm Capel branch crossed the GWR, known locally as Snook's Crossing, which was used as the main access to the copper, silver and lead works, the lifeboat station and the east pier. It was also an alternate route to the Backe, as the area around Glan-y-Mor and Burrows Terraces was called.

There was another road crossing over the GWR at the bottom of Stepney Road, where the present station footbridge is, leading to Neptune Square and on to the pier separating the East and West Docks, terminating at the Custom House. In 1893 this crossing was replaced by a new road bridge (known as the Co-op bridge) a little further west, and the station footbridge was erected to maintain the public right of way. The route onto the docks was crossed by many railway sidings and it is noticeable that photographs always show a gap in the line of wagons on these sidings so as not to obstruct the road.

A reservoir at Cwm Capel on the Dyfatty river which supplied the canal with water was built by the canal engineers in 1834; because the engineers were English the reservoir was known locally as Pownd y Saeson, and had a capacity of 20 million gallons. The water was also used at the docks and was supplied to the copper, lead and silver works. A small feeder reservoir was situated near the north-east corner of the East Dock and was used to keep the dock topped up as the pre-1906 lock gates were extremely leaky. This water was also supplied for locomotive purposes. During the first half of 1888 a portion of the old canal between the engine sheds and the East Dock was turned into a reservoir holding 1,500,000 gallons, a useful reserve during dry weather. A further stretch of the old canal, this time on the south side of the West Dock, became a reservoir during the six months to June 1889, this one holding 487,872 gallons of water. Some of this was made available to the new tinplate works when that opened in 1890. It will be appreciated that these additional water reserves were now required as the former scouring reservoir had been converted into a dock. It was estimated that, if required, 144,000 gallons could now be emptied into the harbour in 24 hours for scouring.

The town of Burry Port relied on local springs for its water supply. By 1878 an enclosed stone-built reservoir filled from the nearby springs was built in Springfield Terrace on the north side of the GWR opposite the 1893 (Co-op) road bridge; Wellfield House was later built in front of this well reservoir. This supplied fresh water to the dock estate and also to the tinplate works. To enable ships in the docks to fill up with this fresh spring water a tank was positioned on top of the Custom House (between the two dock entrances). This building was known as the round house although its shape was actually octagonal.

A site on the East Quay for a new lifeboat house was agreed on 29th November, 1886 with the Royal Lifeboat Institution and the lease signed on 17th January, 1887 for the ground to be let for 60 years at the nominal rent of one shilling per annum. On 25th June it was reported that the new lifeboat station was finished and the boat was ready but there was still a little work to be done on the slipway. This was completed the following month and the old lifeboat station at Pembrey was closed at the same time.

A small building containing a reading room had been erected about 1854 by Thomas Briggs on the West Quay in front of the Coastguard station. It was specifically for the use of the Captains of ships during the time they were in port and others such as brokers, agents and those company servants who wished to be members. Newspapers included *The Times, The Shipping & Merchantile Gazette, South Wales Daily News, The Welshman* and local papers. Outside were a wind and weather chart and a barometer.

In February 1889 it became known that it was about to be closed as the building was required for other purposes. The Directors, at their meeting on 25th February, agreed that a larger room in the Neptune Buildings used as a store could be converted to a new reading room and the old one become an office for the Dockmaster. The new room was known as the Old Band Room and is believed to have been previously used by Elliott's Brass Band. It was re-opened as a reading room on 1st April, 1889 and the membership, then costing 6s. per annum, quickly rose to 90 before dropping after the initial surge of enthusiasm had worn off.

In 1894 the members, with the strong support of John Russell, decided it should become the Reading Room and Club and that they should move to larger premises. The old Congregational Chapel, more recently used as the Seamen's Mission and next to the Neptune Hotel, was available. Built in 1856 with finance from Mr & Mrs John Thompson of New Lodge (the parents of Astley Thompson), the congregation had moved in 1870 to a new chapel in Memorial Square. With the aid of donations totalling £209 14s. 10d. (including £6 17s. 6d. from Russell) and the BP&GV paying the lease, the new club opened on 1st May, 1895 with 40 members. Lord Ashburnham was the first President, Fred Willcocks became the Secretary and Edward Evans the Treasurer. Entertainments and 'smoking concerts' performed by members were under the Chairmanship of George Hancock; on one such occasion even Lord Ashburnham did a turn. After 12 months the name was changed to the Burry Port Reading Room & Club from 1st May, 1896 when a licence was obtained for what was termed 'excisable drinks' and Russell donated a wall clock for the bar.

Having got it up and running, the BP&GV senior staff seem to have quickly ceased to play any active part in administering what locally was called 'Y Clwb Bach', with other members becoming Secretary, Treasurer and Entertainments Chairman. Suffice to say that the club continued to grow in strength; a billiards table was purchased in May 1901 for £25 9s. 1d. In 1903, when subscriptions were increased to 8s. per year, there were 74 members plus 17 ships' officers and 18 visiting members. Sunday opening of the bar commenced in 1904 although Sunday papers were not taken until 1928. A separate reading room ceased to be provided from around 1955 although newspapers including some weeklies such as *Amateur Gardening* and *Angler's Mail* continued to be taken. After many years of trying to buy the premises, the British Railways Board finally agreed to sell them to the club for £3,000 in 1967.

The slow job of removing some of the mud during the low spring tides was continued whenever men could be spared during slack periods. The report to shareholders for the half-year to 30th June, 1896 includes, under the heading of West Dock,

About 3,066 cubic yards of clay and mud have been excavated since March … and banked at the west end of the dock, on which a line has been laid to connect the lines on each side of the dock.

At left the SS *Obsidian* is loading with anthracite at the western steel tip in 1909. There is still sail evident.   *R.E. Bowen Collection*

This fine postcard view is taken looking north-east across the East Dock, with a collier being loaded at the west tip.   *Brian Cripps Collection*

The Docks, Burry Port.

A year later and it was revealed that only £195 18s. 11d. capital had been spent on the West Dock during the previous 12 months because of the urgent necessity to restore the East Pier, badly damaged in the violent storm of 8th October, 1896. The breach was repaired by building a wall 141 ft long, 7 ft thick and 8 ft deep, and against which the pitching rested. The cost of this was put at £1,757 17s. 11d. charged against revenue and which the company could ill afford. There was another terrible storm on 3rd March, 1897 when heavy seas swept over the pier from end to end but the repairs stood firm. The roadway on top of the pier still needed to be filled up with ballast as opportunity offered. In addition to all this, it was even found possible to lay three new sidings, each holding 70 wagons, along the north side of the new dock.

Despite these extra and unexpected costs, Russell was determined to see the bridge eventually replaced, but it was not until October 1898 that a new structure was completed. This was a drawbridge as Fred R. Willcocks, the mechanical engineer, had advised that this would prove cheaper than a swing bridge. The Directors all came down to Burry Port between 4th and 7th November, 1898 to inspect it, having the workings explained to them by Wllcocks, who afterwards was presented with a cheque for £50 in recognition of his good work. Also inspected were the new weighbridge and the grid-iron sidings under construction.

By the beginning of 1899 the finances of the company had considerably improved, the Receiver having been discharged at the end of 1898. It was also all change on the management side with three new Directors - only Lord Ashburnham remaining of the old Board - new General Manager, Harbour Master and Docks Superintendent (Arthur Morgan), new Secretary (Seaton Taylor) and new Engineer (Robert Carr).

One of the first decisions made by the new broom was to sweep away all ideas of retaining the West Dock for shipping; instead it was to revert to its original use as a scouring reservoir. A cofferdam designed by Carr was erected across the entrance to the West Dock, the contract being awarded to George Palmer of Neath on 5th September, 1900 for £2,482. The first pile was driven in on 21st September, through a bed of clay 15 ft thick. The piles had to be from 40 to 44 ft long. The work was completed on 8th May, 1901 and normally the water retained in the former dock (now a reservoir) was left at a depth of 20 ft above the cill. On those occasions when the tide was any higher then the sluice gates were opened, then closed again as soon as the depth dropped below 20 ft.

The Llanelly dredger was hired during the spring of 1902 to remove some 5,000 tons of mud from the East Dock. This dredger continued to be hired from time to time whenever available. Of course, it was also in use at Llanelly so Burry Port usually had to wait for its services; £480 was paid for its hire during September 1907. Morgan's report to the Board dated 15th January, 1914 records,

The Outer Harbour and Dock will require dredging during the coming Spring or Summer, and I hope we shall be successful in getting the hire of the Llanelly dredging plant, otherwise it will be a very expensive matter to get plant from a distance for a such a small job. I am doing all I can with individual members of the Llanelly Harbour Trust and the Harbour Superintendent to get the dredger about April or May, but regret I cannot get a definite promise as so much depends on their Harbour Scheme being carried through.

TELEGRAMS "MORGAN, DOCKS, BURRY PORT." NAT. TELEPHONE Nº 7. 18

Burry Port & Gwendreath Valley Railway.

IN YOUR REPLY PLEASE GIVE THIS REFERENCE

General Manager's Office
Burry Port. South Wales.

IN ANSWER TO YOUR

A. MORGAN,
MANAGER.

1st. August 1914.191

Seaton F Taylor Esq,

5, Gray's Inn Square.

W.C.

Dear Sir:-

I beg to report the following for information of Directors Meeting, August 5th.1914.

Coal Contract. I have made a Contract for Loco Coal @ 16/8 per ton, less 2d.per ton rebate allowed by G.W.R. which is a Nett decrease of 4d. per ton on last Contract.

Approved 4 Aug

Dredger. I have arrange for the Dredger to be here on Wednesday next, August 5th, at an inclusive charge of £12.10.0. per day, when the weather is stormy an allowance will be made. The charge on the last occasion was £11.12. 0. per day, plus £4.15. 0. per week extras for men, overtime and all stores. The terms now arranged are more favourable.

Part of one of Arthur Morgan's monthly reports to the Directors, August 1914.

A power house was built on the north side of the scouring reservoir, close to the spot where the first sod had been turned back in 1868. Work started during the first half of 1900 and was completed in 1901 at a cost of £3,229, charged to capital. Both hydraulic power and electricity were produced. The dynamo in the electric plant was provided by Messrs Crompton & Co. of Chelmsford and was driven by a steam turbine. The workshops, offices etc. were converted to electric lighting, and this was extended to the Neptune Hotel and the Reading Room & Club in April 1905. However it was not until 1919 that the whole of the dock area was lit by electricity, including some powerful arc lamps to allow work to continue at night. After Grouping, in 1922, electricity was purchased from the Llanelly Electric Light & Traction Company.

The hydraulic power was used on the dock estate for machinery including capstans and two new steel-framed coal tips built in 1904, one on each side of the dock, replacing the old timber-framed tips; the first steel tip was brought into operation on 18th June, 1904. Also using hydraulic power were the new steel dock gates fitted in 1906 to allow ships of up to 1,800 tons burthen to use the dock. They were orderd from Edward Finch & Co. of Chepstow at the end of 1905 at an estimated cost of £1,936 with completion forecast for the following July. A modified design was agreed on 21st February, 1906 between Finch and Eager (who had replaced Carr as Engineer) and as a result delivery was not made until the third week in August 1906.

David Lloyd, a local man born in Pembrey in 1827, had been the Dockmaster since 1871 and it was he who had his office from 1889 in the original reading room on the West Pier. His was not a statutory position, like that of the Harbour Master who was appointed under the tems of the original New Pembrey Harbour Act of 10th June, 1825 (6 Geo. IV, cap. 115). He finally retired, aged 73, at the end of April 1899 and was followed by David Rees of Pembrey Road appointed on 1st May, 1899 with a wage of 35s. per week plus the use of a company house at one shilling weekly rental; there was no uniform except for a cap. Later occupants of the position were Capt. Davies from April 1900, then Capt. Morgan from 1st January, 1906, followed by Capt. Hughes. The latter took over as Dockmaster on 20th April, 1920 by which time the wages had been increased to £4 per week. Nowadays the office of the Harbour Master is located in a 'portacabin' by the lifeboat station.

Whilst any proposed expenditure on the dock and harbour was naturally debated by the Directors at their monthly meetings it was only very occasionally that any reference to the ships themselves received a mention. One such occasion was on 16th March, 1915 when an equally rare note of censure on one of their officers was minuted. It was in considering the Dockmaster's report concerning the delay in docking the SS *Aspen* when it was ordered that the 'Secretary write (to) Mr Morgan that the report was not considered satisfactory and that he must be warned not to be absent again in similar circumstances'.

It is not entirely clear if it is Dockmaster Capt. Morgan or the long suffering General Manager and Dock Superintendent Arthur Morgan (no relation) who is being reprimanded here; most probably the former.

An official named Henderson made a report on shipping traffic canvassing on 1st January, 1912 covering the previous 12 months. This is the earliest mention of shipping canvassing at Board meetings and as Mr Henderson's

The original card bears a post mark dated 1913. Of interest is the little 'Clyde Puffer' named *Rushlight* of Greenock sandwiched between two much larger ships. Looking north-east across the East Dock. *Brian Cripps Collection*

Shipping also used the tidal outer harbour as well as the docks, as can be seen in this view looking east with the copper works in the background. *R.E. Bowen Collection*

Many of the original postcard views of Burry Port were taken by the Cardiff photographer Ernest T. Bush and some, as in this July 1912 view, would have his friend Charlie Snook (the local newsagent) featured in some way. Note the coffer dam across the entrance to the West Dock in the centre, the octagonal Customs House on the right and the old Reading Room, now the Dockmaster's Office, prominent on the left.   *Brian Cripps Collection*

Another fine July 1912 Ernest Bush photograph showing the outer harbour with the bowler-hatted Charlie Snook on the right.   *Brian Cripps Collection*

The East Dock with the two-masted brigantine *Hildred* and the SS *Ferguslie* featured in this 1908 view originally taken and published by Charlie Snook. *M.R.C. Price Collection*

The former BP&GV power house some years after closure. The ceremony of cutting the first sod was performed just behind where this building was later erected. *Mrs. M. Davies*

charge does not appear to have been known in advance presumably this was the first occasion he had worked for the BP&GV. He continued to make half-yearly reports, at a fee of £100 each plus expenses, until July 1914 when his appointment as canvasser was terminated at his request. A minute of 30th July, 1913 records that Henderson's suggestion as to a change of Dockmaster was considered, but no decision was taken. On 1st September, 1912 F. John Evans, the local shipping broker, was offered the position of assistant shipping canvasser at £25 per annum plus expenses; this Evans declined but agreed new terms of £40 pa *including* expenses from 1st October, 1912. One hopes his expenses were not as heavy as those paid to Henderson for the second half of 1913 which amounted to £36 17s. for 'printing and other disbursements'.

Evans seems to have succeeded Henderson as canvasser. A Board minute of 27th February, 1920 records that,

> ... in view of the letter from the Railway Executive Committee dated 24th August, 1914 it was decided that Mr Evans' appointment as Canvasser should be terminated.

The REC had taken over control, on behalf of the Government, of all the railways with the outbreak of war on 4th August, 1914 and was not disbanded until 1st January, 1920. It would appear that the BP&GV was unable to end Evans' position whilst the railway continued to be under Government control. However, why it was decided that a canvasser was no longer required now that the war had ended was not explained.

It was on a stormy 22nd January, 1916 that the Norwegian steamship *Smaragd* of 487 tons completely missed the entrance to Burry Port harbour and veered to starboard, sailing to the east of the East Pier and beaching herself next to the copperworks slag bank. All attempts to pull her off with a local tug the following morning on the next and subsequent high tides failed and, fearing she would become a total loss, she was offered for sale by auction in Cardiff and was purchased by the Burry Port ship owner Evan Jones of Penmount. The Secretary reported to the BP&GV Board on 2nd February that the vessel was now considered a total wreck. She was eventually refloated by the Burry Port ship broker (and BP&GV canvasser also at that time) F. John Evans on the high spring tide of 5th March, 1916; remarkably this information was reported to the Directors the following day. Evans then managed the ship for Jones until 1927 during which period she became quite a common sight in the East Dock.

Evans was the son of William H. Evans (1846-79), the Burry Port ship broker. John Evans was also a ship owner, as the report of a shipwreck on 10th September, 1903 confirms:

> The local trader *Heroine* owned by Mr F.J. Evans, ship broker, Burry Port was driven ashore in Angle Bay, Milford Haven, by the severe gale of Thursday last. The vessel was bound for Cork with a cargo of Pontyberem anthracite coal, from Burry Port. The probability is that she will become a total wreck.

At the Directors' meeting held on 18th October, 1920 the solicitor reported on the company's claim against the owners of the SS *Cromwell* for damage to the dock gate. The owners had offered £100 but, after negotiations, the claim had been agreed and paid at £120 in full settlement.

The East Dock in 1923. The dock gates can be seen on the right. The *Afon Dyfi* of Llanelly, 759 tons and acquired from Barcelona in 1922, is moored on the left whilst the *Smaragd,* originally Norwegian but Burry Port-owned since 1916, is in the centre.   *Emlyn Davies Collection*

An aerial view of the docks and outer harbour about 1936. Just one steamer is in the dock whilst the tug moored by the west quay looks to be getting ready for action. At the top right can be seen the Neptune Buildings with the Co-op bridge over the GWR main line prominent just to the left.   *Emlyn Davies Collection*

Other shipwrecks just outside the harbour, notably on the Cefn Sidan sands, were reported at times, although it is possible the boats concerned were not necessarily heading for Burry Port. An early example was the sailing ship *La Juene Emma* of Cherbourg, about 400 tons burthen and bound for Martinique, wrecked on the sands on 21st November, 1828 with the loss of 17 out of the 23 passengers and crew; one was said to be a 12-year-old girl, a niece of Josephine, Empress of France.

During a stormy night on 15th December, 1842 the German galliot *Die Gute Hoffrung* was driven onto the sands. Her cargo included an 8 ft marble statue for the King of Prussia, loaded at Lavinia in Italy. William McKiernan, the Harbour Superintendent, managed to salvage the statue and early in January it was put on display for a week in the centre of Pembrey. McKiernan also purchased the wreck of the barque *Huskisson* which was stranded on the sands on 6th April, 1853 and is reputed to have used her timbers in the construction of several Burry Port houses, including those on Huskisson Row, thus perpetuating the origin of their woodwork.

Another wreck on the Cefn Sidan sands was that of the brig *Daisy* of 311 tons from Bristol, which ran aground on 11th November, 1877. More seriously during a severe storm the iron-hulled and four-masted sailing ship *Teviotdale* of Glasgow, 1,623 tons and only four years old, lost most of her sails and was driven aground on 15th October, 1886 with the loss of 17 men of her complement of 29. The wreck was auctioned on 29th October with the cargo of 2,400 tons of coal (loaded at Cardiff) being sold for £27 and all the rest going for £750. The remains of the hull can still be seen at low tide.

Thick fog on 23rd November, 1888 was the reason that the Austrian barque *Olga B* of 366 tons from Buccan became stranded, the wreck being sold on 25th November. On 30th October, 1925 the German wooden-hulled sailing ship *Paul* became another complete wreck on these treacherous sands. What is believed to have been the last time a ship was grounded here was on 1st December, 1948 when the Norwegian coal-fired steamship *Tungeness* of about 1,800 tons finished up on the sands opposite the 12th hole on the Ashburnham golf links, apparently bound for Llanelly. She was finally refloated, with the aid of three tugs, on the high Spring tide 16 days later and towed to Cardiff for repairs.

Occasional references are found in the local papers to ships arriving safely at the Burry Port docks. One such report of 1877 concerned the *Red Breast* of Grimsby 'will sail this day for Montreal, loaded with Messrs Mason & Elkington's anthracite stone coal (Capel Ifan Colliery, Pontyberem)'. Another said that the *Anthe*, a barque registered in Sunderland which arrived at dusk on Tuesday 2nd December 1884 with about 600 tons of copper ore from Port Nalloth in South Africa, was the second such shipment 'by the same vessel within the last seven or eight months'. The steamship *Cambrian* left the West Dock with what was claimed to be the first cargo to be loaded there, on 8th January, 1889, bound for Liverpool with tinplate from the Gwendraeth Tin Plate Works at Kidwelly. A further report, in the *Llanelli & County Guardian* of 22nd January, 1903, quoted the SS *Lizzie* arriving from Portugal the previous week with over 1,000 tons of copper ore for the Pembrey Copper Works. The names of other interesting ships can be read in photographs taken of the docks. In one, which bears a post-mark date 1913, a diminutive 'Clyde Puffer' is sandwiched between two much larger colliers. She is the *Rushlight* of Greenock, and she must have had to top up with water more than once during her voyage from the Clyde to the Burry River.

It was in the early evening of Monday 18th June, 1928 that another unusual boat, one of the flying variety, berthed in the outer harbour in circumstances that hit the national headlines the following morning. This was because one of the three crew was a woman, the sixth to attempt and the first to successfully fly the Atlantic ocean. Curiously, Miss Amelia Mary Earhart (1897-1937) - a social worker from Boston, Massachusetts with over 500 hours solo flying to her credit - was a late substitute because the Hon. Mrs Frederick Guest, the wife of the former British Secretary of State for Air and one of the sponsors of the flight, had to drop out. It was Mrs Guest who had purchased the seaplane and chosen the name *Friendship*.

The plane was a three-propeller Fokker aircraft with three 200 hp Wright Whirlwind engines and enlarged Junkers duralumin floats, captained by Wilmur (Bill) Stultz and with Louis (Slim) Gordon as flight engineer. The seaplane came out of the low cloud over Burry Port Harbour a little after noon and was low enough for workers below to read the name; indeed she was low enough for Stultz to have to take avoiding action to miss the high Fricker's Metalworks (formerly the Copperworks) chimney, climbing steeply and disappearing into the clouds again. Among those who had witnessed the event was inspector Charles Owen, a former BP&GV man and now in charge of all railway movements at the dock. Owen then received a telephone call from Mr Bevan, who worked in the office at Crown Colliery, to say that the plane, after circling, had dropped again out of the clouds over the Burry estuary, and had touched down on the water. She came to rest almost opposite the harbour entrance and tied up to a bouy; the time was 12.40 pm BST.

They had taken off from Trepassey, Newfoundland at 9.51 am EST on the Sunday, so the flight of 4,449 miles had taken 20 hours and 49 minutes. Owen got in touch with Mr Fisher of Fricker's Metals and together they rowed out to the *Friendship* and brought Stultz back, greeted by a little cheer from just a dozen or so onlookers as he stepped onto dry land. Stultz apparently thought he was in Ireland and was quite surprised to find himself in Wales. He had asked for 'gas' as he had but 25 gallons left in the tank and wanted to continue to Southampton but was persuaded to leave it to the next morning.

So the three flyers all came ashore and had afternoon tea at Fricker's office, then after bringing the *Friendship* into the safety of a mooring in the outer harbour, by which time a much larger crowd had gathered, they had dinner and spent the night at the Ashburnham Hotel, on the road to Pembrey. By next morning, when they were ready to take off for Southampton (and an official reception), the news of their successful flight had spread and well over a thousand onlookers had collected to see the departure. Through this crowd a man, his wife and daughter were passed and introduced to inspector Owen as Sir Arthur Whitten-Brown (who with the late Sir John Alcock had been the first to fly the Atlantic) and family who wished to present a bouquet of flowers to Miss Earhart. Owen quickly arranged for a boat to take the Whitten-Browns out to the *Friendship* and they had almost reached her when the seaplane took off. Owen said afterwards that if he had known in advance he would have made sure that this historic meeting did indeed take place. Later, on 20th May, 1932,

The Fokker seaplane *Friendship* in the outer harbour on 19th June, 1928, the day after the epic flight from Newfoundland. The hipped-roof building in the background is Fricker's offices where the aviators had afternoon tea.   *J. Harper*

Amelia (by this time Mrs Putnam) did fly solo over the Atlantic to Ireland. Just over five years later, on 3rd July, 1937, she was lost over the Pacific.

The railway returns published annually by the Board of Trade unfortunately do not show separately exports and imports through docks, although it is possible the figures are available elsewhere. I have only managed to uncover a selection, mostly covering the Great Western years. Exports only (in tons) through Burry Port are known for the following six-monthly periods:

1/1 to 30/6/1888	17,022	*1/1 to 30/6/1889*	29,152
1/1 to 30/6/1892	34,915	*1/1 to 30/6/1893*	34,382

also available are the import figures just for the latter two half-years (again in tons):

1/1 to 30/6/1892	9,097	*1/1 to 30/6/1893*	20,193

This final figure would appear to be exceptional, with over 8,000 tons being imported just in the January that year, much of it iron ore for Trimsaran as well as copper ore for Elliot's Metal Works. Remember, when comparing these tonnages with the following tabulated figures, that the above are for six-monthly periods whereas the following are for 12 months. In addition another report quotes about 100,500 tons exported in 1912 and 116,500 tons exported during 1913. The former figure is completely different from that for 1912 given in the following table and taken from a different source.

The one-time West Dock seen in September 1964, only used as a scouring reservoir since 1900.
R.E. Bowen

The gates to the East Dock looking in a very sorry state in September 1964.   *R.E. Bowen*

The outer harbour has been made into an attractive marina with floating pontoons and lighting columns, 17th July, 2006.   *Author*

Burry Port Shipping Statistics

Year	No. of ships	Imports tons	Exports tons	Average export tons per ship
1904	402	8,523	129,859	323
1912	156	n/a	78,268	502
1914	n/a	719	98,356	-
1916	67	n/a	32,971	492
1918	n/a	n/a	30,380	-
1919	190	n/a	n/a	-
1920	509	n/a	289,371	569
1921	145	n/a	79,900	551
1922	214	493	138,850	649
1923	308	2,110	198,281	644
1924	275	3,281	159,474	580
1925	189	3,380	98,828	523
1926	43	1,329	25,245	587
1927	65	563	44,817	689
1928	89	2,401	n/a	-
1929	160	997	94,830	593
1930	157	1,341	101,808	648
1931	158	603	102,239	647
1932	157	365	122,225	779
1933	179	n/a	138,068	771
1934	205	736	153,765	750
1935	n/a	838	127,431	-
1936	n/a	423	105,506	-
1937	n/a	496	73,228	-
1938	n/a	288	59,868	-

From August 1914 to the end of 1918 the number of ships using the dock was drastically reduced due to the war; other reductions were affected by the national coal strike in 1921 and the General Strike of 1926. If the average tonnage exported per boat remained at around the 770 mark then the number of ships using the dock will have fallen to only 78 for the year 1938, an average of three every two weeks. With the stay of each vessel in the port normally being limited to 12 hours (between successive high tides) the days when there was a ship in the dock must have been easily outnumbered by those when there was none to be seen. Ships last used the dock for the loading of anthracite in 1939. With the outbreak of war in September and the virtual cessation of exports, Burry Port dock ceased to be used and was officially closed by the GWR in 1940.

As it was not a working port the dock estate did not become a part of British Ports at Nationalisation in 1948, but remained with the Transport Commission under British Railways. The dock, harbour and reservoirs were ceded to local government ownership in 1968, first to the Burry Port Urban District and then, from 1974, to Llanelli Borough who closed the Cwm Capel reservoir in 1980 and proceeded to demolish the dam.

Of course the harbour continued to be used by small boats and yachts, increasingly so into the 1990s. The coffer dam required more and even more maintenance and eventually it was demolished in 1972. The old ('black') girder bridge over the former dock entrance was removed on 4th October, 1989 and replaced by a new concrete footbridge completed on 24th December, the work by Dyfed County Council costing £11,690. The last vestige of the original canal which had been used as a water reservoir was filled in during November 1991. Then, during the winter of 2005-06, the outer harbour was converted into a marina with floating moorings and lighting, with the East Dock receiving similar treatment in the following months. The result, with all the clearance and tidying of the surrounding land that has gone on, is that in place of what had become an area of depressing industrial dereliction Burry Port now has instead a valuable and thriving seaside attraction.

Pembrey & Burry Port, the main-line station, looking west with the Neptune Hotel at extreme left. Between it and the telegraph pole is the Reading Room & Club, then to the right of the nameboard and just peeping over the fence the end of the BP&GV station is seen. To its right the much larger building is Lewis & Sons ships' chandlery with the single-storey GWR station just right of centre on the platform. Above the left end of the footbridge can be seen the Adephi cinema, 16th July, 1951. *R.J. Doran*

View over the Co-op bridge, looking south *circa* 1912. At left centre can be seen the Reading Room & Club, single storey except for the left end, with the back of the BP&GV station building on the right and the goods warehouse beyond. There are two ex-Metropolitan carriages visible, plus plenty of wagons, with the copper works in the distance. *Glyn Davies Collection*

Chapter Six

Up and Down the Line

The designated direction of travel was not as simple as it might have been at the beginning of 1913 when suddenly up became down and at the same time down was changed to up, no doubt to the confusion of rail travellers. At the moment the first passenger timetable was produced, in August 1909, the up trains were shown as running between Pontyberem and Burry Port. This was as expected and complemented the direction of GWR trains which continued in the same up direction towards Llanelly (and eventually on to Paddington).

During the planning of the extension of passenger services to Cwmmawr there was no hint that directions were about to be reversed; the new platform being built at Pontyberem to enable trains to pass was at first referred to as being on the down side (on the left when facing Cwmmawr). Thus when the new timetable appeared in January 1913 it was quite a surprise to find that now it was the up trains that worked to Cwmmawr and the down trains that returned to Burry Port. I have not come across any reason for the change, which appears to be quite illogical. There is no reference to it in any of the Board minutes, contrary to what might have been expected; surely the Directors were at least informed. The decision had evidently been taken by the time a letter was written to the Board of Trade on 14th October, 1912 reporting that the new up platform at Pontyberem was ready; provisional sanction for its use was then given.

Having made the change, it remained up in the direction of Cwmmawr for the rest of the railway's lifetime. Similarly the branches from Cwm Capel and from Sandy Gate (Llanelly) were up to Burry Port, and the line from Kymer's Quay at Kidwelly was up towards Cwmmawr. Even this was illogical as it meant that empty wagons returning from the docks to the collieries travelled down to Cwm Capel, Crown and Pwll, but up to Trimsaran, Carway and Glynhebog. However, in this book, unless otherwise stated, the post-1913 version is used with up being towards Cwmawr.

In that summer of 1922 when the BP&GV became the GWR, or indeed at any time prior to the autumn of 1939, up (eastbound) passengers on the Great Western from Neyland or Southern Ireland alighting at Pembrey & Burry Port station and crossing over the tracks on the footbridge to reach the BP&GV station could not fail to be amazed at the sight that greeted them. Most of the town lay behind them, on the north side of the GWR, whereas in front it would seem like an endless array of coal wagons stretched out like beads on parallel strings, each proudly proclaiming its name. In the mid-distance could be seen the masts and funnels of ships in the dock, with the wide, open Burry River beyond and in the far distance the vast hulk of the Gower Peninsula lying like some mythical giant of a whale in the sea. Over to the left were factory buildings with their tall chimneys, the height of one (285 ft and erected in 1852) being particularly impressive until it fell down without warning on 26th April, 1947, the day before it was due to be demolished. This was in preparation for the

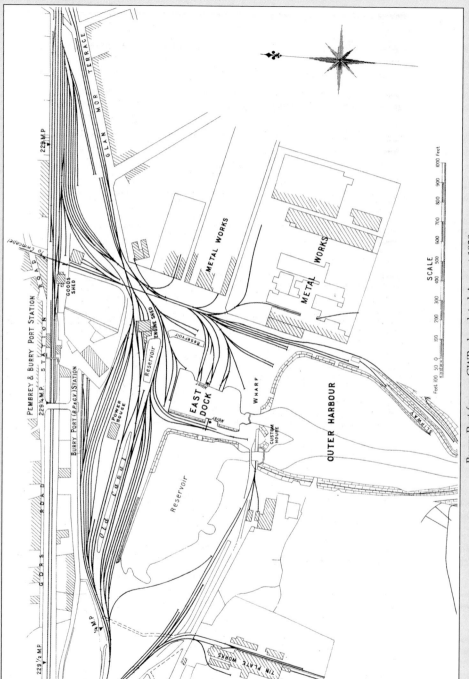

Burry Port from a GWR plan dated August 1930.

Aerial view of Burry Port about 1935 (and before 1937) with the footbridge connecting the two main-line platforms in line with Stepney Road. At the bottom left of the footbridge the white building is Burry Port House, the ships' chandlery of Lewis & Son. At the left end of the platforms is the Co-op road bridge, with the Co-operative Society building facing. Below this bridge is the BP&GV station with several chocolate and cream four-wheel coaches in the siding. Below the main line station building is Neptune Square with the Neptune Hotel being the hipped-roof building. Note the gap left between the wagons for road traffic from the Square to the docks. At the bottom edge, *left of centre*, the power house can be seen, whilst on the extreme right is Snook's crossing where the Cwm Capel branch crossed the GWR and continued off the top edge of the picture.

R.E. Bowen Collection

building of the Carmarthen Bay power station, completed in 1953 and which dominated the skyline until in turn it was demolished in 1991-92.

The footbridge connecting the GWR platforms dated from 1893 and replaced a level crossing guarded by an early Saxby & Farmer signal box, Pembrey West. Until 1893 the platforms were quite short and ended at the crossing; a new road bridge, known as the Co-op bridge, was then built further west allowing the platforms to be extended. Actually the bridge was completed in September 1892 but was found to be unsatisfactory so was taken down and rebuilt, opening to traffic in March 1893. Between the footbridge and the Co-op bridge on the south side stood Burry Port House, the home of the Parkes Brothers, Alexander and Henry the chemical engineers, from 1849 to 1881, then becoming the ships' chandlery of Lewis Bros (later Lewis & Son) until demolition in 1972.

Beyond the Co-op bridge, still on the south side, a later landmark was the Adelphi Cinema, opened in October 1937 and demolished in January 1973. Such information can be useful in helping to date many of the railway photographs taken at Burry Port. In front of the cinema and continuing towards Pembrey is Ashburnham Road (the present B4311); all the buildings are on the north side of the road and facing the West Dock and the BP&GV, with the GWR line at their backs. Prior to the cinema being built, the most prominent of these buildings was the Welsh Baptist Chapel 'Y Tabernacl' built in 1856 and refurbished in 1901, where the BP&GV Accountant Edward Evans was Pastor. Facing the chapel the last portion of the old canal on the dock estate was filled in during the first fortnight of November 1991, according to a diary entry by John A. Nicholson, the Burry Port historian. Previously several sections of the canal could be seen, retained as reservoirs.

Standing on the footbridge and studying the sea of coal wagons for a few moments it would be realised that it was not individual names that were being proclaimed, but owners that were advertising their existence to the world, and further they were arranged in groups of around six to 20 or so trucks all with one name, then a similar group with another name, and so forth; some of the group names being repeated a little further away. With a clattering sound accompanied by the puffing of smoke and steam some of the wagons would be on the move and on panning around possibly one or two other movements and puffings would be detected; this was not a stationary but a continually active scene.

To the half-left (beyond the Neptune Hotel) more smoke revealed a small group of buildings on an island in the sea of coal trucks. Here were the BP&GV engine sheds with perhaps a couple of locomotives on the tracks outside being serviced (grid ref. SN447006). Continuing further back in the same direction but to the far side of the dock a row of houses could be detected, the second one being the BP&GV head office for both the railway and the harbour whilst the nearest - Harbour House - was the home of the General Manager. The fourth, fifth and sixth houses, which were taller, were all occupied by the Coastguard officers and their families. These latter three were demolished about 1985 and replaced by a terrace of three modern houses. Just to the right (west) lay the workshops where all the repairs and maintenance of both locomotives and dock equipment were undertaken.

A little further to the right lay the Ashburnham Tinplate Works served by sidings branching off the line to the workshops; the main building is now the pickle factory of L.A. Parsons & Sons Ltd. In front (on the north side) was the large scouring reservoir that at one time had been the short-lived West Dock. Over to the right and seemingly in the middle of the sidings stood the power house of 1901-02 which until 1922 produced both electrical and hydraulic power, after which electricity was purchased from the Llanelly Electric Light and Traction Co. at a cost of 6d. per unit.

Coming off the footbridge and passing onto the yard on the south side of the GWR station the Neptune Hotel stood in front but at an angle; just to the right and in front was the Reading Room and Club with the BP&GV passenger station a short distance (about 120 yards) further to the right. Unlike the sidings full of wagons and the dockside, here everything was quiet unless it was around the time that a train was due to arrive or depart. Just a single stone-faced platform with a brick-curb edge on the north side of the single track plus a run-round loop sufficed. The station building held only a booking office, a parcels office and a waiting room. Beyond, in a separate brick building, was the toilet block which had been added soon after the passenger service first started. Some spare carriages would be standing on a further track alongside the run-round loop, whilst beyond stood a small goods shed served by a single siding; behind were two more goods sidings which could be used as a run-round loop. Nothing more was required for the local goods traffic.

That is what sufficed as the main terminus of what had been a proud and independent railway. Even after the Grouping and now administered by the mighty GWR it still seemed like a different railway and never succeeded in getting completely away from its light railway image.

Burry Port station, looking west, in 1935 before the delivery of any new bogie carriages.
LGRP 2053

Right: The GWR replacement Dock Junction home signals, with bridge 1 behind, September 1964.

R.E. Bowen

Below: Looking the other way, with Carmarthen Bay power station dominating the background, Dock Junction signal box can be seen round the bend on the left. The line to the right is the Tinplate Works branch. July 1963.

Emlyn Davies

Burry Port to Kidwelly Junction

Setting off towards Cwmmawr from Burry Port, the six tracks in the station area quickly merged into a single line and headed at first westwards, then curved towards the south-west. Alongside, on the up (south) side the tracks of the dock estate ran alongside, gradually merging until only two were left, which combined into one and trailed into the single line at Dock Junction, 23½ chains from the station terminus. Railway distances were always surveyed in miles and chains, one chain being the same as 22 yards (or 20·117 metres); there being 80 chains to one mile (1,609 m.).

At 4½ chains before reaching the junction was the signal box and here the wooden train staff was exchanged for the electric train staff (later token) which for passenger workings was managed without the train having to stop. The line now curved to the right so that up trains were heading north-west; just three chains beyond the Dock Junction was a further trailing junction with the branch from the workshops and the Ashburton Tinplate Works. From early in 1915 until 1917 a private railway branched off the Tinplate Works line and turned west for use during the construction of the munitions factory on Pembrey Burrows. A photograph showing the bridge by which this temporary line crossed the old Pembrey Harbour is reproduced in Volume One on page 114.

Dipping down on a short gradient of 1 in 62, the line curved under the Ashburnham Road (the B4311) which was bridge No. 1 and known as the Gors bridge, having a clearance of 12 ft 7¼ in. in the centre of the original stone segmental arch, then under bridge No. 2 which was the girder bridge (with masonry piers) carrying the GWR main line at a height of just 12 ft 8 in. These two bridges were measured at 29¾ and 31½ chains from the terminus; the remnants of the old canal ran alongside the track under both bridges on its way to feed the dock reservoirs, the S-bend here frequently flooded to cover the sleepers and sometimes the rails as well. In the 1930s the road bridge was replaced by a new concrete girder bridge, the road being raised slightly; the GWR bridge had also been reconstructed, in August 1923.

The line was now in a cutting, the tops of the houses visible on both sides being post-World War II and the course of the original canal could be made out on the down (north) side of the line. At the 46¼ chain mark the connection to the Gwscwm or Pembrey Colliery curved sharply to the north-east, the connection facing towards Burry Port. The branch was about a quarter-mile long. Closed in 1930, the mine entrance was used from 1939 by local people as an air raid shelter, being completely dry. Shortly after the connection, at 51¼ chains, the Gorscombe (old spelling, now Furnace) Road segmental arch bridge, No. 3 with a height of 11 ft 9½ in. above rail level, was passed. This was where George Bowser's tramroad from Gwscwm to Pembrey Harbour had crossed the canal, as discussed in Volume One, page 101. From here the line passed through more open country, still in a cutting and still with the canal on the down side. On the right or south (up) side lay the Ashburnham Hotel, built in 1823 by the Pembrey Iron & Coal Co., after which the line next curved slightly to the left to pass under another old tramroad bridge at 68¾ chains. This was No. 4, Stanley's bridge, also known as the Ashburnham arch, and which had a more generous

Looking east as a loaded coal train approaches the Furnace Road bridge (No. 3), August 1982. The locomotives, from the right, are Nos. 03141, 03119 and 03135.   *Emlyn Davies*

Pembrey Halt, looking to Burry Port, on 31st July, 1955.   *M. Hale*

clearance of 13 ft 3 in. It actually looked more like a short tunnel rather than a bridge with a full semi-circular stone arch. Locomotives stopped here for water, the pipe being attached to the Burry Port side of the bridge which meant that on up trains the engine's chimney was positioned under the arch during the stop. Alongside the tramroad embankment, on its west side and on the up side of the BP&GV, could be seen the Ship Aground Hotel.

The buildings of Pembrey now came into view at the top of the cutting on the south side; on the opposite side they are rather further away at first, and at a higher level, then passing the crenulated square tower of the parish church, St Illtyd's, illustrated in Volume One on page 10, the line passed under the segmental stone arch of the Village bridge, 1 mile 18¼ chains and bridge No. 5. This had a clearance of 12 ft 0¾ in. in the centre and the gouges in the stonework on the south (towpath) side caused by the ropes hauling the canal boats could be clearly seen, as illustrated on page 144 in Volume One. Immediately after the bridge came the brick-faced platform of Pembrey Halt, 1 mile 21 chains, on the south side (SN427011). The word 'Halt' was only added to the station name on 1st July, 1924. There was a small waiting hut which was still standing five years after the passenger closure.

Curving to the north-west the line continued in a shallow cutting with the houses of Pembrey visible on both sides, reaching bridge No. 6 at 1 mile 44½ chains. This is under the Danlan Road (A484) but was known as the Jolly bridge after the neighbouring public house 'The Jolly Sailor' (now a private house); the minimum clearance was 11 ft 11 in. under the centre of the flattish arch. An application was made to the Board of Trade to put in a new goods siding on the up side at 1 mile 45 chains, the points facing Cwmmawr. It is possible the points were actually just under the bridge; however, it is not clear that the siding was ever made, although it received approval from Col Druitt in April 1915. It may be that it was intended to serve the war-time explosives factory of Nobel's, this being about the most adjacent position on the BP&GV, and then removed after the war had ended (1919?). Just beyond the bridge the houses on the down side ceased and those on the up side became more scattered as the outskirts of Pembrey are passed by. At 1 mile 71½ chains from Burry Port the Quarry bridge - No. 7 and bringing the access lane to the Carreg Llwyd Quarry and Brickworks - went over the line. This was a girder bridge, height 12 ft 1½ in., built by the railway to replace a swing bridge over the canal. Immediately beyond was the junction with the quarry siding, on the down side; this had been closed by 1913 but was reinstated in 1937 only to close again by 1947. The bridge has the appearance of having been rebuilt or replaced in 1937; perhaps the original had been taken down.

After another 350 yards (16 chains) a further siding connection trailed in on the down side; this was with the Craiglon Colliery and also served (via a narrow gauge line) the Ffrwd and Bryndias Collieries. These had all closed by 1912 but Ffrwd later re-opened only to finally close in 1934. Immediately after the junction points came the segmental arch of Craiglon bridge, No. 8, at 2 miles 9½ chains and with a generous 12 ft 4½ in clearance in the centre, carrying the B4317 road to Llandyry and Spudders bridge (Pont Spwdwr). At an unknown date the road had been widened over the bridge using straight girders on the

Craiglon Bridge Halt after closure, looking to Burry Port, on 31st July, 1955.   *M. Hale*

Burry Port side, slightly higher above the rails than the original stone arch which had been retained. The 'Butcher's Arms' was on the up side where the main road was joined. Craiglon Bridge Halt (opened in February 1932) was north of the bridge, the timber-faced platform also being on the up side (SN418022).

The line now took the 'Foxhole Curve' to the north then straightened to enter the flat area of the Pinged Marshes, having come out of the cutting to leave the flank of Pembrey Mountain (height some 590 feet or just over 180 metres) behind on the east side. Although dominating the landscape behind Burry Port, it is a very modest mountain indeed which Raymond E. Bowen called 'grossly undersized'. The remains of the old canal continued on the down side of the line for the next two miles, with some stretches being quite prominent. At 2 miles 18 chains the southern end of the Ty Mawr passing loop was reached, the loop line (which closed in May 1947) being on the down side and the signal box, at 2 miles 28 chains, on the up.

Raymond E. Bowen recalls cab rides as a school boy on the engine when his father Oliver Bowen was a driver on the BP&GV in the 1933-35 period. On one occasion when taking empty wagons back to the pits they stopped in the up loop at Tymawr to change the staff. A loaded coal train was waiting in the down loop, so they, together with their fireman and guard, made their way to the signal box which, when they got inside, was found to be very crowded. Besides the signalman and the two train crews with their guards, there were as well a couple of gangers sheltering from the heavy rain outside. Conversations covered diverse subjects, interrupted occasionally by the sound of the block bells, when someone wanted to know how that old tune 'Crugybar' went? Within seconds Tymawr box had been converted into a typical Welsh chapel as all within responded by singing the funeral hymn in the most hearty male voice manner,

O fryniau Caersalem ceir gweled
Holl daith yr anialwch I gyd
Pryd hyn y ....

but by the end of the second verse the crew of the up train had departed the cabin, having collected the staff for the next section, leaving the sound of the third verse fading behind until drowned by the rain. Another time, when the water under one of the bridges was flooding the line to within a fraction of the rail level, Raymond's father threw a piece of coal into the stream resulting in some jacuzzi-like violence as dozens of little fishes swam off in panic.

At the northern end of the passing loop a level crossing (a swing bridge in canal days) was made with the Penybedd to Pinged road just where the route of the Ashburnham canal was crossed. Here was the original terminus of the Kidwelly & Llanelly canal when it opened in 1816. South from this point, through to Burry Port, the canal was constructed much later, in 1837.

In March 1928 about three square miles (nearly 8 sq. km.) of land between the Cefn Sidan Sands and the airfield were purchased from the Ashburton Estate by the Ministry of Agriculture for development by the Forestry Commission as the Pembrey Forest. Planting commenced in 1929 and a seedling nursery was established. Many thousands of young trees were produced which required transplanting in their third year so, from 1932, a surplus was taken at intervals the ¾ mile to the Ty Mawr sidings for loading into wagons and dispatched to Margam and elsewhere, according to the reminiscences of Daniel James Jones, who worked in the Pembrey Forest from 1928. Other young trees, including buckthorn, were brought in by rail from Scotland and unloaded at Ty Mawr.

The siding referred to was not the passing loop at Tymawr (which did not have road access) but a short siding just to the north of the level crossing (at 2 miles 47 chains). Actually the points were just to the south and connected to the down loop so there was double track over the crossing. It is thought that this siding was removed when the Tymawr loop was closed in 1947. Just beyond this siding, on the down side, was Lock Cottage (now much altered) built by the canal company and thus predating the railway. The lock here was originally to prevent any adverse flow of water to the Ashburnham canal, which crossed at virtually the same point as the road crossing, but in 1835 the banks of Kymer's canal had been topped up allowing a rise of two feet in the lock, so deepening the canal on the old section to the north. Before the railway opened, in 1861, a canal labourer named Jonah Jones had been the occupant. In the census of 1881 platelayer George Davies and his family, who all came from Pembrokeshire, lived here. Two sons, William and James, were also platelayers and a 14-year-old daughter Elizabeth was the crossing keeper.

At three miles there was another curve to the right (travelling north) and here, in canal days, was Tywgyn Junction with the Pembrey canal of 1824 trailing in on the up (left) side. To ease the curve the railway left the towpath at the commencement of the bend and crossed over the canal bed, then returned to the towpath as it began to straighten out. By this means the curve was kept to 24 chains radius. Halfway round was mile post 3; like all the mile posts on the line it was on the down side. A photograph at this location, looking north and taken about 1973, appears on page 112 of Volume One; however, the caption needs amending. The course of the Pembrey Canal is marked by the bushes on the extreme left whilst the excavation for pipe laying in the picture follows a drainage ditch and not the canal. Note that the track has been relaid using concrete sleepers and bullhead rail.

The railway now entered a straight and level section of exactly one mile heading north-east across the marshes. At 3 miles 22 chains was Pinged Halt (SN420039) with the platform on the down side and the unsignalled and ungated level crossing immediately to the north at 3 m. 24 ch. There were 10 mph speed limit boards fixed at 9 chains to the south and 8 chains to the north of the crossing. Pinged was hardly even a hamlet with less than a dozen dwellings within a half mile radius; however, it did include the 'Plough Inn' almost opposite the station on the down side. There was a loading basin on the canal at this point to serve the Bryndias Colliery. According to Charles Hadfield 'there seems also to have been a short canal' from here to the colliery but Raymond Bowen dismisses this suggestion, giving his detailed reasons in Volume One on page 90.

Just 6¼ chains before the end of this mile-long straight section was Trimsaran Junction, facing towards Burry Port with the branch curving away to the east. The formation here suggested that a triangular junction may have been intended, but this third 'side' merely indicated the route of the original branch canal. Before the junction, which was at 4 miles 9¾ chains from Burry Port, there was a long siding on the down side with connections to both the main line and the branch. This is not shown on the 1878-79 map but has appeared on the 1913 survey. It was alongside this siding that workmen's trains stopped (or more accurately slowed down to a crawl) to allow colliers to alight; they were then faced with a walk of 1¾ miles to the pit unless they could hitch a lift on a train worked by one of the colliery locomotives.

Beyond the junction the main line curved to the left, crossing the Gwendraeth Fawr at 4 miles 20½ chains by using the original six-arch aqueduct built for the canal in 1815. Still curving to the left, the line is now ruan on the east (down) side of the old canal and a short siding trailed in on this side to the north of the river. This was Nobel's Siding, put in to supply coal to the pumping station erected in 1916 to supply water extracted from the river and piped to Nobel's Pembrey Burrows Explosives Works. Although the points were north of the river, the siding crossed over the aqueduct as the pumping station was on the south bank, just to the east of the line. The BP&GV applied to the Board of Trade for its sanction on 20th May, explaining it was at 4 miles 11 chains (a curious figure, presumably the southern end of the siding) and Col. Druitt gave his approval without any formal inspection on 23rd May, 1916. The pumping station was purchased by the Llanelly Corporation Waterworks in 1920, and closed in 1931; it is believed the siding was lifted soon after. A new pumping station was built here in 1939 to serve the Royal Ordnance Factory but without reinstating the siding.

A short straight section brought the main line to the triangular Kidwelly Junction; the south to west curve, known as the Kidwelly Loop, did not exist in 1878 but had been laid by 1909, following the Kidwelly & Llanelly canal to its junction with Kymer's canal. It seems to only have been used as a siding, it not being possible to use it for through running as the points at each end were controlled by different train staffs. The south end points were operated by the single-levered Kidwelly East Loop ground frame, released by the Tymawr to Kidwelly Junction staff. Here the main line curved to the right to join the line of Kymer's canal with the Kidwelly branch trailing in on the left at 4 miles 59 chains. In 1878 this was known as Mudles-cwm Junction and there was just a short loop siding off the branch along the up side of the line for 6½ chains to where the later Kidwelly Junction signal box stood (on the down side). By 1909 the branch continued until joining the main line at a new Kidwelly Junction at 4 miles 74¼ chains, immediately before the road bridge. Between the two lines there were two siding loops with access to all routes, that at the west end being controlled by the Kidwelly branch ground frame. There were five signals controlling the junction in 1909, but in 1878 only one signal post is shown (in the V of the junction facing Burry Port); the number of arms is not known, possibly two.

Kidwelly Junction signal box and sidings, about 1958.   *R.E. Bowen*

Trimsaran Road station, looking towards Cwmmawr, 9th July, 1958.   *R. M. Casserley 17787*

Trimsaran Road station on 31st July, 1955, looking towards Burry Port. The junction signals for Kidwelly Junction are not very clear in front of the bridge. Beyond can be seen the Junction signal box.   *M. Hale*

Kidwelly Junction to Cwmmawr

The bridge just mentioned carries the Cydweli to Trimsaran Road, now the B4308, and was originally a flattish stone arch with a headroom of 11 ft 8¾ in., the lowest on the main line. It was later replaced by a steel girder bridge which cleared the centre of the track by 14 ft 1 in.; this was bridge No. 10 at 4 m. 74½ ch. Beyond the bridge, on the down side, was Trimsaran Road station at 4 m. 76½ ch.; the stone-faced platform having a brick-curb edge and was provided with a small, corrugated metal, waiting shelter (SN432062). The line now headed north-east and, except for some minor exceptions, kept pointing the same direction all the way to Cwmmawr.

At 5 miles 28 chains came the ungated Parc-y-Llong level crossing (10 mph speed limit); the railway cottages here had been built by the Canal Co. A further 14 chains on was the junction with the Carway line, with a water tank in the V between the two lines. The old canal was now on the up (left) side on both the Carway branch and the main line. Glyn Abbey station (also known as Pontnewydd) was reached at 6 miles 11¾ chains, the timber faced platform being on the up side and just had a small wooden hut (grid ref. SN447073).

There was a lady porter known as 'Owd Mag' at Glyn Abbey and who lived only 100 yards or so from the station, trotting there about 10 minutes before each passenger train was due and returning home immediately after its departure; she performed this ritual for almost 40 years up to the end of the service in 1953. R.C. Riley describes seeing her in August 1951 as a middle-aged lady in best large floral hat, green dress and shopping bag, who locked up the office after issuing tickets. Many of the colliers who lived in Carway used to take the train to Glyn Abbey on finishing their shift, the distance to home being only about a mile and a half. However, there were two public houses in Pontnewydd, as the village around Glyn Abbey station was called, whereas there was none in Carway despite it being more than three times the size of Pontnewydd. As a result most of the men did not commence their homeward trek immediately after alighting from the train.

Glyn Abbey station, looking to Cwmmawr, 9th July, 1958.   *R.M. Casserley 17786*

The holding of eisteddfodau in the grounds of Glyn Abbey, with associated excursion trains, had been a feature since the days when Astley Thompson lived at the Abbey, in the 1870s. Such events were resurrected and continued to be performed until 1940, when the war caused their postponement; the last one was held in 1946. Nowadays the Abbey is home to a commune of up to around 30 people.

At the far end of the station was bridge No. 11 at 6 m. 13¾ ch. carrying the road from Mynydd-y-Garreg to Carway. Built on masonry abutments, the flattish arc girders had concrete infill and the parapet walls were of sheet steel. After the Trimsaran Road bridge was reconstructed, Glyn Abbey became the lowest between Cydwelli and Cwmmawr with a headroom of only 12 ft 0¾ in. in the centre; it was also the wettest on this section, frequently flooding whenever there was much rain. The story of what happened when a locomotive which was too high to go under this bridge was nevertheless sent up the line in 1988 is retold in Chapter Ten.

The railway used the 1836 single-arched stone canal aqueduct at 6 miles 20½ chains to cross the Gwendraeth Fawr just beyond Glyn Abbey station. In 1916 it was proposed to replace it with a girder bridge but under an Order in Council all major building works had been suspended as a wartime economy measure. Works costing less than £500 might be permitted under licence. Accordingly Arthur Morgan wrote to the Board of Trade on 22nd July, 1916 advising that the cost would not exceed £150 and that the steel girders had previously been purchased from the London & South Western Railway some 18 months earlier. The Board referred the BP&GV to the Railway Executive Committee who were able to give their consent. The new bridge was completed in 1917 and 'before and after' photographs are reproduced in Volume One on page 146.

It was hoped that the improved size of the opening would help to alleviate the flooding problem under bridge 11 but it did not make a lot of difference. A tributary of the Gwendraeth - the Clydach - was joined by another stream from the Abbey itself a short distance (about 160 ft) before passing under the station platform and joining the river. It was the overflowing of these streams that seemed to be the principal cause of the flooding and one cannot help wondering if the railway would have been better advised enlarging the culverts under the station; surely this would not have cost more than rebuilding the bridge.

The New Carway Siding connection, on the down side at 6 miles 70½ chains, was put in about 1902. The colliery itself was just over a quarter mile away to the south and was linked to the sidings by tramway. Just beyond, at 6 m. 77 ch., the branch to the Pumpquart Colliery turned off to the north on the up side. This pit closed in 1885 but the connection was retained for access to the Glyn Abbey Storage Siding on the up side; this connection was later referred to as New Carway Middle and it was still in use in March 1962. The line has been climbing firstly at 1 in 68 and then at 1 in 86 to gain height to the top of the two Ynys Fawr Locks on the canal. At the top there was a trailing connection on the down side at 7 m. 29½ ch. with the top end of the extensive colliery sidings, known as New Carway North and installed in November 1914. Immediately beyond (at 7 m. 30¾ ch.) there was, until 1928, a facing connection with the Plasbach Colliery (on the down side) and which also served the Gwendraeth

Pontyates on 4th April, 1953. The crossing gates are open ready for No. 1633 to depart with the 1.35 pm train from Burry Port. *C.H.A. Townley*

Slants. The original connection was further on, at 7 m. 39 ch., but the layout was much altered in 1914-16 and included additional sidings on the up side. The north end connections to both the colliery and the up sidings were at 7 m. 58 ch. adjacent to the down-side Pontyates signal box, but the station loop started earlier, at 7 m. 50 ch., and continued to just over the level crossing which was at 8 miles 5 chains. This is with the old Carmarthen to Llanelly direct road, the B4309, and had the busiest road traffic of all the line's crossings and was one of only three provided with gates.

Pontyates station was on the Burry Port side of the crossing, at 7 m. 61½ ch., both platforms being brick-faced with the booking office and waiting room on the down side (SN470082). The up platform was unusual in later (not originally) having a brick-tiled surface, the only one on the line; it also had a water column, fed by a tank supported on pillars on the Cwmmawr side of the crossing. Alongside the up platform was a goods shed and a single goods siding; this latter was there in 1879 before there was a passenger station or a passing loop. The 1909 signal box had eight levers; in 1916 this was increased to 14 but four of the levers were spare. After 1928, when the collieries closed, this was increased to six spare. After passenger services ceased and the box closed in 1961 the crossing gates were worked by the engine crew, and the regulations included exemption from Rule 99.*

Some 3½ chains beyond the crossing came the facing connection on the down side for the Caepontbren Colliery (New Caepontbren from 1909). There was then a rise at 1 in 256, steepening to 1 in 110, where there had been another lock on the canal. This ended at the down-side facing Ffoy Junction at 8 miles 5 chains with the 30 chain branch to the Ynyshafen Colliery and Brickworks and the Ffoy Colliery. This seems to have been abandoned by about 1909 when the sidings from the New Caepontbren Colliery were extended north-eastwards to cross the former route of the Ynyshafen branch and trail into the BP&GV main line at 8 miles 8 chains from Burry Port. The Caepontbren set-up in turn closed in 1913.

---

* Rule 99 required level crossing gates to be kept closed across the roadway except when necessary to be opened to allow the line to be crossed.

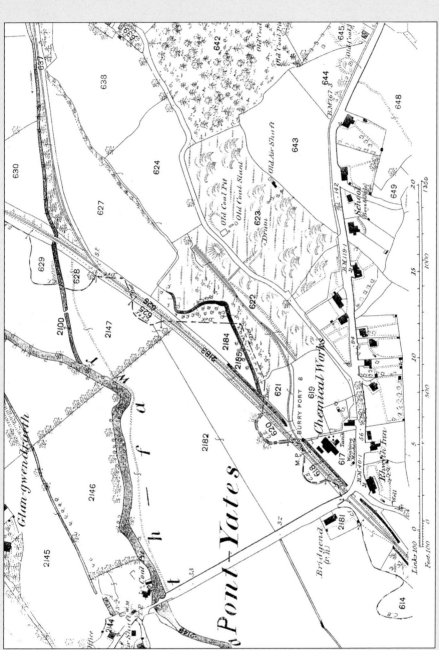

Pontyates. The level crossing is incorrectly shown as a bridge. The sidings branching off by milepost 8 are for Caepontbren colliery whilst the branch at top right served the Ffoy and Ynyshafen collieries and brickworks. There was another lock in the canal by the figures 2183.

Reproduced from the 25", 1880 Ordnance Survey Map

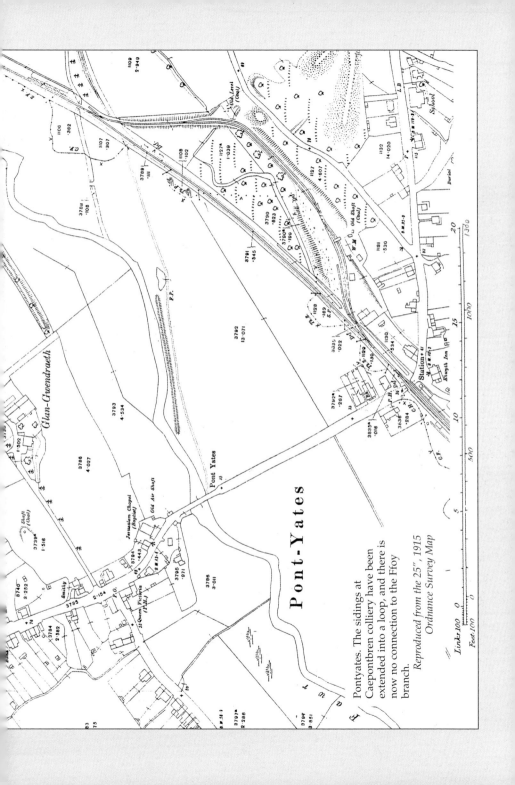

Pont-Yates

Pontyates. The sidings at Caepontbren colliery have been extended into a loop, and there is now no connection to the Ffoy branch.

Reproduced from the 25″, 1915 Ordnance Survey Map

Glan-Gwendraeth

Pont Yates

Pontyates, looking to Cwmmawr after the closure to passengers. The painted name on the signal box has been replaced by something resembling a motor vehicle number plate and the station building has lost the roof extension over the platform.   *R.E. Bowen*

Pontyates on 16th July, 1965, after the line through the station had been singled.   *R.E. Bowen*

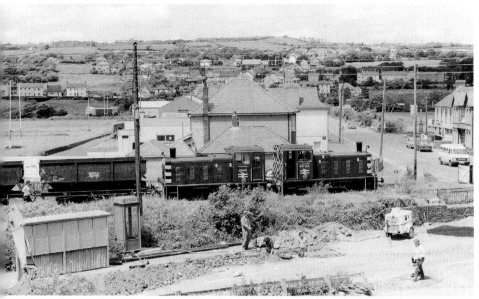

An empty wagon train heading for Cwmmawr has halted before the level crossing at Pontyates on 15th June, 1983. The locomotives are Nos. 03141 (*left*) and 03145 and there are cable connections between them to enable both to be driven from just one cab.   *Tom Heavyside*

Looking south-east later the same day and No. 03141 (*right*) with 03145 plus a glimpse of 03152 take a loaded train for Burry Port across the Pontyates Crossing.   *Tom Heavyside*

The remains of Ponthenry station and platform on left looking to Burry Port in 1952. There is little sign that there was once a platform on the right also. The Incline Hotel is to the right of the bridge.   *R.J. Doran*

Looking to Cwmmawr with the former Ponthenry station on the right and the goods siding in the background, 9th July, 1958.   *R. M. Casserley 17785*

The ½ mile-long incline up to Ponthenry (now spelt Ponthenri) came next, starting at 1 in 56, stiffening to 1 in 50 in the middle and finishing with a severe 1 in 45 at the top, reached just before bridge No. 15 at 8 miles 51½ chains. The masonry segmental arch had a generous clearance of 12 ft 10 in. in the centre; on the west side of the road through the village and the up side of the line was the Incline Hotel, believed to have been so named in the days of the canal, whilst immediately after the bridge came the station at 8 miles 54½ chains (SN477093). This was unusual in that at one time there was a brick-faced platform on both the up and down sides of the single line, that on the up side seems later to have been used mainly for goods traffic, but originally it was the only platform. A down-side platform does not seem to have been provided when the station first opened in 1909 as there is a note in the Board of Trade files which mentions a proposal in August 1911 for a new platform at Ponthenry and that Colonel Druitt reports that the new platform has not yet been constructed. It is not shown on the Ordnance Survey 1913 revision but obviously had been completed by the time the brick-built station building, which was quite different from the Stephens-inspired structures of the other stations, was erected on this down platform; this building is believed to date from 1919. Later the original platform on the up side was reduced to just an earth banking as it was no longer used.

Richard Rowlands, now of Llanelli and who travelled daily by train to and from school in the late 1930s and into the 1940s, recalls a dog waiting on the platform every morning as the first up train arrived at Ponthenry. The guard would alight from his compartment and hand the dog a roll of newspapers, and the dog would immediately set off down the platform to, presumably, deliver the papers to his master. After leaving the platform the short goods siding trailed in on the up side. This was marked as the Station Siding on a plan of September 1930 but is shown as a Mileage Siding on a GWR plan of July 1937; it was still in use in July 1958.

There followed nearly 1½ miles (from the top of the last incline) of level track with the old canal now on the down side. The facing connection to the Pont Henry and Tynywaun Slants on the down side was passed at 8 miles 74 chains. A tramway crossed the line and the river to connect with the Glynhir Slant on the up side; another tramway ran from the colliery south-westwards to the backs of the houses in Bargoed Terrace (the pit had been acquired by the Bargoed Coal Co. in 1906). This was a large colliery in production until 1936 but suffered from gas outbursts which unfortunately cost 10 miners their lives between 1920 and 1928.

A little further on, at 9 m. 49 ch., was the facing connection on the down side with the extensive Pentremawr or Capel Ifan Colliery sidings, known as Pentremawr South. The trailing junction with the sidings at Pentremawr North was at 9 miles 70¾ chains from Burry Port. Being the largest of the collieries served by the BP&GV there have been alterations to the track layout over the years; in September 1930 an additional connection known as Pentremawr Middle was opened, almost opposite the colliery screens. It was at this point that the original canal veered off to the right and the railway pursued an independent course. This was to avoid the canal incline but, even so, the railway

Nos. 1633 and 1607 approaching Pontyberem with the 1.45 pm from Burry Port on 16th July, 1951. The goods siding was converted into a loop in 1911. *R.J. Doran*

Looking back towards Burry Port showing the other end of Pontyberem goods shed. Straight ahead, but keeping to the left of the telegraph poles, can be seen the route of the Field sidings built for the Pontyberem Slants Colliery and lifted in 1957. *M.R.C. Price*

climbed at 1 in 63, steepening to 1 in 53 before the top was reached. Facing the bank on the up side, from 10 m. 21 ch. to 10 m. 26½ ch., was Railway Terrace, a row of 20 cottages built by the Pentrmawr Colliery Co. in 1909; this was just before the canal rejoins the line.

Towards the summit of the bank a goods siding trailed in on the up side at 10m. 38¾ ch. known as Cook's Bridge Siding (later the Mileage Siding); it was in use in 1930 but is believed to have closed about 1940. The route of the old canal had rejoined the line here but as the trackbed had been excavated to a lower level it was in a cutting and rising on a 1 in 142 grade. The Cook bridge itself (Pont Cook), No. 18, was at 10 m. 40 ch. and was not the original canal structure, having a slightly arched ribbed-steel deck on masonry abutments with a clearance in the centre of 12 ft 6½ in.; the parapet consisted of attractive iron railings welded to the deck. The canal bridge referred to a soldier in the 72nd Foot named Derwis Cook who came from Nottingham and was posted to the barracks in Pontyberem during the time of the Rebecca Riots (1839-43), married a local girl and settled down in a cottage next to the canal, which had recently been completed in 1838; he is buried in the village. In the early 1940s a school bus went through the railings and finished up on the trackside, remarkably without any serious injuries. In the post-war period a water pipe was attached to the Burry Port side of the bridge reducing the clearance by several more inches.

A further 7½ chains towards Cwmmawr came the Plough bridge (after a public house, now a private dwelling, which closed when the canal closed in 1868), No. 19, the flat arc having a clearance of only 12 ft 2½ in. in the centre. In 1993 this was replaced by a new reinforced-concrete structure with flat beams and a more than adequate clearance. Known as Pont-y-Plough, it was just on the Burry Port side of the old span. At the same time the Cook bridge was made pedestrian only, vehicles being prohibited.

Continuing in a cutting, at 10 miles 66 chains from Burry Port was the site of the old down-side facing connection to Coalbrook and Pontyberem South Collieries, both closed in July 1880 following the failure of the West of England Bank. A new facing connection at this point to the Pontyberem Goods Siding, thus turning it into a loop, was opened in August 1911. The northern end of the goods (or mileage) siding with corrugated goods shed (probably dating from 1909) and originally the north end of the colliery sidings, followed at 10m. 75ch. and here the up grade levelled out from a modest 1 in 377 and the cutting finally came to an end. The two Field Sidings approached from the north-west at an angle, combined and trailed in at 10 m. 78 ch. They are believed to have been laid down after 1881 to allow pit waste from Pontyberem (Coalbrook) Slants to be dispersed but there were sidings on a different alignment here in 1878 and there may also have been a pit here. A note that the National Coal Board (NCB) Siding was recovered in April 1957 is believed to apply to these Field Sidings.

Immediately after this siding trailed in came the facing point for the Pontyberem station loop, followed by the double-track gated level crossing at 10 m. 78½ ch. and then the station, centered on 11 m. 4¼ ch. (SN507113). Originally, in 1909, there was just a single platform on the down side. The up platform was brought into use in 1913; both were brick-faced. Gates were added to the crossing at a later date. At one time at the house next to the crossing lived

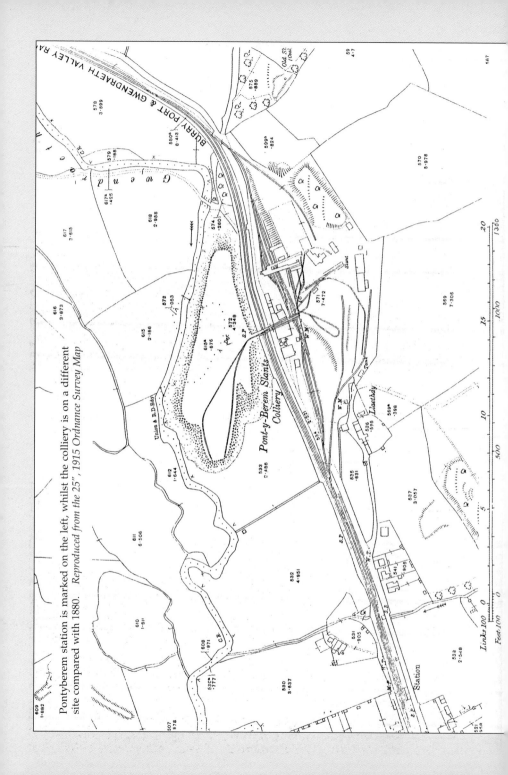

Pontyberem station is marked on the left, whilst the colliery is on a different site compared with 1880. *Reproduced from the 25", 1915 Ordnance Survey Map*

Pontyberem station, looking towards Burry Port on 9th July, 1958. This signal box has also received a 'car number plate' type nameboard.   *H.C. Casserley 93734*

The crossing gates are still there and there is a single track just visible through the weeds in this view of Pontyberem looking to Burry Port on 24th October, 2004.   *Author*

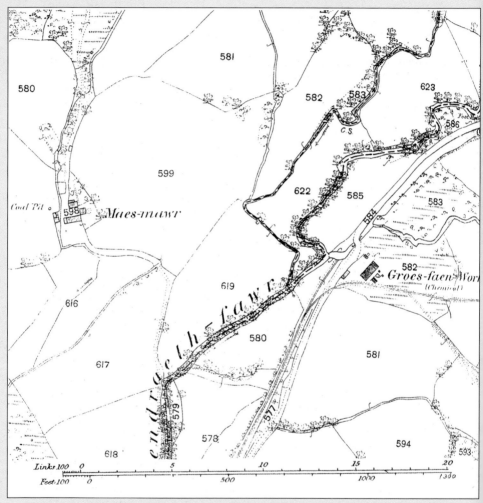

The main line is shown terminating at the canal, one mile short of Cwmmawr. The branch to the right went to the Dynant colliery.   *Reproduced from the 25", 1880 Ordnance Survey Map*

a guard who rejoiced in the name of Nott. He used to delight, whenever he had the opportunity, in announcing to any and everyone within hearing that 'I am *Nott* the guard!' At the Cwmmawr end of the down platform was the signal box (11 m. 6 ch.), dating from 1913, and the loop in 1909 ended here. Later a trailing connection into the down line was put in here with a new down siding and the loop was extended to 11 m. 13 ch. The box was closed and the signal arms were all removed in November 1961; for two years the station loop was retained for the engine to run-round its train and then propel to Cwmmawr. However, the loop and the down side goods siding were recovered in November 1963.

Just before the end of the extended station loop, at 11 m. 11½ ch., came the trailing connection into the down loop line with the sidings for Pontyberem Slants Colliery, established in 1881 and being locally known as Coalbrook Slants. The colliery names can be confusing here. Coalbrook and Pontyberem South Collieries were both to the south-west of Pontyberem station and were closed down by the Pontyberem Colliery Co. in July 1880 whilst Pontyberem Slants (popularly known as Coalbrook Slants) lay to the east of the station and was opened in 1881, also by the Pontyberem Colliery Co. Thus although the names were similar they did not co-exist at the same time. The colliery sidings continued over the acutely angled and ungated Maesmawr level crossing (11 m. 29 ch.) and eventually trailed into the main line at 11 m. 33 ch.

After Pontyberem station the line was level, running alongside the old canal although all traces of the latter had disappeared under the extensive colliery sidings. Just a half chain further from the last junction another, facing, connection appeared for the up-side sidings for the Glynhebog and Closucha Collieries, dating from 1884 and 1908 respectively. The screens for the latter were alongside the BP&GV line but at a lower level at map reference SN528110; the connection to the slant was by a half-mile long tramway. The branch to Glynhebog crossed the Gwendraeth Fawr to the screens at SN517122; there was a 30 chains-long tramway running north to the old slant. Then at 11 miles 45 chains from Burry Port the steeply-graded half-mile branch to the Dynant Colliery curved away to the east on the down side; this was abandoned in 1889.

From here the altered line of 1913 pursued a new course on an embankment slightly nearer the river in order to alleviate the original 1 in 14 gradient of the Hirwaun Isaf bank. Only two wagons at a time were taken up the old line. The inclination of the deviation was originally quoted as 1 in 40 with a length of 1,003 yards, as given in the Inspecting Officer's Report, but the GWR working books show grades of 1 in 44, followed by 1 in 41 and finally 1 in 35; the quoted 1 in 40 is probably an average figure. Partway up the bank at 12m. 2ch. came the ungated Hirwaun crossing, with the similar Tirclay level crossing almost at the top at 12 m. 27 ch.; between the two crossings traces of the old canal could be observed on the down side.

Just after the crossing came the facing connection to the down-side sidings for the New Dynant Colliery, which opened in 1907 and closed in 1939; although part was retained for ventilation and pumping. The shunting neck went over the Tirclay crossing and continued for a short distance on the pre-1913 alignment. The points were at 12 m. 34 ch. and were followed at 12 m. 40¾ ch. by the trailing junction on the up side with the New Cwmmawr Slant, opened

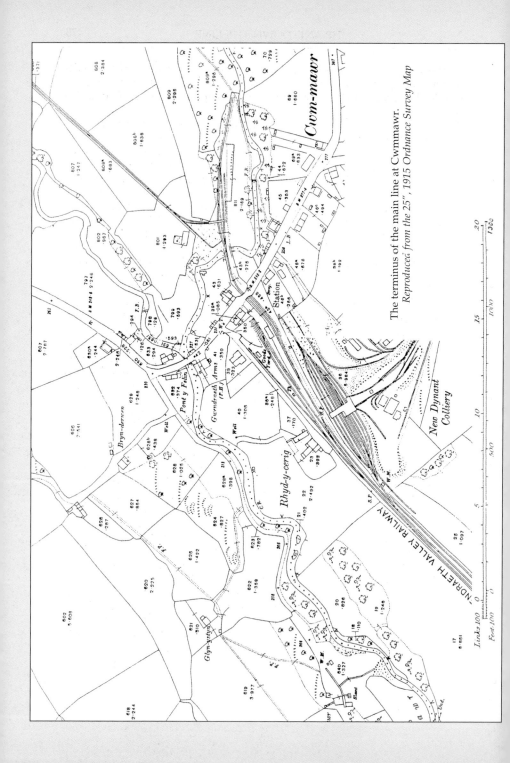

The terminus of the main line at Cwmmawr.
Reproduced from the 25", 1915 Ordnance Survey Map

in a small way in 1901 but still shown without rail connection on the 1913 OS revision. The application to the Board of Trade for a new colliery siding at 12 miles 40 chains was made in April 1915 and was approved by Col Druitt. The colliery closed in 1939.

The facing points for the loop and sidings of Cwmmawr station were at 12 m. 42 ch. Besides the platform line and the run-round loop there were two sidings (one for carriages) on the up side and another behind the platform on the down side. By 1913 the top-end siding connection to the New Dynant lines trailed in to the down station goods siding; at a much later date (probably 1958) this connection was moved to join the main line precisely where the New Cwmmawr Colliery line came in. This would be when the New Dynant site was re-opened as an Opencast Disposal Point. This, incidentally, was always referred to as Cwmmawr (or Cwm Mawr) and never as New Dynant. Despite this, the top-end connection was worked by the New Dynant North ground frame until the day it closed on 1st May, 1967 after which all traffic was worked through the south connection and the tracks in the station area were lifted. The station had closed to all traffic on 12th July, 1965.

At the Burry Port end of the station platform at 12 m. 48 ch. stood the Cwmmawr signal box of 1913. This had closed and the signal arms had all been removed in November 1961. The station itself was at grid ref. SN530126, the single brick-faced platform being on the down side of the track. The terminal buffer stop was measured at 12 miles 52 chains from Burry Port. The brick-faced platform was on the down side of the station loop and had the usual corrugated metal building plus a minimal toilet. From the outset in 1913 water and electricity for lighting was provided by the New Dynant Anthracite Colliery Ltd. Behind the platform on the down side were two goods sidings of which the nearer continued under the road by a very low bridge at 12m. 53¼ ch. to serve the Closyryn Colliery until it was abandoned in 1925.

This segmental arc bridge was No. 22 with a clearance of only 9 ft 7½ in. in the centre; clearly only wagons were allowed to pass under and not locomotives. This bridge has now gone and there is no longer a hump in the road. Curving sharply to the east, the line crossed the Gwendraeth Fawr by using the old canal stone aqueduct at 12 m. 58¾ ch., then divided into several sidings under the loading screens before terminating at the far end of the original canal basin at 13 miles 7½ chains from Burry Port (SN532126). A tramway connected the loading point with the slant 30 chains to the north-east. The area to the east of the slant was later used for opencast mining, the anthracite being taken by road to the Disposal Point opened in 1958 on the site of the New Dynant Colliery; this closed in April 1996 since when there has been no rail traffic up to Cwmmawr. The large Cwm-y-Glo reservoir near Cefneithin, which supplied the canal with its water, was a mile further upstream from Cwmmawr; all trace of this disappeared under the opencast working but the aqueduct over the Gwendraeth Fawr still stands, in use for a road leading to a local industrial business.

No. 03152 is banking its train from Burry Port into the Cwm Mawr Opencast Disposal Sidings on 15th June, 1983.   *Tom Heavyside*

The starting signals at Cwmmawr on 4th August, 1951. The locomotive is 0-6-0PT No. 1618 on the 6.10 pm departure and the young boy is the son of F.K. Davies.   *R.C. Riley*

Cwmmawr showing the starting signals and the screens of the New Dynant Colliery which had closed in 1939. Locomotive No. 1957 is waiting to take off the front two coaches on 7th July, 1947.

H.C. Casserley 49318

The single platform at Cwmmawr showing the 1913 station building, 16th July, 1951.

R.J. Doran

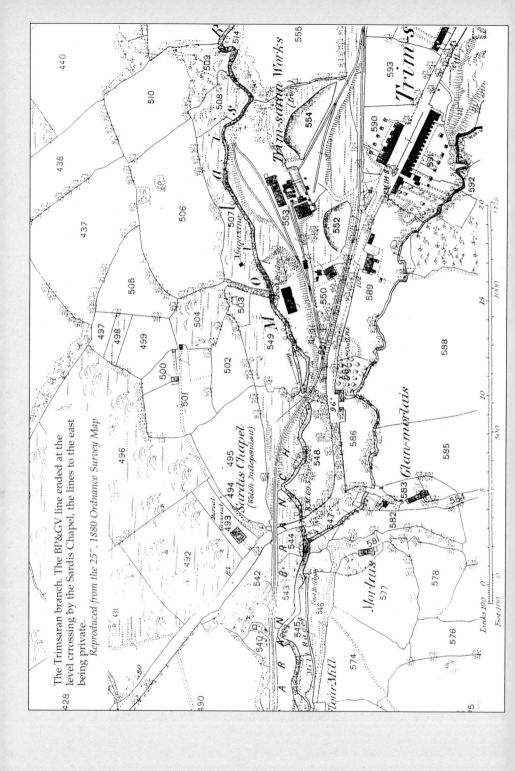

428 The Trimsaran branch. The BP&GV line ended at the level crossing by the Sardis Chapel, the lines to the east being private.

Reproduced from the 25", 1880 Ordnance Survey Map

The Old Carway, Trimsaran and Kidwelly Branches

Turning our attention to the various branches of the BP&GV, the Old Carway branch left the main line at the 5 m. 51½ ch. mark and for the first 25 chains was level alongside the branch canal (on the up side) as far as the Gwendraeth bridge at Pwll-y-Llygod, illustrated on the front cover of Volume One. The canal, which here is the original Kymer's canal, terminated just before the bridge, which was built to take the connecting tram road to the Carway Colliery. Converted to a standard gauge railway near the end of 1870, the branch was about 1 miles 25 chains long in total to the colliery, was not steeply graded, and seems to have closed soon after the new connection was put in about 1902. The track on the first 25 chains as far as the bridge was retained for wagon storage for many years, well into British Railways days, being finally closed and lifted in 1965.

Similarly the first 41 chains of the Trimsaran branch were laid along the north side of the canal so this section was mostly level. To the end of the BP&GV the line followed the Afan Morlais and used the trackbed of the old tram road which rose 46 feet in a length of 56 chains, an average gradient of 1 in 80. Along the first 14 chains there was a loop and a short siding, then at 0m. 29ch. from the junction the line kinked to take to the canal bed under the Moat bridge. This had a segmental arch, almost semi-circular, 11 ft 11½ in. high in the centre.

Now climbing through the wooded valley from the canal terminus, the branch crossed the Llandyry Road (the B4317) at 0 m. 45 ch. by an ungated crossing. This was known as the Colliers' Crossing after the nearby 'Colliers' Arms' public house. After a further 10 chains the branch was immediately north of the Llandyry Slant at Cilrhedyn, about 150 yards away but on the far side of the river. The slant was operative in a small way in 1893-97 and again in 1916-21 but it is doubtful if there was any rail connection, the anthracite possibly being carted to the Colliers' Crossing for loading.

After crossing the Morlais twice in quick succession the branch reached the Sardis Crossing, ungated and named after the adjacent Welsh Independent Chapel, at 1 mile 17 chains. This was the end of BP&GV property, the line continued eastwards in private ownership to the Trimsaran Collieries. At 9½ chains past the crossing came the connection on the north side to the Iron Works at SN448052; the private line continued for almost another 1½ miles serving the Caeduan, Waunhir, Waunhir North, Trimsaran Old and Trimsaran Upper pits, terminating at SN468053. The branch closed in June 1962 and the track had been recovered before the end of the year. Much of the area has since been subject to opencast mining and the latest plans to develop the area with a racecourse are discussed in Chapter Ten.

The Kidwelly branch was also built alongside the Kymer's canal through to its termination at Kymer's Quay on the Gwendraeth Fach. The junction with the main line was at 4 miles 74½ chains from Burry Port, immediately west of the bridge carrying the Trimsaran Road, and the two lines ran parallel (with two sidings between) for 15½ chains to the point of divergence at the former Mudles-cwm Junction. The branch curved to head west and a loop trailed off the siding connection to pass over a weighbridge, then trailed into the branch at 0 m. 27 ch. at Machine Road ground frame. At 0 m. 33 ch. came the Loop West Junction, which was immediately past the old junction of the Kidwelly & Llanelly canal with Kymer's canal. The canal here was on the north side of the line.

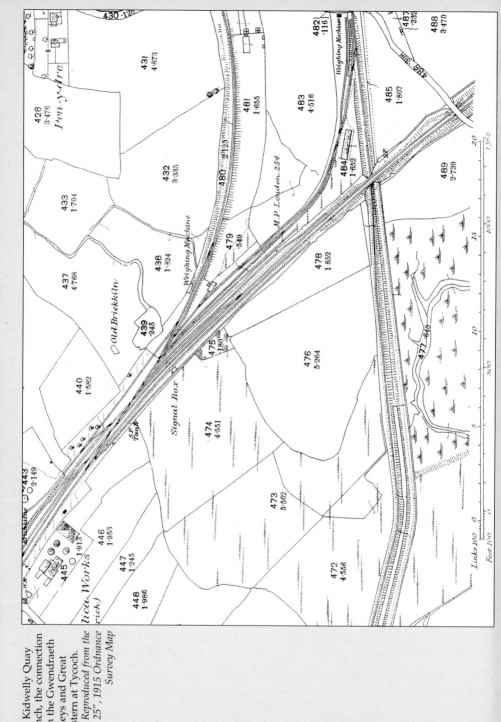

The Kidwelly Quay branch, the connection with the Gwendraeth Valleys and Great Western at Tycoch.

Reproduced from the 25″, 1915 Ordnance Survey Map

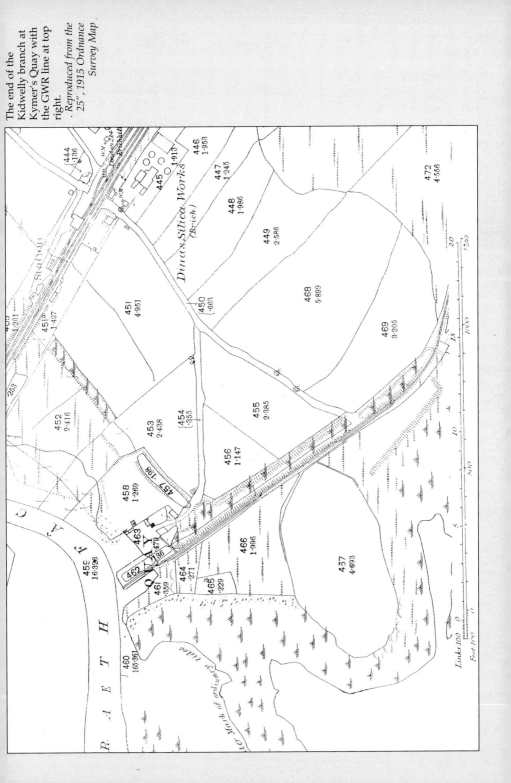

The end of the Kidwelly branch at Kymer's Quay with the GWR line at top right. *Reproduced from the 25″, 1915 Ordnance Survey Map*

Tycoch Halt, the nearest station to Cydweli, after closure looking towards Cwmmawr from the Pembrey Road bridge, in August 1964. The line was supposedly retained for emergency use.   *M.R.C. Price*

The Coed Bach coal distribution site was established in 1953 on the up or north side of the branch, stretching practically all the way from the branch junction until joining the branch at about 0 m. 53 ch., the junction facing Kidwelly. Beyond, and keeping level, the branch curved to the north-west to pass under the modern Cydweli by-pass road, then turned to the west to reach Tycoch at 1 m. 37 ch. (SN408061). The platform was on the north side of the line and there was a single siding also on this side with the points facing Cwmmawr on which the empty stock for the workmen's train used to stand. Beyond the platform was the bridge under the Pembrey Road; I regret I do not have the number or the clearance for this bridge but full-size diesel locomotives were able to pass under.

At 1 m. 42 ch. was the facing junction with the Gwendraeth Valleys Railway over which traffic was worked to and from the GWR at Kidwelly and points west. The BP&GV continued, passing under the GWR (again the bridge number and clearance not known) with the former canal now on the down (south) side before turning north-west, crossed over the canal, and reached the terminus at Kymer's Quay at 2 m. 20 ch. (SN398064). The facilities here consisted simply of a run-round loop, a siding on to the quayside, and another siding accessed via a wagon turntable. There were two small docks, both tidal, each on either side of the terminal, but only the West Dock was served by the quayside siding.

Although ownership of Kymer's canal had passed to the BP&GV, Lord Dynevor had retained possession of the Quay, it having passed to him in 1823 under the terms of Thomas Kymer's will. There was a coal shute and small ships conveyed anthracite for short voyages to such places as Carmarthen, Laugharne and Llanstephan. The *Llanelly Guardian* reported that in 1874 a dozen colliers had been loaded in one week, including one for Cardigan. By the 1890s the locally produced Dinas silica bricks were being shipped from the quay to much further afield. A total of 320 tons were dispatched on the SS *William Dawson* in 1894 for Middlesbrough, and there were 250 ton shipments on each of the *Lynx* for Cumberland, the *Captain Cook* for Glasgow and the *Dunvegan* for Newport. By 1914 this sea-borne brick traffic had ceased, but there was still some coal dispatched this way, the last on boats to Llanstephan in the mid-1920s.

The final rail traffic to the quay is believed to have been roadstone in the late-1920s but whether this was for shipping or unloaded for use on local roads is unknown. The branch beyond Tycoch Junction was closed in October 1929 and the track was recovered during 1933. The West Dock at the quay was much restored, with the aid of MSC funding, in 1983-85, and on 1st August, 1985 a sailing dinghy commanded by Terry James journeyed up the estuary at high tide and anchored in the restored dock, the first vessel to do so for some 60 years. The section from Coed Bach to Kidwelly ceased to carry any traffic from October 1965, but the track was retained for possible emergency use. It re-opened, after relaying, on 19th September, 1983, as will be described in Chapter Ten.

The Cwm Capel Branch

This branch, converted from a horse-drawn tramway in 1876, heads north directly from the East Quay at Burry Port, from alongside the copper and silver works. To reach the branch from the goods station or by the engine sheds a train would first have to cross over the branch into the exchange sidings (with the GWR) before reversing down onto the East Quay and then gaining access to the branch with another reversal. A GWR report on the BP&GV compiled in 1921 mentions 'on one of the branches is a gradient of 1 in 43 a mile in length, very tortuous, on which is one curve of only 93 feet radius' which almost certainly refers to this line. Apart from this the gradients are not otherwise known but the rise was about 130 feet in almost exactly a mile, which gives an average grade of around 1 in 41.

Until 1898 most of the traffic over this branch was worked by locomotives belonging to the Pembrey Copper Works. The branch crossed the GWR on the level just to the east of the goods station, controlled by the Pembrey West signal box on the north-east side of the crossing, then continued over Station Road with an ungated crossing known to the locals as 'Snook's Crossing'. Charlie Snook, a publisher of local view postcards, had a newsagency on one corner here. The rail crossing over the GWR was also used by pedestrians. Climbing steeply, the branch threaded its way between the buildings, part of the route today being a road called 'Old Tramway', the remainder is a footpath.

At 14 chains beyond the GWR crossing comes a facing connection with the Gwendraeth Siding, on the west side, preceded by a short loop. The siding,

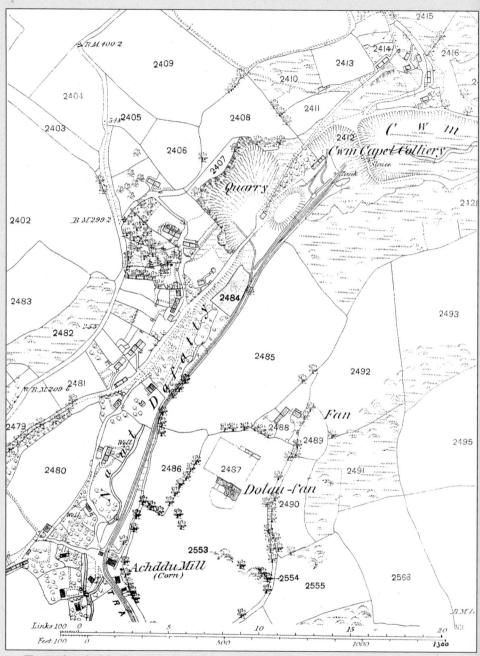

The north end of the Cwm Capel branch.　　*Reproduced from the 25″, 1880 Ordnance Survey Map*

which is not shown on the 1878 map, is thought to have been used to unload building stone brought down from the quarry at Cwm Capel. A further 19½ chains past the siding came the gated level crossing over the Colby Road (the present A484). Named the Pemberton Crossing after the Pemberton Arms Hotel, it was known to the locals as *gâts y cwb* because it was provided with a small cabin, complete with stove, for the use of the crossing keeper.

The branch was in the valley of the Nant Dyfatty which from here became narrower and more steeply sided. At 38 chains after the GWR crossing came the facing point connection with the west-side sidings to the Achddu Slant and Brickworks. This is not shown on the 1878 map and is believed to have been put in about 1905-06. The colliery and brickworks were on the east side of the line on the hillside at SN449016 but the sidings and screens were on the west side; the line here curved towards the north-west. At 48 chains from the GWR the branch made a sharp turn towards the north-east; this will be the 93 ft radius curve mentioned in the 1921 report. On the inside of the bend (east or up side) was the three-storey Achddu Mill. Its water wheel was taken away for scrap metal at the beginning of World War II. Behind the mill were the main colliery buildings, and immediately after the bend came a facing connection to the top end of the sidings (49 ch.).

Continuing up the valley for a further 14 chains the facing points for the Cwm Capel Colliery sidings were reached and the line terminated at the foot of the dam for the Cwm Capel reservoir, 77 chains from the GWR crossing, at SN452021. GWR records gave the length of the branch as 1 mile 11½ chains (probably to the centre of the colliery) and showed the zero point at 18¼ chains south of the GWR crossing; this would place it about midway alongside the Copperworks. The Cwm Capel Colliery buildings were on the west side of the line with the quarry (Cwar Mac) behind. There was a separate siding into the quarry shown on both the 1878 and 1913 maps. On the east side of the line, opposite the colliery, was the loading screen for the small Rhiwlas Colliery, fed by a tramway at a higher level which followed the Dyfatty upstream for nearly ¾ mile to the colliery, active during the 1905 to 1917 period.

There was little if any traffic on the branch after 1931, and the GWR signal box was replaced by a ground lever in 1932; closure duly followed and the track was recovered in July 1940. A footbridge was then erected over the GWR main line by Snook's crossing, enabling the foot crossing to be closed. Today the trackbed is clear enough but apart from the quarry face and the Cwm Capel mine chimney, there is little trace of the former industries in what is now a pleasant wooded valley.

The Sandy (Llanelly) Branch

Considering that this line stood closely to the old shoreline (as it existed before the GWR main line was built) for 3½ miles there were but six very short level sections; the line, which was laid on the track of an old tram road, was built virtually without earthworks and so was continuously up and down with mostly easy gradients, all of them short. The steepest grades, 1 in 66 and 1 in 99 (both very short) were climbed travelling from Sandy to Pwll. In the other direction there were two almost as short sections at 1 in 118 between Pwll and

Sandy. However when it is considered that the lowest and highest points on the line were 12.43 and 23.96 ft above mean sea level, a total climb of less than 12 ft, it will be seen how short the grades were. The 1 in 66 bank raised the line by 5.59 ft, so the climb was only for 123 yards.

Leaving the dock lines, the Sandy branch crossed the Cwm Capel line just to the east of the BP&GV engine sheds and ran alongside Glan-y-Mor Terrace on the south side. The houses in the terrace faced the line were part of the area known as the Backe. There were sidings on either side whilst the interchange sidings with the GWR were on the north or down side. Distances quoted, from the Working Timetables, would appear to be measured from the extreme rail end on the East Pier of the harbour.

At 51 chains was the ungated crossing of Woodbrook Terrace, the road continued northwards to cross the GWR (with a gated crossing) and became Church Road. The Sandy branch next crossed the GWR on the level at an acute angle, known as Dyvatty Crossing, at 57¼ chains and controlled by Pembrey East signal box (still in use) which was on the north-west side of the road crossing. Immediately afterwards the Nant Dyfatty was crossed.

The track layout was altered here in 1940 resulting in the BP&GV branch from Sandy now trailing into the GWR up line instead of crossing it. Access to the branch was now made through the exchange sidings onto the GWR down loop, then crossing over to the up side; this avoided using the Woodbrook Terrace crossing.

Turning towards the north-east, the branch reached the New Lodge Colliery Siding, facing on the down (north) side at 1 m. 11 ch. followed by the brickworks siding with a loop 7¼ chains further on, also on the down side. Until August 1912 the Copperworks engine used to work its own traffic to and from New Lodge. Curving to the east, the facing points for the down side New Pool Colliery Siding loops were reached at 1 m. 57 ch. followed by the up side connection to the Crown Colliery. The workings here extended under the Burry estuary and there was an additional trailing siding connection at 1 m. 75 ch. The Crown shunting locomotive used to travel over the BP&GV to shunt at New Lodge and at New Pool, all being in common ownership, until all three had closed by 1936.

So far the country on the north side of the line had been open, with only scattered housing. There was now a change as the town of Pwll was reached, connected to Llanelly by electric street tramway from July 1911. There was little change on the Burry estuary side; between the former shore line and the GWR embankment (the new shoreline) there was still the mixture of marshland and lagoons. The Pwll Colliery, on the down (north) side, was at 2 m. 15¾ ch. and the siding here included a loop. Like Crown, coal was extracted from under the sea, but this was the only colliery on the branch to last into NCB days, finally closing in 1953. For many years this was the end of the branch, the continuation on to Sandy not being completed until April 1899. The line now curved sharply to the east to reach the Pwll Brickworks, the up side siding connection at 2 m. 23¼ ch. being effective from November 1914.

At the end of the built-up area of Pwll, at 3 m. 5 ch., a tramway passed under the line from the Panthywel Colliery on the north to the brickworks on the south side; there does not appear to have ever been a siding connection here. The colliery closed in 1925. A short open stretch of line followed as the grounds of Stradey Castle lay to the north, but soon the houses of the Sandy district of Llanelli came into view with, on the south side, the industrial buildings of the Llanelly Steel Works. Here lay the Sandy Gate sidings on the down (north) side between 3 m. 31 ch. and 3 m. 42 ch. In GWR days and later all trains from Burry Port terminated here. The short remaining section of the BP&GV to Sandy Junction was worked by locomotives from Llanelly and also those of the local firm of Neville, Druce & Co.

On this final section, at about 3 m. 55 ch the track divided into two and both lines curved round to the south; that on the right trailed into the private Stradey Estate Railway, the other joined the Llanelli & Mynydd Mawr Railway (GWR from 1st January, 1923) at Sandy Junction. With the closure of the Pwll Brickworks all traffic between Burry Port and the Sandy Gate sidings ceased from 4th October, 1962. The final portion of the branch from Sandy Gate to Sandy Junction closed on 22nd December, 1963, although the signal box at the Junction did not close until 25th February, 1968. Three photographs of the trackbed in the Pwll area taken after closure appear in Volume One on pages 134 and 135.

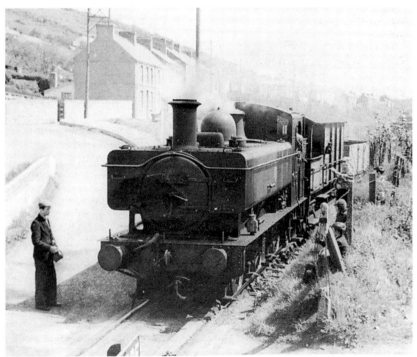

No. 1666 is shunting at the Pwll Brickworks on the Sandy branch on 21st May, 1958, looking towards Llanelli.   *H. Davies*

An illustration in the copperworks sale catalogue of 1912 showing, as well as Dynant, Pentremawr and Ponthenry wagons, a large number bearing the name of Gwendraeth. The good quality of the anthracite in the trucks nearest the camera will be readily apparent.
Brian Cripps Collection

Coal wagon built by the Gloucester Railway Carriage & Wagon Co. It is lettered 'empty to Plasbach Siding, Via Burry Port, G. W. Rly'. *HMRS Gloucester Collection*

Chapter Seven

The Industrial Connections

Having been built to serve the collieries in the Gwendraeth Valley in the first place it naturally followed that it was the various coal mines that provided the most important of the industrial connections to the railway. Coal and coke (probably entirely coal) amounted to 90 per cent of the total tonnage of goods and minerals carried by the BP&GV during 1913 (628,588 out of 699,416 tons) and nearly 96 per cent of originating traffic in 1920 (636,328 out of 663,099 tons), for example. The other connections were to iron and steel, copper, silver, lead, tinplate and brick works, foundries, wagon repair works, quarries and an explosives factory. Of the 26,771 tons of freight carried in 1920 that were *not* classed as coal or coke, 14,757 tons were bricks, 4,833 tons were tinplate, 2,233 tons were iron and steel (over 72 per cent being scrap) and 559 tons were timber (of which over 70 per cent consisted of pit props going *to* the collieries).

The coal mines are in three distinct groups. In the south, along the northern shore of the Burry River, a bituminous or ring (soft) coal is extracted and this provides good steam, manufacturing and household coals, being the eastward end of the Llanelly (spelt Llanelli since 1966) coalfield. These are the upper coal measures containing 11 seams with an aggregate thickness of 21 ft 10 in. and extending south under the Burry Estuary. The middle coal measures, which contain less bitumen, outcrop on the southern flanks of Pembrey Mountain and consist of eight seams totalling 13 ft 10 in. in thickness. The collieries concerned are Achddu, Bryndais, Craiglon, Cwm Capel, Ffrwd, Gwscwm and Rhiwlas; in this work these upper and middle series pits are all grouped together as bituminous collieries. None of these mines was particularly large but both Cwm Capel and Gwscwm produced good steam coal (which was purchased by the BP&GV for use in their locomotives); the others produced household and manufacturing coals.

In the north, along the Gwendraeth Valley, is the anthracite belt consisting of 16 seams of lower measures amounting to 47 ft 8 in. in aggregate. This belt extends eastwards across the upper Amman, Swansea, Dulais and Neath valleys as far as Glynneath, and sweeps westwards into Pembrokeshire probably (but not proven) by continuing under Carmarthen Bay. Many of the collieries did not use the familiar shafts and winding headgears seen in other coalfields but drove slants directly along the coal seams from the points where they outcropped at the valley sides, what in other areas are called drift mines. This type of mine required less capital to establish so was preferred when conditions were favourable. Such slants could incline downwards towards the south at grades of 1 in 4, steepening to as much as 1 in 2 in the Trimsaran area, and could be driven as far as two miles from the entrance.

Anthracite consists of over 80 per cent carbon and is very hard, commonly known as stone coal (*glo carreg* in Welsh), and when burning is flameless and smokeless and does not soil the fingers when handled. In 1854, when there were 41 collieries at work in the whole anthracite coalfield, only about 750,000 tons in total were produced. Separate figures just for the Gwendraeth Valley are not available but would amount to about 13 to 14 per cent of the total. At that period much of the production went towards lime burning, hop drying and malting; only a small quantity went for export. After 1865 there was a steady annual increase in the amount exported and this was closely related to the growth in mining in the anthracite coalfield. The development of the anthracite burning stove in the 1880s, especially in the Baltic States and Scandinavia, increased exports. In the main these also went to Guernsey (for the hot-houses), France, Italy, Germany, the Low Countries, USA, Canada and Argentina. Examples of the increase in exports are shown by comparing the tonnages sent to France and Italy, 14,369 and 558 respectively, in 1868 with the amounts in 1921 - 848,297 and 238,474 tons. By 1921 about 62 per sent of the total output was going for export but had been a rather higher proportion prior to the 1914 war breaking out. Whilst some of that mined in the Gwendraeth Valley was shipped through Burry Port there was also a proportion (about half in 1922) sent by rail to Llanelly and to Swansea for shipping.

Some idea in the growth of anthracite production can be gained by comparing the total mined for selective years, the proportion just for the Gwendraeth district alone amounted to around 14 per cent of these figures:

Year	1,000s of tons	Year	1,000s of tons
1890	1,221	1913	4,778
1895	1,678	1920	4,232
1900	2,204	1923	4,873
1910	4,032	1930	5,568

The big increase in production occurred between 1895 and 1910 and this is closely related to the change in profitability achieved by the BP&GV during the same period. The year 1934 was to prove the peak for anthracite mining when 6,133,934 tons were produced.

Of course greater investment was required for the necessary increase in plant and equipment to produce this continuous rise in output. The deeper seams had to be tapped and the product needed grading for different users, requiring crushing, screening and washing plants to be installed. Some consolidation in the industry had been first mooted as early as 1903. By 1911, when there were about 80 independent anthracite mines, amalgamation to produce larger colliery groups was being actively proposed, but it was not until 1923 that action was at last taken. Then, in the same year that most of the railway companies embraced groupings, the Amalgamated Anthracite Collieries Ltd (henceforth referred to as AAC Ltd) was registered, on 16th June, 1923. By the end of that year AAC Ltd, with a share capital of £2,500,000, had acquired the 10 anthracite mines of Cleeves Western Valleys Anthracite Collieries Ltd, Gelliceidrim Collieries Ltd and Gurnos Anthracite Collieries Ltd. Also at this time the Great Mountain Collieries Ltd (formerly John Waddell & Sons and so intimately connected with the Llanelly & Mynedd Mawr Railway) and who had purchased a controlling stake (£60,000) in the New Dynant Anthracite Colliery (1914) Ltd, now acquired two anthracite pits of the Ammanford Colliery Co. Ltd and which also included Glynhebog pit of Pontyberem Collieries Co. Ltd. This combined undertaking was then acquired by the newly-formed United Anthracite Collieries Ltd (with John Waddell Jnr a Director) on 25th August, 1923, also with an authorized capital of £2,500,000. This group is referred to as UAC Ltd for short; by 30th June, 1927 Caerbryn Anthracite Colliery Co. Ltd, Carway Collieries Ltd, Gwendraeth Valley Anthracite Collieries Ltd, New Rhos Anthracite Collieries Ltd and the United National Collieries Ltd (formerly the Pentremawr Colliery Co. Ltd until February 1925) were all included in UAC Ltd.

Pwllbach, Tirbach & Brynammon Anthracite Collieries Ltd was registered on 12th February, 1924 to combine the three mines. Welsh Anthracite Collieries Ltd was formed on 15th January, 1926 to take over Trimsaran Collieries and the New Cwmmawr Colliery of Ashburnam Collieries Ltd. The Blaina Colliery Co. Ltd at Pantyffynnon combined in 1925 with the Raven Colliery at Garnant to form the Blaina & Raven Anthracite Collieries Ltd. These three new firms then combined in May 1928 to form Henderson's Welsh Anthracite Collieries Ltd. In the meantime AAC Ltd had taken over UAC Ltd with effect from 1st July, 1927 giving them a total of 23 pits and then went on to acquire Henderson's Welsh Anthracite and the Llewellyn group in August 1928 so that they now had control of about 80 per cent of the anthracite production. This left the Ponthenry Colliery, operated by the Bargoed Coal Co. and much troubled with outbursts, as the only pit of any consequence to remain in operation (until it closed in 1936) in the Gwendraeth Valley that was not a part of the AAC Ltd combine. It is interesting to note that although he was not one of the original Directors, John Waddell was on the board of AAC Ltd by 1935.

Lists of the collieries existing in 1884, 1896, 1909 and 1923 are given in *Appendix Six*. Of those at work in 1909, Caepontbren closed in 1913 followed by the small Achddu and the equally small Rhiwlas, both in 1917. Pontyberem Slants, also known as Coalbrook Colliery, was closed by the Coal Commission (due to inefficiency) in 1918 leaving 17 rail-connected pits (11of them mining anthracite) still in operation when the BP&GV became a part of the enlarged GWR in July 1922. The small Panthywel closed in 1925 as did the larger Closyryn (Closyrhyn), although the latter was to re-open in 1930 for a couple of years. Plasbach followed in 1927 whilst the closure of Gwendraeth Slants in 1928 was a severe blow to the life in the valley. Two years later the Gwscwm pit in Pembrey ceased to work and, as mentioned, Closyryn closed its gates for the last time in 1932.

After 1934's peak output, the subsequent decline was accompanied by more pit closures in the Gwendraeth Valley as well as most of the smaller bituminous (soft) coal mines along the Burry River. Crown, New Cwmmawr Slant and New Pool all succumbed during 1934, the little New Lodge Colliery and the big Pont Henry Slants finished in 1936. There was still over extraction in the anthracite industry requiring AAC Ltd to weed out their least productive pits and this included New Dynant, closed in 1939. Cwm Capel also closed at this period but re-opened during the war in a small way, without any rail connection. On vesting day, 1st January, 1947 when the NCB came into being, only six collieries were still in production. Of these Pwll, Trimsaran and Cwm Capel (for the final time) all stopped working during 1952-54, although the washery at Trimsaran remained in use until 1960. It was in 1960 also that Carway Slants finally closed, followed in 1961 by Pontyberem (Glynhebog) leaving Pentremawr (Capel Ifan) as the sole remaining colliery connected to the former BP&GV. Rail traffic here ceased about 1970 although the mine remained in use until March 1974 and was actually retained as an emergency access to Cynheidre Colliery (to which it was linked underground) until early in 1989. Cynheidre is higher up the valley side to the south of Capel Ifan and is on the route of the former Llanelly & Mynedd Mawr Railway from Llanelli to Cross Hands.

This was not the end of coal extraction in the Gwendraeth Valley for opencast mining had commenced in the Trimsaran area in 1953 and near Cwm Mawr in 1958 with the main sites at Carway (Ffos Las) and Saron (Gilfach Iago) being opened by Wimpey Mining from 24th October, 1983 and 13th June, 1988 respectively. These workings were undertaken on behalf of the Opencast Executive of the NCB until 29th December, 1994, when Celtic Energy Ltd became responsible. A disposal depôt with screens for loading both road and rail wagons was built in 1953 at Coed Bach (at first known as Cefn Bach) on the north side of the Kidwelly branch, with another loading point erected on the site of New Dynant colliery at Cwm Mawr in 1958, these being operated by contractors. Rail traffic from Trimsaran ceased in June 1962 and henceforth the opencast coal was forwarded to Coedbach by road. It also arrived at New Dynant from the Gilfach Iago site, Saron, by road and thence forwarded to Coedbach by rail until rail traffic to Cwm Mawr ceased on 1st April, 1996. From then road lorries were used all the way from Gilfach Iago to Coedbach travelling via Cross Hands and Carmarthen to avoid the congested valley roads until the closure of Coedbach on 23rd March, 1998 after the opencast workings had ceased. It should be pointed out that road traffic had at times previously had to be used when the line near Pontnewydd was badly flooded. About half the output from Coedbach went away by road; much of that taken away by rail went to Swansea Docks, for shipment to such places as Immingham and Belfast. Since closure the odd very small colliery (slant) has continued to operate in the valley under licence, such as at Dynant Fach, but there has been no contribution to rail traffic.

There were several brickworks associated with the bituminous coal workings in the Burry Port area. These were to be found at Achddu, Craiglon, New Lodge, Panthywel and Pwll (Pool) collieries as well as one in the copper works complex. That at Pwll was in use until rail traffic ceased in 1962. There were other brickworks at Trimsaran and at Pontyates (the Ynyshafen Brickworks next to Caepontbren Colliery) in the anthracite belt which produced silica firebricks. These all contributed to the traffic on the BP&GV as did the silica brickworks on the Gwendraeth Valleys Railway, connected to the BP&GV at Tycoch Junction, Kidwelly (now Cydweli), which lasted until 1959. Other rail sidings were provided to the various works involved with some form of metal working. The Pembrey Copperworks was first established by Birmingham financiers at Burry Port in 1849, before the BP&GV was formed (after 1912 it was replaced by a zinc-oxide works). Yet another brickworks was included in the Copperworks complex; next door was the Pembrey Lead and Silver Works, plus a separate White Lead Works, whilst nearby was the Burry Port Foundry.

All these establishments were on the east side of the docks. Over on the other side of the docks was the Ashburnam Tinplate Works and a further tinplate factory was connected to the BP&GV via the Gwendraeth Valleys Railway at Kidwelly.

At the eastern (Llanelli) end of the Sandy branch there were connections with the private Stradey Estate Railway, the Llanelly Foundry and Engineering Co. Ltd and with the Sandy Works of the Cambrian Wagon Works Ltd. Locomotives of Nevill, Druce & Co. Ltd of Llanelly worked their own traffic over the Stradey Estate line and thence from Sandy Junction to Sandy Gate Sidings (and at one time through to Pwll Colliery) over the BP&GV. Private sidings were also provided for wagon repairers in Burry Port - Owen & Bevan & Co. and the North Central Wagon Co. who erected a repair shed in 1894 and which had become Wagon Repairs Ltd by March 1921 when their rent was reduced from £70 to £60 per annum - essential businesses when virtually all the rail-borne coal traffic was conveyed in privately-owned wagons and not those belonging to the railway companies. A feature of these wagons was the name of the operating colliery emblazoned on the sides with as large a lettering style as possible. The shorter the name, the larger the print could be; 'CROWN' thus had a distinct advantage over competitors such as 'GWENDRAETH' and 'PENTREMAWR'. Much later, after 1937, a new wagon works was established on the dockside at Burry Port by Marcrofts which lasted until 1983, latterly seeming to be more concerned with scrapping rather than repairing wagons.

The full list of all the industrial connections with the BP&GV which follows commences with the anthracite mines, arranged alphabetically, followed by the two opencast disposal sites, then by the bituminous (soft) coal mines, the metal and other associated industries and finally the works served by the Gwendraeth Valleys Railway in the Kidwelly area. Following each name a grid reference (prefixed SN) is given as the locations for many of the sites are not at all obvious today or shown on modern maps. An attempt is also made to give some details of ownership from about 1868 plus periods of operation and, where known, the number of employees is also quoted for various years to give an indication of the size of the undertaking at different periods. Note that for the Welsh colliery names there are many alternative spellings, especially in earlier years. For example Pumpquart can also be found listed as Pump Quart, Pump Ewart, Pump-cwart and (as on the 1879 25 in. OS map) Pum-cwart.

The Anthracite Collieries

Bryn Forest at grid reference SN448066 on S. side of the Carway branch. Bryn Forest Colliery Co. Ltd was registered on 12th May, 1903. Abandoned 11th April, 1905, plant for sale by auction on 8th June, 1905.

Caeduan SN453048 on S. side of the Trimsaran branch. Shaft sunk 1908 by the Trimsaran Company (owner Mr Clarke), slant added. 'Haulage accident on 26/4/1923 at Caeduan Slant, one of three drifts at Trimsaran Colliery, ten dead, owner Evan Jones'. Abandoned 13th January, 1934. A total of 200-300 men were employed from 1913 to 1932. *See Trimsaran for further details.*

Caepontbren SN472083 (pit), SN475083 (slant) above Pontyates on down side. Shaft sunk 1888 by H. Lloyd & Co., from 1890 H.E. Smart & Son, from 1894 H.E. & H. Smart. Abandoned 24th June, 1897. Maximum 71 employed in 1894. Slant from 1900 Caepontbren Colliery Co. (Alfred Stephens) (Ltd from 4th April, 1902), acquired in 1908 with Gwendraeth Colliery by United Gwendraeth Collieries Ltd who set up the New Caepontbren Colliery Ltd, registered 22nd September, 1909. Abandoned 15th Jaunaury, 1913. There were 111 to 152 employed from 1906 to 1912. The Ynyshafren Brickworks was next to the slant site. Believed operated by the Cwmparc Silica Brick Co. of Swansea (J.W. Rogers) in 1886-87. Smart and Stephens were both much involved with the silica works at Kidwelly, see the end of this chapter. *See also Ynyshafren Colliery for earlier history.*

Capel Ifan Slant, *see Pentremawr.*

Carway Slants SN461069 (old), SN465064 (new), SN463066 (**Wembley Slant**), SN461071 (pit) on Carway branch. Carway & Duffryn Steam Coal Co. Ltd registered 1st January, 1858 (Owen Bowen the major shareholder). For sale by private contract in 1868. Carway Coal Co. formed by Thomas Cadman in 1871, became Carway Anthracite Colliery Co. Ltd on 3rd January, 1872. Tenders sought for sinking new pit in August 1873. 'Carway Collieries on strike since 6th March, 1874, latest report that colliery is fast filling with water' per *Engineering* 13th March, 1874 and advertised for sale in *Mining Journal* 9th May, 1874. Acquired 1876 by the Hon W.H. Yelverton (who was the landowner) but 'Sale of whole of plant and material at Carway Colliery took place on 5/12/1879, purchaser Mansel Rees' (the Burry Port lawyer, so probably acting for someone else). Again for sale by auction on 9th February, 1881 and again on 7th November, 1883. Thomas Fenard formed the Wheal Gwendreath Valley Collieries Co. Ltd on 10th June, 1881 and seems to have acquired Carway at this time, but closed in 1887 (company dissolved 17th July, 1888). The New Slant was started by Joseph Birkenshaw (of Derbyshire) in 1896 and a report of 5th September, 1898 (*Coal & Iron Review*) stated,

> The Carway region is about to be re-opened. The original Carway Pit has been closed for years, but the railway is now being relaid and a new pit is at once to be set going, coal of a splendid quality having been found.

A new company - Carway Ltd - was registered on 26th October, 1901, renamed Carway Collieries Ltd on 20th July, 1908. A washery was added in 1915. By this time the colliery was connected by tramway running northwards to the screens on a loop of the BP&GV main line (known as Glyn Abbey Sidings) at SN461074, so traffic had ceased on the original Carway branch line, which closed early. The collieries were acquired by UAC Ltd in 1924, and passed to AAC Ltd on 1st July, 1927. Closed 1st July, 1960 but rail traffic continued for some years (via the Glyn Abbey Sidings) to dispose of the stockpile of coal. Less than 100 employed prior to 1910, then well over to 1959 with maximum of 330 in 1935. On closure in 1960 some 220 men were transferred to Cynheidre Colliery.

About 1929 an 0-6-0T shunting locomotive was transferred to here from Trimsaran Colliery by AAC Ltd. This carried the numerals '51' and had been built by Dick, Kerr & Co of Kilmarnock in 1915 with 14 in. by 20 in. outside cylinders and 3 ft 2½ in. wheels. She was still at Carway on vesting day (1st January, 1947) but went to Great Mountain Colliery soon after (where scrapped in February 1952), and was replaced by *John Waddell*, a Hudswell, Clarke & Co. 0-6-0ST (No. 912) built in 1912 with 15 in. by 22 in. outside cylinders and 3 ft 7 in. wheels and believed to have previously had a short spell at Carway prior to 1944. Her second period here was also short as she only lasted until July 1949 (but was not scrapped until about 1964) when the shunting duties at Carway were taken over by British Railways' locomotives. Became a coal stacking site after closure until 1982 when rail traffic ceased.

An alighting point for the colliers' train was opened in 1898; this was in the Glyn Abbey Sidings alongside the main line at SN459075 and not up the branch. It was closed at the end of passenger workings on 30th September, 1953.

Cilrhedyn, *see Llandyry.*

Closucha Slant SN521127 below Cwmmawr on up side. Small mine operated by Jones & Harry from 1878 until closed in 1880. Re-opened 1908 by Closucha Colliery Co. Ltd from 25th January, 1910, siding agreement approved by BP&GV on 28th June, 1910, abandoned 20th July, 1917. Never more than 33 men employed.

Closyryn Slant SN535121 (Closyrhyn) above Cwmmawr and connected by private line to the BP&GV. Opened 1884 by N. Harris & Anthony but closed 30th September, 1888. Re-opened 1903 by D. J. Griffiths & M. Gray trading as the Closyryn Colliery Co, became Limited from 3rd May, 1905. Sold to New Dynant Anthracite Colliery (1914) Ltd registered 25th April, 1914. In September 1923 became, with Great Mountain, Glynhebog and New Dynant pits, part of United Anthracite Collieries Ltd, first registered 25th August, 1923. Abandoned 30th May, 1925. Around 100-130 employed 1911 to 1923. Re-opened by Thomas Griffiths in 1930 but abandoned 28th July, 1932, maximum of six men only employed.

Coalbrook SN507112 less than ¼ mile SW of Pontyberem station on down side. Worked by David Watney in 1867, by D. Lloyd & Sons in 1873-74, from 1876 by Thompson, Wise & Co. (who also worked New Lodge) and after 1st October, 1878 by the Pontyberem Colliery Co. but had closed down (owing the BP&GV £461) and was put up for sale at auction on 29th September, 1880 following the failure of the West of England Bank on 1st July, 1880. *For later history see Pontyberem South.*

Cwmmawr SN528127 just below station on up side. Revd D. Parry Thomas owner from 1854. 'For sale at Auction on 30th May, 1873 by trustees of late Revd D.P. Thomas'. Capt. Henry Rees took over lease in 1873 to 1880 (also D. Jones, Thomas, Sons & Davies, and J. Harry). In 1896 being worked by the Cwm Mawr Colliery Co. (20 men) but soon closed. *See also New Cwmmawr (from 1901).*

Danybanc SN477077 E. of Plasbach, Pontyates. Smith & Squire in 1873, John & Phillip Davies in 1893-4, T. Carted granted lease 30th October, 1894, abandoned 27th February, 1896. Max. of six men employed.

Dyffryn SN476063, *see Carway.* Probably not worked after 1860.

Dynant SN527117, also **Old Dynant** SN523116 below Cwmmawr on down side. Benjamin Jones in 1865-68, R.H. Harris in 1874, D. Harris & Co in 1875-77,

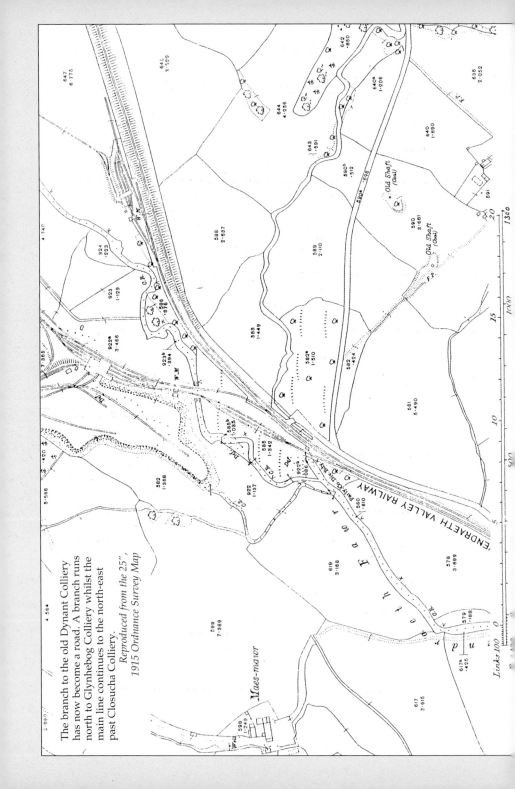

The branch to the old Dynant Colliery has now become a road. A branch runs north to Glynhebog Colliery whilst the main line continues to the north-east past Closucha Colliery.

Reproduced from the 25″,
1915 Ordnance Survey Map

'ENDRAETH VALLEY RAILWAY

Maes-mawr

then the Dynant Colliery Co. 'First cargo of coal from Dynant Colliery was shipped on 14th August, 1878'. N. Thomas was the proprietor in November 1884. Eighty were employed in 1888. Abandoned 1889, 'For sale by auction plant and materials at Dynant Colliery'. On 10th July, 1908 it was reported (per *Iron & Coal Trades Revue*) that a new company had been formed to acquire Dynant Colliery - *see under New Dynant*.

Ffoy SN481081 to E. of Pontyates. Small concern started by Smith & Squire by 1869 (leases of 25th March, 1867, 4th April, 1872 and 23rd April, 1872) but failed several times; advertised to be sold at auction on 21st April, 1875, by auction on 27th January, 1876 and again by auction on 21st February, 1878, abandoned in 1880. The siding connection to Ynyshafen and Caepontbren collieries was originally known as Ffoy Junction.

Glan Gwendraeth SN469085. Small concern on up side above Pontyates worked by William Evans from 1856; despite coal train dispatched on 23rd June, 1869 seems to have closed in 1870. Re-opened 1900 by Glangwendraeth Colliery Co. (maximum of nine men). Brook's Anthracite Syndicate Ltd (Frederick Brook) registered on 22nd November, 1904 to work this colliery but was not successful.

Glyn Abbey SN446075, SN453078 and other sites on up side above Pontnewydd. Opened 1897 by James Hansard with max. of 17 men but seems to have closed in 1901. Glyn Abbey Colliery Co. Ltd formed 21st January, 1909 but does not appear to have done any mining.

Glynhebog Slant (Pontyberem) SN518124 (old), SN517122 (new) on up side between Pontyberem and Cwmmawr. Commenced 1884 by Glynhebog Colliery Co., became with Pontyberem Slants (Coalbrook) the Pontyberem Collieries Co. Ltd from 4th January, 1887 with George Herring a major shareholder. There were 59 men in 1888 rising to 142 in 1910. Acquired in 1911 by the Ammanford Colliery Co. Ltd (formed 24th September, 1890, a subsidiary of the Wigan Coal & Iron Co. Ltd) washery built by 1923, 240 to 400 men 1911-23. Known as Pontyberem Colliery after 1918. Combined with New Dynant, Great Mountain and others on 25th August, 1923 to form the UAC Ltd. Became AAC Ltd from 1st July, 1927 and vested in the NCB on 1st January, 1947. 300 to 500 men 1924-38 and still 249 in 1945. Closed 15th October, 1949 but re-opened 1958 to 1961 as Cynheidre No. 3 Slant and also a training centre. *See also Pontyberem Slants.*

An alighting point for the colliers' train was opened in 1898 in the sidings for the new slant; this was in use until the colliery closed in 1949.

Glynhir Slant, *see Ponthenry*

Gwendraeth Slants SN472073 S.E. of Plasbach (to which connected by tramway) below Pontyates on down side. This was Watney's Colliery, worked by Alfred Watney (of the Kent brwing family) in 1852-53. There had been a tragic roof fall here entombing 26 miners on 10th May, 1852. David Watney by 1866 and Daniel Watney in 1869-72. Astley Thompson took over, forming the Gwendraeth Colliery Co. but this failed in 1878. In 1899 J.E. Burnell formed the Gwendraeth Anthracite Collieries Co. (Ltd from 17/3/1900). Became Gwendraeth Valley Anthracite Collieries Ltd from 18th March, 1913, acquired by UAC Ltd about 1925, to AAC Ltd 1st July, 1927. Abandoned 31st July, 1928. Men employed: 28 in 1900, 134 in 1901, over 200 from 1904 to 1927 with maximum of 333 in 1923. There was a washery installed prior to 1923.

Gwendraeth Valley Anthracite Collieries, Ltd.

HEAD OFFICE:

2, Cambrian Place, Swansea.

Telegrams : " Gwendraeth," Swansea.   Telephone : 1205 Central Swansea

PRODUCERS OF

Best Big Vein Anthracite Coals for Malting, Hop-drying, Horticultural and Lime Burning. Also Cobbles and Nuts for Stoves

Specially prepared Machine-made and Washed Nuts, Beans, and Peas for Suction Gas Producers.

Lambert's SN461073, small concern on the site of the later Carway screens S. of Glyn Abbey Sidings. Lambert's Collieries Ltd was registered on 29th March, 1893 to acquire the mine of T.H. Lambert, maximum of 14 men employed before closure in 1895.

Llandyry Slant (or Cilrhedyn) SN437052 on S. side of Trimsaran branch. A small slant started in 1893 by the Llandyry Anthracite Colliery Co. Ltd (registered on 24th December, 1892), abandoned December 1897; 27 to 38 men employed. Prospecting with a view to re-opening the colliery took place in December 1913. Re-opened 1916 by the Cilrhedyn Anthracite Collieries Ltd (registered on 3rd November, 1916) and closed at start of coal dispute on 1st April, 1921 never to re-open. Fourteen to 19 men were employed 1918-21.

Nantddu Slant SN527115 below Cwmmawr on down side S. of New Dynant. Small mine abandoned in 1888, re-opened 1910 by John Davies & Co., from 1913 the Nantddu Colliery Co., maximum of 12 men, abandoned 6th July, 1918.

New Carway, *see Carway.*

New Cwmmawr Slant SN526125 on up side below Cwmmawr station. Lloyd & Treharne formed the New Cwmmawr Colliery Co. in 1901 with maximum of 24 men employed in 1911. A siding agreement of 13th December, 1919 was made between the BP&GV and Mrs Louisa Arnaud Wheldon trading as the New Cwmmawr Colliery Co. Acquired by the Ashburnham Steamship & Coal Co. Ltd on its formation in December 1921, then by Ashburnham Collieries Ltd by April 1922 when 81 men employed; washery installed about this time. In 1926 became part of Welsh Anthracite Collieries Ltd (registered 15th January, 1926), then to Henderson's Welsh Anthracite Collieries Ltd on its formation in May 1928. To AAC Ltd in August 1928. Over 100 men 1928 to 1933. Abandoned 15th October, 1934 when still 91 men employed.

New Dynant SN530125 below Cwmmawr on down side. Despite a siding agreement being reached on 17th April, 1905 it was not until 30th October, 1907 that the New Dynant Anthracite Colliery Ltd was formed to open a slant, with a shaft being added by 1913. Became New Dynant Anthracite Colliery (1914) Ltd on 25th April, 1914 and a washery was added, to UAC Ltd 25th August, 1923, then AAC Ltd on 1st July, 1927. Closed 1939, except for ventilation and pumping, due to the policy of AAC abandoning its most inefficient mines as a result of over production. This colliery was sufficiently large to employ its own shunting locomotive - *Edith* - an 0-4-0ST built in 1908 by Andrew Barclay (No. 1164) and obtained from Oliver H. Thomas Ltd, Gellihir Colliery, Lletty Brongu. She was still at New Dynant when the pit closed in 1939 but where she went next is not known. She was seen standing, in early August 1948, at an old tinplate works in Pontardulais. *See also Closyryn Slant. For Old Dynant see Dynant.*

Pentremawr or Capel Ifan Slant SN494104 (slants), SN502108 (pit) below Pontyberem on down side. 1872-75 T. (Thomas) Harries & Co., (Harries & Redford), 1876-82 Mason & Elkington Ltd (evidently still with Harries involved), from 1883 Pentremawr Colliery Co. (W.W. Walters), the Pentremawr Colliery Co. Ltd (George Herring & Thomas Pilkington) from 16th April, 1890. Washery built by 1923 and there was also a pithead baths. Acquired by United National Collieries Ltd in February 1925 and had become a part of UAC Ltd by 30th June, 1927, merging with others to form AAC Ltd from 1st July, 1927. Under 300 employed up to 1909, then 500 to 750 to 1968. Closed March 1974 (merged with Cynheidre) but rail traffic ceased about 1970.

An alighting point for the colliers' train was opened in 1897-98 at the colliery sidings at SN493106; this was in use until 1953.

A Gloucester built wagon for the Pentremawr Colliery Co. This one says, 'Empty to Burryport, G.W.R. South Wales.' *HMRS Gloucester Collection*

The Pentremawr Colliery screens at Pontyberem, looking towards Cwmmawr, July 1951.
R.J. Doran

Plasbach Colliery at Pontyates looking east about 1921; it closed down in 1927.
GWR Magazine

Plasbach SN469079 (slant) and SN47008 (**Gras** or Upper Pit) below Pontyates on down side. Operated by Wolfram & Co. from 1856 until closure in 1867, re-opened 1874 by Roberts & Evans but closed again 1884. From 1886 worked by Richard Thomas & Co. (30 men in 1888) and became the Pentremawr Colliery Co. Ltd (registered on 16th April, 1890) but closed again from 10th July, 1892. Restarted by the Plasbach Colliery Co. from 1893 until the next abandonment on 12th June, 1896 (55 to 57 men employed 1894-95). Re-opened in 1903 by Gwendraeth Anthracite Collieries Ltd (31 men) but again closed from 20th September, 1906. Re-opened 1913 by the Gwendraeth Valley Anthracite Collieries Ltd with over 100 men employed from 1917 to 1922. Twenty outbursts of gas were recorded between 1920 and 1926, fortunately without any loss of life. Became part of UAC Ltd about 1925, then to AAC Ltd on 1st July, 1927 who promptly closed the mine on 22nd September, 1927 when there were still 95 wage earners. *See also Gwendraeth Slants*, to which connected by tramway.

Ponthenry Slants SN481097 above Ponthenry station on down side; also included were **Tynywaun** at SN480096 (also on down side) from 1892 and **Glynhir Slant** SN479099 (on up side) from 1893, all worked as one colliery. It was being operated by T. Lloyd by 1872, then from April 1873 by Arthur, Jenkins & Co. trading as the Ponthenry Coal Co. Came into sole possession of John Arthur from 11th June, 1875 who formed the Ponthenry Colliery Co. (an order was placed with the Gloucester Wagon Co for rail wagons on 11th April, 1876), became Limited from 4th July, 1891 when apparently re-opened (max. 205 men in 1898, 192 in 1896). Acquired by the Bargoed Coal Co. on 24th November, 1906 and a washery later installed. This mine was prone to outbursts of gas, particularly in the Pumpquart seam, with 26 being experienced in 10 years. Between 1920 and 1928 10 miners lost their lives in four separate outbursts with five men killed by an escape of gas in 1924. Maximum of 650

Bargoed, Evan Davies and Ponthenry wagons are visible on the east pier at Burry Port outer harbour. The Bargoed Coal Co. operated the Ponthenry Slants from 1906. In the left background is the Harbour View Hotel of 1896 with the coastguards' houses on the right.
Author's Collection

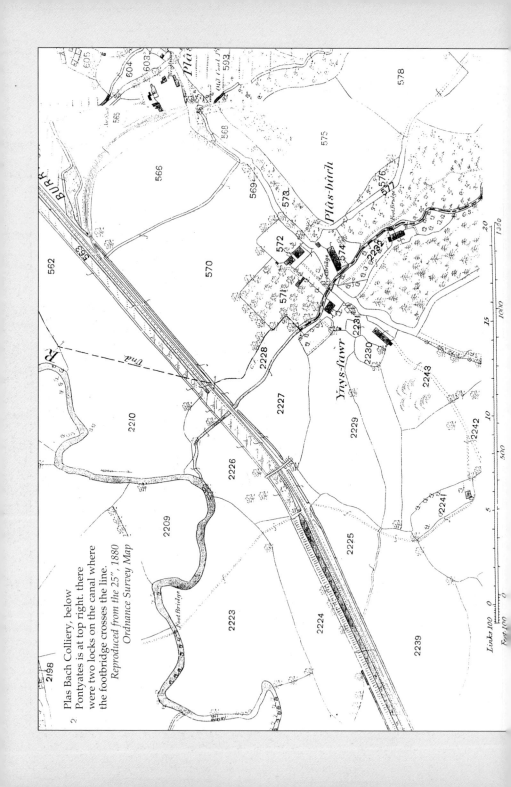

2   Plas Bach Colliery, below
    Pontyates is at top right. there
    were two locks on the canal where
    the footbridge crosses the line.
    Reproduced from the 25″, 1880
    Ordnance Survey Map

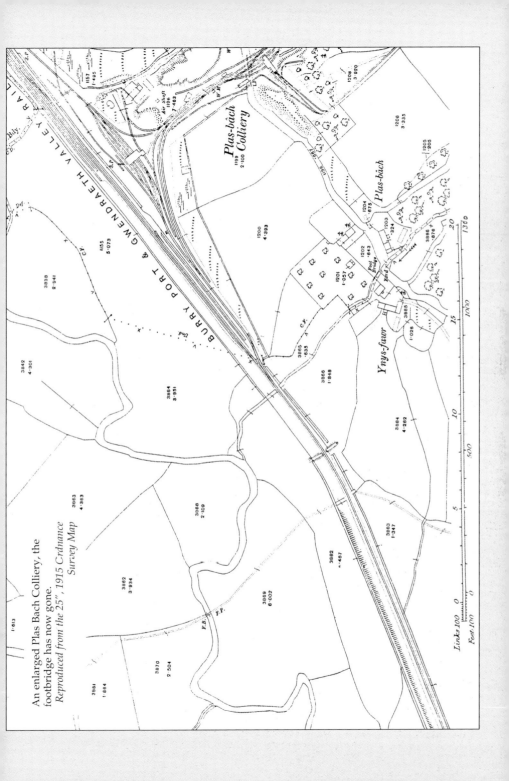

An enlarged Plas Bach Colliery, the
footbridge has now gone.
*Reproduced from the 25", 1915 Ordnance
Survey Map*

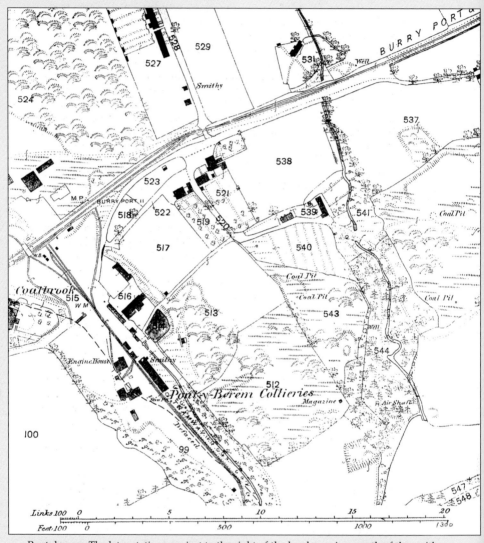

Pontyberem. The later station was just to the right of the level crossing, south of the smithy.
Reproduced from the 25″, 1880 Ordnance Survey Map

men employed in 1927. The Bargoed Coal Co. did not get involved with the amalgamations of the 1920s. George Robling, said to be Cardiff's first mining graduate, was manager from 1913 to 1929 when he was appointed Agent to the Swansea Valley Group of AAC Ltd. The colliery closed on 15th August, 1936 when there were still 451 men employed.

An alighting point for the colliers' train had been opened in the pit sidings at SN492097 in 1897-98; it lasted until the colliery closed in 1936.

Pontyberem Slants SN513114 above station on down side. After a period of closure was re-opened in 1881 by the reformed Pontyberem Colliery Co., which became Limited from 4th January, 1887 (also operated Glynhebog), George Herring and Major (later Sir) Thomas Pilkington - who both became Directors of the BP&GV - were Directors and major shareholders. A washery was built and from 220 to 355 men employed between 1894 and 1909. Acquired in 1911 by the Ammanford Colliery Co. Ltd (formed 24th September, 1890) but was gradually run down and closed on 23rd March, 1918 (by the Coal Commision due to gross inefficiency). Used by UAC Ltd and AAC Ltd for pumping until 1929. *See also Glynhebog.*

Pontyberem (South) SN508108 between the station and Pontyberem Slants on down side, also known as **Gwendraeth Colliery**. Worked by David Watney in 1867, by D. Lloyd & Sons in 1873-74, from 1876 by Thompson, Wise & Co. (who also worked New Lodge) and after 1st October, 1878 by the Pontyberem Colliery Co. but had closed down (owing the BP&GV £461) and was put up for sale at auction on 29th September, 1880 following the failure of the West of England Bank on 1st July, 1880. *For subsequent history see under Pontyberem Slants, see also Coalbrook.*

Pontyates unknown location but may be the same as **Woodbridge** (SN474084) which see. Operated by Evans & David in 1858-59 and by W. & D. Evans in 1865-67, followed by J. Hughes & Co. (of Pontardulais) 1871-72. Not listed from 1873 but note that Woodbridge opened in 1872.

Pumpquart SN460078 between Pontnewydd and Pontyates on up side. Started by Onslow & David in 1870, then from 1871 by D.A. Onslow & J.D. Thompson (by 1875 Astley Thompson, son of John) trading as the Pumpquart Coal Co. Pumpquart was the name of one of the anthracite seams. It was Douglas Onslow's wife - Caroline - who had turned over one of the first sods in that 1868 ceremony. Evidently closed by 1885 as the plant and materials at Pumpquart Colliery were for sale by auction on 24th July, 1885.

Rhydycerrig is marked on a BP&GV small-scale map produced in September 1898 a little to the S. of Cwmmawr on down side opposite Glendebog [*sic*] Colliery, which would position it about the site of Dynant Colliery (which had been abandoned in 1889). It is presumed that there was no production.

Star SN453043 on Trimsaran branch S. of Caeduan, small pit not obviously ever rail-connected. Worked by Harris & Co. 1854-57, by Edwards & Co. 1858-67 (for sale per the *Colliery Guardian* of 8th June, 1867), Henry Pratt in 1868-69 and the Star Coal Co. until that failed in 1870 with all plant & materials to be sold by auction on 2nd August, 1870, but evidently re-opened by T. Davies in 1871. It was included as part of the Trimsaran Coal, Iron & Steel Co. Ltd from its formation in 21st February, 1872 and not subsequently listed separately.

Peckett & Sons class 'B2' locomotive No. 1051 before delivery on 20th October, 1905 as *Trimsaran No. 2'* to the Trimsaran Colliery. This engine was transferred to the Great Mountain Colliery in 1954.   *F. Jones Collection*

Trimsaran, a complex including the oldest pit, an ironworks and brickworks at SN458045 which was abandoned from 13th March, 1905 (89 to 131 men at the colliery from 1888 to 1905). **Trimsaran Top** or **Upper** at SN467053 which commenced in 1922 and was closed on 7th April, 1954 except for the washery (at SN457051) retained for opencast coal until 1960 (reported in the *Colliery Guardian* on 21st January, 1960 that it is 'to close shortly'); 50 to 80 men in 1923-26 but greatly expanded after the closure of Caeduan and Waunhir in 1934 with between 217 and 285 men 1934-45 and 138 to 217 during 1946-54. It was being worked by Williams, Smith & Co. in 1858-63 when the Trimsaran Anthracite Coal & Iron Co. Ltd (registered on 17th January, 1863) took over but had closed down by 1870. The Trimsaran Coal, Iron & Steel Co. Ltd was formed on 21st February, 1872 and it was reported on 10th May, 1872 (*South Wales Daily News*) that 'Trimsaran collieries are being re-opened' but despite the nine foot seam being struck on 10th February, 1876 seems to have also struggled as yet another firm took over in 1877 - The Trimsaran Colliery Co. Ltd (registered on 17th May, 1877) - but in turn does not appear to have been very active after 1879. Next to try was the Trimsaran Co. Ltd (first registered on 18th March, 1882) and was more successful with from 89 to 144 men being employed in 1888-1901. The **Waunhir Slant** was added in 1895 (15 men in 1896) replacing the original Trimsaran Colliery and Caeduan followed in 1908 (*see separate entries*). The ironworks including two blast furnaces appear to have been operated separately at this period by the Trimsaran Anthracite Iron & Steel Co. Ltd but the whole estate was evidently in common ownership as it was put up for sale by auction on 25th January, 1901 (per *Coal & Iron Review* 14th January, 1901) - two locomotives were included in the sale.

Whatever the outcome of the sale, the Trimsaran Co. Ltd continued to work the pits, the ownership in 1908 being quoted as a Mr Clarke. In 1915 it was reported in the *Colliery Guardian* on 5th November, 1915 that Evan Jones, owner of Achddu and New Pool Collieries, had purchased the Trimsaran Estate, including collieries and brickworks. On 19th December, 1924 it was announced in the *Colliery Guardian* that the Trimsaran Collieries of Evan Jones had been sold on 13th December, 1924; these properties included Caeduan and Waunhir Collieries. The next owner noted is the Ashburnham Steamship & Coal Shipping Co. (*South Wales News* 30th November, 1925, *Colliery Guardian* 4th December, 1925) who transferred the collieries to their subsidiary - Ashburnham Collieries Ltd. Another change occurred on 31st March, 1926 with acquisition by the newly-formed Welsh Anthracite Collieries Ltd (registered on 15th January, 1926). They in turn formed part of a new group - Henderson's Welsh Anthracite Collieries Ltd - on its formation in May 1928, then from August 1928 became a part of Amalgamated Anthracite Collieries Ltd. There was no subsequent change before vesting in the National Coal Board on 1st January, 1947.

Several locomotives were employed over the years at Trimsaran on shunting duties. The first, known originally as *Trimsaran* and later as *Trimsaran No. 1*, arrived new on 30th December, 1872 from Manning, Wardle & Co of Leeds (No. 418), an 0-6-0ST of class 'M' with 13 in. by 18 in. inside cylinders and 3 ft 0 in. wheels. Although offered for sale on 25th January, 1901 she appears to have remained at Trimsaran until about 1929. *Trimsaran No. 2* was a similar maker's

A Trimsaran wagon supplied by the Gloucester Railway Carriage & Wagon Co. in 1893, when the style was to include plenty of lettering on the side. It is branded, 'Empty to Pembrey G. W. R^y'.   *HMRS Gloucester Collection*

By 1902 the style was to have the name emblazoned with letters as large as possible.
HMRS Gloucester Collection

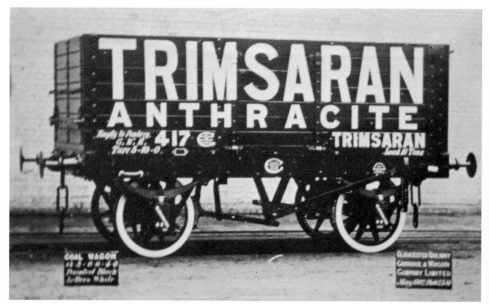

class 'M' purchased from Hudswell, Clarke & Co. on 27th November, 1890, having previously worked for the Wheldale Coal Co. Ltd, Castleford, and was a few weeks older than her sister having been built by Manning, Wardle (No. 381) on 11th December, 1872. Also offered for sale in 1901, she was replaced on 20th October, 1905 by a new *Trimsaran No. 2*, an 0-6-0ST built by Peckett & Sons Ltd of Bristol (No. 1051) of class 'B2' with 13 in. by 20 in. outside cylinders and 3 ft 7 in. wheels. She remained here until the colliery closed in 1954, then went to nearby Great Mountain Colliery before being scrapped in 1957-58.

Next to arrive, during 1920, was the Dick, Kerr & Co. 0-6-0T already mentioned at Carway Colliery. Built in 1915 and known as '51' she was used by her makers to construct the National Filling Factory at Hackney Wick, London for the Ministry of Munitions and seems to have remained at Hackney until munitions production was wound down in 1919, was evidently offered for sale and came to Trimsaran. After Amalgamated Anthracite took over in 1928 various of their locomotives were transferred as required between the collieries they controlled. Thus No. 51 found herself being sent to Carway in 1929. The replacement, which arrived before September, 1929, was an 0-6-0ST named *Pantyffynnon* which came from the colliery of that name. She had been built by the Avonside Engine Co. of Bristol (No. 1507) in 1906 and had 14 in. by 20 in. outside cylinders and 3 ft 3 in. wheels. She had been sent back to Pantyffynnon Colliery by the beginning of 1935, where she lasted until 1965-66. AAC Ltd then transferred their 1912-built Hudswell, Clarke & Co. 0-6-0ST *John Waddell* (No. 912) from Great Mountain Colliery to Trimsaran about 1935, and she stayed (apart from a short spell at Carway) until about 1944 before returning to Great Mountain. She was again at Carway in the 1947-49 period.

In January 1939 AAC Ltd purchased from the GWR the last to be built of their '1901' class 0-6-0 pannier tanks No. 2020 with 16 in. by 24 in. inside cylinders and 4 ft 1½ in. wheels, built at Wolverhampton works (No. 562) in 1895 (originally as a saddle tank). After use at Ammanford Colliery, she came to Trimsaran some time before July 1944 and remained here until after the pit closed, latterly being used to shunt the washery. She was scrapped some time after March 1957 and before May 1958. Another Peckett (No. 465) a class 'B1' 0-6-0ST with 14 in. by 20 in. outside cylinders and 3 ft 6 in. wheels arrived during NCB days. Lettered *D.M.D. L^{TD} No. 10*, she had had a most interesting history having been built in 1890 for the Alexandra (Newport & South Wales) Dock & Railway, becoming GWR No. 679 in 1922 and was sold in November 1929 via the agency of Charles Williams of Morriston to Davies, Middleton & Davies, the contractors. They used her on the construction of the branch to the Hook Anthracite Colliery near Johnston and she subsequently passed into the hands of Watts, Watts & Co., the colliery owner, and then to the NCB. She came to Trimsaran after Hook closed in November, 1951 and had arrived by July 1952. She lasted until scrapped about 1956 and before April 1957.

Her replacement at Trimsaran was an Avonside (No. 1893) named *John* which came from Blaenhirwaun Colliery, Cross Hands soon after June 1954. Of class 'B5' with 14½ in. by 20 in. outside cylinders and 3 ft 3 in. wheels, she had been built in Bristol in 1921 for the Emlyn Anthracite Colliery Ltd, passing into the ownership of AAC Ltd in April 1939. She moved on to Brynlliw Colliery,

Former GWR locomotive No. 2020, built at Wolverhampton in 1895, shunting at Trimsaran in 1950.   *M.R.C. Price*

Another Trimsaran locomotive was this Peckett class 'B1' of 1890 which the NCB transferred here from Hook Anthracite Colliery in 1952. The cab-side plate reads 'D.M.& D. L^{TD} N^{O} 10'.

M.R.C. Price

Glamorgan, in late 1959 or early 1960. There is still one more standard gauge steam locomotive to record at Trimsaran; this is Sentinel Waggon Works No. 9569 which came new from the Shrewsbury builder on 31st March, 1954. She was a four-wheeled geared locomotive with a horizontal water-tube boiler, vertical cylinders 6¾ in. by 9 in. and 3 ft 2 in. wheels, rated at 200 hp. She was used at the washery until that closed and was transferred away in late 1960, going to nearby Cynheidre Colliery. She was scrapped in September 1969. There is also one narrow gauge locomotive to consider, an 0-4-0T of 2 ft 7 in. gauge of which not a lot is known. She was built by Fox, Walker & Co. of Bristol (No. 203) in 1873 with 9 in. by 14 in. outside cylinders of class 'M', and came from the Llanharry Ironstone Mine, Llantrisant, at some time prior to March 1880. She was advertised for sale in *Machinery Market* in July 1881 but whether she was sold or remained at Trimsaran I have not been able to discover.

Tynywaun, *see Ponthenry.*

Waunhir Slant SN458050, also **Waunhir North** at SN462047, between Caeduan and Trimsaran on S. side of branch. Worked as part of Trimsaran Collieries, started in 1895 and closed on 13th January, 1934. There was a haulage accident here on 16th February, 1907 resulting in the death of six miners. A stoppage lasting 18 months was settled on 24th February, 1912 (*Colliery Guardian* 1st March, 1912) whilst on 14th October, 1920 it was reported (in the *Llanelly Star*) that 'the colliery was flooded and the main slant greatly damaged; colliery has been rendered idle'. Then on 23rd September, 1921 it was claimed that Cilrhedyn and Waunhir had not restarted since the settlement of the coal dispute on 4th July, 1921 (per *South Wales News*). The number of men employed was quite small at first but rose from 41 in 1901 to 240 in 1905. Thereafter, apart from 1910-12, it was between 64 and 169 until 1933.

Wembley Slant, *see Carway Slants.*

Woodbridge SN474084 on down side just S. of Pontyates station. Probably the same as Pontyates Colliery. The Gwendraeth Valley Colliery Co. Ltd was registered on 4th July, 1872 to acquire this colliery to which a siding would be provided. The previous owner was believed to be Hughes & Co. The new owner seems to have failed by 1875 as the 'plant and materials are to be put up for sale by auction on 17/1/1876 by Court Order', following the postponement of a previous sale.

Ynyshafren SN479087 above Pontyates on down side. Worked by Joseph Everett 1858 to 1873. For sale by auction on 9th December, 1873. Later a brickworks was established here and Caepontbren Slant was opened in 1900 on almost the same site. In 1886-7 the Cwmparc Silica Brick Co. of Swansea had a brickworks in this area.

The Anthracite Opencast Disposal Points

Coedbach SN424059 on N. side of the Kidwelly branch to the W. of Trimsaran Road. Was known as the **Cefn Bach** Disposal Point when first opened. Established in 1953 by the National Coal Board Opencast Executive, which became the British Coal Corporation from 5th March, 1987. Ownership passed to Celtic Energy Ltd

The Coed Bach washery and screens, looking to Cwmmawr, on 8th October, 1983.

M.R.C. Price

The Cwm Mawr screens just after closure in 1996.   *R.E. Bowen*

from 29th December, 1994. It was operated by contractors, the first being William Pepper & Co. Ltd. Sir John Jackson took over from about 1958, followed by Wilson Lovatt & Sons Ltd from *circa* 1961. *Circa* 1968 Powell Duffryn Fuels Ltd took over and had changed their name to Powell Duffryn Coal Preparation Ltd by the time the owner - Celtic Energy Ltd - decided also to operate the site from October 1995. The disposal point closed on 23rd March, 1998.

Two steam locomotives were used at the site during the period that William Pepper & Co. Ltd were in charge, both believed to have belonged to the Opencast Executive and been on hire to Peppers. The first to arrive was an ex-War Department 'Austerity' 0-6-0ST No. 75056 with 18 in. by 26 in. inside cylinders and 4 ft 3 in. wheels, built by Robert Stephenson & Hawthorns Ltd (No. 7092) in 1943 for the Ministry of Supply, and transferred here from the Glyn Neath Disposal Point by July 1953. After about a year here she went away to the Blaensychan Disposal Point and was replaced by a much smaller 0-4-0T numbered and named *95 Honfleur* with 16 in. by 22 in. outside cylinders and 3 ft 10 in. wheels built by the London & South Western Railway at Nine Elms Works in 1893. She came from the Gwaun-cae-Gurwen Disposal Point at some time before August 1954 and went back again by June 1957. Her replacement was a diesel shunter and around 15 of these small diesels were eventually used at differing times at Coedbach before closure in 1998 .

Cwm Mawr SN530125 on the site of New Dynant Colliery S. of station on down side. Established in 1958 by the NCB Opencast Executive, which became the British Coal Corporation from 5th March, 1987, then Celtic Energy Ltd from 29th December, 1994. As at Coedbach, William Pepper & Co. Ltd was the first contractor to operate the site, until the end of 1964 when Stephenson, Clarke Ltd took over. From about 1968 the contractor was Powell Duffryn Fuels Ltd, subsequently Powell Duffryn Coal Preparation Ltd, until Celtic Energy took over at the end of 1994. The Disposal Point closed on 1st April, 1996. The contractors employed about eight small diesel locomotives in all (only two or three at any one time) for shunting here.

A view of the Cwm Mawr Opencast Disposal Point looking north-east on 15th June, 1983. The locomotives, from the right, are Nos. 03141, 03145 and 03152 and are ready to depart with a loaded hopper train.   *Tom Heavyside*

Another view of the Cwm Mawr site with a train of loaded hopper wagons waiting for collection, 2nd March, 1990.   *R.E. Bowen*

Cwm Capel Colliery, looking south-west, just after final closure in 1952. Rail traffic had ceased some years before. The edge of the quarry can be made out at the top right.   *Author's Collection*

The Bituminous Collieries

Achddu Slant SN449018 Small pit on E. side of Cwm Capel branch, probably developed about 1905 and by 1906 (the lease of water rights to the Achddu Colliery Co. Ltd was approved by the BP&GV Board on 16th July, 1906), subsequently operated by R. Watkeys Ltd until 1911, later (by November 1915) owned by Evan Jones. Closed on 28th February, 1917, re-opened c.1925 for a short period by Evan Davies & Co. Ltd. There was also a brickworks here.

Ashburnham, *see Cwm Capel.*

Ashburnham Level, *see Craiglon.*

Bryndias SN435035 connected to a branch of the Ashburnham canal, N.W. of Craiglon bridge. The Bryndais Colliery Co. failed on 27th March, 1911 and a sale of 23rd July, 1912 included 1½ miles of 2 ft gauge tramway laid with 30 lb. per yard rails, 60 coal drams with wooden buffers and one locomotive. The tramway would appear to have run via the Ffrwd (or Cape) Colliery to the BP&GV at Craiglon bridge. The narrow gauge locomotive was an 0-4-0 well tank with 6 in. by 8 in. outside cylinders built by Orenstein & Koppel AG of Berlin (No. 1377) and sent new to the Bryndias Colliery Co. on 2nd August, 1904. What happened to this little engine after the sale is not known.

Cape, *see Ffrwd.*

Craiglon SN419021 behind the Butcher's Arms, E. of Craiglon bridge and also known as the Ashburnham Level, was a small pit sunk in 1864 by John Stanley and John Swire, which closed in 1871. Re-opened by Mason & Elkington Ltd and passing to Elliott's Metal Co. Ltd in 1884, this colliery was finally abandoned on 31st December,1907. Subsequently a siding at the site of the colliery connection was provided for Carreg Llwyd Quarries in 1937 for Charles Harding of The Links, Pembrey and mostly supplied chippings for builders and contractors; a brickworks was also developed but quickly failed. The quarry did not last very long either and the rail connection had closed by 1947.

Crown SN473011 S. of Sandy branch at Lower Pwll. Started about 1900 and worked by the Crown Colliery Co. but was out of use in 1913. Acquired by Evan Davies & Co. in December 1915; closed 30th June, 1934. A second-hand locomotive was acquired by Davies, possibly in 1923 or a little later, and was also used to shunt at Davies' other collieries at New Lodge and New Pool, running over the BP&GV to reach them. This was an 0-6-0ST built by the Leeds firm of Hudswell, Clarke & Co. (No. 1283) in February 1917 for the National Filling Factory of the Ministry of Munitions at Holbrook, Coventry but left in late 1922 for work with the Kidwelly Tinplate Co. before coming to Davies, who gave her the name *Dyvatty*, the river that flows down to Burry Port. She had 13 in. by 20 in. inside cylinders and 3 ft 3½ in. wheels and, after the closure of the Evan Davies' collieries, was put up for sale in June 1936 but her fate is not known.

Cwm Capel SN452021 at the end of the tramroad N. from Burry Port, converted to a railway in 1876, the largest of the bituminous collieries. Originally sunk by George Bowser in 1830, this pit was worked by Mason & Elkington Ltd from 1865 to 1884, then Elliott's Metal Co. Ltd to 1898 when closed (107 men in 1896). Re-opened in 1900 by Daniel Williams and David Rees, followed after a few years by John Rowlands and Richard Jones, then Rowlands alone, worked by the

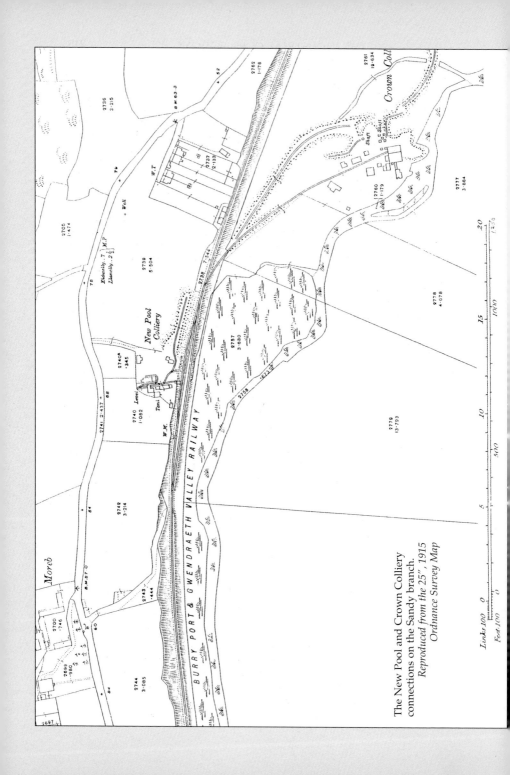

The New Pool and Crown Colliery
connections on the Sandy branch.
Reproduced from the 25", 1915
Ordnance Survey Map

Ashburnham Collieries Ltd by 1922 until 1931. Closed and re-opened several times until final closure in 1952. Rail traffic had ceased by July 1940. Next to the colliery was McKiernon's Quarry (*Cwar Mac*), from which the large stones in the dock walls at Burry Port were quarried. William McKiernon, whom we first came across in Volume One, had been Manager and Engineer of the harbour company and also the first licencee of the Neptune Hotel. Stone from here was also used for the building of the Ashburnam Tinplate Works from 1889 and definitely was conveyed by rail. From January 1915 Walter Scott & Middleton Ltd worked the quarry and the stone was conveyed by rail to the new Explosives (Munitions) Works being built by them on Pembrey Burrows (*see later*).

Ffrwd SN428027 also known as **Frood** and the **Cape** Colliery, N.W. of Craiglon bridge. Possibly connected to the BP&GV by the narrow gauge tramway from Bryndias, this small colliery closed on 17th February, 1906, again on 29th January, 1915 and finally in 1934. Latterly worked by Pembrey Collieries Ltd.

Gwscwm SN440013 also known as **Pembrey** Colliery. Connected by a short branch to the down side of the BP&GV between Burry Port and Pembrey. Mason & Elkington Ltd leased this pit from 1869 until 1879. Re-opened in 1890 by Rees, Parry & Roberts (their application for a siding approved on 12th March, 1890); to Evans & Williams by 1903, became Thomas Evans & Co. in 1910 and passed to the Pembrey Collieries Ltd by 1923. Finally closed during Whit Week 1930. Mr Thomas Evans' locomotive caused some damage to a bridge on the BP&GV on 30th June, 1910; I have not been able to identify this engine.

New Lodge SN459012 on N. side of Sandy branch, had re-opened in 1863 under the aegis of Astley Thompson (1837-87), then Thompson, Wise & Co. who were associated with Pontyberem South Colliery and the Burry Port Smelting Co. until they failed in 1877 - 'temporary stopped but now working again' per *Llanelly & County Guardian* 24th May, 1877. Mason & Elkington Ltd worked this pit from 1877 until 1884 using their own locomotives, then by the New Lodge Brickworks Co. (15 men in 1896). Had closed by July 1909 but by 1913 this and Pemberton were worked as one colliery with the attendant brickworks separate. Had become Evan Davies & Co. Ltd by 1923. From then the locomotive at Crown Colliery also shunted this site; indeed Evan Davies & Co. Ltd regarded both this pit and Crown as the one colliery. The closure date is not certain but is believed to have been early in 1936.

New Pool SN467013 on N. side of Sandy branch. Pool is an Anglicised spelling of Pwll. Worked by J.G. & E.A. Thomas in 1884, by the New Pool Colliery Co. (J.G. Thomas manager, 18 men) in 1896, abandoned 17th December, 1910. Re-opened by Evan Jones by November 1915, the New Pool Colliery Co. in 1922 and until 13th August, 1928, later Evan Davies & Co. Closed 30th June, 1934. The locomotive at Crown Colliery also shunted this site.

Panthywel SN487013 ¼ mile N. of Sandy branch and connected by tramway which passed under the BP&GV to reach the brickworks on S. side of branch. Also known as Pwll Level and Panthowell, this small pit was being worked by David Jones in 1896 and later, but in July 1923 by D. Griffiths of Llanelly. Abandoned 31st March, 1925. May never have had a rail connection.

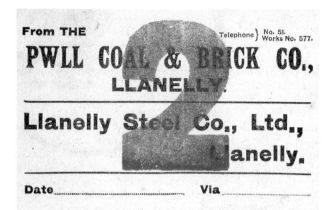

From THE

Telephone } No. 51.
Works No. 577.

PWLL COAL & BRICK CO.,
LLANELLY.

Llanelly Steel Co., Ltd.,
Llanelly.

Date.................................... **Via**......................

Pemberton Level SN458012, on N. side of Sandy branch. Was being worked by Rees, Harry & Roberts in 1896 with 18 men, not listed in July 1909. Rees and Harry had both been involved with the Cwm Mawr Colliery Co. Subsequently worked as part of New Lodge.

Pembrey, *see Gwscwm.*

Pwll (or Pool) SN475009 on N. side of Sandy branch. Worked by Mason & Elkington Ltd from 1865 until 1879, then by Nevill, Druce & Co. Ltd of Llanelly Copper Works. Colliery shown as disused in 1913 and not listed in 1922. Subsequently (by July 1923) re-opened by the Pwll Coal & Brick Co. Ltd. The rail connection to the brickworks on S. side of branch was put in during November 1914. The colliery, but not the brickworks, was vested in the NCB from 1st January, 1947, and finally closed in January 1953. The bulk of the workings were under the sea. The brickworks continued to perform until October 1962; the engine house was not demolished until 1986.

Rhiwlas SN456024 to the N. of Cwm Capel and connected to it by private tramway. Opened by Evan Evans and David Harry trading as David Harry & Co. in 1905 until closed in 1912. Restarted 1916 by Morris & Williams but finally abandoned 19th October, 1917.

Before leaving the collieries, mention has to be made of 'Mabon's Day', named after the bardic title adopted by William Abraham (1842-1922) the miner's leader, elected MP for Rhondda in 1885 and the first President of the South Wales Miners' Federation. He was responsible for the introduction of a scheme to limit the output of coal in South Wales in order to maintain the wages of the miners. In 1892 an agreement was reached with the colliery owners that the South Wales miners would not work on the first Monday of every month and it was this non-working or 'free' day that became known as 'Mabon's Day'; this agreement lasted until 1898. Several times a year during the summer months the Gwendraeth miners and their families would use the train on these days for an excursion to Burry Port; of course at that period the train on the BP&GV consisted of open wagons which had to be specially cleaned by the miners' wives. Some temporary seating would also be fitted - it was probably considered all part of the fun.

Similar miners' excursions had operated before 1892. One such occasion was on Saturday 30th June, 1883 when the men employed by the Pontyberem Colliery Co., accompanied by their families and a brass band, took the train to Burry Port for their annual trip, arriving just after 10 o'clock by the BP&GV. The time of their return train is not recorded but 'they amused themselves in the usual way of excursionists by parading the docks and sands, seeming to enjoy their holiday and change of air'.

Similar trips were organised on Whit Monday in 1887 and 1888 when arrangements were made with Mr Herring of the Pontyberem Colliery 'put the line and a locomotive at his disposal'. Special trains also used to run to Pont Newydd for the benefit of the miners and their families in connection with the well-attended eisteddfodau held at Glyn Abbey during the period when Astley Thompson owned the estate; this would be from the late 1860s to about 1878. The eisteddfodau were later revived and continued until 1939; it is not known if the resumption was before or after the start of regular passenger trains in 1909.

The Metal and Other Works

Ashburnham Tinplate Works SN443004 on the S.W. side of the West Dock at Burry Port. Founded by a group of industrialists including Lord Ashburnham, David Griffiths and William Bevan (who operated a small chemical works in Llanelly) who formed the Ashburnham Tinplate Co. Ltd in 1889. The works opened on 15th April, 1890, the rail connection being put in before the end of the year. Five acres of land, with an option on a further 10, were leased from Lord Ashburnham at £10 per acre per annum but to reach the site another two acres had to be rented from the BP&GV for which the annual charge was £20 per acre. The 1891 census records 223 tinplate workers then residing in Pembrey Parish, which included Burry Port. Griffiths left in 1893 to become manager of the Kidwelly Tinplate Works. Bevan was a Director of the BP&GV from March 1892 until the end of 1896. The industry had been badly hit by the introduction in the USA of a damaging import tax on tinplate (the 'McKinley Tariff') with the result that the works closed at the end of 1896 and the company was wound up in April 1897. Fortunately it re-opened in July 1898 under the auspices of Thomas Bowen & Co. of the Morriston Tinplate Works, near Swansea, with Bowen's son-in-law Arthur Lewis as works manager. There was a long stoppage in 1913 and again in 1915. Ownership passed in July 1915 to the Ashburnam Tinplate Co. (a subsidiary of Baldwins Ltd); Director Daniel Williams was also a Director at the Old Castle Tinplate Works in Llanelly as well as Chairman of both the Kidwelly Tinplate Works and the Gwendraeth Valleys Railways Co. Production resumed in August 1915. The Ashburnham works became a part of the South Wales Tinplate Corporation from March 1924 but there was a four-month closure that winter and so frequent were the subsequent closings and openings it was given the title of 'The Umbrella Works'. Then from April 1939 it became the Llanelly Associated Tinplate Co. Ltd, which with others combined in September 1947 to form the Steel Company of Wales. During World War II and just afterwards the factory was closed and was used for Government storage, from August 1941 to March 1946 (vital wartime stocks of tobacco are believed to have been stored here!). The final closure came in 1965.

At its maximum about 300 workers were employed. From about 1903 their own locomotive is known to have shunted at this tinplate works, with a second added about 1931. The first was an 0-4-0ST built by the Hunslet Engine Co. of Leeds (No. 386) in 1885 for the contractor J.T. Firbank with the name *Groombridge*. She had 9 in. by 14 in. outside cylinders and 2 ft 8½ in. wheels and was first employed on building the London, Brighton & South Coast Railway line from Hurst Green Junction to Ashurst Junction in 1885-86, Groombridge being a village near Ashurst. After helping on many other contracts, this little engine finished work for Firbank on his Cirencester to Andoversford widening for the Midland & South Western Junction Railway, completed in 1902, and was sold to Thomas Bowden & Co. about 1903 or shortly after. She remained at Burry Port until scrapped in 1949, by the September of that year. The second engine here was a larger 0-4-0ST by Peckett & Sons of Bristol (No. 1191) named *Dunkerton* and built in August 1910 for Dunkerton Collieries Ltd (E. of Camerton, Somerset) with outside cylinders of 10 in. by 15 in. and 2 ft 9 in. wheels. She was sold after the last coal was raised on 30th May, 1925 (the pit subsequently re-opened in a small way but for only a short period) and passed to Walter Scott & Middleton, the public works contractors, before coming to the Ashburnham Tinplate Works around 1931. The locomotive was still at Burry Port in August 1950 but had been transferred away to the Teilo Tinplate Works in Potardulais by July 1953.

Burry Port Foundry SN448007 was started by William Roberts of Llanelly in 1874 as iron and brass founders to serve local industries including ship repairing and boiler scaling. There were 23 employees in 1881. Roberts developed a forge which could use anthracite as fuel and used steam to blow as well as blast, being granted a provisional patent in 1882. Details of his invention seem to have been the magnet for two burglaries at the foundry in a week! The foundry later closed (possibly around the time the copper works closed in 1912) but was re-opened during Word War I by the Burry Port Foundry & Engineering Co. (Messrs J. Eager, F.J. Evans, E. Jones and A. Morgan), and finally closed in 1925. (Note that John Eager, F. John Evans and Arthur Morgan were respectively Engineer, shipping canvasser and Manager of the BP&GV.)

Burry Port White Lead Works SN448006 was established by Risley and Burgman in 1870 on a site covering 1.75 acres leased from the copper works; John Wilkins (a Wiltshire man) was the Manager. In the 1881 census there are 50 employees, 20 of them women. After the death in 1902 of John Risley (who came from Oxfordshire) aged 68, a limited company was formed, but this seems to have ceased business in 1910.

Pembrey Copper (later Zinc Oxide) Works SN448004 was started as early as 1849, which is well before the railway came and is why the name Burry Port was not adopted. The founders were the Birmingham industrialists Josiah (later Sir Josiah) Mason (1795-1881) and George Elkington (1801-1865). The Burry Port Co. offered them a 20 acre site on the east side of the dock free of charge but 10 acres only were all they then needed (a few years later they had to purchase these extra 10 acres when an extension was required! Eventually 34¼ acres were owned but the copper works itself only occupied 18 acres). Smelting began in

November 1849; a feature of the works was the 280 ft-high brick chimney, completed in 1852 (when it was the third tallest in Britain) and which suddenly fell down without warning on 26th April, 1947, the day before it was due for demolition! In 1856 the partnership was dissolved and Elkington and his five sons became sole proprietors although the trading name was kept as Mason & Elkington. In 1884 it was merged with the Elliott's Metal Co. Ltd of Solihull (Henry W. Elliott) with Gerard Elkington (the grandson of the founder) as Managing Director until March 1903. Gerard's father, Frederick Elkington, had previously been Manager of the works. A later Director and Chairman of the company was Neville Chamberlain (Prime Minister 1937 to 1940).

Much of the copper ore originally (until the mid-1860s) came from Anglesey or Cornwall, coming by sea direct from Amlwch or Portreath to Burry Port; some also came from southern Ireland. Later the ore came from further afield, such as Portugal, Chile and South Africa (shipments, each of 600 tons of ore, have been recorded as arriving at Burry Port during 1884 from Port Nalloth, South Africa). Most of the coal used in the copper works came from the company's own Craiglon, New Lodge and Cwm Capel collieries. The latter was connected to the copper works by a 4 ft 2 in. gauge, horse-worked tramway originally belonging to the Kidwelly & Llanelly canal. The tramway was converted to a standard gauge branch of the BP&GV in 1876. Under an agreement of 26th February, 1876 the copper works was enabled to use its own locomotives to convey its coal traffic between the works and the Cwm Capel colliery (with the BP&GV being allowed to use the copper works' crane and stage on the inner dock when not required for unloading ore). This enabled the copper works to dispose of its Gwscwm and Pwll collieries in 1879, although those at Craiglon and New Lodge (only acquired in 1877) were retained and the traffic to and from them worked by the copper works' locomotive.

Examination of the census returns for Pembrey Parish, which then included Burry Port, Pwll and Trimsaran, reveals that for the years 1851, 1861, 1881 and 1891 the number of men who recorded themselves as copper workers totalled 33, 101, 128 and 213 respectively. Of course, there will have been further employees who gave other occupations so these figures will not represent the total workforce (which in the 1870s amounted to as many as 500 for this and the Silver Works together) but do give some idea of size and growth. Copper smelting involved using sulphuric acid which was taken between vats through rubber tubing, the rubber gradually being dissolved. It was noticed (it is said by accident) in the Pembrey Works that the dissolved copper could impregnate cloth and the resultant processing rights were sold to Charles Macintosh & Co. for them to develop successfully for waterproof clothing in place of using coal-naphtha.

The locomotives used at the copper works, over the dock lines and over the lines to Craiglon, Cwm Capel and New Lodge were all small 0-4-0STs with outside cylinders built by the Leeds firm of Manning, Wardle & Co. The first to arrive was *Merlyn* (No. 47), sent new from Leeds on 8th August, 1862 (and thus before the BP&GV had any track laid), and was of the maker's class 'E' with 9½ in. by 14 in. cylinders and 2 ft 9 in. wheels. Next to come was *Norah* (No. 397) on 12th June, 1872, a larger class 'H' with 12 in. by 18 in. cylinders and 3 ft. 0 in. wheels. This engine was involved in a fatal accident by the level crossing over

Looking east across the outer harbour to the Pembrey Copper Works. A screw tug is moored
waiting for action on the left.   *R.E. Bowen Collection*

One of the copper works' narrow gauge locomotives employed to take the slag out to the shore
line. This is *Anita* which arrived new from Manning, Wardle & Co. in March 1904 and was sold
in July 1912 when the works closed.   *Author's Collection*

the GWR main line when taking empty wagons back to the colliery; a boy of eight being run over. Later the locomotive stock was increased from two to three with the arrival of *Curlew* (No. 1247) on 2nd February, 1892; she had 10½ in. by 16 in. cylinders and 2 ft 9 in. wheels and was of class 'F'. Also of this class was *Elsie* (No. 1671), sent new on 16th December, 1905 and which seems to have replaced *Merlyn*, which was scrapped.

In addition to the standard gauge, the Pembrey Copper Works also operated an internal 18 in. gauge railway (no locomotives) and a 3 ft 0 in. gauge system with locomotives to take the slag produced in the works to the shore for tipping. The embankment produced by the tipped slag protected the works, built on land only just above sea level, from any very high tides. The first of two 0-4-0ST narrow-gauge locomotives was *Stanley* which arrived about 1898-99. Built in Leeds in February 1886 by the Hunslet Engine Co. (No. 391) as *Winnie*, this engine had 9 in. by 14 in. outside cylinders and 2 ft 6 in. wheels. She was new to the contractor J.P. Edwards at Ripley, subsequently passing to S.E. Bentley - presumably for Kellett & Bentley who were contractors for the Christchurch to Brockenhurst line of around 1887 - then by August 1897 to a third contractor - James Nuttall - who used her on his Lynton & Barnstaple contract completed in May 1898. After this she came to Elliott's Metal Co. and had her name changed. She was still with Elliott's in February 1903, when spares were ordered for her, but seems to have been disposed of after the second engine was purchased. She was at the works of her maker's, the Hunslet Engine Co., in September 1904 when the order (No. 27399) was issued for her to be cut up for scrap. Her replacement was *Anita*, dispatched new from Manning, Wardle & Co. (No. 1630) on 21st March, 1904. *Anita* was of the maker's class 'E' with 9½ in. by 14 in. outside cylinders and 2 ft 4 in. wheels.

The Pembrey Copper Works was one of the largest employers in the district and it had a devastating effect on the locality when the works closed down in 1912, the last copper being smelted on 30th March, 1912. An auction took place on 2nd July, 1912 to dispose of the works and contents, including four steam locomotives (one narrow gauge), one electric locomotive, 56 wagons (12 narrow gauge) and 4,552 yards of sidings. All the steam engines went on to other work except for *Norah*, which latter is believed to have been scrapped. *Curlew* went to W.W. Holmes & Co., Killan Colliery, Duvant, Swansea (later Killan Collieries Ltd and was sold in 1925 to George Cohen, Son & Co. Ltd, probably for scrap). *Elsie* went to A. Lyle & Son Ltd, Silvertown Sugar Refinery, Essex. The narrow-gauge *Anita* had a most varied career. She passed to William Underwood & Brother, the Dukinfield contractors, who used her (by April 1913) on their Grwyne Fawr Reservoir contract, passing to the Abertillery & District Water Board in December 1916, to the contractors Lehane, Mackenzie & Shand Ltd in June 1928 becoming their *Derby*, subsequently with Pauling & Co. and finishing up at their Swansea (Crymlyn Burrows) Depôt where she was scrapped about 1951.

After the copper works was partially dismantled the site was purchased by Evan Jones & Plews who formed the Metallic Chemical Co. Ltd and erected a factory to make zinc-oxide. This had some success during World War I but went into liquidation in 1921. A sale on 28th June, 1922, which included the 33½ acre site, received a bid of £12,500 but this was refused; however, later in 1922 Fricker's Metal Co. Ltd (of Luton) bought the site and recommenced the production of zinc-oxide in 1923. Some coal was delivered to the works by rail. From 1952 Fricker's was incorporated into the Imperial Smelting Corporation, then from 1973 was a subsidiary of the Rio Tinto Zinc Corporation. From 1991 the works was owned by Grillo Zincoxide (UK) Ltd, whose parent company is in Germany, but subsequently closed and the site was completely cleared in 2006. The eastern portion of the old copper works site (13 acres) was used in the building of the coal-fired Carmarthen Bay power station (which occupied 214 acres) which commenced generating on 28th June, 1953 but closed down 31 years later in 1984 and was demolished in 1991-92. At its peak about 500 workers were employed and a maximum output of 363,000 kilowatts was produced.

Pembrey Lead & Silver Works SN448005. A Silver Works on land (4½ acres) leased from the copper works was set up by Alexander Parkes in 1853 and who formed the Burry Port Smelting Co. Ltd. About 1860 Astley Thompson became Chairman with Douglas Onslow as manager from 1865, when lead smelting was added. The firm failed in May 1877 and was declared bankrupt two months later. The New Lodge and Pontyberem South Collieries and the Burry Port Steamship Co. were also operated by this firm. The factory, which included chimney stacks 152 ft and 80 ft high, remained unused until the copper works sale in 1912 but New Lodge Colliery was re-opened later in 1877 by the copper works owners (Mason & Elkington).

A speculative venture was reported in the *Morning Post*, London on 6th February, 1888 which read, 'Gold Smelting in Wales - A Syndicate have decided to erect a gold smelting works at Burry Port, Carmarthenshire for the purpose of smelting gold, several hundred workmen will it is said be employed in the smelting'. It was believed at the time that one of the Parkes Brothers was involved. If the date of the newspaper had been 1st April it would be more understandable; needless to say such a works was never built.

Pembrey Burrows Explosives Works SN416003 was established in this isolated spot in 1881 by the Stowmarket Explosives Co. Ltd of Suffolk (and Penrhyndeudraeth) through a subsidiary called the Explosives Co. Ltd to manufacture dynamite, production starting in 1882. There was no main line rail connection, but there was a mile long narrow (2 ft 6 in.) gauge tramway to Pembrey Old Harbour (not Burry Port). According to *The Llanelly & County Guardian* of 23rd November, 1882 over £6,000 was expended on the construction of this line and its rolling stock, which included a diminutive locomotive named *Rocket* (possibly a nickname). The company failed and the assets were sold in June 1885, a New Explosives Co. Ltd being formed to take over. This in turn was acquired in 1888 by the Nobel Dynamite Trust Co. Ltd, part of Nobel's Explosives Co. Ltd, which promptly ceased all production here.

After many years of dereliction, construction of a new works was commenced in October 1914 and rail connections this time were made with both the GWR and the BP&GV, the latter running over the old tramway, crossing over the Pembrey Old Harbour, and joining the BP&GV near the tinplate works; negotiations for the junction were 'proceeding' according to the Manager's report of 28th November, 1914 to the Directors and the new siding had been 'laid down' according to his next report dated 13th January, 1915. A photograph showing the harbour bridge appears on page 114 in Volume One. Trinitrotoluene (TNT) was produced, followed by

cordite from March 1916. It would seem that the BP&GV branch was mostly used
for materials to be brought in for construction. The contractors building the new
factory (which became known as the Munitions Works) were R. Thorburn & Sons
and Walter Scott & Middleton Ltd who employed several 0-6-0ST locomotives, those
of Scott & Middleton certainly worked over the BP&GV branch and through to the
quarry they were working on the Cwm Capel branch. A particularly high and
stormy tide in February 1915 washed away a section of line by the Old Harbour
(Pembrey) with one truck loaded with rails actually falling into the sea. This suggests
the branch was then still under construction. It had a short life, being closed in 1917
(the Manager's report to the Directors dated 11th September, 1917 says the
agreement for the junction expires in December next but it 'will shortly be taken up
- probably in about a week's time'). From the beginning of that year the works had
come under the control of the Ministry of Munitions and was classed as a filling
factory. Production duly ceased during 1919 after the end of the war.

A Royal Ordnance factory was built on the site for use in World War II, but the
only rail connection this time was with the GWR main line. Working in an
explosives factory was not without risk; there had been a small explosion at the
works on 11th November, 1882 in which fortunately no one was killed. This was
followed by a much more serious one on 17th November, 1882, killing seven, and
which was heard as far away as Tenby (18 miles distant). A third explosion occurred
in July 1917 which this time included six fatalities. Finally, on 10th July, 1940 a
German air-raid on the plant unfortunately resulted in the deaths of 10 workmen.

Trimsaran Iron & Steel Works at SN458045 was part of the colliery complex
and further details have been given earlier under Trimsaran in the listing under
Anthracite Collieries. The iron and steelworks, with its two blast furnaces
(which dated from April 1843), seems to have closed in 1900 and was put up for
sale on 25th January, 1901 (C&I 14th January, 1901). The 1891 census quotes
only 12 men in the locality who gave their occupation as steelworker. Carl
Sandalil (?), born in Sweden, was then the works manager.

The Kidwelly Industries

Some information next follows of the industries served by the Gwendraeth
Valleys Railway, which was worked by the BP&GV as a part of its own system
from 1876 until 1905. After Grouping the GWR, from June 1923, again worked
the GVR as a part of the BP&GV. Limestone and silica stone quarries, silica
brickworks and a tinplate works were served and full details of their quite
complex histories and ownerships (which also involved the ownership of the
GVR) are given by M.R.C. Price in *The Gwendraeth Valleys Railway, Kidwelly to
Mynydd-y-Garreg* (Oakwood Press, 1997) and which also gives details of the
privately-owned shunting locomotives.

Graig Silica Brickworks SN435094 opened in 1900 by William Young, who
also operated the Penymynydd Lime Works, which see for subsequent changes.

Kidwelly Tinplate Works SN422079 worked by Jacob Chivers to 1877, then by
his son Thomas Chivers until he failed in December 1887. Taken over by the
Gwendraeth Tinplate Co. Ltd in 1888. The works closed in June 1892 but resumed

early in 1893 when David Griffiths came in from the Ashburnham Tinplate Works. The factory closed again in 1896, then was re-opened in 1899 by the Kidwelly Iron Sheet & Tinplate Co. which in July 1904 became the Kidwelly Tinplate Co. Ltd (partly financed by Baldwins Ltd). It was taken over by the Llanelly Associated Tinplate Co. Ltd in March 1939 and closed for the last time in July 1941.

Mynydd-y-Garreg Limestone & Silica Stone Quarries SN431083. Daniel Stephens, who operated an existing brickworks on the south side of Kidwelly GWR station (and which lasted until 1965), with his brother Alfred (later Sir Alfred) formed Stephens & Co. which started the quarries here about 1913 (they had been involved with forming the Caepontbren Colliery Co. Ltd in 1902). This became the Stephens Silica Brick Co. Ltd, which passed to Rock Products Ltd in 1943. Rail traffic to the quarry ceased in 1954.

Mynydd-y-Garreg Lime Works SN428084 opened in 1872, then acquired by Edward Threlfall and others in 1876 who formed the Mynydd-y-Garreg & Kidwelly Railway & Lime Co. This was wound up in 1894. From 1895 the lime kilns here were leased to Daniel Stephens (*see above*).

Penymynydd Lime Works SN440096 was established by Alexander Young in 1877, connected to the GVR by a private line. About 1900 the business passed to his son William Young. In 1908 this and the Graig Silica Brickworks were taken over by the A.Y. Dinas Silica Brick & Lime Co. ('A Y' for Alexander Young) and by 1921 was in the hands of the Amalgamated Dinas Silica & Lime Co., which was wound up in 1929. Young's locomotive had been hired by the BP&GV during 1899; also previously, in 1887, what is presumed to be the same engine had been repaired by the BP&GV at Burry Port when Russell (BP&GV Receiver) wrote to Mitchell (traffic manager) on 6th July, 1887, 'Please forward Mr Young's application to have his locomotive repaired by the Company, you can tell him the application will be allowed … how will Mr Young work his traffic in the meantime?', which is a clear indication only the one engine was owned. It is believed that this was a 12 in. 0-6-0ST named *Carmarthen*, built in 1877 by Manning, Wardle & Co (maker's No. 640) and purchased by Young on 31st May, 1878; she was advertised for sale in July 1905 but her eventual fate is not known.

R. Dinas Silica Brick Works SN410062 had been formed by George Redford (hence the 'R') as the R. Dinas Fire Brick & Silicate Works. On 3rd September, 1886 this was taken over by the Kidwelly R. Dinas Fire Brick Co. Ltd, which lasted until November 1893 when it was wound up. The works was acquired by Henry Smart (who seemed to have had an interest of some sort in the previous ownership, and who then traded as H. & H.E. Smart; worked also the Caepontbren Colliery above Pontyates) and it later (by June 1930) became Smart's Dinas Silica Brick Co. Rail traffic ceased in February 1959 and the brickworks closed soon after.

The original Young's silica brickworks was at Dinas Rock, to the north of Glyn Neath, close to where the silica was quarried. It was first established by W.W. Young in 1822 and it is believed that his brother is the ancestor of Alexander and William. Several members of the Young family operated silica brickworks, especially in the Neath area, all using the word 'Dinas'. This term became synonymous with a quality firebrick made with silica and lime and which was particularly suitable for lining furnaces. Thus the 'Dinas' as used in the Kidwelly (now Cydweli) area refers to the type of brick and is not used as a place name.

Chapter Eight

Motive Power

A detailed account of the engines owned by the BP&GV was produced in Part 10 of *The Locomotives of the Great Western Railway* pages K212-K218, published by the Railway Correspondence & Travel Society in 1966. Although the present writer was responsible for two of the chapters therein (those covering the Brecon & Merthyr and the Cambrian), the section on the BP&GV was entirely the work of my friend the late Ken Davies of Neath. Nevertheless much further information has come to light since 1966 so this chapter will not be all repetition.

The first two locomotives, named *Lizzie* and *Gwendraeth*, were supplied by Henry Hughes & Co. of Loughborough in 1868, well before the opening of the line on 23rd June, 1869. As mentioned in Chapter One it would seem likely that both were ordered by the BP&GV Engineer, Henry Robinson, and they may have been hired to the contractor Frederick Furniss until the railway was complete. It is believed that *Lizzie* was named after Robinson's 17-year-old fiancée Elizabeth Newton (they were married in Newcastle-upon-Tyne in 1872); Robinson was a Londoner and some 14 years her senior. Rumour has it that the name *Gwendraeth* was chosen by a Cornish Director because the meaning in Cornish was similar to that in Welsh, i.e white sands in English; the 'Cornish Director' will have been Captain John Luckraft, the Superintendent of the canal and railway. John Nicholson, who came from Portsmouth, was the first driver employed by the BP&GV but it is not known if he also drove for the contractor; he would then have only been 18 years of age in 1868 but the Portsmouth connection would suggest he was one of Furniss's men.

Who actually paid for the engines is not exactly clear. Managing Director (later Chairman) General Malcolm seems to have paid for *Gwendraeth* as he was re-paid £1,050 in 14 monthly instalments of £75 each between 31st August, 1869 and 30th September, 1870, but did the General pay Hughes & Co. or Furniss? What would appear to be the payment for the diminutive *Lizzie* was made on 31st March, 1870 when £700 was paid for a 'Railway Construction Engine' but to whom? The next two payments recorded in the company's cash book are £287 17s. 0d. to 'Furniss' and £4 to 'Hughes & Co. Materials', all on the same date, which suggests that the £700 payment was to someone else. This amount also is suggestive of a second-hand price rather than a new engine so perhaps Furniss was the original owner of *Lizzie* but not of *Gwendraeth* for which it appears that the full price was paid.

What little is known of the dimensions of these two engines has come from an anonymous article in the monthly magazine *The Locomotive* for December 1909; acknowledgment for information being given to Henry Court, the recently retired BP&GV Engineer who had first started with the railway in 1870. Both were 0-4-0STs with outside cylinders and open cabs. The cylinders of *Lizzie* were 12 in. by 20 in. and her wheels were only 2 ft 9 in. in diameter so clearly she was not really capable of operating over an 11 mile main line. The saddle tank fitted over the barrel only, there was a dome on the firebox, a front spectacle plate bent over to provide a short cab roof, and no buffers. She had disappeared by 28th May, 1870, when there were definitely only two engines in stock. As she was possibly only two years old she was presumably sold or retained by Furniss, but unfortunately it is not possible to trace any later owner with any certainty because Hughes' locomotives did not record any identifying number on their builder's plates. Curiously, Furniss used another 0-4-0ST by Hughes on his Hayling Railway contract which was even smaller, having only 10 in. by 15 in. cylinders; she was sold to the second-hand locomotive dealer I.W. Boulton of Aston under Lyne after being repaired in Brighton works in October 1868.

The other Hughes engine, *Gwendraeth*, although also an 0-4-0ST, was more powerful with 3 ft 9 in. wheels, cylinder size unknown but presumably larger than 12 in. In a report to the Directors on 30th May, 1893 it is stated that 'the Gwendreath [*sic*] dock shunting engine had been taken into the shop for repairs, but on examination it was found that the boiler was dangerously worn', so clearly a new boiler was needed, also the wheels required new tyres, which would take at least three months. At the shareholders' meeting on 29th August, 1893 it was stated that the shunting engine was awaiting a new boiler, expected to be ready in November. It is possible that it was during this rebuilding that the engine received the proper cab which appears in a photograph taken about 1898, when working what looks like an engineer's train over the Pwll branch. Alternately the cab might have been fitted during further repairs, when it was reported to shareholders on 27th August, 1897 that during the half-year ending 30th June,1897 'the Gwendreath [*sic*] had been practically rebuilt'.

It was in 1899 that this engine received the number '2' when BP&GV locomotives were numbered for the first time, but very quickly was altered to '3' in August 1900 when the previous number was given to a new engine. It is not at all clear why '3', and also '1', had been left blank when the new numbers were first allocated. One suggestion is that they had been left for the two new engines which were ordered in 1900. Whatever the reason, *Gwendraeth* found her identity changed yet again to '6' when a third new engine arrived in September 1901. To have been renumbered twice in two years when numbers in addition to names had only just been implemented suggests a serious degree of indecision. Anyway, No. 6 *Gwendraeth* soldiered on, mainly shunting around the docks and sidings at Burry Port, until the Engineer's report of 28th August, 1905 advised that, rather than spending more money on her repair, it would be better if she were sold; to this the Board on 11th September, 1905 agreed. Accordingly in July 1906 she was sold to the Avonside Engine Co. of Bristol for just £90 in part exchange for a new locomotive. Presumably she had not worked since the previous August.

Robert Fairlie had in 1864 patented his design of double boiler articulated locomotive and by 1870 early examples had been at work on the Brecon & Merthyr, Monmouthshire and Neath & Brecon railways so that the BP&GV would at least have known a little about the type when offered the chance to test one for itself. The double Fairlie comprised two boiler barrels, one each end of a central firebox, mounted on two identical power bogies with the cylinders outermost (under the two smokeboxes and chimneys). The cab was central and these early examples all had a single central dome fitted on top of the firebox, on the opposite sides of which stood the driver and fireman, the firebox being fed from one side.

The Fairlie Engine & Rolling Stock Co., which had taken over the Hatcham Ironworks, New Cross in London from George England & Co., built two of the type for the Nassjo-Oscarshamn Railway in Sweden but only one was delivered. The other, completed in December 1869 with the name *Pioneer*, instead came during 1870 to the BP&GV, running trials in February and June. She quickly showed her worth, being capable of taking twice the loads worked by *Gwendraeth*, and was taken into stock with the new name of *Mountaineer* (the same name was in use on another Fairlie locomotive on the Neath & Brecon Railway). £1,800 was paid for this engine on 30th September, 1870 and on the same day a further cheque for £22 2s. 0d. was made out to 'Fairlie', presumably to Robert Fairlie for the use of his Patent.

Mounted on four-wheeled bogies and described as an 0-4-4-0T, *Mountaineer* had four outside cylinders (two pairs) 10 in. by 18 in. and 3 ft 6 in. wheels, bogie wheelbase 5 ft 0 in., total wheelbase 19 ft 6 in., boilers 2 ft 10 in. by 8 ft 6 in., heating surface (in sq. ft.) of 763 tubes plus 70 firebox, grate area 11 sq. ft, water 700 gallons, coal 15 cwt and total weight 25 tons. Along the footplate angle under the cab was a narrow plate worded 'Fairlie Engine and Steam Carriage Co. London. 1870'. The report that this plate also showed the maker's number is incorrect. In or about 1877 it is believed that the GWR borrowed this engine for trials on its steeply graded Pantyffynon to Rhos line, presumably the GWR lent the BP&GV an engine in exchange, but what sort has not been recorded. The *Mountaineer* returned to continue working on the BP&GV until withdrawn during the six months ending 30th June, 1891 when described as worn out, being broken up at Burry Port, and the locomotive stock was reduced from five to four as a result. The boiler shell was later used as a culvert on the dock estate (and was still there in 2004) whilst the two bogies were kept to be used to convey any heavy loads such as boilers.

Impressed with the prowess of their Fairlie double engine the BP&GV quickly said 'yes' when offered another, and even larger, example by the Yorkshire Engine Co. of Sheffield in 1873. This was a 12-wheeler of type 0-6-6-0T and was one of three built by James Cross & Co. of Sutton, St Helens to the design of Charles Douglas Fox for the 3 ft 6 in. gauge Southern & Western Railway of Queensland, Australia in 1866 as works numbers 28, 29 and 30. The water was carried in well tanks, capacity 1,030 gallons, the sides of which formed the bogie frames which meant that the valve gear was placed *outside* the frames but *inside* the wheels. Fox had departed from some of Fairlie's specifications in several important details (Fairlie himself disclaimed them) and the result was that when the first engine (believed to have been No. 29) was assembled after arrival in Queensland it turned out to be a miserable failure and all three were promptly laid aside; one not even being unpacked from the shipping crates. Under the instigation of Robert Fairlie they subsequently (1872-73) returned to Britain and were sent to the works of the Yorkshire Engine Co., Meadow Hall, Sheffield for complete rebuilding. They were reconstructed to the standard gauge, the well tanks were discarded and new side tanks (capacity 1,000 gallons) fitted and the Stephenson's motion transferred to the normal

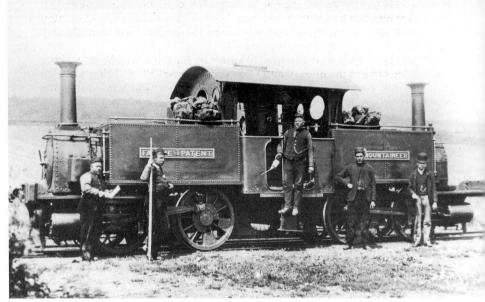

The 8-wheel Fairlie locomotive *Mountaineer* seen at Kidwelly Junction on 24th May, 1890.
LGRP 18181

The larger Fairlie *Victoria*, which had 12 wheels, is seen at Burry Port in 1899.   *LGRP 18207*

position between the frames. New wheels of 2 ft 9 in. diameter (previously 3 ft 0 in.) were attached and at the same time the springing and (most importantly) the steam and exhaust pipe connections to the bogies were considerably improved.

Two of the rebuilds were exported to Uruguay; the third, which was maker's number 29, came to the BP&GV and received the name *Victoria*, being added to stock during the six months ending 31st December, 1873; increasing the locomotive stock to three. Other dimensions of this 12-wheel Fairlie were wheelbase 6 ft 6 in. (bogie) and 23 ft 4 in. (total), outside cylinders (four) 11 in. by 18 in., boilers 3 ft 0 in. by 9 ft 10 in., heating surfaces of 1,037.4 sq. ft (tubes) plus 72.1 sq. ft (firebox) and grate 17.4 sq. ft. As rebuilt the weight was 37 tons empty and 41 tons in working order.

As the largest engine on the line the *Victoria* did a considerable amount of work and it is not surprising that after more than 18 years she was declared to be worn out and laid aside during the first half of 1892, being replaced in the locomotive stock by a new engine from Peckett & Sons. However, she was not broken up but kept waiting until funds would be available for her rebuilding. This was under way at last by 3rd December, 1895 when it was reported to Shareholders that 'great progress has been made in rebuilding the *Victoria*'.

Great progress it might have been but it was 22nd May, 1896 before the work was completed, the Directors being informed on 9th June, 1896 of the successful trial with this 'reconstruction'. Shareholders were informed on 8th September, 1896 that *Victoria* had 'worked heavy traffic daily since, up to 790 tons'.

The reconstruction included fitting two new boilers of Low Moor iron and a new copper firebox. Taking her back into stock increased the number of locomotives from five to six. She received the number '8' in 1899 (remember there were two blank numbers). Then on 7th February, 1900 it was reported that the engine had broken down.

Fred R. Willcocks, the company's Engineer until he resigned on 29th August, 1899, seemed to know how to get the best out of the Fairlie design whereas the impression is gained that his successor, Robert Carr (appointed 11th September 1899), had little time for it. His report to the Directors dated 15th September, 1900 mentioned that he proposed to sell and got the Board to agree to consider offers for any of the old locomotives just two days later. However, it was not until 23rd June, 1903 that George Herring (a Director) informed his fellow Board members that he had sanctioned the sale of *Victoria* for £200, presumably since the date of the previous meeting which was on 20th April, 1903. Despite this, the locomotive stock total was not adjusted until the six-month period ending 31st December, 1903; perhaps payment was not received until after the end of June. By this time Robert Carr was no longer with the BP&GV, having resigned on 20th April, 1901. It is understood that the old double engine was sold to a scrap merchant and was duly cut-up on the dock estate at Burry Port. When the boiler shell of *Mountaineer* was unearthed in 2004 during foundation work for a new road on the estate, part of another boiler was revealed which was likely to be off the *Victoria* but further excavations would be required to confirm this.

After a period of soured relations with the neighbouring Gwendraeth Valleys Railway, mainly concerning the use of the rail connection at Tycoch and culminating in the GVR taking legal action against the BP&GV in 1875, a period of much closer working between the two companies was soon arranged. This resulted in an agreement formalised on 30th November, 1876 whereby the BP&GV took over the working of the GVR and its only locomotive was also taken over at a cost of £1,000. This was an 0-6-0ST named *Kidwelly* which had been built new for the GVR by Fox, Walker & Co. of the Atlas Works, Bristol in 1872, works number 150, and had 13 in. by 20 in. cylinders (probably outside) and 3 ft 6 in. wheels. So the locomotive stock of the BP&GV increased from three to four in the half-year ending 31st December, 1876 and the GVR was worked as a branch of the BP&GV. This working agreement lasted until 1905.

The engine received extensive repairs in 1883. Then shareholders were told at their half-yearly meeting on 7th March, 1893 that the *Kidwelly* had been rebuilt (with a new boiler) in the Burry Port shops at a cost of £436 6s. 4d. charged to revenue and was back in service on 8th November, 1892, after which she was reported to have been 'in constant service, and gave complete satisfaction'. She had another overhaul in the second half of 1896 and was given the number '5' in 1899. When due for more repairs, it was agreed on 12th July, 1899 that due to pressure of work at Burry Port the overhaul should be put out to tender, Mr Willcocks to prepare a specification. There is no trace of any such repair being effected and presumably the appointment of Robert Carr resulted in a change of plan. She was one of the old locomotives up for sale in September 1900 and was eventually sold for £275 to the Avonside Engine Co. in November 1902 in part exchange for a new engine which took the same name but curiously a different number ('4'). She was actually not taken out of stock until the first half of 1903 which was when her replacement was received (during May).

In the first half of 1886 another 0-6-0ST engine was added to stock. This was the *Susan* purchased second-hand for £650 and previously with the Bishwell Coal & Coke Co. Ltd at Gowerton, Glamorgan. She was completed on 6th August, 1874 at the Boyne Engine Works, Leeds of Manning, Wardle & Co. (maker's No. 459) and delivered to the Bury contractor John Barnes (formerly of Barnes & Beckett) at Chatburn for use on his Chatburn to Hellifield contract for the Lancashire & Yorkshire Railway (L&YR) with the name *Edith Mary* after Barnes' two-year-old daughter. Due to financial difficulties, Barnes ceased work on 28th March, 1877 and the contract was re-let to T.J. Waller on 28th April, 1877, with this locomotive now working for Waller. The ownership is not clear, she may now have been the property of the L&YR (as a creditor) and been on hire to Waller. After the completion of the contract (the line opened to traffic on 1st June, 1880), this engine was sold to the Bishwell company who gave her the new name of *Susan*. She was of the maker's standard class 'M' with 13 in. by 18 in. inside cylinders, 3 ft 0 in. wheels and a wheelbase of 11 ft 3 in. The heating surface was 418 sq. ft (tubes), 47 sq. ft (firebox), grate area 7·5 sq. ft, the working pressure was 140 lb./sq.in. and the weight 24 tons.

She was still named *Susan* on 19th October, 1889 but soon after had become the *Burry Port* and was given the number '6' in 1899. She was reported on 27th January, 1900 to have broken down and may not have returned to work. The offer of £400 for her off the cost of a new locomotive from Chapman & Furneaux of Gateshead was accepted on 21st January, 1901 and on 13th June, 1901 the

Board agreed to dispatch the engine to Gateshead; however, as the new engine
was not received until 10th September, 1901 it may be that *Burry Port* was not
sent away till then; according to the stock returns it was after the end of June. In
later years this locomotive was named *Copshawe* and before the end of 1901 was
working for the contractor G.K. Waghorn of Hull before being offered for sale at
Easington Colliery (where presumably Waghorn had a contract) on 15th April,
1905. After that all trace of her is lost and she might well have been scrapped.

In a letter sent by Secretary Russell to Mitchell, the traffic manager, on 13th
June, 1889 is the intriguing statement, 'I agree to accept half fare for the return
journey of *Velindre* locomotive'. Quite what this means I just do not know. This
was the name of the engine supplied in September 1880 to J. Chivers & Son of
the Kidwelly Tinplate Works; perhaps she was returning from repair. There is
no suggestion that she was ever used by the BP&GV. She was built by Manning,
Wardle & Co (No. 753) as one of their class 'M' 0-6-0ST locomotives.

The locomotive stock was reduced from five to four during the first half of
1891 by the withdrawal of *Mountaineer*; later in the year the Directors were
informed on 26th November, 1891 that only two engines were now working.
Kidwelly required a new boiler and another (probably *Gwendraeth*) a new
lubricator and new tubes. A new locomotive was now 'absolutely necessary'
and one would have to be hired until it was delivered. The tender of Peckett &
Sons of the Atlas Works, Bristol (who had taken over the works from Fox,
Walker & Co. in 1880) for a suitable engine quoted £1,525 or £525 on delivery
and 12 quarterly payments of £92 14s. 0d. (totalling £1,634 8s. 0d.), with the
owner's plate to remain on the locomotive until fully paid. After agreeing that
a lower deposit of £385 would be accepted, the Directors instructed the
Secretary to make the arrangements and request the Receiver to petition the
Court of Chancery to allow such payment to be made out of revenue.

The new engine, named *Dyvatty* (the name of the river that flows past Cwm
Capel to Burry Port), was completed in December 1891 but was not officially
added to stock until the following half-year after the deposit had finally been
paid. It had been intended that £350 received for a strip of land sold in December
1891 would go towards the deposit; instead it was retained by the solicitors to
offset what was owed to them and was never received by the BP&GV! The
Dyvatty was the maker's No. 498 of their standard class 'X' of 0-6-0ST with
inside cylinders 16 in. by 22 in., 3 ft 10 in. wheels and a wheelbase of 11 ft 0 in.
The polished brass dome enclosed the safety valves on top and the saddle tank
was of full length, covering the smokebox. The maker's official photograph,
taken before delivery, showed a taller chimney compared with the copper-
capped one on the engine in service. Perhaps the original was too high for some
of the low BP&GV bridges.

On 22nd December, 1893 the Secretary reported to the Directors that *Dyvatty*
had been laid up since the 23rd ultimo with serious defects in the tubeplate. It
was inspected on the 28th by Mr George Peckett on behalf of the makers who
repeatedly exclaimed that 'he could not account for it' adding that 'he never had
seen or heard of such a thing happening to such a plate' but the next day Peckett
& Sons wrote refusing to make good the defects except at the company's
expense. The Secretary, as Receiver, called in Mr Tom Hurry Riches, the

The Peckett locomotive *Dyvatty* as first built in 1891 and before receiving nameplates.
Author's Collection

locomotive superintendent of the Taff Vale Railway, for an independent report and he held that the makers were responsible. This acrimonious dispute dragged on for almost two years. When the final payment (of £105) was due the Directors, on 17th September, 1995 rejected an offer of a £20 allowance for settlement and instead agreed to send just £50 as final payment. As nothing further seems to have been recorded about this dispute then presumably this last amount was accepted as final. It is perhaps not surprising to note that the BP&GV had no further business dealings with Peckett & Sons, who thus missed out on the chance of supplying up to 16 new locomotives for the line.

During the six months ending 30th June, 1897 shareholders were informed that 'the *Dyfatty* [*sic*] was thoroughly overhauled'. She then underwent a bewildering succession of re-numberings being, in turn, '4' in 1899, changed to '5' in November 1902, finally to '7' in 1905. A new axle had been authorized at a cost of about £80 on 7th February, 1900 and new tyres were ordered on 10th April, 1901 so she was evidently being kept in good repair. However, by September 1906 she required repairs estimated to cost £500 and the Board referred to Morgan and Eager the question that, rather than spend more money on what by then had become the oldest engine of the fleet, would it not be better to have a new engine? Accordingly she was sold to the Avonside Engine Co. for £200 in part-exchange for a new locomotive ordered on 7th December, 1906, being taken out of stock in the following half-year. Subsequently the engine worked at the Maerdy Colliery, Glamorgan of Lockett's Merthyr Collieries (1894) Ltd, then passed via the Darlington dealer John F. Wake to the Burradon & Coxlodge Coal Co. Ltd, Northumberland.

Before this dispute the BP&GV did attempt to buy another locomotive from Peckett & Sons, although she was second-hand. On 30th May, 1893 the Directors minuted that 'the proposal to purchase the locomotive *Phœnix* at the works of Messers Peckett & Co., [sic] Bristol, when rebuilt by that firm, meets with their approval and subject to the sanction of the Court, they also approve the terms the Manager …' has arranged. The cost was £645 but as the Receiver did not have the funds, arrangements were instead made to hire her at 10 per cent per annum, payable in advance, the BP&GV to keep her in repair. It is likely, but not absolutely certain, that *Phœnix* was Peckett No. 444 of 1885, an 0-6-0ST of the maker's class 'B1' with 14 in. by 20 in. outside cylinders and 3 ft 7 in. wheels. She had been hired out before, when new, from December 1885 to October 1886 to the Liskeard & Caradon Railway (Cornwall) before being sold to the Nailstone Colliery Co., Bagworth, Leicestershire in December 1886 and who later returned the engine to Peckett & Sons. The length of time spent on the BP&GV is not known but seems to have been quite short, at the very most 12 months.

Although unable to buy *Phœnix,* just over one year later the Receiver did allow the purchase of another second-hand locomotive, added to stock during the six months ending 31st December, 1894. This was Manning, Wardle No. 731, an 0-6-0ST of class 'M' just like *Burry Port* and with the same dimensions. She was new on 4th May, 1881 with the name *Resolute* and had been delivered to the contractor J.M. Smith at Bury, Lancashire. Her next owner was Gabbutt & Owen who used her on a contract at Huddersfield, then she went to work at the Yniscedwyn Colliery, Gurnos, Glamorgan before coming to the BP&GV; she was promptly given the new name *Cwm Mawr* and received in addition the number '7' in 1899. Early in 1900 she had broken down, per a report to the Directors on 7th February, 1900. She was duly repaired and soldiered on until April 1905 when she was taken by Avonside in part-payment (£200) for a new engine of the same name (but not the same number). Avonside resold her to the Weston, Clevedon & Portishead Light Railway the same year, where she became *Weston* and lasted until that railway closed, being scrapped in 1940.

During 1899, when evidently short of locomotive power (*Kidwelly* was under repair for part of the year), the BP&GV paid Alexander Young of the Penymynydd Lime Works for the hire of his locomotive; she was probably used mostly on the GVR line from Mynydd-y-Garreg to Kidwelly. This was not the first time Young had been involved with the BP&GV for his engine had been repaired at Burry Port workshops during 1887. Some notes about Young appear under the entry for Penymynydd Lime Works at the end of Chapter Six. His engine was a small 0-6-0ST built by Manning, Wardle & Co. (No. 640), Leeds of class 'K' with 12 in. by 17 in. inside cylinders and 3 ft 1½ in. wheels, new on 20th March, 1877 to the contractors Logan & Hemingway at Medbourne, Leicestershire for work on the construction of the Great Northern & London & North Western Joint line; subsequently returning to Manning, Wardle's after about a year. She was resold on 31st May, 1878 to Alexander Young and given the name *Carmarthen.* The last known spares order was sent to her in August 1900. An advertisement appeared in the *Western Mail* from the 6th to 12th July, 1905 for a 12 in. 0-6-0ST locomotive for sale, 120 lb. pressure - apply A. Young, Kidwelly; almost certainly this is the *Carmarthen.* No purchaser is known, but she was possibly bought for scrap as she is not heard of again.

No. 1 *Ashburnham* is seen shunting at Burry Port in 1909.   *LPC 3137*

GWR No. 2192 *Ashburnham* after receiving the Swindon treatment in 1928.   *Photomatic 1795*

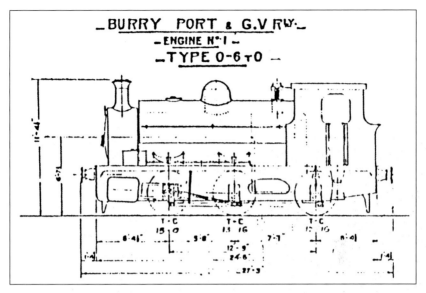

Later in 1899, on 25th October, the Directors instructed their Manager to find a suitable second-hand locomotive and report back. Less than three months after this the finances had sufficiently improved for the railway to instead place an order on 13th January, 1900 for a completely new large engine from Chapman & Furneaux (formerly Black, Hawthorn & Co.) of Gateshead. The price quoted was £1,575 which the BP&GV felt should include the cost of fitting the Eames automatic vacuum brake. In the event this brake was not fitted (it was on the next engine to be ordered instead). Five months were quoted for delivery but on 15th June the Directors were told there would be a delay which resulted in the builders being told 'their breach of contract might necessitate the hire of a locomotive , in which case the cost of hire would have to be debited to them' then on 11th July, 1900 the Board heard that Mr R. Carr (the BP&GV Engineer and Locomotive Superintendent) was 'about to go to Gateshead and test the boiler' of the new locomotive. Finally, on 28th August, 1900 they were informed that the 'trials and running of *Ashburnham* (for that was her name, after the Chairman) were 'most satisfactory' so this new engine had probably arrived in mid-August. She was a standard Chapman & Furneaux design with that firm's characteristic shape of flat-sided saddle tank, a slight forward extension of the lower cabside sheets and a rather small cabside opening above the doorway; she also was embellished with a copper-capped chimney. An 0-6-0ST with 16 in. by 24 in. outside cylinders and 3 ft 8 in. wheels, she was much larger and more powerful than the other saddle tanks. The trailing axle boxes allowed 1¾ inch side play with a swivel joint being provided between the driving crank pin and the rear coupling rod, the wheelbase of 12 ft 9 in. being much longer than any of the older locomotives. A single coal rail was added to the bunker not long after delivery.

B 49

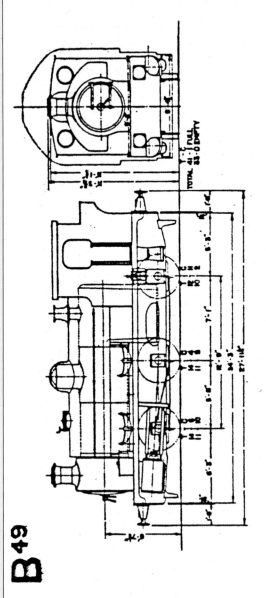

DESCRIPTION.

CYLINDERS —— DIAM. 16". STROKE 24".
BOILER —— BARREL 9'-8". DIAM. OUTS 4'-1" & 4'-2".
FIREBOX —— OUTS. 4'-10⅜" X 3'-10⅝INS. 4'-3⅜" X 3'-3⅜" HEIGHT 5'-5⅝".
TUBES —— N°174. DIAM. 1¾". LENGTH 9'-11⅝".
HEATING SURFACE —— TUBES 795·5 SQ. FT. FIREBOX 78 SQ.FT. TOTAL 873·5 SQ.FT.
AREA OF FIREGRATE —— 14·0 SQ. FT.
WHEELS —— COUPLED 3'-8".
WATER CAPACITY OF TANK. 950 GALLONS
WORKING PRESSURE —— 140 LBS□"
TRACTIVE EFFORT —— 16620 LBS.

LATE B.P.& C.V.R. N°1,

ENGINE N°2192
TYPE 0-6-0

A final payment of £1,400 was made on 12th November, 1900, sufficient debenture stock being issued to cover the cost. She received the number '1', the next six new engines being numbered from '2' to '7' in turn as they were received and, although no two were exactly alike, all had the feature of having outside cylinders with all their six wheels coupled and with the smokebox uncovered by the saddle tank. *Ashburnham* was the maker's No. 1197 and was provided with a new boiler, firebox and smokebox costing £958 10s. at Burry Port workshops during 1917, delivery from R. & W. Hawthorn Leslie & Co., Newcastle, being expected in a fortnight according to a report of 11th September, 1917, with the 'machinery' stated to be in good condition. She was the oldest BP&GV engine to be handed over to the GWR in the Amalgamation of 1922, being recorded as 'rebuilt 1917' in the new owner's records.

Under the provisions of the Railways Act of 1921 the BP&GV was grouped into the enlarged Great Western system and the GWR duly absorbed its smaller neighbour on 1st July, 1922; 15 locomotives belonging to the BP&GV were added to the GWR locomotive stock during the four-week period ending 8th October, 1922, being given new numbers that were vacant in the GWR list on 13th August, 1922. These were Nos. 2162 to 2168, 2176 and 2192 to 2198. They were supposed to be allocated according to the calculated tractive effort in descending order for each engine. So these GWR numbers should correctly have been applied to the BP&GV locomotives Nos. 2, 9, 11 to 15, 6, 7, 1, 8, 10 and 3 to 5 in that order. In actuality the order was 2, 9, 11 to 15, 7, 1, 3 to 6, 8 and 10.

The clerk entrusted with deciding the actual order should not be blamed entirely for getting it wrong as there is evidence that he may have been given some inaccurate figures, especially those of boiler steam pressures, which affected the calculations of tractive effort. The Great Western locomotive department at this period had a fixation with tractive efforts, which in reality were only indicative ratios.

Anyway, *Ashburnham* became GWR No. 2192, her comparatively new boiler was given the number 211 and her dimensions were recorded on diagram A113 in the T0-6-0 series. She received repairs at Carmarthen, completed on 17th March, 1925, then was sent to Swindon for a heavy overhaul on 29th September, 1927. When she emerged from the works on 20th January, 1928 her appearance was changed with a new dome cover, safety valve casing, smokebox handrail and bunker extension, the latter being of typical GWR shape for tank engines. The boiler was retubed, the new tubes being slightly smaller in diameter at 1¾ in. These changes were recorded on a new diagram - B49 - which also showed alterations in the weight distribution.

No. 2192 returned to Burry Port to work, spent a fortnight at Carmarthen in mid-May 1928, then was transferred to Neath shed on 19th July, 1928 where she spent the rest of her active life. She received intermediate or general repairs at Caerphilly on 15th November, 1932 (these are all completion dates), 17th March 1938 and 14th February, 1945, also light repairs at the same factory on 16th July, 1948 which did not involve a repaint so she never received the British Railways livery. She was withdrawn from service on 30th April, 1951, being recorded with having run 246,931 miles since September 1922 (the GWR did not record the mileage worked in BP&GV days) and was scrapped at Swindon during the week ending 19th May, 1951.

The BP&GV Board were urged on 6th March, 1900 the necessity of obtaining a second new locomotive and Carr was instructed to obtain prices. Accordingly, on 28th March quotations from the following manufacturers were considered:

Avonside Engine Co.	£1,295
Peckett & Sons	£1,350
Robert Stephenson & Co.	£1,480
Chapman & Furneaux	£1,575
Manning, Wardle & Co.	£1,650
Ford & Company	£2,200

The minutes make no mention of size of locomotive required and it would appear that like was not being compared with like insofar as the Avonside quote was obviously for a 14 inch engine whereas Chapman & Furneaux's price was for a larger 16 inch machine.* Robert Carr, who attended the meeting, recommended acceptance of the Chapman & Furneaux tender but the Board directed that Carr should 'inspect the Avonside engine and report'.

Although there is mention at the next Board meeting of Carr having visited Bristol, there is no reference to his report nor to any order being placed with Avonside. Nevertheless, the order was placed and Carr reported to the Directors on 12th November, 1900 that the trials of the new locomotive were satisfactory, so she must have been received from Avonside by then. She was a standard design of the makers except that the normal wheel diameter of 3 ft 3in. was increased by three inches. She was given the number 2, named *Pontyberem* and, notwithstanding the quotation, a cheque for £1,400 was drawn on 6th December on Capital Account in payment. She was equipped with the Eames automatic vacuum brake which will have accounted for some of the additional cost.

Pontyberem was Avonside No. 1421, an 0-6-0ST of their standard design with 14 in. by 20 in. outside cylinders, 3 ft 6 in. wheels, a wheelbase of 11 ft, a 700 gallon saddle tank and a weight of 29 tons. Presumably the vacuum brake was fitted to enable her to work the colliers' trains, and she was the only locomotive so fitted until 1905. She had a polished brass dome with the safety valves mounted on top, a copper-capped chimney and, most unusually, the smokebox door hinged on the left (as viewed from in front of the locomotive). In service the front vacuum stand pipe was lowered as it got knocked when emptying ash out of the smokebox and a single coal rail was added to the bunker. In November 1913, when requiring heavy repairs, it was decided that, as she was now too small for future requirements, she would be replaced by a larger locomotive. She was sold in January 1914 to the locomotive dealer P. Baker & Co. Ltd, Albion Works, Cardiff for £225. They in turn resold her in 1915-16 to Nixon's Navigation Co. Ltd at Mountain Ash Colliery, ownership changing to Llewellyn (Nixon) Ltd in 1929. After passing to the National Coal Board in 1947, she was transferred to Penrikyber Colliery in 1962, was noted as being the spare engine in May 1968 and out of use in June 1969. By now she was the sole surviving BP&GV locomotive and her significance was appreciated, so in 1970 she was purchased on behalf of the Great Western Society and that July was moved to Taunton, then taken to the Society headquarters at Didcot in June

---

* These dimensions refer to the diameter of the engine's cylinders.

Avonside's photograph of *Pontyberem* before final painting in 1900.   *Author's Collection*

1977 to await restoration. A photograph taken in 1952 shows that she then had a smokebox door that hinged on the left (viewed from the front) and the rear of the cab now extended to the back of the bunker; of course she had also lost her vacuum brake.

Carr reported to the Board on 23rd November, 1900 that three of the older locomotives had now broken down and he clearly was hoping to persuade them that it was time to order another. At the Directors' meeting on 21st January, 1901 they considered Chapman & Furneaux's letter of 8th January, offering £400 for *Burry Port*,

> ... provided an order was given by the 31st for the building of another engine of the 'Ashburnham' class. Mr Morgan's and Mr Carr's letters on this proposal also read and the Board directed the Secretary to write accepting Messrs Chapman & Furneaux's proposal the order to be for a new 15 inch engine of a class midway between the 'Ashburnham' and 'Pontyberem' locomotives as recommended by Mr Carr.

The manufacturer received the finally agreed order on 21st January, 1901, the price being £1,470 less £400 part exchange, and five months were quoted for delivery. On 27th August the issue of further debenture stocks was authorized to cover the cost and this, the latest locomotive on the line, had arrived by 23rd September, 1901 when she was reported to have had a satisfactory trial. No. 3 *Burry Port* was Chapman & Furneaux No. 1209, an 0-6-0ST with 15 in. by 22 in. outside cylinders and 3 ft 6 in. wheels; she also had the increased side play to her rear axle as on No. 1 and resembled her bigger sister in appearance. A new firebox and tubes costing £1,081 15s. were ordered for this locomotive on 8th April, 1919.

She became GWR No. 2193 in September 1922, her boiler became No. 469 and, evidently because she was never sent to Swindon, she was one of the least altered of any BP&GV locomotive by her new owner. A new dome cover and

B10

ENGINE No 2193
— TYPE 0-6-0
T
LATE B.P&G.V.R. No 3

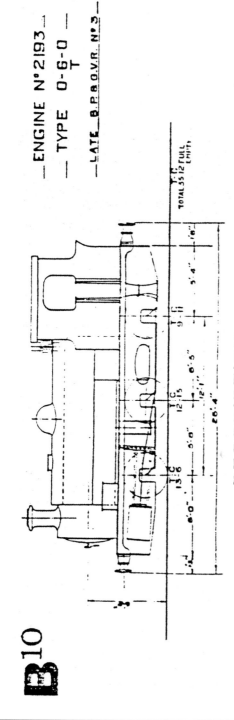

TOTAL 55 12 FULL
EMPTY

T.C
13-6

5'-0"

T.C
12-15

12'-1"

6'-5"

26'-4"

T.C
9-11

3'-4"

6'-0"

1'-8"

DESCRIPTION

CYLINDERS	DIAR: 15" STROKE 22" STEAM PORTS	EXHAUST
BOILER	BARREL	DIAR: OUTS:
FIREBOX	OUTS:	INS: HEIGHT
TUBES	No DIAR LENGTH	
HEATING SURFACE	TUBES SQ FT FIREBOX	SQ:FT TOTAL
AREA OF FIREGRATE	SQ FT	
WHEELS	LEADING 3'-6" DRIVING 3'-6" TRAILING 3'-8"	
WATER CAPACITY OF TANKS	850 GALLONS	
WORKING PRESSURE	140 LBS	
TRACTIVE EFFORT	14025 LBS:	

SQ FT:

No. 3 *Burry Port* became GWR No. 2193 and was photographed at Llanelly engine shed in 1948.   *Author's Collection*

safety valve casing of typical Great Western appearance were fitted but the coal bunker was only slightly enlarged and not given the usual extension; also the smokebox handrail was not altered. Her details were recorded on diagram B10 in the T0-6-0 series and she received heavy repairs at Carmarthen, completed on 14th May, 1924; otherwise all major overhauls were undertaken at Caerphilly - on 12th February, 1929 costing £711, on 22nd May, 1935 costing £708 (after which she was transferred from Burry Port to Llanelly shed), on 16th April, 1943 and lastly on 12th January, 1949. She was withdrawn from Llanelly on 27th May, 1952 having covered 321,312 miles since September 1922, and was cut up at Swindon during the week ending 19th April, 1952.

The company went back to Avonside for the next new 0-6-0ST locomotive ordered on 10th November, 1902 at a cost of £1,600, with an allowance of £275 for the old Fox Walker No. 5 taken in part exchange. The old name *Kidwelly* was transferred to the new engine which was given the number 4. She was of similar appearance but larger than *Pontyberem* having 15 in. by 20 in. outside cylinders; wheels and wheelbase were the same but the saddle tank capacity and the total weight were increased to 750 gallons and 32 tons 1 cwt. Delivered in May 1903, *Kidwelly* was Avonside No. 1463 and just like her smaller sister was soon given a coal rail to increase the bunker capacity. Late in 1917 her boiler was sent to Avonside for the fitting of a new firebox whilst the wheels went to Swansea for new tyres; the thorough overhaul being completed in 1918.

In September 1922 she became GWR No. 2194 and her boiler was numbered 330; diagram A114 recorded her particulars. She was sent to Swindon on 25th July, 1923 where she waited a long time before the decision was taken to rebuild her. She emerged on 18th March, 1926 with new boiler, firebox and smokebox, new saddle tank, Great Western style chimney, dome, safety valves and extended bunker and was equipped with train steam heating gear and the

A 114

— BURRY PORT & G.V.R LY. —
— ENGINES Nᵒˢ 4 & 5. —
— TYPE 0-6-0 —

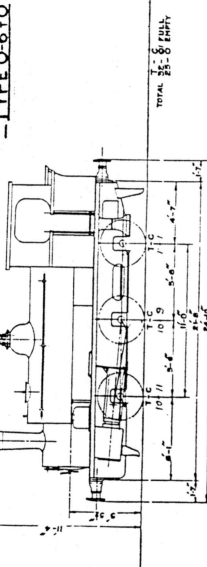

TOTAL 32-6 FULL
25-8 EMPTY

— DESCRIPTION —

Cylinders	DIAR: 15" STROKE 20" STEAM PORTS EXHAUST
Boiler	BARREL 8-0" DIAR: OUTS: 3-5½"
Firebox	OUTS: 4-0" X 5-0". INS: 3-4¾ X 2-11". HEIGHT 4-4½"
Tubes	Nᵒ 125. DIAR: 1¾". LENGTH 8-2".
Heating Surface	TUBES 515. SQ:FT: FIREBOX 60 SQ:FT: TOTAL 575 SQ FT:
Area of Firegrate	10-2 SQ FT:
Wheels	LEADING 3-6" DRIVING 3-6" TRAILING 3-6"
Water Capacity of Tank	750 GALLONS
Working Pressure	150 LBS:
Tractive Effort	13960 LBS:

B 22

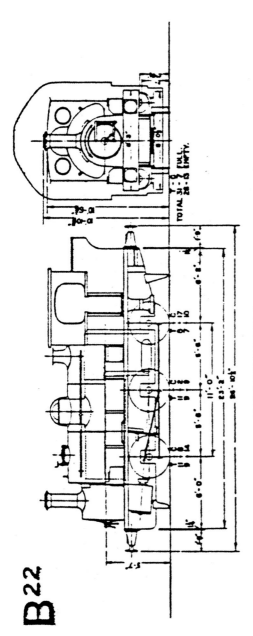

DESCRIPTION.

CYLINDERS	DIAM 15″. STROKE 20″. STEAM PORTS 10″ x 1⅛″. EXHAUST 10″ x 2⅛″.
BOILER	BARREL 9′- 0″. DIAM. OUTS. 3′- 5½″& 3′- 5″.
FIREBOX	OUTS. 3′- 9″ X 3′- 6″. INS. 3′- 2″ X 2′- 11⅝″. HEIGHT 4′- 2″.
TUBES	Nº 129. DIAM. 1⅝″. LENGTH 9′- 2⅛″.
HEATING SURFACE	TUBES 506·4 SQ. FT. FIREBOX 54·6 SQ.FT. TOTAL 561·0 SQ. FT.
AREA OF FIREGRATE	9·27 SQ. FT.
WHEELS	COUPLED 3′- 6″.
WATER CAPACITY OF TANK	745 GALLONS
WORKING PRESSURE	150 LBS.
TRACTIVE EFFORT	13660 LBS.

2194 CLASS

TYPE O·6·O
T

LATE B.P.& C.W.R. Nº 4 & 5.

No. 4 *Kidwelly* was built by Avonside in 1903 and is here seen at Burry Port in 1909.

LPC 3139

GWR No. 2194 *Kidwelly* is pictured in later years shunting at Taunton around 1950.

M.R.C. Price Collection

vacuum brake complete with crosshead driven pump on the right-hand side. The new boiler was No. R330 of class 'YF' and was identical to that fitted in 1915 to GWR No. 1377 and, apart from the dome position, similar to the older boiler on the sister ex-Bristol & Exeter locomotive No. 1376. The only difference was that this 1926 version was given an extra 1½ inch of water space at the lower sides of the firebox resulting in a small reduction in the grate area from 9.45 to 9.27 square feet. Two more of these boilers were also built and fitted in 1926, to Nos. 795 (in September) and 2195 (the next locomotive to be described, during March). The same firebox, but with a barrel six inches shorter and classed 'YG', was used in the rebuilding of the former Barry Railway No. 783 in February 1926 and the Swansea Harbour shunter No. 942 in November 1926. It is believed that these five boilers fitted in 1926 were the last of the round-top pattern to be built at Swindon.

For some reason on leaving Swindon she was sent to Cathays, the former Taff Vale engine shed in Cardiff, but after a few days No. 2194 moved on to Weymouth for working the Quay Tramway through the streets; for this purpose she was fitted with a warning bell on the left-hand footplate just ahead of the firebox and subsequently (in 1929?) with a step plus handrail for the red flag-man on the right side in front of the cylinder. The sight of this small locomotive working a train of eight to ten corridor bogie coaches on a Channel Islands Boat Express, dodging the road traffic along the way, was an experience never forgotten.

Major overhauls were completed 1st July, 1929 (£349), 5th January, 1933 (£306), 28th April, 1936 (£555), 3rd May, 1943 and 3rd December, 1948 - all at Swindon except that the 1943 repairs were at Newton Abbot. Before that, as the Channel Islands traffic had ceased owing to the war, *Kidwelly* left Weymouth on 20th March, 1941 and was sent to Taunton where she remained allocated for the rest of her life, duly losing the steam heating connections. Curiously she was noted back at Cathays, Cardiff in November 1941 (not recorded in the records so evidently considered a short term loan). At Taunton she regularly worked at Dunball Wharf and on other yard duties, and also deputised when required at Bridgwater Docks - the known periods being February to May 1946, January and February 1947, July to August in 1948 and for a rather longer period in 1952. I saw her at Taunton on 6th March, 1948 and she was finally condemned on 3rd February, 1953, being credited with having run 356,532 miles since September 1922, and duly scrapped at Swindon during the week ending 21st March, 1953.

On 10th August, 1904 another locomotive was ordered from the Avonside Engine Co., virtually identical to the *Kidwelly* except that a longer smokebox was fitted and she was equipped with the Eames automatic vacuum brake. She was Avonside No. 1491, cost £1,305 (less £200 part exchange) and was delivered in March 1905; a report to the Board dated 29th March, 1905 recorded that her trial was satisfactory and payment was agreed to be made on 17th April. She became No. 5 and as usual took the name of the replaced engine - *Cwm Mawr* - and was soon (by 1909) equipped with a bunker coal rail. On 16th October, 1918 it was proposed to order a larger replacement engine but by the time this was ready for delivery (August 1919) there had been a big increase in the shipping trade so it was decided there was enough work to keep the smaller locomotive after all.

The third small Avonside saddle tank was No. 5 *Cwm Mawr*, built in 1905 and seen at Burry Port in 1909. Note the name spelt as two words whereas the station name was a single word.

LPC 3141

GWR No. 2195, no longer named and withdrawn from service in January 1953, is at Swindon on 20th September that year awaiting her fate. *Author*

Cwm Mawr became GWR No. 2195 in September 1922, with boiler No. 331, entering Swindon on 15th November, 1922 and eventually emerging on 18th March, 1926 having undergone exactly the same treatment as No. 2194 *Kidwelly,* her new boiler being numbered R331. As she now had steam heating presumably the intention had been to send her to Weymouth, but instead she first went to Gloucester, then on to Neath on 17th April before finally arriving at Weymouth on 5th July, 1926. She had overhauls completed on 30th March, 1929 at Swindon costing £307 (possibly when the front right step and handrail were fitted), and on 25th January, 1936 for £343, also at Swindon. Apart from a short spell at Westbury in March and April 1930, she remained at Weymouth until 18th March, 1939 when she was withdrawn from service. Like others withdrawn at this period, she was not scrapped but placed in reserve (minus her name plates) in case war broke out. When this happened she was taken into Caerphilly works on 8th November to be put into good order with repairs costing £377, emerging nameless and without bell, front right step and handrail but with new horizontal handrails on the upper smokebox sides on 20th December, 1939 and was sent first to Swindon, moving on to Bristol (St Phillips Marsh) in February 1940. Two months later she began a period of just over two years on loan to the Ministry of Supply and was used at the ordnance factory at Tidworth. She returned to the GWR before the end of 1942 and became the Carriage & Wagon works shunting engine at Swindon. She had a six-month return visit to Weymouth between December 1945 and 15th June, 1946 for which the steam heating hoses were reinstated, then it was back to being the works' shunter. She was generally repaired at Swindon on 27th November, 1947 smartly repainted in green and with the large initials 'G' and 'W' on either side of the missing nameplate (I recall seeing her like that a couple of weeks later). No. 2195 was withdrawn for the second, and final, time on 16th January, 1953 having been credited with 346,332 miles since September 1922, not bad considering she had been thought as surplus to requirements back in 1918. She was not broken up straight away and I photographed her intact and still lettered 'G W' at Swindon on 20th September, 1953. Her number plates had been removed and in the paintwork under the left-hand plate the shape of her original BP&GV oval number plate could be clearly seen. She was actually recorded as being scrapped during the week ending 26th December, 1953, presumably at the beginning of that week rather than at the end!

The Engineer's report of 28th August, 1905 advised that, rather than spending more money on old No. 6 *Gwendraeth,* it would be better if she were sold. Another locomotive like *Burry Port* was required but Chapman & Furneaux had ceased manufacturing in May 1902 following the death of Chapman and the resignation due to illness of Furneaux. So the BP&GV turned to the Avonside Engine Co. and asked them to build a similar machine. Their tender of £1,730 less an allowance of £90 for the old locomotive in part exchange was approved by the BP&GV Directors on 23rd April and the order was given on 2nd May, 1906. On 24th September it was reported that the new *Gwendraeth* had now arrived and was working satisfactorily; the cheque in payment was signed on 22nd October, 1906. She was Avonside's No. 1519 and was given the BP&GV No. 6.

– BURRY PORT & G.V. Rly. –

– ENGINE Nº 6 –

– TYPE O-6-O –

A 111

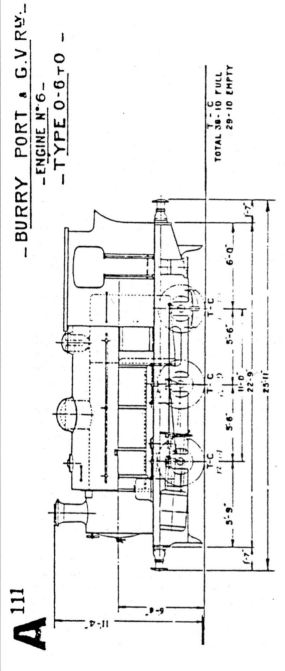

TOTAL 38-10 FULL
29-10 EMPTY

T-C

EXHAUST

T-C

T-C   T-C

1'-7"

6'-0"

5'-6"

11'-0"

22'-9"

25'-11"

5'-6"

5'-9"

1'-7"

11'-4"

6'-6"

— DESCRIPTION —

CYLINDERS	DIAR: 15" STROKE 22" STEAM PORTS
BOILER	BARREL 8'-0" DIAR: OUTS: 4'-1".
FIREBOX	OUTS: 4'-10" X 3-11¼. INS: 4'-2⅝ X 3'-5"HEIGHT 5'-3" 2 4'-5".
TUBES	Nº 164 DIAR: 1⅝ . LENGTH 8'-3¼.
HEATING SURFACE	TUBES 758 SQ: FT: FIREBOX 80 SQ: FT: TOTAL 838 SQ: FT:
AREA OF FIREGRATE	15·2 SQ: FT:
WHEELS	LEADING 3'-6⅝. DRIVING 3'-6⅝. TRAILING 3'-6⅝.
WATER CAPACITY OF TANKS	950 GALLONS.
WORKING PRESSURE	170 LBS:
TRACTIVE EFFORT	16850 LBS:

Avonside produced a design featuring the same wheelbase, 11 ft 0 in. as on their previous models, despite the larger boiler which needed to be pitched 12½ inches higher so that the bigger grate could clear the rear axle. The result was a humpy, top-heavy looking locomotive accentuated by the need to keep the overall height down to 11 ft 4 in. The outside cylinders were 15 in. by 22 in. the wheels 3 ft 7 in. in diameter and she had Ramsbottom safety valves and a steam brake.

When the GWR took over the BP&GV locomotive stock in September 1922 *Gwendraeth* was undergoing repairs in the Burry Port shops. On completion, on 5th February, 1923, she was sent as No. 2196 to Llanelly (Sandy) shed to help out over the former Llanelly & Mynedd Mawr section but had returned to Burry Port in June. Her details were recorded on diagram A111 which now showed the wheel diameter as 3 ft 6½ in.; the boiler was numbered 326. Then on 7th January, 1925 she was selected to go to Kitson & Co., Leeds for a complete overhaul under Lot 238 costing £2,644 (considerably more than the engine had cost new in 1906). It is thought that this is when the nameplates were repositioned slightly lower on the sides of the saddle tank so as to leave room for the legend *Great Western* under the handrail. Apart from the removal of the lubricator nipple behind the chimney, there was no other alteration to her appearance. Leaving Leeds on 17th December, 1925 she was sent to Swansea (Prince of Wales Dock) engine shed, moving to nearby Danygraig in October 1926 and finally to Llanelly on 5th October, 1936. From time to time she was outstationed at Sandy (as in 1942) and at Burry Port (as in 1947-48).

Other major repairs were undertaken at Caerphilly; that completed on 13th May, 1931 is believed to be when *Gwendraeth* received her GWR style bunker, handrails to the smokebox sides and round the front top of the saddle tank, plus GWR safety valves (without cover) in place of the BP&GV Ramsbottom type. Later repairs were finished on 16th January, 1935, 9th September, 1940, 6th May, 1947 (when she was repainted green with the large initials 'G W R' on the tank sides) and 22nd October, 1952 (British Railways black with smokebox number plate and, surprisingly, GWR safety valve casing fitted for the first time). She was condemned on 9th January, 1956, having completed 437,967 miles since December 1925, and was broken up at Swindon (her only visit to the place) during the week ending 25th February, 1956. One of her nameplates was purchased by Mr R.S. Wilkins. Remarkably she retained her original chimney and dome cover to the end.

Avonside were asked to quote for another locomotive like *Gwendraeth* but with the wheelbase increased by 15 inches so that the firebox could sit in front of the rear axle and enable the boiler to be pitched six inches lower. The rear axle was to fit in sliding axle boxes, like the two Gateshead-built engines. The tendered price of £1,800 (later increased to £1,820 to include the vacuum brake) less £200 allowance for the *Dyvatty* taken in part-exchange was accepted on 7th December, 1906. Rather than reuse the old name, it was decided on 12th March, 1907 that the new locomotive should be named *Pembrey* and she was delivered before the end of June. She was Avonside No. 1535, BP&GV No. 7, and far better proportioned than her humpy sister. Being vacuum-fitted she frequently took her turn working the regular passenger trains following their introduction in

No. 6 *Gwendraeth* was a big, humpy saddle tank, photographed at Burry Port on 15th May, 1919.
LCGB Ken Nunn Collection 2212

Gwendraeth, by now GWR No. 2196, is standing in the sunshine at Burry Port in August 1947.
Author

1909. In December 1915 repairs, including fitting a new boiler ordered from Avonside, were due to be completed in a few days, according to the Engineer's Report of 7th December. However, it is likely that it was her original boiler (only 8½ years-old) that had been fitted with a new firebox and some new tubes and not a completely new boiler.

The livery of the Avonside engines was dark green with black bands edged with a yellow line on each side of the band; the corners of panels were radiised; wheels also were green with black and yellow lining. Buffer beams were signal red with black edging lined in white. Frames were crimson edged in black with an ochre lining. Cabs were buff inside with black and red lining. The two Chapman & Furneaux engines were also green with similar lining. All BP&GV locomotives had a second whistle - low pitched and referred to as a 'hooter' - which was used for signalling instructions to the train guard.

In September 1922 *Pembrey* became GWR No. 2176, with the boiler being numbered 421, and her details were recorded on diagram A112. This shows the wheel diameter was now 3 ft 6½ in. and the slimmer saddle tank held 900 gallons (50 less than No. 2196). She was sent to Swindon in June 1923 and was hanging around for a long time before the decision was made to rebuild her with a new GWR Belpaire boiler No. R421. This was a modified 'U' class boiler as used on some of the '517' and on the '2021' classes but with the barrel shortened by 12 inches and the firebox by three inches; the flat grate was also changed to the sloping pattern, as shown on new diagram B39. A new saddle tank of 850 gallons was required so as to fit over a Belpaire firebox and, with her GWR chimney, dome and safety valve covers, plus her extended bunker and crosshead driven vacuum pump, she presented quite a different appearance when she emerged from the works on 22nd February, 1927. A curved handrail at the top, front of the saddle tank was now fitted but the sides of the smokebox never had rails. She was now without her name, apparently victim of the policy that precludes locomotives bearing the same titles as main line stations (it was thought that one day a passenger might be confused!).

Major repairs were completed at Swindon on 10th June, 1929, with others all at Caerphilly on 7th September, 1937, 4th January, 1944 and 1st October, 1948. In her last years she is said to have been fitted with a smokebox number plate; this was probably when light repairs were undertaken at Barry works on 24th July, 1952. Going back to 10th July, 1931 this engine was officially transferred from Burry Port to Llanelly (with occasional return visits to Burry Port), the only change of shed recorded before her withdrawal on 14th March, 1955 after covering 369,645 miles since September 1922. She was sent to the Swindon pool, but not for long, being scrapped during the week ending 21st May, 1955.

The decision taken on 28th September, 1908 to go ahead with the introduction of a regular passenger service (they started on 2nd August, 1909) meant that a new locomotive would be required. Tenders were invited and were considered by the Board on 23rd November, 1908; that from Hudswell, Clarke & Co., Leeds to be accepted subject to an explanation of their quotation. On 14th December the Directors were told by the Secretary that the order had been given to Hudswell, Clarke at the tender price of £1,670 provided that 'this sum included metallic packing'. This style of packing, to the glands where the piston and

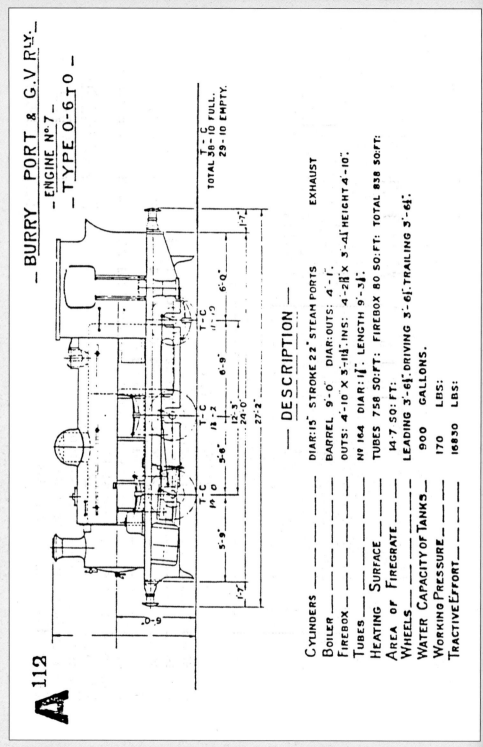

A 112

BURRY PORT & G.V R^LY.

ENGINE Nº 7

TYPE 0-6 T 0

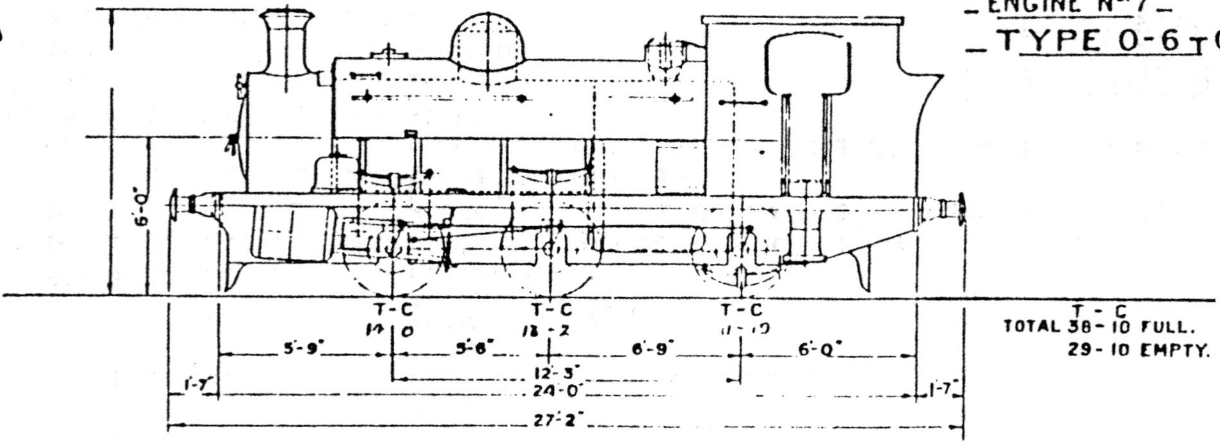

— DESCRIPTION —

CYLINDERS	DIAR: 15" STROKE 22" STEAM PORTS EXHAUST
BOILER	BARREL 9'-0" DIAR: OUTS: 4'-1".
FIREBOX	OUTS: 4'-10" X 3'-11½". INS: 4'-2⅞" X 3'-4½" HEIGHT 4'-10".
TUBES	Nº 164 DIAR: 1⅞". LENGTH 9'-3⅛".
HEATING SURFACE	TUBES 758 SQ:FT: FIREBOX 80 SQ:FT: TOTAL 838 SQ:FT:
AREA OF FIREGRATE	14·7 SQ: FT:
WHEELS	LEADING 3'-6½". DRIVING 3'-6½". TRAILING 3'-6½".
WATER CAPACITY OF TANKS	900 GALLONS.
WORKING PRESSURE	170 LBS:
TRACTIVE EFFORT	16830 LBS:

B 39

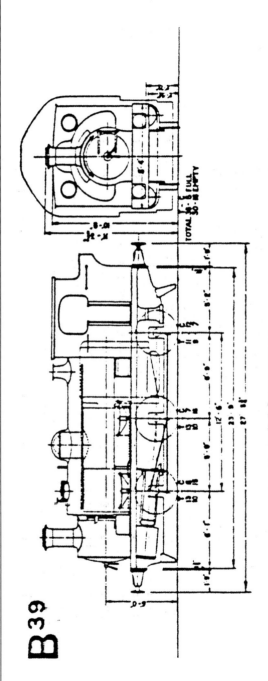

DESCRIPTION.

CYLINDERS——————DIAM. 15". STROKE 22".

BOILER——————BARREL 9'- 0". DIAM. OUTS. 3'- 10" & 3'- 8½".

FIREBOX——————OUTS. 4'- 10" X 3'- 10". INS. 4'- 1½" X 3'- 2". HEIGHT 5'- 11¾" & 4'- 3½".

TUBES——————N°193}. DIAM 1⅝"} LENGTH 9'- 3½".
              N°2½}. DIAM 5½"}

HEATING SURFACE——————TUBES 785·90 SQ. FT. FIREBOX 73·9 SQ. FT. TOTAL 859·8 SQ. FT.

AREA OF FIREGRATE——————13·8 SQ. FT.

WHEELS——————COUPLED 3'- 6½".

WATER CAPACITY OF TANK——850 GALLONS

WORKING PRESSURE——————165 LBS"

TRACTIVE EFFORT——————16335 LBS.

ENGINE N°2176

TYPE O-6-O

LATE B.P.&G.V.R. N°7.

No. 7 *Pembrey* was a much better balanced looking engine, as can be seen in this 1909 view at Burry Port.   *LPC 3140*

As GWR No. 2176, and now nameless, the engine is seen inside Llanelly engine shed *circa* 1937.
Real Photographs 353

valve rods enter the cylinder casting, was quite new having been developed following the introduction of superheated steam. The traditional 'soft' packing consisted of asbestos strips dipped in tallow and coiled around an India rubber core.

The locomotive ordered was remarkably different from existing BP&GV saddle tank designs in that it was a handsomely proportioned side tank with 15 in. by 22 in. outside cylinders, 3 ft 9 in. wheels and a wheelbase of 10 ft 9 in. It is possible to discern the influence of the engineer H.F. Stephens in this order. Stephens had had some mechanical experience as a pupil of J.J. Hanbury at the Neasden works of the Metropolitan in 1888-90, and he was locomotive superintendent of several of the lines of which he was also Engineer, so he will have been aware of metallic packing. Although his lines are associated with the purchase of old, second-hand locomotives, there were several new engines on such as the Selsey Tramway (1897), Rother Valley Railway (1900) and Bere Alston & Calstock Light Railway (1908) which were all smart and well-proportioned side tanks with outside cylinders.

The detailed design work of the new 0-6-0T was left to Hudswell, Clarke & Co. It was the maker's No. 871 and was dispatched on 24th March, 1909 as BP&GV No. 8 with the name *Pioneer*. As a passenger engine she was fitted with the Gresham combination vacuum ejector and steam brake valve with the Vacuum Brake Co.'s train braking. She was painted in 'Midland' red, with similar lining to the Avonsides except the corners were indented. The finish included a copper-capped chimney, brass dome and brass ring between smokebox and boiler. Unfortunately when first delivered this locomotive developed a propensity for running 'hot' resulting in the Directors insisting, on 20th August, 1909, that the maker's should put her 'into proper working order'. In November 1914 the boiler was dispatched to Hudswell, Clarke for a new firebox to be fitted.

When *Pioneer* was taken into GWR stock in September 1922 she was undergoing an overhaul in the Burry Port workshops. It would appear that the Swindon authorities halted work for a time whilst they appraised the situation as it was not until 9th April, 1924 that she emerged, renumbered 2197 and with the boiler numbered 176. She was smartly repainted in green and lined out in a simplified style but whether the green was the Brunswick shade as used by the GWR is not known. She was unlettered except for the GWR initials on the new number plates, fixed on the cabside instead of the maker's plates which had been moved to the bunker to replace the BP&GV number plates. She retained her original safety valves and dome but was fitted with a new smokebox and GWR copper-capped chimney, also GWR lamp fixings. It was not until light repairs at Swindon on 24th March, 1928 that she received her GWR style safety valve casing; the diagram B11 depicted her in this condition. Other major repairs were all at Caerphilly, on 19th July, 1934 (cost £511), 16th February, 1938 (£691), 11th October, 1943 and finally on 14th November, 1947 when the large initials 'G' and 'W' were applied, one each side of the central nameplate. These initials remained to the end. On 1st September, 1931 this engine was posted to Kidderminster for working the Ditton Priors branch as both the regular locomotives were being repaired. After this, on 22nd February, 1932 it was next

B¹¹

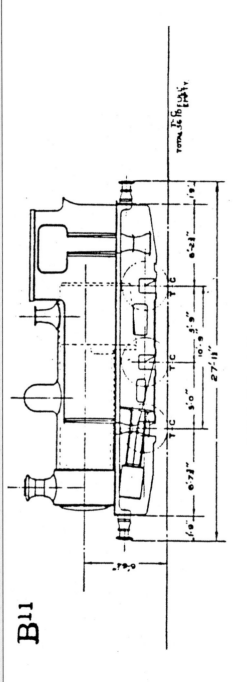

—DESCRIPTION—

CYLINDERS	DIAR.15" STROKE 22" STEAM PORTS EXHAUST
BOILER	BARREL 9'-1" DIAR. OUTS. 4'-6⅝. 4'-0".
FIREBOX	OUTS.5'-0¾"X3'-11".INS. 4'-5"X3'-4". HEIGHT 4'-7" 8.4'-0".
TUBES	N°163.DIAM.1⅞" LENGTH 9'-4⅛"
HEATING SURFACE	TUBES 749.8 SQ.FT.FIREBOX 76.50 SQ.FT.TOTAL 826.3 SQ.FT
AREA OF FIREGRATE	14.80 SQ.FT.
WHEELS	LEADING 3'-9".DRIVING 3'-9". TRAILING 3'-9".
WATER CAPACITY OF TANKS	800 GALLONS.
WORKING PRESSURE	160 LBS.
TRACTIVE EFFORT	14960 LBS.

—ENGINE N° 2197—

—TYPE 0-6-0 T—

—LATE B.P.&G.V.R. N° 9—

The first of the new breed of side tanks, No. 8 *Pioneer*, is resplendent in her red livery at Burry Port about 1910.   *Author's Collection*

A nice broadside view of *Pioneer* as GWR No. 2197 at Pontardulais in 1948.
                                                                    Author's Collection

A110

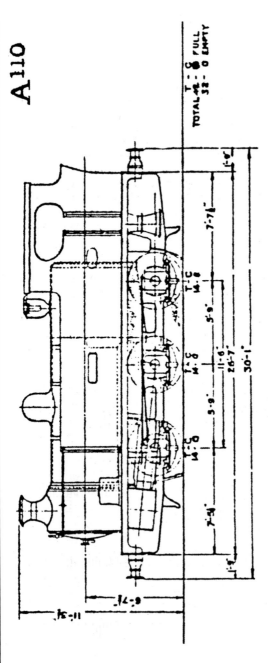

— DESCRIPTION —

Cylinders	DIAR: 16" STROKE 24." 3 STEAM PORTS EXHAUST
Boiler	BARREL 10'-1". DIAR: OUTS: 4'-2".
Firebox	OUTS: INS: 4'-11½" X 3'-5". HEIGHT 4'-10"& 4'-3".
Tubes	Nº 167 DIAR: 1⅞". LENGTH
Heating Surface	TUBES 830.03 SQ:FT: FIREBOX 88.41 SQ:FT: TOTAL 918.44 SQ:FT:
Area of Firegrate	18.87 SQ: FT:
Wheels	LEADING 3'-2". DRIVING 3'-2". TRAILING 3'-0".
Water Capacity of Tanks	1000 GALLONS.
Working Pressure	180 LBS:
Tractive Effort	18570 LBS:

BURRY PORT & G.V. Rʸ

— ENGINE Nº 9

to Llanelly and she remained here to the end, although outstationed at Burry Port from February to April 1942 and at other times. The end came on 27th October, 1952, having run 278,378 miles since April 1924 and she was broken up at Caerphilly, still with her original tanks and bunker and displaying her maker's plates, during the week ending 21st February, 1953.

The passenger service was less than a month old when a second Hudswell, Clarke locomotive was ordered, this time a larger machine. The quotation of £1,750 was accepted by the Directors on 30th August, 1909 and the maker's No. 893 was dispatched from Leeds on 30th November, as BP&GV No. 9; she was without a name as would be all future deliveries. Although larger, she was still a handsome, well proportioned 0-6-0T in the same red livery with copper-capped chimney and polished brass dome; the number plate was positioned in the centre of the side tanks as there was no name plate. The outside cylinders were 16 in. by 24 in., the wheels the now standard 3 ft 9 in. diameter and the wheelbase 11 ft 6 in. The capacity of the water tanks was increased from 800 to 1,000 gallons. Clearly she was intended for harder work than jogging along with a light passenger train, even though vacuum brakes were fitted.

Coming to the GWR in September 1922 she became No. 2163, with her boiler being numbered 513. She underwent heavy repairs at Neath, completed on 4th March, 1925, and her details were recorded on diagram A110. She was very little altered; apart from her new livery (her dome was now painted over) and her change of number plates, she now had GWR buffers and lamp brackets plus a connecting strap over the top of the boiler just in front of the dome attached to the top of each side-tank. She was sent to the Prince of Wales Dock shed in Swansea in December 1925, was transferred to Neath in October 1926 then was back in Burry Port the following December.

BP&GV No. 9 became GWR No. 2163 but, apart from the new numberplate and lamp brackets, is largely unaltered in this picture taken by H.L. Hopwood inside Neath shed on 12th August, 1924.   *LCGB Ken Nunn Collection H4040*

Old No. 10 is also virtually unaltered except for the No. 2198 GWR numberplate in this 1923 picture.   *R. Daniels Collection*

No. 2198 was much altered by her Swindon 1927 rebuilding, as seen in this 1955 view taken in Llanelly shed.   *Real Photographs R5561*

On 31st March, 1928 she came out of Swindon after overhaul looking quite different. She now had new tanks, extended bunker, smokebox and chimney, Western type safety valves and cover, whilst the number plates were moved from the tanks to the bunker sides and she lost the lubricator behind the chimney. She still had her original boiler and dome, however. Further overhauls were performed at Swindon on 31st March, 1937, and at Caerphilly on 29th April, 1932 plus 6th August, 1941, but without any additional changes. In July 1928 she was transferred to Llanelly shed, spending periods outstationed at Burry Port such as in January 1934 and at the beginning of 1938. In the earlier part of World War II she was loaned to the Ministry of Supply working at the Pembrey Ordnance Factory - between 28th August, 1940 and 30th April, 1941 - then she was sent back to Burry Port on 6th August, 1941 where she remained until condemned on 4th March, 1944. She was credited with having covered 268,130 miles since September 1922 and she was broken up at Caerphilly during April 1944.

The next locomotive, No. 10, was delivered from Hudswell, Clarke (their No. 924) on 5th December, 1910 at a cost of £1,695. The quotation had been discussed by the Board on 28th June but the decision taken then was to postpone placing the order just for the present. She was like No. 9 *Pioneer* but with the wheelbase increased from 10 ft 9 in. to 12 ft 6 in. Not only did this allow the boiler barrel to be lengthened from 9 ft 1 in. to 9 ft 7 in., it allowed the rear of the firebox to clear the rear axle so that the grate could be flat instead of sloping. Another difference was that the leaf springs for the front axle were placed above the footplate. The brake apparatus remained the same but there was a reversion to the green livery. She was regularly used on passenger services and a new firebox was fitted during 1916 at a cost of about £400.

In September 1922 she became GWR No. 2198 and her boiler was numbered 499; diagram B12 was prepared which showed an incorrect wheelbase of 12 ft 9 in.; this was corrected when the next diagram, B40, was issued after her rebuilding. For this she was sent to Swindon works in December 1923 but it was not until 24th February, 1927 (over three years later) that she emerged freshly rebuilt with a new modified 'U' class Belpaire boiler No. R499. This was similar to the one built for No. 2176 (BP&GV 7) except that the barrel was 8 inches longer. She also had new smokebox, tanks, extended bunker, buffers, crosshead vacuum pump (right side only) and of course chimney, dome and safety valves. The number plate was transferred to the bunker sides and the lettering 'GREAT WESTERN' applied to the tanks.

No. 2198 was posted to Llanelly shed on 9th March, 1934 where she officially remained; however, she was outstationed at the sub-shed at Pantyffynnon for two years (October 1935 to September 1937) and also at times at Burry Port, as she was in September 1939 and December 1947. All other major overhauls were at Caerphilly works, completed on 19th May, 1933, 30th August, 1938, 1st October, 1943, 9th September, 1947 and 28th May, 1952; on this last repair she was fitted with a smokebox number plate. When she was sent to Caerphilly on 9th June, 1958 for inspection she was by then the last of the BP&GV locomotives still in service (not counting *Pontyberem* at Mountain Ash Colliery) but unexpectedly she was given a heavy repair completed on 1st August looking very smart repainted in black with the second style of British Railways emblem

B12

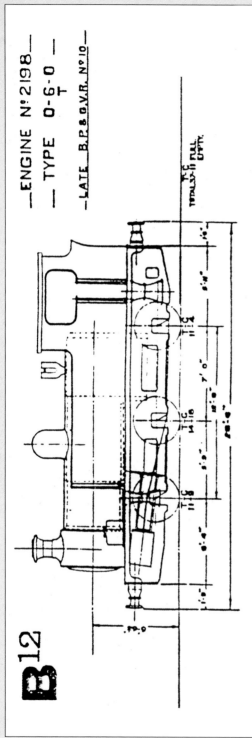

ENGINE Nº 2198

TYPE 0-6-0$_T$

LATE B.P.&G.V.R. Nº 10

T.C. TOTAL 33'-11" FULL EMPTY.

DESCRIPTION

CYLINDERS——————DIAR. 15. STROKE 22". STEAM PORTS   EXHAUST

BOILER——————BARREL 9'-7" DIAR. OUTS. 4-1⁄8 & 4'-0⁄4".

FIREBOX——————OUTS. 5-0⁄4" X 3'-9⁄4 INS. 4'-5" X 3'-2⁄4" HEIGHT 4'-7".

TUBES——————Nº 163. DIAR⁄4". LENGTH 9'-10 1⁄2".

HEATING SURFACE——————TUBES 791·5 SQ.FT. FIREBOX 81·0 SQ.FT. TOTAL 872·5 SQ.FT.

AREA OF FIREGRATE——————14·00 SQ.FT.

WHEELS——————LEADING 3'-9". DRIVING 3'-9". TRAILING 3'-9".

WATER CAPACITY OF TANKS——800 GALLONS.

WORKING PRESSURE——————160 LBS.

TRACTIVE EFFORT——————14960   LBS.

The 1922 weight diagram of GWR No. 2198 showing the flat grate and incorrect wheelbase.

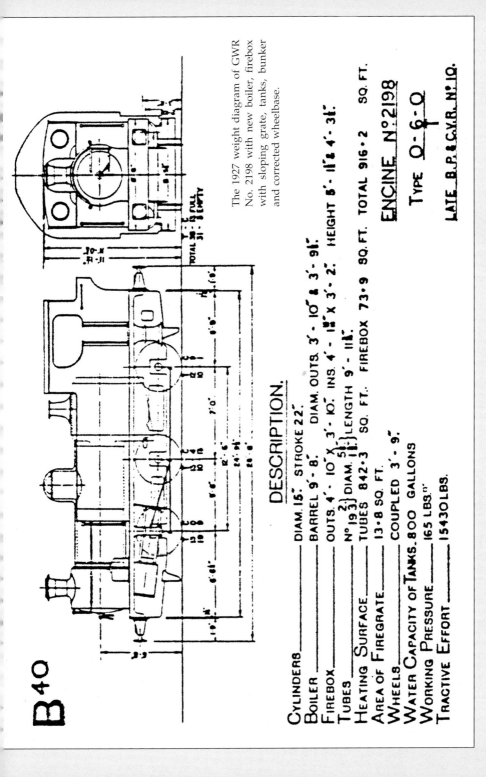

B40

The 1927 weight diagram of GWR No. 2198 with new boiler, firebox with sloping grate, tanks, bunker and corrected wheelbase.

DESCRIPTION.

CYLINDERS — DIAM. 15". STROKE 22".

BOILER — BARREL 9'-8". DIAM. OUTS 3'-10" & 3'-9½".

FIREBOX — OUTS. 4'-10" X 3'-10". INS. 4'-1½" X 3'-2". HEIGHT 5'-11½ & 4'-3½".

TUBES — N° 193 DIAM. 1⅝". (2) DIAM. 5". LENGTH 9'-11½".

HEATING SURFACE — TUBES 842.3 SQ. FT. FIREBOX 73.9 SQ. FT. TOTAL 916.2 SQ. FT.

AREA OF FIREGRATE — 13.8 SQ. FT.

WHEELS — COUPLED 3'-9".

WATER CAPACITY OF TANKS. 800 GALLONS

WORKING PRESSURE — 165 LBS."

TRACTIVE EFFORT — 15430 LBS.

ENGINE N°. 2198

TYPE 0-6-0

LATE B.P. & G.V.R. N°. 19.

G.W.R.
ENGINE HISTORY.

No. **2198** Engine.

B.67.10

BUILT	*1910* AT *Hudswell Clarke* LOT
Type	*0.6.0.T* Cost £ *1698* (Including £ for Boiler. ......) Tank Capacity *800*
Weight { Empty *29 10*	Tractive Effort *11960* Cylinders *15 x 22*
W.O. *37 11*	

REPAIRS.

Tender Attached	Date Stopped	Date set to work	No. of days stopped	Station	Date Report received	Classification of Repair and Miles	Boiler Change or Renewal
						H8 18,137 20,335	499 R499
19	4 29	25 5 29	36	Burry Port	8 6 29	L	
13 8 29	17 9 29	35	do	28 9 29	R	
14 1 30	1 2 30		do		R	
8 3 30	24 3 30	44		12 4 30	R	
31 6 30	9 8 30	46	do	30 8 30	R	
2 2 31	7 4 31	64	Carmarthen	11 4 31	L	
29 10 31	15 12 31	47	Burry Port	19 12 31	R	
24 5 32	2 6 32	34	Carmarthen	2 7 32	L	
11 10 32	26 10 32	15	Burry Port	19 11 32	R	
9 32	5 1 33	27		14 1 33	R	
24 3 33	19 5 33	56	Caerphilly Fac	19 6 33	I	102,430
9 3 34	8 5 34	60	Llanelly	2 6 34	R	
28 12 34	15 1 35	18	"	9 2 35	R	
35	16 10 35	91		19 10 35	R	
11 12 35	2 1 36	22	Pantyffynnon	11 1 36	R	
11 5 36	20 6 36	40	"	27 6 36	R	
18 37	3 9 37	108		18 9 37	R	
27 6 38	30 8 38	64	" Caerphilly Fac	27 9 38	I	181,487
23 1 41	3 2 41	11	"	1 2 41	R	
2 42	9 3 42	47	"	21 3 42	L	
19 1 43	24 4 42	36	"	3 10 42	R	
29 3 43	22 5 43	54	"	12 6 43	R	
28 6 43	1 10 43	95	" Caerphilly Fac 9/8		I	251,585
21 3 45	9 4 45	19	"		R	
10 11 45	13	"		R	
22 7 46	13 3 46		Burry Port		R	
6 12 46	20 12 46	14	"		R	
11 5 47	9 9 4	121	Llanelly Caerphilly 18/6 Fac/7 Cast 3/12 Fac/12		I	311,998
14 11 47	7 1 48	54			L	
4 4 48	6 5 48	32	" 574		R	
27 8 49	10 49	43	"		U	
18 2 50	5 8 50	20	"		U	

Part of the GWR engine history card for No. 2198.

on her tanks. Unfortunately, seven months later (on 28th February) she cracked a cylinder block and was withdrawn on 2nd March, 1959. Her mileage (since September 1922) was 437,705 and she was broken up at Swindon during the week ending 16th May, 1959. According to the Engine History a maker's plate was purchased by Mr K.M. Buckle in March 1959 although none would appear to have been carried on the locomotive since 1927.

Growing traffic meant that even more locomotive power was required so on 18th September, 1911 another engine was ordered from Hudswell, Clarke & Co., the tendered price being £1,810 and payment was to be in two halves - the first by 30th June and the second before 31st December, 1912; delivery was promised for early that year. She was the maker's No. 969 and she was delivered as BP&GV No. 11 on 15th January, 1912 in the green livery with brass dome and back smokebox ring plus copper-capped chimney. She had the same boiler as No. 9 but the wheelbase had been lengthened by 13 inches which enabled the firebox to have a flat grate; the tanks, cab and bunker were all set back a similar amount in the frames, thus widening the cab space (between firebox and bunker) which the enginemen greatly appreciated. The leading springs were placed above the footplate as on No. 10. These were the last alterations to the design of BP&GV locomotives; all subsequent ones ordered were exactly the same as No. 11.

At Grouping this engine became GWR No. 2164 in September 1922 and her details were recorded on diagram A109. She was transferred to Neath shed about February 1927; then, in December 1928, she was sent to Swindon works for overhaul but, after examination, it was decided that further expense was not justified and she was withdrawn in February 1929, being cut-up at Swindon the following month. Her mileage as a GWR engine was quoted as 80,141. Unfortunately her GWR Engine History card has not survived, presumably because of her early demise, so that it is not possible to quote her GWR boiler number or any repair details. However, she was not greatly altered apart from repainting (including the dome) with the words 'GREAT' and 'WESTERN' on either side of her new number plates, GWR style buffers and lamp brackets, and a strap over the boiler connecting the side tanks as was done on No. 2163 (BP&GV 9). This would suggest that she had been repaired at Neath but there is no confirmation.

With passenger services due to be extended to Cwmmawr early next year the Board decided on 19th September, 1912 that it was time to enter negotiations with Hudswell, Clarke & Co. for a new locomotive to cost approximately £1,870 for delivery next May, with a first payment of £1,000 in June and the balance payable in Sept 1913. They were far too optimistic about the price, and had to agree to the cost being £2,075. Note that no attempt was now being made to go through the motions of obtaining competitive tenders; clearly the BP&GV was happy to stick with this existing design. So Hudswell, Clarke No. 1024 was dispatched from Leeds as promised on 24th May, 1913 as BP&GV No. 12 and was identical to No. 11. In September 1922 she became GWR No. 2165 and her boiler was numbered 321, with details on diagram A109.

She entered Swindon works on 21st April, 1926 and was kept waiting for a whole year before the decision was taken to rebuild her completely with a new

BP&GV No. 11 was new in 1912 and photographed outside Burry Port shed on 15th May, 1919.
LCGB Ken Nunn Collection 2213

The next engine, No. 12, came in 1913. With the driver and fireman sitting on the sandbox, the three young cleaners look pleased with their work. Burry Port about 1920.   *J. Harper*

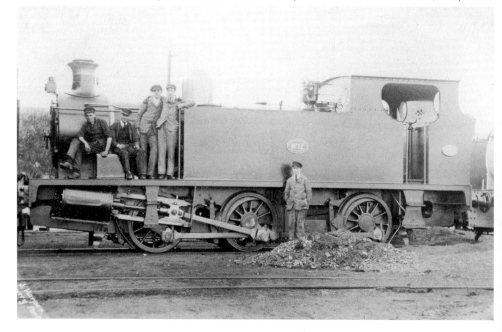

boiler, the same as that just fitted to No. 2162 (ex-BP&GV No. 2, the next engine to be detailed). This boiler was a modified version of the GWR class 'LA' (or standard No. 11) parallel Belpaire boiler as used on the ex-Midland & South Western Junction Railway 2-4-0s Nos. 1334-36 and later (with altered smokebox) on the '5400' class tanks. The modifications consisted of a shortening of the barrel by 4½ inches and a reduction in the height at the front of the inner firebox by five inches with a sloping grate. This new boiler was given the number C321 and other alterations included a new extended bunker, chimney, dome, safety valves and crosshead driven (on right-hand side only) vacuum pump; the original side tanks were retained.

No. 2165 received heavy repairs at Caerphilly works on 3rd April, 1932, 4th July, 1940 and 2nd July, 1945. In the 1940 repair she was also fitted up with the necessary equipment to be used as a stationary boiler in the event of a wartime emergency, in particular to be able to operate pit-head winding gear. In the event she was never called upon to perform such a duty. She was last overhauled at Swindon on 20th October, 1948, but was not given a smokebox number plate. On 3rd April, 1932 the engine was sent to Neath shed, but returned to Burry Port the following month, then was officially posted to Llanelly on 26th September, 1935. Here she was from time to time outstationed at Burry Port, for example in September 1939 and December 1947, and at Sandy (from July to September 1938). She was at Burry Port when withdrawn on 17th March, 1955 with 446,864 miles since September 1922 to her credit, and she was sent to the Swindon pool where she was scrapped during the week ending 21st May, 1955.

Becoming GWR No. 2165, old No. 12 was rebuilt at Swindon in 1927 and is seen at Llanelly in the Summer of 1949.   *Author*

On 12th November, 1913 the Board decided that *Pontyberem*, with its 14 inch diameter cylinders, which needed heavy repairs and had become too small, should be sold and tenders be invited for a replacement 16 inch locomotive. The result was that the new number 2 was dispatched by Hudswell, Clarke & Co (maker's No. 1066) on 30th April, 1914. The quotation was for £2,200 but only £2,197 was paid as she did not have a copper-capped chimney. She also had a painted dome and back smokebox ring. She became GWR No. 2162 in September 1922 and the boiler was given the number 380. Then in January 1924 she was sent to Swindon works and there was kept waiting for over three years for the decision to be made to rebuild her with a modified 'LA' Belpaire boiler (as on No. 2165) No. R380 together with new side tanks, extended bunker, chimney, dome, safety valves plus right-hand crosshead vacuum pump. Unusually she retained her Hudswell, Clarke maker's plates on the bunker and had the GWR plates on the cabsides. She left works in this condition on 21st April, 1927 and returned to Burry Port.

There were major repairs, all undertaken at Caerphilly works, completed on 28th May, 1931 (at a cost of £527), 10th May, 1937 (almost identical costing of £526), 6th March, 1942 (probably when the sliding cab shutters were fitted), 22nd December, 1945 and lastly on 25th February, 1949. On this last occasion she was repainted in British Railways black complete with smokebox number plate. In July 1928 she was officially transferred to Llanelly shed where she remained for the rest of her career, spending frequent intervals outstationed at times to Burry Port as in January 1930, January 1938, September 1939 and March 1955; she also spent a month or so at Landore (Swansea) in August-September 1948. She was withdrawn on 15th March, 1955 whilst at Burry Port, having completed 432,519 miles since September 1922, and was scrapped at Swindon during the week ending 21st May, 1955.

A new locomotive was completed by Hudswell, Clarke (No. 1222), but just as it was ready to be sent to Burry Port on 20th October, 1916 it was commandeered by the War Office. However, just over a month later, the new engine was released and finally came to Burry Port on 25th November, 1916. Unfortunately, due to inflation, the cost had risen to £3,008. She received the number 13 and, apart from the number plates, was devoid of any polished brass or copper work. She was, however, fully vacuum-fitted. BP&GV No. 13 duly became GWR No. 2166 in September 1922, her boiler being numbered 328. She was sent to Kitson & Co., Leeds on 7th January, 1925 for overhaul under Lot 238 at a cost of £2,005, returning to Burry Port on 28th May, 1925 with her appearance unaltered except the number plates were on the bunker and GWR style lamp brackets were fitted. Subsequent major repairs were completed at Caerphilly on 28th September, 1929, 7th March, 1933, 13th October, 1936 and 3rd September, followed on 15th June, 1945 at Wolverhampton (the only known visit by an ex-BP&GV locomotive) and finally on 21st January, 1949 at Swindon. A GWR chimney was fitted in or by 1933, later she lost her vacuum brake connections and a smokebox number plate was attached in 1949 ; otherwise she was hardly altered, retaining her original boiler, tanks, bunker, dome and even safety valves (without cover) till the end. Regarding allocation, she was posted to Neath shed in July 1928, spending part of the time at the sub-shed at Riverside (the former Neath & Brecon Railway shed) before being transferred in November 1929 to Swansea East Dock - her last depôt - where I managed to see

The next engine, No. 13, became GWR No. 2166 and was observed working at Swansea East Dock in October 1949. *Author*

her on 29th October, 1949. She was there condemned on 10th May, 1955, having covered 509,393 miles since May 1925, the highest figure recorded for any BP&GV locomotive, and was sent to the Swindon pool from where she was cut up during the week ending 16th July, 1955.

A replacement for No. 5 *Cwm Mawr*, which was to be sold, was ordered on 16th October, 1918 from Hudswell, Clarke & Co.; the quoted price had rocketed to no less than £4,185 due to the high rate of inflation at that period. The maker's No. 1385 was completed and dispatched on 22nd August, 1919 as BP&GV No. 5 but, as soon as she was received at Burry Port, her number was altered to 14. A big increase in the amount of traffic at the dock following the end of the war caused the railway to change its decision and keep the older locomotive after all. She was in the plain livery without any polished brass or copper. On coming to the GWR in September 1922 she was renumbered 2167, her boiler becoming No. 158. She received a heavy overhaul at Carmarthen on 8th May, 1924, but her appearance was hardly altered. She entered Swindon works on 5th March, 1928 and was rebuilt, emerging on 21st September that year with a modified 'LA' Belpaire boiler No. R158, new smokebox, chimney, dome and safety valves, new tanks, extended bunker and right-hand crosshead pump; the number plates were now on the bunker sides.

No. 2167 received major repairs on 18th August, 1932, 21st January, 1938, 10th October, 1945 and 29th October, 1948, all at Caerphilly except that in 1938 which was at Swindon. She also received a light repair at Caerphilly on 15th November, 1940 when she received the modifications to be able to operate colliery winding gear in an emergency. Regarding allocations, she was sent to Carmarthen shed on 21th September, 1928, then moved to Llanelly in December 1931. Like other locomotives attached to Llanelly, she was from time to time outstationed at Burry Port, as in January 1934, September 1939 and December 1947. She was withdrawn whilst at Llanelly on 9th February, 1953, still without a smokebox number plate.

The last new locomotive to be built for the BP&GV, No. 14, is seen at Burry Port in 1920 still in wartime austerity finish without polished brasswork.   *Author's Collection*

Becoming GWR No. 2167, old No. 14 is here standing outside Llanelly shed on 4th August, 1951.
R. C. Riley

Her mileage was recorded as 428,062 since September 1922 and she was sent to Swindon where she was broken up during the week ending 13th June, 1953.

The locomotive just described was the last to be obtained new by the railway but one more of the standard design was added to stock which had been built for the line but was actually obtained second-hand. As detailed in Chapter Four, an engine had been ordered in February 1915 but requisitioned by the Ministry of Munitions when completed by Hudswell, Clarke & Co. on 24th February, 1916. This was the maker's No. 1164 which, after completing her Government service, was released and returned to Hudswell, Clarke in February 1920. After being put in good order she was offered to the BP&GV for £2,800, who accepted and in May was duly dispatched to Burry Port as the new No. 15, becoming the sixth member of her class on the railway.

She became GWR No. 2168 in September 1922, with her boiler numbered 226. She was sent to the Swindon factory on 31st August, 1926 and emerged in rebuilt form on 18th May, 1927. Her new Belpaire boiler No. R226 was of the modified 'Metro' or 'LA' pattern, and she had a new smokebox, chimney, dome, extended bunker and right-hand crosshead-driven vacuum pump. It was this latter feature that made the characteristic 'spitting' sound when the engine was moving. She appears to have retained her original side tanks which were lettered 'GREAT WESTERN' and the number plates were moved to the cab sides. Major repairs were completed on 6th October, 1931, 13th April, 1937, 21st June, 1941 and 30th May, 1945 - all at Caerphilly - plus 20th December, 1948 at Swindon and finally on 13th January, 1954 at Caerphilly. On this last occasion she was repainted in black with the second style of British Railways' emblem on her tanks plus a smokebox number plate. A curiosity of her 1945 overhaul was that she received the latest Brunswick green livery with the initials 'G W R' positioned just below the horizontal centre line of the tanks and thus out of line with the number plates. Perhaps the painter at Caerphilly was short in stature! There seems no obvious reason, indeed the insignia were perfectly placed on the centre line in the 1927, 1954 and other repaintings. On 12th June, 1923 No. 2168 was transferred to Neath shed, but returned to Burry Port on 19th December that year. Then in July 1928 she was posted to Llanelly, where she remained to the end but, like many of the inhabitants of Llanelly shed, she was quite often to be found outstationed at Burry Port, as she was in January 1934, December 1937, September 1939 and December 1947. She was at Burry Port on 28th May, 1956 when she was condemned, being credited with having worked 479,839 miles since September 1922, and was dispatched to Swindon where she was broken up in the week ending 17th July, 1956.

In 1921 the Directors decided to have one of their engines overhauled by one of the manufacturers and quotations were invited. These were considered on 21st June and a contract for '£1,140 for heavy locomotive repairs' was approved. Unfortunately the identity of the engine concerned is not revealed in the surviving minute books and reports of the railway, but I believe it to be No. 9 that was sent to Hudswell, Clarke in Leeds for repair. This suggestion should be treated with caution without further corroboration, however. On 23rd January, 1922 the Board further authorized the 'usual extras amounting to £227 to [the] locomotive under contract repairs at Leeds'. Again there is no explanation as to what these 'usual extras' might be.

Ordered by the BP&GV, this engine was requisitioned by the Government on completion in 1916 and sent to the Shoeburyness Military Tramway, where she is seen together with a load of celebratory troops on Armistice Day, 11th November, 1918.   *NEL*

Released by the Government, the locomotive became BP&GV No. 15 in 1920, then GWR No. 2168, and here is waiting by Burry Port engine shed in August 1948.   *Author's Collection*

The GWR assumed responsibility for the working of the BP&GV system on 1st July, 1922, although it was not until the four-weekly period ending on 8th October that the BP&GV locomotives were taken into GWR stock. The engine shed at Burry Port came under the control of the Llanelly shedmaster, An allocation of around eight to 10 or so engines was retained at Burry Port with additions, which were changed rather more frequently, being supplied by Llanelly from its own pool. With so many of the BP&GV engines spending so much of the early post-Grouping years either awaiting or undergoing repairs (in February 1925 there were no less than nine inactive out of the 15, mostly at Swindon), there was an urgent need to send replacements to work from Burry Port. The newcomers were of three generally similar classes, all originally built and designed as 0-6-0 saddle tanks at Wolverhampton; the GWR '850', '1901' and '2021' classes of which a large number had been rebuilt since 1910 with Belpaire boilers and pannier tanks.

The '850' class dated from 1874-77 and originally had 4 ft 0 in. wheels, a wheelbase of 13 ft 8 in. and 15 in. cylinders. The '1901' class were built between 1881 and 1895, had different boilers, 4 ft 1½ in. wheels and 16 in. by 24 in. cylinders. By 1922 they were virtually the same class, all having the larger wheels and cylinders. The main difference was the wheels with the '850s' having wrought-iron wheels with round section spokes whereas the later engines had cast-iron wheels with 'H' section spokes. The '2021' class, built 1897 to 1905, had a longer wheelbase of 14 ft 8 in. (the longest on the BP&GV engines was 13 ft 7 in.) so as to accommodate a larger firebox, also having 16½ in. cylinders and steel wheels. This longer wheelbase meant that the '2021s' were not as popular as the older classes over the sharp curves of the BP&GV, despite their increase in power, so were never very common.

In June 1922 Nos. 989, 1907, 1926, 1981, 2111 and 2134 were stationed at Llanelly, with 859 arriving soon after. At this period the four with the highest numbers were still saddle tanks, but were soon converted and it is believed that only the pannier rebuilds were to be seen at Burry Port after about 1928. An arrival at Burry Port shed in June 1923 was No. 26, the former GVR Hudswell, Clarke inside cylinder 0-6-0ST transferred from Kidwelly when that shed was closed; by all accounts she continued to work to Kidwelly and Mynydd-y-Garrer for a few years but in 1927 was sent away to Neath and was sold early the following year, eventually reaching Uruguay.

Reverting to the '850/1901' class pannier tanks, those known definitely to have worked over the BP&GV in the late 1920s include Nos. 861, 872, 1916, 1920, 1979 and 1988. In January 1934 Nos. 1907, 1929, 1936, 1937, 1978, 1979 and 2002 were all allocated to Burry Port with Nos. 859, 872, 997, 1941, 1948, 1988, 1991 and 2018 in the back-up stock at Llanelly. Most of these engines had the back of their cabs open to the elements except Nos. 859, 872, 989 and 1948 which had backs with spectacle plates fitted. One other engine, of a completely different class, which was at Llanelly at this period and which might have been expected to have been tried out over the BP&GV, was No. 1371. She was the last of the '1366' class of 0-6-0PT which had outside cylinders 16 in. by 20 in., 3 ft 8 in. wheels and an 11 ft 0 in. wheelbase. Built at Swindon in February 1934, she was sent new to Llanelly and remained there for over two years before moving on to Danygraig.

Inside Llanelly shed on 31st May, 1936 is GWR '850' class pannier tank No. 872; she was withdrawn less than four months later.   *F.K. Davies*

No. 2012 was a member of the '1901' class and had been converted to a pannier tank as early as 1910. She was stationed at Burry Port in 1938 and again in 1947. Note the flat-faced 'H' section wheel spokes.   *LPC 4311*

During 1935-36 Nos. 872, 1929, 1936 and 1978 were all withdrawn; newcomers to Burry Port shed by the end of 1937 included Nos. 1903, 1988, 1991 and 2012 (only 1903 and 2012 had backs to their cabs), 2002 was still here. Looking at Burry Port's allocation at the end of 1947, we find six of the '1901s' working here - No. 1907 had returned and Nos. 2002 and 2012 were joined by 1957, 1967 (both with enclosed cabs) and 2019 (with backless cab); soon after No. 1991 also returned. By 1951 all of these old stagers had left the district, to be replaced for a short period by some of Llanelly's '2021s', followed by the first new locomotives to come to Burry Port since 1919. Nos. 2027, 2081 and 2126 were all working here in 1949-51, indeed No. 2081 was unusually sent from Burry Port to Derby for repairs, returning on 28th November, 1949 with an LMS style smokebox number plate.

The new engines were introduced from 1949 by British Railways as a modernised version of the '2021' class, enabling the older engines to be withdrawn. The replacements were called the '1600' class and had the same general dimensions; indeed the main differences were to be found in the more modern Collett style cab with a rounded roof and the footplate raised so as to be level with the tops of the buffer beams, resulting in shallower splashers. There was a slight reduction in water capacity (875 instead of 900 gallons) but the wheelbase remained unaltered at 14 ft 8 in. In November and December 1949 Nos. 1607, 1609, 1614 and 1618 were sent new to Llanelly and the latter three certainly were soon working from Burry Port, No. 1614 being so noted on 5th August, 1950. They were followed by several of the 1950-51 built batch, including Nos. 1633 and 1638, also later 1623 and 1644. More of this class were built in 1954-55 (at Swindon, like the others) and Nos. 1654, 1655 and 1666 were those that were delivered to Burry Port brand new. The last of the old brigade, No. 2168 (formerly BP&GV 15) was condemned at Burry Port on 28th May, 1956 and sent off to Swindon for scrapping, leaving No. 2198 (old BP&GV 10) working from Llanelly shed as the sole survivor. However, we should not forget to mention No. 2120, the last built of the '1901' class of pannier tanks, which the GWR had sold in January 1939 to the Amalgamated Anthracite

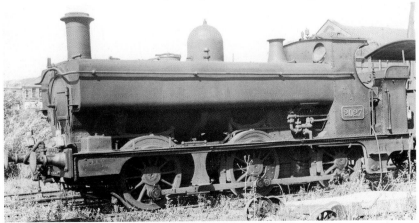

No. 2027 of the larger '2021' class is seen in the sunshine at Burry Port on 4th August, 1951.   *R. C. Riley*

Collieries Ltd at Ammanford Colliery, and had been transferred to Trimsaran Colliery by July 1944 and remained there until scrapped under NCB ownership some time between March 1957 and May 1958.

By 1959 there were no less than 17 of the '1600' class panniers at Llanelly, of which from 8 to 10 would normally be deployed over the BP&GV lines. Burry Port engine shed closed in March 1962 and henceforth all the engines were now kept at Llanelly. Steam working finally ceased on 1st November, 1965; only Nos. 1607, 1623, 1643, 1651 and 1669 remained in the last few months and all were promptly withdrawn when diesel traction took over all workings. No. 1607 was sold in 1965 in full working order to the NCB at Cynheidre Colliery, just north of Llanelli (the new spelling was adopted in 1966); unfortunately she was scrapped after suffering a cracked frame in 1969. Meanwhile No. 1638 - which had arrived new at Burry Port but subsequently had moved north to Croes Newydd - was also sold in running order to the Dart Valley Railway in 1967. After several years operating in Devon she was resold in 1992 to the Kent & East Sussex Railway and is thus the second locomotive to be preserved which had BP&GV associations.

Although 1st November is usually given as the date that steam working from Llanelli ceased, it is believed that diesel locomotives took over on the BP&GV line slightly earlier, on 4th October, 1965. Landore Diesel depôt (Swansea) was now responsible; six of their 204 hp Gardner-engined 0-6-0 diesel-mechanical engines, Nos. D2141 to D2146, were modified to enable them to be worked cab-to-cab in pairs by one driver, thus requiring 12 cable connections between each pair. They also had the cab roof and exhaust chimneys reduced in height by 4½ inches from 11 ft 10 in. and electric headlamps fitted front and rear. These locomotives had been built at Swindon in 1961-62 and had a top speed of 28 mph, more than enough for the BP&GV overall limit of 25 mph. The larger 350 hp diesel-electric locomotives (later known as class '08') were considered unsuitable as the low-slung electric motors could be damaged when using any flooded stretch of line (which could occur quite frequently). At first just one pair of the 204 hp diesels was used on the service of up to four trains each way per day, but as many of the trains had to be split into two to climb the steep bank up to Cwmmawr, a third locomotive was later rostered to bank the empty trains with the returning train of loaded wagons being triple-headed. The third engine also increased the braking power available. The three engines actually in use were normally stabled at the Llanelli goods yard (not the old steam shed) and only returned to Landore for attention or replacement.

No. D2146 had gone from Landore by July 1967 and D2143 followed in June 1968, both going into store pending withdrawal. They were replaced by Nos. D2119, D2120 and D2121, the latter two being fitted with radio telephones. This equipment was soon added to the others. About this time the locomotives were repainted in the blue livery and, from October 1968, the 'D' prefix to the numbers was omitted; they were also given the classification '03'. During 1973-74 they were renumbered by altering the first figure '2' to the class figure '03'. Thus the engine which used to be No. D2141 now became No. 03141. New arrivals at Landore in June (and cut-down in September) 1974 were Nos. 03151 and 03152, both from Hull, followed by No. 03382 (ex-D2382) which came three months later from Bristol, whilst No. 03121 was sent away. In 1969 No. 2142 was coupled with D2145 and they were still together in March 1973; at the end of 1974 the pairings were Nos.

Sometimes a down coal train would have as many as three of these class '03' diesels at the front, as on 15th June, 1983 when *(from the right)* Nos. 03141, 03145 and 03152 were involved. The train is approaching Dock Junction.   *Tom Heavyside*

03119+144, 03141+145 and 03151+152 plus 03120 and 03142 as the engines operating singly. Note that these pairings were altered from time to time according to availability. On 15th June, 1983 No. 03152 was being used singly as a banker; the following month No. 03120 was noted banking the partnership of Nos. 03119+141, whilst on the last day of working from Burry Port, 17th September the same year, Nos. 03144+151 were coupled as a pair with No. 03120 still acting as the banker.

At this period the stock of suitable engines to work the Coedbach to Cwmmawr section of the BP&GV was further diminished by the withdrawal of Nos. 03142, 03152 and 03382 before the end of 1983, and by April 1985 there were only four cut-down '03s' still in service at Landore. No. 03141 subsequently was acquired by the Gwendraeth Railway Society and in June 2007 was undergoing restoration on the Swansea Valley Railway.

Replacements were needed as soon as possible. If any had still been in service, the D9500 series (later class '14') of 650 hp Paxman-engined diesel-hydraulic 0-6-0s built at Swindon in 1964-65 would have been ideal having been designed for branch and trip work with a maximum speed of 40 mph. Unfortunately all 56 built had been withdrawn by 1970 with 48 of them being sold to industrial users. BR engineers turned their attention instead to redundant 620 hp Rolls Royce-Sentinel 0-8-0 diesel-hydraulics which British Steel at Ebbw Vale had on offer. After inspection, agreement was reached for BR to hire two of the locomotives for one month for trials over the BP&GV line which, if successful, could result in four engines being purchased for £40,000 in total. It was hoped that no alteration would be required to alter the 11 ft 8 in. height of the centre cab; unfortunately the civil engineer refused to allow the engines over the BP&GV until the track had been relaid to a higher standard, so what would have been an interesting idea had to be dropped.

Several of the '03' class diesel locomotives had their height specially reduced to work over the BP&GV. One such was No. 03145 captured at Burry Port in the Summer of 1983.
Emlyn Davies

As the prone to flooding section of line at Burry Port and Pembrey was now closed, it was decided in June 1984 to give a trial to a cut-down class '08' diesel-electric locomotive and Landore selected No. 08259 (previously D3329 and originally 13329 when built at Darlington works in 1956) for the treatment, as the locomotive had been withdrawn from operating service at the end of March 1984. The cab, fuel header tank and radiator were all altered so as to reduce the overall height by 10 inches. A section along the bottom of the body sides was removed to allow the body to sit lower down and the radius of the cab roof was increased to give a flatter curve; a headlight was attached at each end to existing lamp brackets. The class '08' locomotive was fitted with English Electric motors rated at 350 hp but the top speed was limited to 20 mph. The engine re-entered service in July and was tried in the yards at Burry Port on 27th July as well as working from Coed Bach to Cwmmawr. The trial was successful so two further engines were given the same treatment, Nos. 08203 (formerly D3273, originally 13273, built Derby works 1956) was modified at Swindon in January 1985 followed by 08592 (originally D3579 when built at Crewe works in 1959) altered at Landore in March 1985. These two conversions were permanently fitted with sealed beam headlights both front and rear.

These modified locomotives formed a new sub-class known as '08/9'and accordingly were given new numbers 08991 to 08993 on 13th April, 1984. Subsequently they were also bestowed with names on neat, oval, cab-side combined name and number plates, in much the same style as on some of the GWR 'Bulldog' 4-4-0s that used to work years previously through Pembrey station. The details are:

No. 08203 became 08991 and was named *Kidwelly* on 18th January, 1986
No. 08259 became 08992 and was named *Gwendraeth* on 21st September, 1985
No. 08592 became 08993 and was named *Ashburnham* on 18th January, 1986

No. 08992 was named at Landore diesel depôt whilst the other two had their names unveiled at a ceremony on Llanelli station. No. 08993 was dual-fitted with both vacuum and air (Westinghouse) brakes; all three had horns instead of the usual whistles. The introduction of air-braked wagons on the line resulted in Nos. 08991 and 08992, which were vacuum-braked only, being withdrawn on 23rd June, 1987; indeed 08992 had already been stripped for spare parts by 20th May. They were replaced by two air-braked engines which were in store at Derby; these were dispatched to Landore for conversion on 18th February, 1987. One was to take the number and name 08994 *Gwendraeth* (previously No. 08462 and originally D3577, built Crewe works in 1958) whilst the other would become 08995 *Kidwelly* (previously 08687 and originally D3854, built Horwich works in 1959). Both conversions were completed on 4th September, 1987, originally with painted numbers, the combined name and number plates being affixed at Landore in November 1987. No. 08995 incorporated some parts from the withdrawn No. 08991; both had the horns taken off the replaced locos and both had sealed beam headlights. No. 08994 was turned out in the latest *Railfreight* livery of grey with red footplate angle and yellow coupling rods; the other four conversions had all been painted plain blue but in August 1990 No. 08995 received the *Railfreight Coal* two-tone livery. On 20th March, 1994 No. 08995 was sent away to Cardiff leaving the other two locomotives to share the duties for the final two years; they were the last two engines to work over the BP&GV to Cwmmawr before the line closed on 1st April, 1996. The big main line locomotives continued to operate between Kidwelly and Coed Bach until this final section of the BP&GV closed on 23rd March, 1998.

Three of the cut-down class '08/9' diesel-electric locomotives continue to operate for EWS Railways. No. 08995, formerly *Kidwelly*, is seen at Bury, Lancashire on 22nd May, 2007.
Author

Chapter Nine

Carriages, Wagons and Train Services

After the introduction of authorized passenger trains from 2nd August, 1909 the workmen's trains on the main line became regular service trains; however, the Ponthenry and Pentremawr halts for the collieries were not shown in the public timetable, and only certain trains stopped there. The halt at Trimsaran Road became a regular stopping place. Additional halts were opened to serve other collieries at Trimsaran Junction and Carway Colliery Sidings (between Glyn Abbey and Pontyates). I have seen it suggested that this latter halt was first opened in 1898 but it would seem unlikely that the owners of the two coaches in use before 1909 would allow them to serve a rival establishment. More likely there was a halt established at the site of the later Pontnewydd (Glyn Abbey) station for miners who lived in the locality and the nearby village of Carway. Also excursion trains are known to have run to Pontnewydd dating back to the 1870s in connection with the eisteddfodau held in the grounds of Glyn Abbey. This does not mean there was a platform here before 1909 but there must have been a suitable trackside space for passengers to use and a means of access with the road. Another halt was later opened to serve Glynhebog Colliery, probably when the passenger service was extended to Cwmmawr on 29th January, 1913. Workmen's trains continued to run to Tycoch on the Kidwelly branch but these were not shown in the public timetable.

The GWR 1927 working timetable showed workmen's trains arriving at Tycoch at 12.15 am and 4.25 pm on Mondays to Fridays, and at 3.25 pm on Saturdays with departures at 5.50 am weekdays and 2.00 pm Mondays to Fridays. For many years some branch coaches were attached to or detached from 'main line' trains at Trimsaran Road. Many of the main line public passenger services included workmen's coaches and made additional stops at the colliery halts which were not advertised in the public timetable. Even trains starting at Tycoch were included as if they started at Trimsaran Road, the first public stopping place!

Not all those trains carrying workmen stopped at all the colliery halts. For example in 1927 the 7.45 am down from Cwmmawr stopped only at Pentremawr Colliery besides the regular stations and the 12.45 pm down called only at Trimsaran Junction. Later the 4.15 pm down from Cwmmawr was shown in the working timetable as calling at Glynhebog and Pentrmawr Collieries 'when required to pick up colliers'. Note that no platforms were provided at these colliery halts although there was one at Tycoch. It was usual (at least in later days and perhaps always so) for the men to start to alight well before the train came actually to a halt, despite the lack of a platform.

The first passenger carriage to be owned (as distinct from used) by the BP&GV was one purchased second-hand in late 1904 for the princely sum of £20. The Lambourn Valley Railway in Berkshire had decided that the GWR should in future operate its line and was disposing of its locomotives and rolling stock. The three engines quickly went to the Cambrian Railways but the four passenger carriages had to wait to be disposed of by auction sale.

These were four-wheeled saloons with end entrance verandahs, 26 ft 4 in. long (the saloon bodies were 21 ft 7 in. long) and with a handbrake at one end. They had been built by Brown, Marshall & Co., Birmingham in 1898 and reputedly were the result of a failed export (South America?) order. There was no third class on the Lambourn so three of the coaches were second class (one had been altered with first class at one end) and had 12 windows on each side. The fourth coach, which was originally No. 1, was built as a first class coach but had been altered to a first and second composite and had only seven windows each side. It was this latter that the BP&GV acquired, the purchase being approved by the Directors on 28th November, 1904. The actual recorded minute makes interesting reading.

> The Board decided that the Coach should be purchased for £20 & if possible for two as well if both could be got for £50. Secretary to write Mr Morgan as to the user of these Coaches.

Arthur Morgan was the Manager of the BP&GV; evidently he was not successful with any further bids as the other three saloons all went instead to the West Sussex Railway (Hundred of Manhood & Selsey Tramway), of which concern H.F. Stephens was the Engineer; this was 3½ years before Stephens was introduced to the BP&GV.

In later years, from 1913, the BP&GV classified this vehicle as an inspection coach but it would seem that as the original intention was to buy more than one perhaps it was to have been used for other purposes, such as on the colliers' wives Thursday market trains. It was first shown in the BP&GV stock for the half-year ending 30th June, 1905 as a composite carriage, but from December 1909 was listed under carriages of uniform class, subsequently as stated becoming an inspection coach from the half-year ending 31st December, 1913.

The inspection saloon, purchased from the Lambourn Valley Railway, at Swindon after withdrawal in March 1925. The carriages on either side are ex-Cambrian Railways. *GWR*

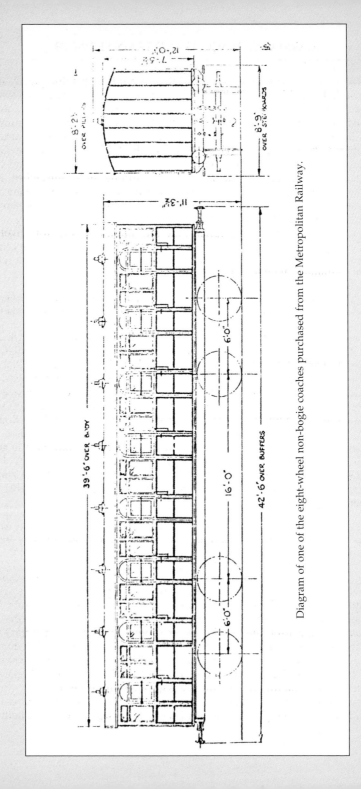

Diagram of one of the eight-wheel non-bogie coaches purchased from the Metropolitan Railway.

The original livery was varnished wood (teak?) but it may subsequently have been painted a mid-brown. The numeral 1 was shown towards the left end of the waist panel but whether this indicated the vehicle number or the class at that end is not known. After Grouping the GWR allocated the new number 80945 in its service stock series to this saloon but it was never actually renumbered, being condemned on 21st March, 1925. Curiously the GWR Register shows it as a composite seating eight first- and 24 second-class passengers in two compartments; a rather curious statement when it is considered that the BP&GV only ever carried third class passengers and workmen; they never had any first or second class tickets printed or showed any receipts for such tickets in their accounts.

It is not clear if Holman F. Stephens, the consulting engineer, was involved with finding any suitable carriages for the commencement of the official passenger service in August 1909. The Directors, at their regular Board meeting on 28th September, 1908 minuted,

> Mr. Stephens revised estimate further discussed also the tenders for signalling & proposed inspection by Mr Morgan & Mr Eager of second hand carriages now on sale.

Subsequently it was Stephens who obtained tenders from four signalling contractors so he might well have suggested where suitable coaches might be purchased. After all, he had at one time worked for the Metropolitan Railway and it was this company to which the BP&GV turned for their carriages. On 23rd October, 1908 Arthur Morgan (the General Manager; John Eager was the Engineer) reported to the Board stating that six coaches 'had been secured'; three days later the Secretary was instructed to obtain more information. A further report dated 22nd November, 1908 recommended to the Board the purchase of 10 coaches for £600 and quoted a further £700 to put them in good order. The next day the Board approved the purchase but not the cost of the repairs. A quotation was then obtained from the Gloucester Carriage & Wagon Co. for the repairs required. It was not until 4th February, 1909 that the Directors rejected the Gloucester tender and,

> ... decided to accept the previous tender of the Metropolitan Railway Co. if they would engage to complete repairs by early in May - Mr Morgan to see Mr Selby [sic] & endeavour to arrange accordingly.

Robert Selbie (correct spelling) was the General Manager of the Metropolitan and their carriages were surplus following the delivery of new electric stock.

Early May came and went; so did early June. Delivery of the first four was promised before 30th June; eventually it was reported on 5th July, 1909 that the new coaches were inspected that day by Sir Thomas Pilkington (Chairman) and Mr Morgan and were ready for delivery. Clearly they arrived in time for the start of the new service on 2nd August, 1909. The livery was varnished teak with white roofs and gilt lettering, they were fitted with the vacuum brake and were lit by acetylene roof lamps with a gas generator for each coach.

These 10 carriages thus cost an average of £130 each; it was reported on 15th March, 1909 that a cheque for £600 had been paid to the Metropolitan Railway

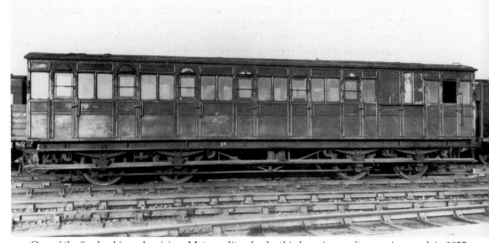

One of the 8-wheel (non-bogie) ex-Metropolitan brake third carriages after ceasing work in 1925. The number is not discernible but is probably 20 or 24. *GWR*

An empty train in the loop at Pontyberem in 1909, before the second platform was added. The first two carriages are former Metropolitan, the third is ex-LSWR. The locomotive, appropriately, is *Pontyberem* with the smokebox door hinged on the left. *LPC 17472*

so presumably they were actually BP&GV property from then. The Metropolitan numbers and the builders of the 10 coaches are known although unfortunately the order in which they became BP&GV Nos. 1 to 10 is not. Metropolitan Railway Nos. 188, 191, 197 and 207 were built by the Ashbury Railway Carriage & Iron Co. in 1879-80; Nos. 225, 229 and 286 by Brown, Marshall & Co. in 1883-84; Nos. 253 and 255 by Cravens Ltd in 1884 and No. 267 by the Gloucester Carriage & Wagon Co., also in 1884. On the BP&GV they were originally marshalled into two trains each of five coaches, thus requiring four to have brake ends for the guards. Nos. 1, 6 and 10 had two compartments given over to the guard and luggage whereas No. 3 only had one compartment available to the guard. Otherwise each coach had eight compartments with the distance between the partitions of only 4 ft 10⅝ in. resulting in a space between knees of somewhat less than nil - clearly a degree of interlocking would be required! Later they were arranged into one rake of four carriages for the ordinary passenger service and one set of six for the workmen's train.

The new coaches were flat sided with a low arc roof, had iron frames, a body length of 39 ft 6 in. (42 ft 6 in. over buffers), a width over stepboards of 8 ft 10 in. and a height of 11 ft 3 in. They were mounted on eight wheels of 3 ft 7½ in. diameter but these were not fitted to swivelling bogies; the inner axles (8 ft from the vehicle centre) were fixed to the frames but the outer axles (14 ft from the centre) were in radial boxes with the springs attached to the frames by flexible links. The doors had the semi-circular tops usual on coaches designed to work in tunnels (to allow them to open fully without striking the tunnel wall) and a bar was fitted across all droplights except those for the guards. After the delivery of further carriages in 1920 only Nos. 3 and 4 were used for ordinary passengers; the rest were reserved for workmen. Nos. 1 to 10 had new numbers 4360 to 4369 in the same order allocated to them when the GWR took over the BP&GV stock on 1st July, 1922, but none were actually renumbered as all had been condemned by early 1924.

As well as these 10 Metropolitan carriages and the former Lambourn Valley saloon, the BP&GV returned another three passenger vehicles for their stock total at 31st December, 1909; numbered 11 to 13 it would seem that they were obtained to replace the two colliery-owned bogie coaches rather than for any increase in services. On 30th September, 1909 Morgan was instructed by the Directors 'to negotiate for three more coaches from the Metropolitan Co.' but evidently what was offered was not suitable and instead three six-wheeled gas lit carriages were obtained, through the agency of Edmunds and Radley of Cardiff, from the London & South Western Railway (LSWR). Each was 28 ft 1 in. long over body which had the curved turn-under sides (as on GWR coaches) and doors with the normal square tops. All had the centre wheels removed before delivery, converting them to four-wheelers with stronger springs and larger axle boxes being fitted to the outer axles. Three partitions in each coach were cut down making two groups of compartments in each. By the Grouping Nos. 11 and 12 were five-compartment carriages and No. 13 was a brake third with three compartments; this latter would appear to have been a modification as all three were quoted as being five-compartment thirds when purchased. Unlike the Metropolitans, which were finished in varnished teak, the three

LSWR carriages were painted a dark brown (presumably the same shade of brown that the LSWR used for the lower half of carriage sides) and they were allocated (but did not receive) the GWR numbers 4349 to 4351.

The initial passenger service in 1909 consisted of four down and three up trains on Mondays to Fridays, with five each way on Saturdays. There was not, and never would be, a service on Sundays. The down trains left the new terminus at Burry Port at 5.30, 9.40 am, 2.00 and 5.25 pm; with the additional train on Saturdays at 8.20 pm. The up return workings from Pontyberem were at 7.45 am, 12.25 and 3.30 pm Mondays to Fridays; and 7.45 am, 12.25, 4.00, 6.40 and 9.30 pm on Saturdays. The 6.40 pm up also ran on weekdays but was a workmen's train and was unadvertised. The direction of travel had been changed by 1913 with 'up' being from Burry Port to Cwmmawr. Much the same sort of times were still being practised when the passenger service was extended in 1913 except that the afternoon and evening down departures from Cwmmawr now ran about an hour later and the Saturday evening up train set off at 9.00 pm from Burry Port. By 1920 this extra late train was also running on weekdays but the early morning up train had become workmen only and was unadvertised.

On 24th January, 1911 approval had been given for the purchase of another Metropolitan Railway eight-wheel carriage, this time at a cost of £100 plus an additional £70 for refurbishment. This was added to stock during the half-year to 30th June, 1911 as No. 14 and at Grouping was listed as a seven-compartment brake third, the GWR allocating it the number 4370. With the extension of passenger services to Cwmmawr expected shortly (this took place on 29th January, 1913) Arthur Morgan was given authority on 15th October, 1912 to negotiate for three additional carriages; and on 19th November, 1912 the purchase of three more of the LSWR six-wheelers (altered to four wheels) at £91 apiece was sanctioned, again through the agency of Edmunds & Radley, although they were not shown in the stock return until the second half of 1913. Given the numbers 15 to 17, they were just like the previous trio; No. 17 being the brake third, but differed in that none were designated for workmen. The GWR numbers 4352-54 (not bestowed) followed on from the other four-wheelers.

Still more carriages were required in 1914 with an additional night-time train for colliers (arriving at Tycoch at 12.15 am) being added and increased traffic generally. The company was able to return to the Metropolitan for more surplus eight-wheelers with the straight sides. Authority was given on 17th December, 1913 to purchase three second-hand coaches at £94 each; the purchase of an extra workmen's coach at £100 was sanctioned on 21st January, 1914; then on 12th June, 1914 Mr Morgan's 'purchase of three coaches at £55 each confirmed and authority given to purchase two more at same figure'. This adds up to nine vehicles but only eight more were added to stock, BP&GV Nos. 18 to 25, all during the second half of 1914. They appear to have arrived on the line in late July 1914 as the Manager's Monthly Report to the Directors dated 1st August, 1914 quoted the new coaches 'have been received and will be required next week, when I expect we shall have a record passenger traffic. The workmans [sic] coaches are not fit for ordinary passenger traffic'.

At Burry Port on 16th May, 1919 locomotive No. 10 is ready to depart with the 9.50 am train of Metropolitan stock to Cwmmawr.   *LCGB Ken Nunn Collection 2214*

Nos. 20 and 24 were six-compartment brake thirds and the others had the full eight compartments. The allocated GWR numbers were 4371 to 4378 in the same order as the BP&GV numbers. Altogether there were now 19 of these ex-Metropolitan eight-wheeled carriages on the line.

One further set of second-hand carriages was purchased before Grouping, five of the North London Railway four-wheel suburbans made redundant by electrification. They received the new numbers 26 to 30 (GWR 4355-59 were later allotted in the same order) and were added to stock during the second half of 1920. Curiously, their purchase and cost were not minuted by the Secretary during any Board Meetings, although it was recorded that on 11th November, 1919 the 'Manager reported as to further train facilities' without going into any more detail. They were all five-compartment coaches with square top doors and turn-under sides like the LSWR stock, bodies 27 ft 11 in. long, fitted with the automatic vacuum brake and electric lighting (the first on the BP&GV) and all were overhauled by the LNWR at Wolverton in varnished teak livery before delivery. In addition No. 30 had two end-compartments converted into a guard's and luggage compartment, the others being unaltered.

After Grouping it did not take the GWR long to replace the assortment of 31 passenger carriages it acquired from the BP&GV; the last two being condemned in March 1926. The actual dates were as follows but in many cases the vehicles will have already ceased work pending inspection and the decision taken to scrap rather than authorize the cost of repairs:

On 28th January, 1923 BP&GV carriage 3.
On 25th March, 1923 BP&GV carriages 1, 4, 6, 7, 13, 14, 15, 22.
On 20th May, 1923 BP&GV carriage 8.
On 1st December, 1923 BP&GV carriages 2, 5, 9.

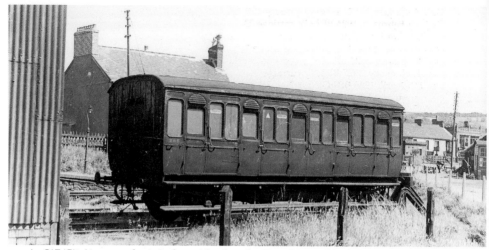

An S17 'City' type coach, six inches wider than the 'Branch' type, No. 285 at the terminal buffers at Burry Port station on 7th July, 1947. The GWR monogram is to the right of the central door, whilst that on the left is marked 'GUARD'. There was no official recognition that the vehicle was ever a brake third or that guards were allowed to smoke!   *H.C. Casserley 45303*

Smartly repainted by British Railways in chocolate but without any lettering, No. W180 is another S17 'City' type coach photographed at Burry Port on 4th August, 1951.   *R.C. Riley*

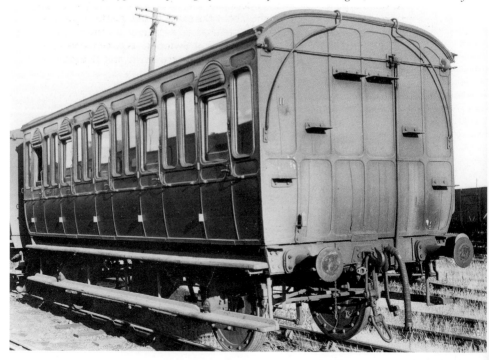

On 26th January, 1924 BP&GV carriages 10, 17.
On 23th February, 1924 BP&GV carriage 23.
On 19th April, 1924 BP&GV carriage 15.
On 17th May, 1924 BP&GV carriages 11, 12.
On 21st March, 1925 BP&GV inspection coach.
On 24th January, 1925 BP&GV carriage 24.
On 18th April, 1925 BP&GV carriage 25.
On 13th June, 1925 BP&GV carriages 18, 19, 20.
On 5th September, 1925 BP&GV carriage 21.
On 28th November, 1925 BP&GV carriages 26, 27, 30.
On 20th March, 1926 BP&GV carriages 28, 29.

The replacement vehicles, as well as being standard Great Western in construction, also used the GWR vacuum brake system which differed from that used by the BP&GV, which would thus have required modification. The new imports were all Dean four-wheel suburban coaches dating from the 1890s and were about 25 to 35 years old. All had the low three-centre roof with the middle of the roof almost flat due to a large radius of arc being used. There were plenty available, some 605 having been built with many displaced by new bogie stock during the 1920s; there were still 491 running at the end of 1934 and 335 in GWR stock on 31st December, 1936.

There were two types; some were built for the 'City' services over the Metropolitan to Moorgate and Liverpool Street and had round-top doors (so that they could be fully opened in the tunnels during any emergency) and reduced height droplights. These were all built to a width of 8 ft 6¾ in. over mouldings whereas the other type for 'Branch' services had a width of 8 ft 0¾ in., square-top doors and droplights of normal height (about the same as the quarter lights on either side of the doors). It was the 'City' type that was far more common on the BP&GV section; around 200 had been built (all at Swindon) between 1894 and 1898. The tare weights of these four-wheelers varied between 10 and 12 tons.

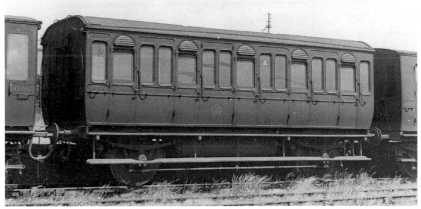

GWR S9 'Branch' type workmen's carriage No. 2774 in the chocolate livery at Burry Port on 7th July, 1947. Note the GWR monogram to the left of the central door and only one compartment for non-smokers.   *H.C. Casserley 45310*

A wartime economy, commencing at the beginning of 1917, was a reduction by one train in the Saturday service, but this had been restored by 1920. At the time of Grouping (1922) the basic passenger service as advertised in the public timetables showed departures from Burry Port at 9.50 am, 1.30, 4.20 and 9.00 pm on weekdays and 9.50 am, 2.10, 6.10 and 9.00 pm Saturdays only. In the down direction trains left Cwmmawr at 7.45 am, 12.30, 5.25 and 10.00 pm weekdays and 7.45 am, 12.30, 3.55, 7.10 and 10.00 pm on Saturdays. The imbalance was due to the early morning up workmen's not being advertised - 5.35 am from Burry Port with a through portion from Tycoch at 5.50. There was also a through coach from Tycoch at 1.45 pm attached to the early afternoon up train (not Saturdays) and a down workmen's at 3.45 pm from Cwmmawr (2.45 on Saturdays) which also had a through portion for Tycoch. It is believed that the carriages for this train and also the 5.25 pm from Cwmmawr were combined to form the double-headed 1.30 pm up departure, a practice that continued until the end of passenger working in 1953.

In 1922 there was still the 'night' train for workmen, 11.45 pm from Cwmmawr with carriages for Tycoch. The engine which arrived at 12.15 am Saturdays excepted with the night workmen's train must have then taken the empty stock forward to Kidwelly yard in order to run round, then returned to Tycoch to leave the carriages in the siding there, afterwards continuing as a light engine to Kidwelly Junction arriving at 12.40 am. The main line timetable for 1927 then showed it departing the Junction at 12.42 with a goods working to Burry Port, due in at 1.00 am. It is believed that workmen's trains ceased to call at Trimsaran Junction from 1927.

By the mid-1930s the basic service still consisted of four up and five down trains on weekdays, with the extra working on Saturdays. However, the unadvertised up early morning train now ran much later on Saturdays, departing from Tycoch at 8.25 am, and was shown in the public timetable as starting at Trimsaran Road at 8.30. The times of the other up trains were 9.35 am, 1.52, 5.50 (5.30 on Saturdays) and 9.30 pm from Burry Port; from Cwmmawr at 7.10, 11.10 am, 3.10 (3.00 Saturdays), 4.35 and 10.45 pm (10.15 Saturdays), with the extra down Saturdays train at 6.30 pm. By this period it is believed that all passenger trains now included at least one workmen's carriage (without any upholstery) in its makeup.

Oliver Bowen, the father of the author of Volume One, often used to take his '1901' class locomotive on this early morning up train in the 1933-35 period when it loaded to 14 four-wheel coaches. It then returned to Pontyberem with empty stock after which the locomotive spent the day banking goods trains to Cwm Mawr before collecting the coaching stock for its return working to Burry Port.

The workmen's trains to and from Tycoch ran for the last time in May 1949. For the last years from then until passenger services ceased in 1953 the up departures from Burry Port set off at 5.50 (unadvertised workmen's train), 8.00 am (8.10 Saturdays), 1.45 (two train sets, double-headed, on Mondays to Fridays), 5.25 Saturdays only and 9.30 pm (9.20 on Saturdays). The corresponding down trains left Cwmmawr at 6.55 am, 12.0 noon, 3.20, 4.15 and 10.45 pm. On Saturdays the last three trains departed at 3.10, 6.20 and 10.15 pm instead. Passenger trains generally took 45 to 50 minutes for the full journey. A detailed log of a journey by the 1.45pm up train in 1951 is given in *Appendix Four*.

At the beginning of 1939 the BP&GV received some brand-new carriages for the first time since the two Ashbury workmen's vehicles arrived around 1897; what is more they were bogie coaches, a previously unknown luxury for third class fare-paying passengers of the Gwendraeth Fawr valley. Lot 1611 at the Swindon carriage works consisted of six vehicles built to Diagram D129 numbered 1323 to 1328, the last coming to the line on 4th March. These were brake thirds with seven compartments seating 70 passengers and were similar to the standard 57 ft 0 in.-long GWR suburban carriage of the period except that they were built three inches narrower at 8 ft 8 in. wide and no less that 18 inches lower with a maximum height of 11 ft 3 in. They also were equipped with Churchward 9 ft light 'fishbelly' bogies to keep the weight down; these had previously been used on other vehicles.

One other bogie coach was also built, to the same specification, in 1939; this was an all-third class with nine compartments, 55 ft 3½ in. long and seating 90. No. 1329 was completed on 25th March, 1939 under Swindon lot 1612 to Diagram C80. On delivery these seven bogie coaches replaced some old four-wheel coaches on the regular passenger services, although about 11 old ones were retained (for workmen's trains) stripped of all upholstery and painted all chocolate (no cream for the workers!).

The numbers of 19 of the GWR four-wheel coaches which worked over the line prior to 1939 have been recorded; five of them continued to run during the 1940s when another eight examples came to the line. At least another eight - probably more - examples will have been used whose numbers and identities are unknown. There were still eight of these old four-wheelers left running when British Railways was formed in 1948, including three that had been on the line since the 1930s. Two survived to the very end of passenger services on 20th September, 1953, by which time they are believed to have been the last standard gauge four-wheeled passenger carriages in use on British Railways; they certainly were the last on the former Great Western system.

The details of the known 19 carriages in use during the 1930s are:

Diagram S17 'City' type 5-compartment third class, body 25 ft 0¼ in. x 8 ft 6¼ in.

No.					
238	built Swindon	1896	50 seats	altered to workmen only.*	
340	built Swindon	1898	?	altered to workmen and guard.	
341	built Swindon	1898	50 seats	altered to workmen only.*	
2719	built Swindon	1893	30 seats	altered to third class and guard.	
2780	built Swindon	1896	50 seats	not altered.	
2781	built Swindon	1896	50 seats	not altered.	
2783	built Swindon	1896	50 seats	not altered.	
2790	built Swindon	1897	50 seats	not altered.	
2793	built Swindon	1897	50 seats	not altered.*	
2794	built Swindon	1897	50 seats	not altered.*	
2799	built Swindon	1898	34 seats	altered to workmen and guard.*	

* These five carriages remained on the BP&GV section after 1939; presumably Nos. 2793/4 were altered to workmen's coaches in 1939. Nos. 238 and 2799 had been transferred away to Glyncorrwg by 1949. It is interesting to note that 238 had previously been at Glyncorrwg for the Cymmer Corrwg-North Rhondda Colliery workmen's service from *circa* 1909 until 1920; so had probably been altered to a workmen's carriage before coming to Burry Port.

One of the bogie brake thirds, No. W1324, built at Swindon specially for the BP&GV, seen at Burry Port on 9th September, 1951.   *H.C. Casserley 75778*

Note the difference in the other side of the bogie brake thirds, and the branding on the end. This is No. W1323 with a multi-tank gas transporter on the right and a Dean clerestory coach on the left. What this out-of-gauge vehicle was doing here on 9th September, 1951 is not known.   *H.C. Casserley 75780*

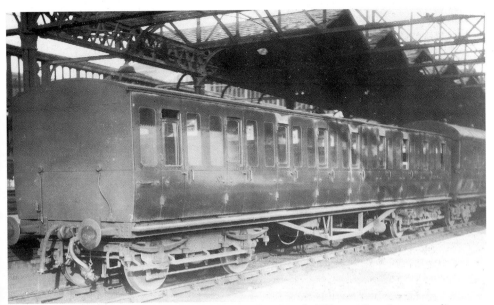

The only bogie all-third carriage, No. W1329 built in March 1939, seen here in maroon livery after leaving the BP&GV. *Author*

The 5.20 pm train to Cwmmawr on 4th August, 1951 is composed of pannier tank No. 1618 and three smartly turned-out bogie carriages, seen here ready to depart from Burry Port. *R.C. Riley*

On arrival at Cwmmawr the 1.45 from Burry Port was divided into two. On 7th July, 1947 No. 1967 (*on right*) is ready to set off with the 3.20 pm departure whilst 1957 (*on left*) will form the 4.15 train with the remaining two coaches.

H.C. Casserley 45314

Diagram T59 'City' type 3-compartment brake third, body 31 ft 0¾ in. x 8 ft 6¾ in.
No. 337   built Swindon   1898   44 seats   alterations not known but remained third class and guard.
    2698   built Swindon   1897   45 seats   altered to workmen and guard.
    2699   built Swindon   1898   50 seats   altered to workmen (no guard?).

Diagram S11 'Branch' type 5-compartment third class, body 30 ft 0¾ in. x 8 ft 0¾ in.
No. 2748   built Swindon   1895   50 seats   not altered.

Diagram T32 'Branch' type 3-compartment brake third, body 31 ft 0¾ in. x 8 ft 0¾ in.
No. 2611   built Swindon   1894   30 seats   not altered.

Type not identified
No. 228   30 seats   remained third class and guard.
     284   49 seats   altered to workmen and guard.
     309   30 seats   remained third class and guard.

The eight further carriages used during the 1940s were:

Diagram S17 'City' type 5-compartment third class, body 25 ft 0¾ in. x 8 ft 6¾ in.
No. 180   built Swindon   ?   50 seats   altered to workmen, later W180, survived until 9/1953.
     285   built Swindon   ?   50 seats   altered to workmen, later W285, sent to Caerphilly by 5/1951.
     303   built Swindon   1898   50 seats   altered to workmen.
    2796   built Swindon   1898   50 seats   altered to workmen, survived until 9/1953.
    2800   built Swindon   1898   50 seats   altered to workmen.

Diagram S9 'Branch' type 5-compartment third class, body 28 ft 0¾ in. x 8 ft 0¾ in.
No. 2774   built Swindon   1895   50 seats   altered to workmen, later W2774, sent to Caerphilly by 8/1951.

Diagram U6 'Branch' type 4-compartment third class, body 28 ft 0¾ in. x 8ft. 0¾ in.
No. 734   built Swindon   1898   40 seats   altered to workmen.

Type not identified
No. 195   No details known other than altered to workmen.

The reason why it has not been possible to identify some coaches even though their numbers are known is due to them having been re-numbered at some time, probably when downgraded from composite or second class to third class. For example No. 734 mentioned above was built as a composite in 1898 with the number 1887, was renumbered firstly 7887 in 1907, and again to 734 in 1936 when downgraded to third class. Some of the seating capacities quoted seem unreal; was the number of seats in coach No. 284 really only reduced by one to accommodate a guard? The two carriages sent to Caerphilly were for use on the Senghenydd-Llanbradach Colliery workmen's service.

All the four-wheel carriages had ceased to work after the end of passenger services on 20th September, 1953, but the seven specially constructed bogie coaches of 1939 were all transferred to other services in South Wales, mostly on the Trecwn (near Fishguard) branch and from Tredegar; some were still active in 1964 and afterwards were used during a film-making exercise in 1965 at Bath Green Park station.

In between the scheduled passenger trains the BP&GV had to accommodate the working of as many goods trains as possible on the single line. The term goods trains covered mineral trains and the returning empty wagons which constituted the vast bulk of the traffic on the line. There were no specific trains shown in the timetables just for minerals or empties, all were classified as goods. Looking at the tonnage figures for goods traffic originating on the line during 1920 the amounts for the next highest categories carried after coal and coke are very small:

Coal and coke	636,328 tons	=	95·96%
Bricks	14,757 tons	=	2·23%
Tinplate	4,833 tons	=	0·73%
Iron and steel	2,233 tons	=	0·34%
Timber	559 tons	=	0·08%
All other goods	4,499 tons	=	0·67%

After Nationalisation in 1948 the American term freight was introduced instead of goods but the actual traffic carried remained the same. At the time of the introduction of regular passenger services in 1909 the first place along the line from Burry Port where trains could pass was Kidwelly Junction (two goods trains or a goods and a passenger train could pass, but not two passenger trains), followed by Pontyates (any trains could pass) and Pontyberem (again two passenger trains could not pass). Another train (passenger or goods) could cross with a goods train held in the colliery sidings at Pentremawr. In 1913 Pontyberem became a full crossing place where all trains could now cross, and Cwmmawr a place where two goods, or a goods and one passenger, trains could cross. On 21st July, 1914 an additional crossing loop was opened at Ty Mawr (between Burry Port and Kidwelly Junction, no platforms) which could be switched out before the last two 'night' trains were due. This latter loop ceased to be used from 1940 although not officially closed until 1947.

As the number of 'paths' for trains was limited by the single line and the passing places it became essential to load the trains with up to 60 wagons each at the busiest periods (until about 1936) which meant working some trains with two locomotives; this included even when having to shunt the various colliery sidings. Not all the goods trains ran the full length of the line. In the 1920s the first up morning goods got to Cwmmawr at 7.25 am (returning at 7.55); then the next only travelled as far as Pontyberem arriving at 8.45 (departing back to Burry Port at 11.35 am); the third up goods also worked only a shorter journey, as far as Pontyates, arrive 8.37 (and return to Burry Port at 9.20 am). It was not until 12.29 pm that Cwmmawr witnessed the next goods to arrive from Burry Port (and which set off back at 12.55).

An even shorter working along the main line was performed by two trips to Gwscwm (Pembrey) Colliery, departing Burry Port at 8.50 am and 1.20 pm getting back 50 minutes later. The colliery closed in 1930. It is suspected (but not known for certain) that the engine from the morning working went on to take the 9.50 am to Sandy Gate, calling at Crown Colliery and Pwll Brickworks.

Evidently the Crown shunting locomotive collected the traffic from the other collieries on the line and assembled it all at Crown. The Sandy Gate terminal was at sidings some 30 chains (⅜ mile) short of the junction with the line from Cross Hands, so the full length of the branch was not worked. The return was at 11.36, getting back to Burry Port at 12.07 pm (in plenty of time for the second trip to Gwscwm Colliery). There was no afternoon working on the Sandy Gate branch. All these trips were scheduled to run on Saturdays as well as weekdays. Generally there were about 15 wagons taken to Sandy Gate whilst as many as 30 would be collected at Pwll and Crown for taking to Burry Port.

There was also just one daily train, including Saturdays, on the Cwm Capel branch, departing at 11.00 and getting back to Burry Port at 11.40 am. The train was not booked to call at Achddu Colliery in this 1927 timetable. On the Kidwelly branch the 10.17 am down departure from Kidwelly Junction was shown as working the whole length of the branch to the Quay, arriving at 10.45. Curiously no return working was shown, but evidently after getting back to Tycoch Junction, the train would have continued to Kidwelly yard and the engine then would have spent the rest of the day working the former Gwendraeth Valleys line to and from Mynydd-y-Garreg before leaving the Yard for Trimsaran Road, arrive 6.30 pm on Mondays to Fridays only, running round and continuing to Burry Port at 6.50. The main line timetable in 1927 showed another goods for Tycoch setting off from Trimsaran Road at 2.05 pm, (including Saturdays) but the branch page depicted only a light engine from Kidwelly Junction at 2.15 pm daily with a return goods from Tycoch at 3.45 pm weekdays and 2.55 Saturdays only.

The Kidwelly Quay line closed completely beyond Tycoch Junction on 11th October, 1929, the track being lifted in 1933. The last traffic had been to deliver roadstone. In earlier days, before the harbour became too silted up, a few wagons of coal would be brought down whenever a small ship called. On the Cwm Capel branch rail traffic had ceased by about 1939 and certainly by July 1940 when the track was recovered. In later years it became the practice to propel the wagons of down trains (to Cwm Capel) with the guard acting as flagman over the level crossings.

It was in 1940 that the flat crossing of the Sandy Gate branch with the GWR main line at Pembrey East was done away with and instead access to the branch could only be made by a new junction put in on the up side of the GWR main line. It was also about this time that the line beyond Pwll Brickworks was closed for one mile; access to Sandy Gate Sidings henceforth could only be made from the Llanelly end. The daily goods now left from the sidings alongside the GWR main line at Pembrey and Burry Port, departing at 11.40 am for Pwll and getting back at 12.30 pm. The timetable as late as 1949 still showed the train as calling at Crown Colliery if required, even though the pit had closed in 1936.

By this time (1949) there was also just the one daily freight working on the Kidwelly branch. This left Burry Port at 8.25 am and reached Kidwelly Junction at 8.46 where the locomotive ran round the train, setting off for Kidwelly Yard at 8.55. The engine then spent the rest of the day on the former Gwendraeth Valleys line to Mynydd-y-Garreg and shunting at Kidwelly before leaving the yard at 5.45 pm (3.00 on Saturdays), running round at Kidwelly Junction, calling for 15 minutes at Trimsaran Junction to deal with the branch traffic (which over the branch was actually worked by the colliery locomotive) and returning to Burry Port at 6.40. On Saturdays the freight had to spend no less than 55 minutes at Kidwelly Junction before calling at Trimsaran Junction if required and finally reaching Burry Port at 4.25 pm. Presumably this was to allow the mid-afternoon down passenger working (due Trimsaran Road at 3.36) to clear the single line section, but if the freight had set off from Kidwelly Yard just 10 minutes earlier the long wait could have been avoided, but only if it was not required to call at Trimsaran Junction. Note that the loop line at Kidwelly Junction (the S. to W. curve) was not used and is believed to have closed some years previously, perhaps another of the 1940 economies.

There were three freight trains running each way on the main line in the 1940s although one, the 6.10 am from Burry Port, only went as far as Pontyberem (due 7.57) or to Glynhebog Colliery when required. This mine closed in 1949. The return working was due back at Burry Port at 11.08 but would have been later if Glynhebog was visited. The engine off the 9.30 am up goods from Burry Port returned on the 12 noon down passenger train from Cwmmawr. Similarly the locomotive off the 8.00 am up passenger (Saturdays excepted) next took the 9.30 down freight from Cwmmawr, due Burry Port at 1.26 pm. The third freight working was also Saturdays excepted, 11.40 am from Burry Port and 1.50 pm from Cwmmawr, which eventually got back to Burry Port at 5.35. Some 61 minutes were spent at Pentremawr Colliery, from 2.44 to 3.45, allowing the 3.20 pm down workmen's train to call at 3.33; 40 minutes at Pontyates from 4.03 to 4.43 so that the 4.15 down passenger could pass at 4.31; by comparison the 21 minutes allowed at Carway Colliery Siding was commendably short. By 1952 the timings for this third freight had been considerably altered with departure from Burry Port now at 2.00 pm, returning from Cwmmawr at 3.30 and getting into Burry Port again at 6.00 pm.

Photographs taken at Burry Port in the 1920s and 1930s show many hundreds of coal wagons in the sidings around the dock area and all seem to have the name of a colliery or its owner emblazoned on the sides; hardly to be seen are any with the names of other operators or with railway company initials. This is the result of a railway and dock built to serve the coal industry and reflected the huge tonnages of coal carried as shown in the annual BP&GV returns; 636,328 tons (or 96 per cent) out of a total of 663,099 carried for all originating goods on the line during 1920 for example. The names of the collieries were, after about 1890, frequently shown as a single word using lettering as large as possible along the upper sides, with additional information such as the product carried (as BEST ANTHRACITE), the wagon number and an address in a much smaller size print lower down.

Familiar names to be seen over the years on the wagons around Burry Port included ASHBURNHAM, CARWAY, CROWN, DYNANT, GWENDRAETH, PENTREMAWR, PEMBREY COLLIERY, PONTHENRY, PONTYBEREM, TRIMSARAN, H & H E SMART and also later BARGOED, UNITED ANTHRACITE and EVAN DAVIES & C⁰. L^D which latter firm was the owner of the Crown, New Lodge and New Pool collieries. Bargoed operated Pont Henty Slants after 1905. From 1928 one operator in particular became increasingly common having AMALGAMATED in a curve at the top, ANTHRACITE in a larger straight style beneath and L^TD under that. A photograph of about 1908 shows a partially-obscured wagon with a name that looks like J.W. PATON plus, in much smaller lettering below, *Coal Exporter*, so evidently this was an agent and possibly of Llanelly. Up the valley, but not in Burry Port, could be seen the wagons labelled STEPHENS & C^O (or sometimes just STEPHENS in the large lettering) used to collect anthracite from the pit head and transport it to their Dinas Silica Works at Kidwelly (by the GWR station).

Coal wagons from collieries not served by the BP&GV could also be observed at Burry Port, arriving over the GWR line. A photograph taken on 18th June, 1904 of a coal tippler on the dockside shows a wagon lettered (in two lines) SAMUEL THOMAS/BROADOAK COLLIERY (*see page 124*); this mine was at Loughor, about four miles east of Llanelli so could be considered nearby, raising manufacturing and steam coals. The BP&GV purchased its locomotive coal from this colliery. More surprising is a photograph taken in 1912 showing three wagons lettered GLENAVOR on one of the sidings next to the BP&GV station in Burry Port, so perhaps not for shipping at the dockside. This colliery was much further away at Cymmer, north-east of Port Talbot, and mined household and steam coals so the contents of the wagons may well have been for local consumption.

There are intriguing references to the BP&GV having operated some of its own coal wagons in the early days, and not just using the colliery companies' vehicles. The following payments for wagons are known to have been made on the dates shown, presumably purchases and not hirings.

	£	d.		
30th June, 1870	567	18	4	(probably about 12 to 14 wagons)
31st August, 1870	56	15	10	(probably only 1 wagon)
30th September, 1870	240	0	0	paid to Gen. Malcolm (about 5 or 6 wagons)
31st October, 1870	170	7	6	paid to Bristol Wagon Co. (about 4 wagons)

A little later an agreement was made with the Trimsaran Coal, Iron & Steel Co. Ltd dated 22nd September, 1871 for them to lease 50 second-hand coal wagons from the BP&GV for three years at £17 per year. The lease was renewed for a further three years from 20th July, 1874. The wagons were of the Taff Vale 8 ton pattern numbered 120 to 170 inclusive (which totals 51 wagons!) built for the BP&GV by Hennell & Spink of Bridgwater, Somerset. The Taff Vale pattern is believed to mean a short wagon with six-plank sides and only one door - at the end also provided with spring buffers - the non-door end having dumb (wood) buffers; there were no doors in the sides. They were essentially for shipping coal by end tipping.

Another early agreement was made on 18th December, 1872 with the Bristol Wagon & Carriage Works Co. of Lawrence Hill, Bristol for the BP&GV to hire 32 of their 7½ ton wagons numbered 598-617, 659, 660, and 704-712 (this totals 31 wagons!) at a rent of £17 13s. 0d. per wagon per year payable quarterly, the BP&GV to be responsible for their repair and maintenance. Expectantly these are the Bristol Wagon numbers and not those of the BP&GV's own fleet!

The earliest wagon stock return, as reported in the half-yearly accounts of the company, show a total of 104 vehicles being operated up to the end of 1873. These consisted of two goods brakes, one covered wagon, one open wagon, 92 trucks and eight ballast wagons. How the trucks differed from the open wagon is not stated and presumably the figure includes the Bristol wagons rented but not the 50 (or 51) hired out to the Trimsaran Co. The return for 31st December, 1874 showed only 42 trucks, with the total being reduced to 54 vehicles. A year later the total was 50, with only 40 trucks in stock, and this remained the position until 30th June, 1884 when the number of trucks increased to 50 and the total to 62 wagons.

From the end of 1885 the total had been reduced to 53, made up of 41 trucks and one open wagon, two goods brakes, eight covered wagons but no ballast wagons; however, there was now a goods transfer wagon shown in the returns for the first time. Despite only eight covered wagons being shown in the stock totals there were, during 1887, 10 'covered tin wagons' leased to Thomas Chivers of the Kidwelly Tinplate Works for £60 pa. Due to non-payment the vehicles were collected back in December 1887. Why did a tinplate works need covered wagons? The half-yearly stock returns remained unchanged until 31st December, 1894 when the figures were now made up of the usual two goods brakes, 10 covered wagons, 29 trucks, nine ballast wagons and three timber trucks but no transfer wagons, the total being the same. 18 months later the total and number of ballast wagons had dropped to 51 and seven and instead of the timber trucks there were now three goods transfer wagons (might they have been the same vehicles re-classified?). Whilst struggling to make sense of stock figures it should be remembered that these returns would have been completed by a clerk in the office and a change in personnel could easily result in a change in interpretation. However, it is difficult to explain how the wagon fleet could suddenly drop from 51 to only 20 in the space of six months. But that is what the return for 31st December, 1896 suggests, the details being two brakes, three covered, five trucks, seven ballast and three transfer wagons. It is not known if vehicles that were hired (as distinct from owned) were included in the stock returns; it is perhaps pertinent to mention that the Directors approved on 1st May, 1899 the suggestion to discontinue the hiring of wagons.

The number of covered goods wagons - three - is what would be expected at that period for a line the size of the BP&GV. Could the eight to 10 vans returned in the period from 1885 to 1896 (which seems extraordinarily high) reflect the position that colliery workers (and their wives) were regularly carried and the vehicles concerned were being disguised as covered goods wagons in the accounts? It was about 1897 that the first bogie workmen's coaches were hired from the colliery companies, so that the extra vans if used for that purpose would no longer be required.

The next change in the goods stock occurred on 31st December, 1898 when the three goods transfer wagons were exchanged (or reclassified?) for timber trucks. The transfer wagons were never to reappear in the statistics again and the three timber trucks were shown for the last time on 31st December, 1899. The bulk of the timber carried by the BP&GV consisted of pit props, which were usually carried in the colliery companies' own coal wagons.

The quantity of trucks increased from five to eight during the second half of 1899, rising to nine in the following half year. It rose further to 12, then 14 and finally 16 in the half-years ending December 1908, 1909 and 1912. New vehicles presumed to have been purchased during 1904 were evidently replacements for old wagons as there was no alteration to the stock totals at this time. A letter dated 25th June, 1904 was received from the GWR Locomotive & Carriage Dept, Swindon (and signed by G.J. Churchward) agreeing to the sale of three open goods at £18 each and two covered goods at £22 each (total £98), the opens presumably being included in the BP&GV stock of trucks.

At the Board Meeting of 1st October, 1895 the Secretary reported he had purchased 10 side-tip wagons at £7 12s. 6d. (presumably each). But the number of ballast wagons in stock remained at seven, altered to six at the end of 1899, then dropped to just a single specimen during the first half of 1900 and remained at that total until 30th June, 1908 after which they never again appeared in BP&GV statistics. There is nevertheless a suggestion that there were still ballast wagons around; on 24th January, 1911 the Board approved the purchase of three of them for £28 10s. each and three months later told A. Morgan the Manager that he could purchase 12 tip wagons at a price not exceeding £12 per wagon. From 1913 the 16 goods trucks appear to have been reclassified as open goods wagons with the totals changing to 13 on 31st December, 1919 and to eight 12 months later. The GWR Wagon Registers show that these final eight open wagons were all allocated new GWR numbers but were all condemned without being renumbered, the details being:

BP&GV No.	GWR No.	Load	Condemned
1	72325	10 tons	14th June, 1924
2	72346	10 tons	14th June, 1924
4	72374	10 tons	14th June, 1924
6	72386	10 tons	14th June, 1924
7	72402	10 tons	14th June, 1924
11	72427	10 tons	14th June, 1924
14	72444	10 tons	14th June, 1924
15	72461	10 tons	14th June, 1924

No dimensions or building details are recorded.

The number of covered wagons (vans) remained at three until 1899, then dropped to two in the first half of 1900, doubling to four in the first half of 1908, five by 30th June, 1909, eight by 31st December, 1909 and rising to 10 in the six months ending 31st December, 1912. These last two additions would appear to have been second-hand as earlier in the year Morgan was given approval to negotiate for two covered goods vans at £35 each. Twelve months later the total was reduced to nine, followed by a return of eight for 31st December, 1919, at which figure it remained to Grouping. The GWR records of these final eight vans are:

BP&GV No.	GWR No.	Load	Condemned
10	101663	10 tons	12th July, 1924
20	101564	10 tons	8th October, 1925
21	101565	10 tons	6th August, 1927
22	101566	8 tons	24th March, 1923
23	101567	8 tons	24th March, 1923
24	101568	10 tons	17th May, 1924
25	101569	8 tons	24th March, 1923
26	101570	8 tons	24th March, 1923

Only Nos. 20 and 21 are recorded as actually being renumbered by the GWR, both at Swindon on 15th April, 1923. These two are quoted as having the lever brake with wood body and wood frames, 14 ft 6 in. long, 6 ft 10 in. wide and 5

After a hundred years using traditional small wooden (and later steel) open wagons with an end door plus a single door on each side, larger wagons were at last introduced. Here we see type 'MCO' and 'MDO' double-door wagons heading from bridge 3 at Pembrey towards Burry Port behind locomotives Nos. 03141, 03119 and 03145 (from the front) in the summer of 1982. The Carmarthen Bay power station, for which the coal is probably destined, dominates the skyline.

Emlyn Davies

By the time this photograph was taken, 15th June, 1983, type 'HTV' and 'NTV' vacuum-braked hopper wagons were now in use. Here Nos. 03145 and 03141 pause before the Pontyates level crossing with a train of empties for Cwmmawr.

Tom Heavyside

ft 9 in. high (presumably inside dimensions), four wheels of 3 ft 2 in. diameter and 9 ft 0 in. wheelbase. Both are recorded as built at Saltley (this would presumably be by the Metropolitan Amalgamated Co. unless this is a transcription error for Saltney where the GWR had a wagon works) and having tare weights of 5 t. 13 c. 0 q. (No. 20) and 5 t. 14 c. 0 q. (No. 21). No dates are shown and no further particulars are quoted for the other vans.

Before discussing the goods brake vans, mention is made of the tool vans and a miscellaneous wagon. This latter was shown in stock during 1921 only and it is not known what it was unless it was a reclassified tool van; just one tool van is shown for the years 1913 to 1918, 1921 and 1922, whilst two are given for 1919 and 1920 only. The one that remained at Grouping was an ex-Great Eastern Railway four-wheel passenger brake van with the guard's compartment altered to a mess with seats but retaining the hand-brake; the luggage compartment held the tools and packing. Presumably this vehicle was acquired during either 1913 or 1919. It was allotted the GWR number 160 and shown to have a body length of 27 ft 0 in. It lasted until 17th March, 1928.

Turning attention to the goods brake vans, for many years two only sufficed, then in the second half of 1899 the number was increased to four by the purchase on 23rd September, 1899 of two old brake vans from the GWR, their numbers 17621 and 17675. Another, GWR 17828, was purchased on 3rd May, 1902 but as the stock total remained the same it is presumed that an older brake was withdrawn at the same time. The stock was further increased to six during the half-year ending 31st December, 1906. The purchase of a goods brake for £36 was sanctioned on 19th November, 1912. Two more brake vans were obtained at a cost of £79 15s. 6d. (so presumably second-hand) during the second half of 1913 but the stock total was only increased by one (to seven) suggesting that another older brake was then withdrawn. (or possibly became the first of the two tool vans). On 1st August, 1914 the Manager reported to the Directors that two of the oldest goods brakes were beyond further repairs and that he was negotiating for the purchase of replacements at a price of about £35 each; however, it is thought this deal never took place. Eventually two additional brake vans were ordered from Hurst, Nelson & Co. Ltd of Motherwell (Manager's report of 11th September, 1917) but due to the war were not delivered until 1919. This brought the total of goods brakes up to nine and all came to the GWR at Grouping; on the BP&GV they were numbered in their own series from 1 to 9 and the GWR allocated new numbers 68914 to 68922 to them in the same order, although only four of them actually received (at Swindon works) their new numbers:

BP&GV No.	GWR No.	Date Renumbered	Tare	Condemned
1	68914	-	10 t. 0c. 0 q.	20th May, 1923
2	68915	-	-	24th March, 1923
3	68916	9th June, 1923	12 t. 0c. 0q.	24th December, 1927
4	68917	-	-	12th July, 1924
5	68918	16th June, 1923	12 t. 0c. 0q.	4th August, 1928
6	68919	-	-	11th August, 1923
7	68920	-	-	25th February, 1923
8	68921	23rd February, 1924	16 t. 1c. 0 q.	31st May, 1949
9	68922	26th April, 1924	15 t. 0c. 0q.	20th August, 1938

Goods brake van No. 9, of Great Central Railway design, built new for the railway in 1919 and
which lasted until 1938. *HMRS Pickering Collection*

The GWR always used Pembrey as the name of their main line station in Burry Port, and this
was perpetuated in the early years of British Railways. Here ex-GWR goods brake van No.
W68957, with reduced height chimney, waits in the exchange sidings branded 'PEMBREY R.U.
NOT IN COMMON USE'; the R.U. standing for restricted user. *M.R.C. Price*

Numbers 3 and 5 were former GWR vehicles and numbers 8 and 9 were the two built in 1919. The GWR Registers record some dimensions for these four brakes which were the ones that were renumbered. All had steel or iron frames (as did No. 6 also). No. 3 had an 11 ft 6 in. wheelbase and internal dimensions of 17 ft 6 in. length, 6 ft 9 in. width and 6 ft 7½ in. height. On 9th June, 1923 when renumbered the tare weight was altered (or corrected) to 10 t. 17 c. 0 q. It was included with other GWR brakes on diagram AA16 which covered old (pre-1889) 18 ft-long brake vans built with X-braced outside framing. No. 5 was the same except that the width and height were recorded as ½ in. and 1½ in. more, four wheels of 3 ft 0 in. diameter and oil axle boxes are shown and at the time of renumbering the tare was altered to 10 t. 16 c. 0q.

The two 1919 vans were built to a standard Parker design of the Manchester, Sheffield & Lincolnshire (later Great Central) Railway, current until about 1905 when replaced by the larger Robinson six-wheel type. It is presumed that Hurst, Nelson & Co. had previously built some and had all the drawings and patterns available, the Great Central Railway not raising any objection. These had a vestibule at one end, a 16 ft 6 in.-long body with 10 ft 0 in. wheelbase and the height of the stove chimney on the roof was considerably reduced for working on the BP&GV! No. 8 was recorded by the Great Western as having internal dimensions of 15 ft 7 in. length, 6 ft 10½ in. width and 6 ft 6 in. height, four wheels of 3 ft 2 in. diameter and a tare of 16 t. 1 c. 0 q. In GWR days it was branded 'PEMBREY' on the sides. No. 9 differed only in that the wheels were shown as being of 3 ft 0 in. diameter and the tare weight was recorded by the GWR as 15 t. 0 c. 0 q. At a later date it was renumbered 35785. Hurst, Nelson & Co. photographed it brand new before leaving their works; it would appear to be painted grey with white lettering, the buffers, couplings and all parts below the solebar in black except for the footboards and tyres. The tare when new was shown as 15 t. 2 c. 2q. and there were oil axleboxes fitted.

Standard GWR vehicles (except for reduced height chimneys) replaced the old BP&GV wagons as they were withdrawn. Some of the goods brake vans used on the line during the 1930s and later included the GWR numbers 17510, 35186, 35805, 35859, 56157 and 56356, all branded 'PEMBREY' on the van sides. All this time old No. 8, as GWR 68921, kept soldiering on and became the last item of BP&GV rolling stock to survive, lasting into British Railways days. In its last years it was allocated to Llanelly Dock, receiving the branding 'LLANDILO JUNᶜ R.U.' (which stood for 'Restricted user') and was not finally condemned until the end of May 1949. In later years standard British Railways design goods brake vans with shortened chimneys were used, appropriately branded 'BP&GV', until wagons fully fitted with the automatic brake took over in 1985 and brake vans were no longer required.

In July 1978 the BR standard goods brake B955049 has been branded 'LLANELLI BP&GV WORKING ONLY'.   *R.E. Bowen*

In the summer of 1982 diesel No. 03145 attaches cut-down brake van No. B953218 to the rear of a train at Burry Port; by now the designation is simply 'B.P.+G.V. ONLY', straight and to the point.   *Emlyn Davies*

Chapter Ten

From Grouping to the End, 1922-1998

The proposed GWR Scheme of Absorption received general approval by the BP&GV Board on 20th March, 1922 subject to the position of the Directors and staff being further defined, the Secretary being required to continue the negotiations. The Wharncliffe and Extraordinary Shareholders meetings were held on 10th July to formally agree to the scheme; this was followed by the attendance of the Secretary and Solicitor at the Railway Amalgamation Tribunal on 24th July, 1922 when the absorption scheme was legally approved. The BP&GV was now a part of the Great Western Railway. Although 24th July, 1922 is the legal date when the GWR absorbed the BP&GV, for practical purposes the change over was backdated to 1st July as this coincided with the start of a new half-year period. Messrs Morgan, Eager, Wenham and Hancock had all decided to retire but the amounts of their pensions to be offered by the GWR were still under discussion on 22nd May even though all the other terms for the take-over had by then been agreed. Other employees transferred their services to the new regime but the BP&GV Directors expressed regret that the remuneration of some officials (believed to be Messrs Williams, Owen and Harries) 'must stand as fixed by the Great Western Rly'.

Arthur Morgan did not enjoy a long retirement as he died on 21st April, 1925 at the age of 65. His widow Emma was 78 when she died in 1940. Elizabeth Hancock was also aged 78 when she died in 1952 but husband George eclipsed them all by surviving until 7th July, 1961 when aged 92.

The distribution of an interim dividend of 2½ per cent on preference shares and 3 per cent on ordinary shares for the first half-year of 1922 was decided on 20th June but, at the request of the GWR, payment was not to be made until approved by the Railway Tribunal. The terms for shareholders agreed with Paddington were for 10 GWR preference shares to be exchanged for every one BP&GV preference share (of which there were 3,312) and for 143 GWR ordinary shares to replace every 10 BP&GV ordinary shares (36,214 GWR for 2,535 BP&GV with a balance left over of £39 3s. 1d.); the £80,000 of BP&GV 4 per cent debentures and £60,000 of BP&GV 4 per cent debenture stock was to be converted to an equal amount of GWR 4 per cent debenture stock.

There was also a cash payment of £23,500 received from the GWR which was placed in a separate bank account called 'The Winding Up A/C' and the whole of this was distributed by the payment of 93 cheques signed on 14th September, 1922. The individual amounts and to whom these payments were made are not known but it may well have included loss of office compensation to the company Directors and Secretary as well as the settlements completed with all creditors.

The last Board meeting of the BP&GV was held at 5 Gray's Inn Square on 14th September when the Directors agreed to contribute equally to gratuities of £25 to each of Charles Herbert Owen (traffic inspector, age 54) of Gors Road, Thomas Williams (permanent way inspector, age 52) and William Richmond

The grave memorial to Arthur Morgan and his wife Emma in Pembrey churchyard, 11th July, 2007.

Author

Harries (dock clerk, age 37) of Church Road. Williams is thought to be the son of locomotive driver Henry Williams and who lived in the flat above the Harbour Office. These payments were deducted from the Directors' personal fees so did not come from the GWR. It was Owen who was to greet Amelia Earhart and the co-pilots of the seaplane *Friendship* on its arrival at Burry Port in 1928 after the historic non-stop flight from Newfoundland (*see Chapter Five*).

Interestingly, included in the list of subscribers to the Burry Port and Pembrey Nursing Association for the year ending 31st December, 1938 can be found the names of Mr & Mrs Eager of Cae Helyg, Elkington Road; Mrs G. Hancock of Elkington Road; Mrs W.R. Harries of Church Road; Mrs C.H. Owen of Gors Road and Mrs A. Morgan of Harbour House. There is also a sizable donation from the GWR Employees and smaller ones from the Burry Port Reading Room & Club, the GWR Directors and the Dock Coal Trimmers (were these not also GWR employees?).

Of the Directors who lost their positions Col Atherton E. Jenkins was aged 63 and was not averse to retirement; Col the Hon. Sidney C. Peel DSO, whose address had by now changed to 6 & 7 King William Street, EC4, was 52 and also had ceased to be an MP in 1922. He became a CB in 1929, a baronet in 1936 and died in December 1938; he had married Lady Delia Spencer in 1914. Col Sir Thomas Pilkington Bt was 65 in 1922 and died in February 1944; his wife - Lady Kathleen - died in 1938. Major the Rt Hon. Earl of Dunmore VC, DSO, MVO, the youngest of the Directors, was 51 when the GWR took over, saw the railway Nationalised and then lose its passenger service, and died in 1962 at the age of 91. The Countess died in 1966 aged 88; she was Lucinda Dorothea Kemble before her marriage in 1904. Their only son was killed in 1940 but there was a grandson to continue the title.

The responsibility for operating the line passed to the GWR on 1st July, 1922 although the locomotives and rolling stock were not taken into GWR stock until the four-weekly period ending on 8th October, after which the 15 engines all received their new number plates and were allowed to carry on with their normal duties until they required anything more than the lightest of repairs. The authorities at Swindon considered them as non-standard and would not allow any costly maintenance to be carried out until they had been thoroughly inspected. As previously mentioned, all this took time and by February 1925 no less than nine of the 15 locomotives were inactive either awaiting or undergoing repairs, other GWR engines having been drafted in to keep the trains running.

Of course all the BP&GV engines had been well looked after and eventually the GWR undertook extensive repairs to all but one of them, several receiving new boilers. Indeed no less than 13 of them continued to work until well into the 1950s. In contrast none of the passenger carriages lasted any later than March 1926. None were repainted and none received GWR numbers, all being replaced by GWR four-wheel suburban coaches. Of the wagons, two only were renumbered but neither survived beyond 1927; a tool van (not renumbered) lasted until March 1928. Four of the nine guard's vans received GWR identities; one ran until August 1938 and another actually continued in use long enough to be Nationalised, finally being condemned in May 1949.

The neighbouring Gwendraeth Valleys Railway was taken over by the GWR on 1st January, 1924. Of the two locomotives, one was retained by the Kidwelly

The Burry Port Locomotive Department Mutual Improvement Class of 1923, photographed by J. Harper. Left to right in the back row are E. Williams, B.L. Bowen, T. Thomas, C. Lewis, W.J. Williams, W.S. Evans. In the middle row are W.J. Tierney, W.H. Lewis, S. Thomas, W.J. Davies, W.D. John, T.J. Bonnell, Will Davies. The front row consists of B. John (Treasurer), J. Williams, W.M. Knudson, J.J. Davies (Secretary) and T.J. Jenkins. Of those seated John Williams was 46 and a fitter from Burry Port, William Marker Knudson was the chief instructor and workshop foreman, age 47 and the son of a Llanelly grocer, whilst Thomas Jenkins was a carpenter, 42, from Pembrey. Of the others Thomas Thomas (back row) was 21 and started as an engine cleaner in 1916, became a fireman and then a driver, later transferred to Llanelly and retired in 1963. His grandson Stuart Thomas is now Chairman of the Gwendraeth Railway Society. *S. Thomas*

The last locomotive to be repaired at the Burry Port workshops with a group of present and recently retired staff on 9th April, 1924. In the seated row John Eager, the retired Engineer, is third from the right; fourth is William Knudson, the works foreman; seventh is Thomas Jenkins, a carpenter in the shops. As well as a new numberplate, the engine has been fitted with a GWR smokebox, chimney and lamp brackets but the lining of the paintwork is distinctly non-Great Western. *Emlyn Davies Collection*

Tinplate Co. and the other was taken into GWR stock. At first it continued to operate as before the take-over, but in June 1924 the little engine shed at Kidwelly was closed and henceforth the line was operated as a branch of the BP&GV, using an engine from Burry Port shed, just as it had been during the 1876 to 1905 period.

The Burry Port engine shed came under the control of the shed master at Llanelly, with the Divisional headquarters at Neath. The locomotive workshop at Burry Port was closed after the last engine (the *Pioneer*) was repaired on 9th April, 1924; henceforth the engines were usually sent to Neath, Caerphilly or Swindon for repairs with regular maintenance being carried out at Llanelly.

Neath was also the headquarters of the divisional engineer as well as the locomotive superintendent; however, Swansea was now the office of both the divisional superintendent and the district goods manager; the Burry Port Dock and Harbour also came under the docks manager at Swansea. The signalling on the line came under the control of the signal inspector at Carmarthen whilst Burry Port station was now the responsibility of the GWR Pembrey & Burry Port station master. Despite all these administrative changes the former BP&GV section still seemed to operate very much as it had in its independent days and one doubts if the authorities at Paddington HQ ever gave it a second thought. No 'best kept station' or any other kind of award was ever won by anyone or anywhere on the BP&GV. Only the report of an unusual incident would bring the line into public notice, such as during the night of Friday 27th November, 1925 when thieves broke into a loaded van in the Pontyates goods yard and stole valuable goods including pairs of high-grade boots.

It would seem that some of the single line electrical signalling soon needed replacement. In 1926 the electric train staff for the Pontyberem to Cwmmawr section was replaced by new electric token instruments. This was after complaints that the Cwmmawr signalman was receiving low-voltage electric shocks when operating his block bell! The next section, Pontyates to Pontyberem, was also converted to token operation not long afterwards. However, the remaining sections of single line continued without further alteration until 1957.

As with other country branch lines the passenger takings were eroded by the competition with local motor omnibus services as these developed during the 1920s and 1930s. This particularly applied between Pontyates and Cwmmawr where the Gwendraeth Transport Co. was operating and other services ran from these places to Carmarthen or Llanelly, more convenient than Burry Port for business, shopping and other transport connections. This in a large part was due to the GWR itself which was operating its own road motor services, although the valley train remained the best means of transport for many of the colliers.

The GWR had opened a bus garage in Carmarthen as early as May 1909 and a service through Cwmmawr and Cross Hands to Llandebie had commenced on 2nd October, 1909. Subsequently many of the buses continued on to Ammanford and even, from July 1922, through to Neath. Note that this service started from outside the LNWR (later London Midland & Scottish Railway) station in Carmarthen and that Cwmmawr had a railway bus service nearly four years before it got any passenger trains. A garage was opened in Cross Hands in 1913 and a service from Llanelly instituted on 19th March that year, extended to Carmarthen or to Ammanford from 12th July, 1920. It is believed that this Carmarthen service used the direct road from Cross Hands to Drefach and did not run via Cwmmawr.

A new service from Pontyberem to Carmarthen was started in April 1929. A little later that same year, 1st August, 1929, all these motor bus services were taken over by the Western Welsh Omnibus Co. which had been formed on 1st April, 1929 jointly by the GWR and South Wales Commercial Motors (part of the National Electric Construction Co. Ltd); eventually - by the end of 1933 - the GWR ceased to run any of its own buses. On 10th June, 1935 another of the local services which was being operated by J.H. Bacus & Co. was taken over by the South Wales Transport Co. Ltd. An indication of how these motor bus services affected train travel is found by comparing the number of third class train tickets issued on the BP&GV in 1920 - 190,972 - with those issued in 1938 - 83,965 - which amounts to only 44 per cent of the 1920 figure.

In 1922 there were 17 active collieries with siding connections to the BP&GV, of which 10 of them extracted anthracite. The other seven pits, mostly small, mined bituminous coal and were all spaced along the north bank of the Burry estuary. Panthywel closed in 1925 followed by Gwscwm in 1930 and Cwm Capel in 1931. The latter was to re-open later in a small way but without offering any rail traffic. Crown and New Pool both went in 1934 followed by New Lodge in 1936. This left Pwll as the only remaining bituminous colliery, together with its brickworks, still providing traffic for the railway.

The anthracite pits were generally much larger and, apart from Trimsaran, were spaced along the Gwendraeth Fawr valley. Plasbach closed in 1927 and Gwendraeth Slants went in 1928. Closyryn had shut down in 1925 but had re-opened in 1930 only to close finally in 1932. New Cwmmawr followed in 1934, Pont Henry in 1936 and New Dynant in 1939. This left just Capel Ifan, Carway, Glynhebog and Trimsaran still in production.

Just as there had been a grouping of the major railway companies, so in 1923 there was a similar grouping in the anthracite industry. That year two large combines were formed, the Amalgamated Anthracite Collieries Ltd (AAC) and the United Anthracite Collieries Ltd, with the two amalgamating (as AAC) in July 1927. By August 1928 Pont Henry was the only colliery of any consequence in the Gwendraeth Valley not controlled by AAC. Greater investment was attracted for new plant and equipment so that, despite the reduction in the number of collieries, production actually increased each year until 1934, which was the peak year for the mining of anthracite.

Despite the increase in production, the amount being exported through the Burry Port Dock was dropping considerably. A total of 289,371 tons of coal were shipped out during 1920, which amounts to around 112 wagons per day. In 1925 this had fallen to 98,828 tons whilst in the following year - the year of the General Strike - the figure was but 25,245 tons. There was some recovery from 1928 but even in the peak year of 1934 only 153,765 tons was sent out this way and this was the only year that more than half of the 1920 total was reached. The year 1939 proved to be the last in which any anthracite was shipped from Burry

Port as the commencement of war in September meant the end of exports and the little dock was officially closed in 1940.

With less and less coal being loaded onto ships at Burry Port it meant that more and more was being sent away by rail over the GWR main line, much of it to Swansea Docks. One result was that the exchange sidings at Burry Port became full with wagons waiting to be taken either forward on to the main line or for return to the collieries for reloading. To alleviate the bottleneck some traffic was deviated to connect with the GWR at Kidwelly via Tycoch, a route previously only used for coal travelling westbound to Milford, Pembroke etc. There was plenty of capacity this way; in 1920 only 9,255 tons of coal had been passed to the GWR this way, about four or five wagons per day. Indeed the total goods and mineral traffic exchanged with the GVR that year was 19,027 tons or only about eight to 10 wagons daily. Further up the valley the output from the Capel Ifan (Pentremawr) Colliery was growing requiring increased siding capacity so new South and Middle ground frames were brought into use there in August 1930 and January 1932 respectively.

Due to the silting of the Gwendraeth estuary the little quay at Kidwelly was used less and less after 1920 and thus required but a few occasional wagons of coal over the branch. By the late 1920s the line was becoming quite overgrown with vegetation and it is believed that the last traffic to use it before closure in October 1929 was roadstone. The track from Tycoch Junction to the quay was recovered in 1933.

The signalman at Dock Junction had a nasty accident early in 1929, and William W. Cooke of the Ministry of Transport investigated. Charles James Mortby, aged 32, had signed on duty at 5 pm on 29th January and at 12.20 am the next morning he accepted the 11.30 pm passenger train from Cwmmawr. On hearing the engine whistle he left the box to exchange the train staffs. The locomotive crew saw Mortby leave his box but he failed to change the staffs. The train was brought to a stand and the crew ran back to find Mortby lying injured by the line (he recovered later). The inspecting officer concluded that Mortby had probably fallen asleep sitting in front of the fire in his box, was startled by the whistle and, on hurriedly leaving the box, had forgotten it was a passenger train approaching so started to cross the track thinking the locomotive would be on the dock line. He was knocked down due to his own negligence; if he had realised it was a passenger train he would not have had to cross any track, being able to exchange the staffs from the banking at the side of his cabin.

Following the closure of Cwm Capel Colliery in 1931 there was virtually no traffic on this branch so, in 1932, the GWR signal box at Pembrey West (on the up side just east of the crossing) was closed and the level crossing of the branch over the main line (Snook's Crossing) was subsequently controlled by a ground lever released by Pembrey East. It would seem that the track on the Cwm Capel branch remained for a time in case the colliery re-opened, but was eventually lifted in 1940 and those pedestrians that used the crossing as a short cut to the dock were provided with a footbridge.

The Sandygate (Llanelly) branch also crossed the GWR main line on the level, at an acute angle just to the east of Pembrey East signal box (also on the up side).

The competition lines up for a publicity shot by Ernie Griffiths of Llanelly not long before J.H. Bacus & Co. were taken over by the South Wales Transport Co. Ltd on 10th June, 1935. The destination blinds are showing 'PEMBREY', 'KIDWELLY', 'LLANELLY' and 'CARMARTHEN'. The Gwendraeth Hotel in Burry Port was previously Gwendraeth House and the home of General Malcolm, Chairman of the BP&GV 1872-88; it is now part of the Royal British Legion Club and there is a single-storey extension where the three right-hand buses are standing.

Brian Cripps Collection

Normally engines worked chimney first towards Cwmmawr, however, No. 1967 is an exception. The coaches, all in plain chocolate, are Nos. 180, 1325, 2775 and 1327 at the rear, 7th July, 1947.

H.C. Casserley 49313

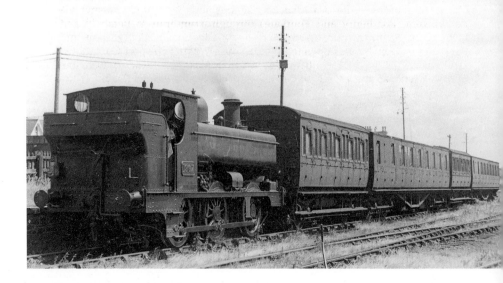

In 1940 this crossing was removed and the branch now trailed into the main line instead. Trains from Burry Port henceforth had to use the exchange sidings for access onto the main line before turning off to the branch. It was also in 1940 that the signal box at Ty Mawr was used for the last time, on 14th November. The loop and the box remained in position, but disused, for some years but eventually were officially closed on 20th May, 1947 and removed.

During the 1939-45 war women were employed on various duties to alleviate staff shortages; at one time on the BP&GV section there was a lady porter and several signalwomen and at one period there were women operating all the signal boxes except Ty Mawr and Cwmmawr. They found that some of the point levers were difficult to operate, especially those at Dock Junction and Kidwelly Junction boxes, with each lever working both the points and the locking. The station master at Pembrey & Burry Port made complaints on their behalf and after some attention had been given to the Dock Junction lever he reported in May 1943 that:

> ... an improvement has certainly been effected, which makes it easier for the lever to be pushed back into the frame. The pulling portion is, however, about the same as it was before, and although Miss Melton can manage it fairly well, Miss Morgans, who is slightly built, has a little difficulty in doing so ... after the sun had been shining brightly on the rodding, even Miss Melton was having problems,

then a few months later the station master was reporting that the signalwomen were complaining they felt vulnerable at night as they were unable to lock the signal box, so please could a bolt be fitted to the door (it was).

During the war the anthracite trains continued to run, although none of the coal was now shipped at Burry Port; much of the output was used to keep the power stations working and the position was little changed after 1945. The number of ordinary passengers, not colliers who were classed as workmen, had dropped considerably during the war and showed no signs of recovering to the pre-war figures. In the 1940s there was further competition from J. James & Sons Ltd of Ammanford who provided an omnibus service from Cwmmawr via Pontyberem, Ponthenry and Pontyates through Trimsaran to Pembrey and Burry Port. Another route from Drefach via Cwmmawr, Pontyberem and Pontyates to Llanelly was operated by the South Wales Transport Co. Ltd. On 1st January, 1948 all the railways in Great Britain were Nationalised, the BP&GV section being placed under the control of the Western Region of the Railway Executive.

Consideration of the closure of the line had begun as early as January 1951, when surveys of the number of passengers using certain trains and stations began. During 1949 71,397 passenger journeys were recorded, with 37,076 tickets (mostly returns) being issued. The passenger receipts totalled £1,499 and the Executive claimed this resulted in a loss of £1,144 for the year. However, this could have been offset by the net parcels receipts of £1,290, the 7,756 parcels concerned all travelling by the passenger trains. In 1952 the approximate populations of the places served by the BP&GV stations was quoted in a Western Region report as:

The east end of the Burry Port engine sheds on 17th April, 1949. The locomotives on show are Nos. 2019 and 2167.   *Bill Potter*

The sheds on 16th July, 1951 with No. 1618 standing outside. The photographer recorded that No. 2012 was inside.   *R.J. Doran*

Pembrey	1,800	Pontyates	2,000
Craiglon	80	Ponthenry	700
Pinged	80	Pontyberem	3,500
Trimsaran Road	200	Cwmmawr	2,250
Glyn Abbey	150		

After the intention to close was announced objections were received from all the local government councils concerned and from the Pentremawr Pit Consultative Committee; there were no legal objections and none from the Licensing Authority nor (surprisingly) from the Transport Users' Consultative Committee. A meeting with representatives of the objectors was held by the Railway Executive on 6th December, 1951. The main objections were that the inhabitants of Glyn Abbey and Pontnewydd would be left without any alternative bus service whilst the Pentremawr Committee was also concerned that the 9.30 pm train from Burry Port was being replaced by a motor bus leaving at 10.00 pm which it was claimed arrived at the Capel Ifan Slant too late for the miners starting their shift at 11.00 pm.

The Executive subsequently pointed out that the average number of daily passenger journeys to and from Glyn Abbey in 1949 was 15½ and that this did not justify the continuance of the passenger service over the line. Regarding the 9.30 pm train from Burry Port, surveys conducted during five different weeks in 1951-52 showed that an average of 11 passengers alighted at Pentremawr daily (the maximum was 14 on two occasions). An arrangement had been agreed with the James' Bus Co. to advance its 10.00 pm service to start at 9.50 pm which would get to Capel Ifan at 10.40 pm; this the NCB agreed was suitable. The Miners' Committee pressed for a 9.30 pm departure but the James' Bus Co. could not do this without introducing a special bus and it was not prepared to do this for the small number of passengers involved.

The Western Region Branch Lines Committee's report of June 1952 on the effects of closure estimated that 16 staff would be made redundant with an annual saving of £3,942, the positions being two each of station masters, checkers and leading porters, eight signalmen, one porter signalman and one female porter. The staff representatives, whilst accepting the inevitability of the closure, expressed concern at the redundancies and the Secretary of the Burry Port branch of the National Union of Railwaymen wrote to the local Member of Parliament, James Griffiths, emphasising the hardship that would result.

The last trains ran on Saturday 19th September, 1953 and, as there was no Sunday service, the closure of the line to passengers took place on Monday 21st September, 1953. Pontyberem and Pontyates stations remained open for 'station to station' parcels traffic and luggage in advance. All other parcels traffic was now collected or delivered by road lorry based at Llanelly.

The new Carmarthen Bay power station, to the east (and partly on) the copper works site at Burry Port, commenced working in June 1953 and, although never admitted, it is likely that the anticipated extra coal traffic that would be required, together with the commencement of opencast mining the same year, hastened the decision to end passenger working over the single line. Although the tonnage of freight being handled annually rose to over 250,000 (it was still around 240,000 in the late 1980s) it had not increased all that much as 243,461

Withdrawal of Passenger Train Service Burry Port & Cwmmawr

(GWENDRAETH VALLEY BRANCH).

The Railway Executive hereby give NOTICE that on and from Monday, 21st September, 1953, the passenger train service between Burry Port and Cwmmawr will be permanently withdrawn and the undermentioned Stations and Halts will be closed to passengers :—

Burry Port	**Glyn Abbey Halt**
Pembrey Halt	**Pontyates**
Craiglon Bridge Halt	**Ponthenry**
Pinged Halt	**Pontyberem**
Trimsaran Road	**Cwmmawr**

Alternative Omnibus Services are operated by Messrs. J. James & Sons, Ltd., Ammanford, between Burry Port, Pembrey, Trimsaran, Pontyates, Ponthenry, Pontyberem and Cwmmawr.

Facilities for the collection and delivery of Parcels will be available by a Lorry Service operated to and from Llanelly. Parcels and Passengers' Luggage in Advance will be collected upon request being made to Llanelly Station ; or to Pontyates or Pontyberem, which stations will be opened at certain periods of the day for dealing with Parcels traffic.

Paddington Station, W.2.
August, 1953.

K. W. C. GRAND,
Chief Regional Officer.

Printed in Great Britain by Swansea Printers Ltd., Swansea.   TE. 802

tons had been handled during 1949 when the full passenger service was operating. Remember that the amount carried back in 1913 was 699,416 tons, and 663,099 tons in 1920, both also being handled alongside passenger trains.

As mentioned, it was in 1953 that the Opencast Executive of the National Coal Board started to develop new opencast sites in the Carway and Trimsaran areas, followed by another site near Cwmmawr from 1958; their development was to lead to the closure of all the deep mines in the Gwendraeth Valley by 1961 except for Capel Ifan Colliery at Pontyberem. This latter pit continued to provide rail traffic until 1970; after this it was purely the opencast sites that kept the railway busy, the high quality anthracite that was extracted being in demand. To service the sites a disposal depôt was opened in 1953 alongside the Kidwelly branch to wash and grade the coal, the junction (facing Kidwelly) for the sidings being a half-mile from the branch junction at Trimsaran Road. Named Cefn Bach at first, the more familiar title Coed Bach was adopted in 1956. Another rail-loading depôt was opened in 1958 on the site of New Dynant Colliery which was named Cwmmawr.

Following the cessation of passenger services in 1953 there was little change in the working of the line at first and it was not until November 1961 that the proposed economies at last were put into effect. It was then that the single line instruments in the signal boxes at Pontyates, Pontyberem and Cwmmawr ceased to be used, the boxes were closed, the arms were removed from all the signals, the various passing loops were removed and the main line above Kidwelly Junction worked by the 'one engine in steam' regulations. The three tokens for the three single-line sections were now permanently tied together and used as one token. A new single staff for the extended section was eventually introduced on 21st September, 1965. Actually the loop at Pontyberem was retained for run-round purposes, trains now being propelled from there to Cwmmawr. The signal box at Kidwelly Junction was replaced with a new building in 1957; the old lever frame was retained but was re-locked using stud locking. This must have been one of the last occasions on British Railways when tappet locking was *not* used for mechanical signalling. A new signal box was also provided in 1959 at Dock Junction, this time with tappet locking.

The last of the former BP&GV locomotives, old No. 10, suffered a cracked cylinder on 28th February, 1958 and had to be withdrawn. By this time all the workings over the BP&GV were being handled by the new '1600' class pannier tanks, built at Swindon in 1949-55, and they remained in charge until diesel locomotives took over on 4th October, 1965.

Regular traffic to and from Trimsaran ceased in 1960, but the track retained some use for wagon storage after that until the branch finally closed in June 1962 and had been lifted by end of that year. The New Carway Colliery connection was also closed about this time, by September 1962, the colliery having closed in July 1960. The stub of the Old Carway branch was still intact on 6th March, 1962, being level it was suitable for wagon storage, but is believed to have closed by 1965 and the track lifted. Goods traffic to Pwll Brickworks ended on 4th October, 1962 and regular traffic to Kidwelly (for Smart's Dinas Silica Brickworks) ceased in February 1959. The Kidwelly branch was little used

Another view of the east end of the locomotive sheds taken on 31st May, 1958.   *V.R. Webster*

The 1959 replacement signal box, of GWR pattern, at Burry Port Dock Junction. This closed after only six years of life on 27th June, 1965 and is seen on 16th July the same year with the signal arms already removed.   *R.E. Bowen*

after that apart from some coal traffic to Stephens & Company's works at Kidwelly but was also retained as an emergency route after closure beyond Coed Bach in October 1965 when Stephens' works finally shut down. However, the track, being without use, gradually deteriorated to the stage were it would have been unsafe to use again even in an emergency. As the junction with the Coed Bach sidings faced towards Kidwelly, a train's length of the branch beyond the junction was retained as it was required to be used as a shunting neck.

Burry Port engine shed was closed in February 1962 and the locomotives now travelled 'light engine' to and from Llanelly shed. The diesel-mechanical locomotives that replaced steam on the line from 4th October, 1965 were specially modified Gardner-engined 204 hp units, later known as class '03'. The Plasbach Colliery siding at Pontyates was closed and the ground frame removed in July 1964. Pontyates, Ponthenry, Pontyberem and Cwmmawr were closed to goods except for coal on 7th June, 1965, followed by complete closure to all traffic on 21st July, 1965. This meant that the only traffic now on the line was anthracite collected from the private sidings and the station buildings, no longer required, were demolished. At the Pentremawr Colliery Sidings the Middle ground frame was closed and replaced by hand levers in January 1966; however the North ground frame remained in use until about 1970. Next the short section from the New Dynant North ground frame to the Cwmmawr terminus was closed 1st May, 1967, although the coal depôt at New Dynant continued to be referred to as Cwmmawr. The former BP&GV workshops near the harbour offices were demolished about 1972; the engine sheds lasted until early 1990 before being pulled down, having stood forlornly without track for nearly six years.

The short isolated eastern section of the BP&GV from Sandy Gate sidings to Sandy Junction, worked from the Llanelly end, closed on 22nd December, 1963, although the box at Sandy Junction did not close until 25th February, 1968. The locomotives of the Llanelly firm of Neville, Druce & Co. also worked over this portion of the BP&GV to Sandy Gate. Back in Burry Port it was time for Dock Junction signal box, only six years old, to be closed on 27th June, 1965 followed by Kidwelly Junction box on 5th March, 1967, allowing the whole of the remaining BP&GV to be worked as one section under the 'one engine in steam' regulations with a wooden train staff and a 'B' key attached for operating the ground frames. Trains to Cwmmawr now set off from Burry Port at 6.15 am and 1.40 pm, reversing at Kidwelly Junction to pick up empties from Coed Bach. The return workings ran direct to Coed Bach, then to Kidwelly Junction and reverse to continue to Burry Port. It is believed that the Kidwelly Loop (the south to west curve), although not used for through running, was closed at the same time; it was intact on 18th September, 1962. Some of the anthracite carried at this time was for use locally, at the Carmarthen Bay power station until it closed in 1984, entailing a short trip alongside the ex-GWR main line from Burry Port before reversal into the generator's sidings.

The Kidwelly branch beyond Coed Bach was re-opened (after re-laying the track) on Monday 19th September, 1983 and for the first time large main line locomotives (mostly classes '33', '37', '47' and '56') began to use the portion,

This section of the old canal, in front of Y Tabernacl (the dark building on the right) seen in October 1965, was the last piece of the canal at Burry Port to be filled in during November 1991.

R.E. Bowen

Kidwelly Loop South Junction from the train in October 1975. The main line to Cwmmawr curves to the right; straight on is the loop line which clearly has not been used for some time. The Coed Bach Opencast Disposal Point is in the distance, stretching right across the picture from left to right.

R.E. Bowen

admittedly very short, of the BP&GV as far as Coed Bach. It should also be mentioned that classes '33', '37' and normal-height '08' had used the exchange sidings at Burry Port, the western ends of which were former BP&GV tracks, until 1983. There was a formal (re-)opening ceremony of the Kidwelly branch on 27th October, 1983 which involved using two corridor carriages for the officials and guests which was attached to a freight train worked by No. 37180 *Sir Dyfed - County of Dyfed*. The re-opening enabled the original section of line from Burry Port to Kidwelly Junction to be completely closed (from 19th September, 1983) and any remaining track on the main line and the docks was recovered during the following 12 months except for the line to Marcroft's Wagon Works, which lasted about another year. The remaining line was now worked in two sections; Kidwelly yard to Coed Bach and Coed Bach to Cwmmawr (New Dynant formerly).

Special excursion trains carrying passengers have operated from time to time. One, with the passengers in open wagons in the traditional manner plus a low-chimney goods brake van at each end, traversed the line to and from Cwmmawr on 25th September, 1965. Between 1975 and 1983 five such trips, organised by the Pembrey historian John A. Nicholson and with commentary by Raymond E. Bowen, ran between Burry Port and Cwmmawr with stops at places of interest such as Lock Cottage (Ty Mawr), comprised of a train of two or three goods brake vans with shortened stove chimneys, 20 passengers per van, and hauled by one of the line's special '03' class locomotives. On the last occasion, 23rd July, 1983, the train also ran to and from Kidwelly yard. Another excursion, this time using diesel railcars, ran from Kidwelly to Coed Bach and return on 8th October, 1983.

From 1983 there were still two return freight trips operated each weekday. Trains now generally consisted of up to 15 hopper wagons, empties Coed Bach to Cwmmawr and loaded returns. After the cut-down class '08s' took over (1985) up to 18 wagons were taken. These type 'HEA' hopper wagons could each hold about 26 tons of anthracite, and containers on type 'FPA' wagons were also used. The class '08/9' diesel-electric locomotives only worked their trains between Coed Bach and Cwmmawr; for a few years engines from Llanelly travelled light to and from Kidwelly over the GWR main line, and thence to Coed Bach. The two trains each way daily from Mondays to Fridays were now operated by Transrail.

It was on 9th November, 1988 that diesel-electric locomotive No. 08995 *Kidwelly* failed when working a train at Pontyates and Landore (Swansea) rather foolishly dispatched unaltered 08898 cab-first on a rescue mission. This engine was too high to go under the lowest of the BP&GV structures with the result that the top of the cab struck the Glyn Abbey road bridge, moving the bridge by four feet and fracturing the water main. The resulting cascade of water caused the driver to believe for a moment that the locomotive had fallen into the river! Fortunately the driver (Max Elmer Cadman of Llandybie) and his assistant (Nigel Morgan of Ammanford) escaped any injury. In contrast, the damage received by the engine was sufficient to have her withdrawn. No. 08995 on the other hand was overhauled and shortly afterwards re-appeared smartly painted in the latest Railfreight Coal Section two-tone grey livery. By this time Landore had taken

Five open wagons were needed to augment the two brake vans for a visit by the Branch Line Society. The special train is seen at Pontyates on the return journey on 25th September, 1965.
R.M. Casserley 21156

Between October 1975 and July 1983 local historian John A. Nicholson arranged five excursions from Burry Port to Cwmmawr using class '03' locomotives and two or three goods brake vans. Stops were made at interesting places with Raymond Bowen supplying the commentary. Here we see No. 03142 on the first of these special trains with the passengers about to climb on board opposite Pembrey East signal box; clearly sunny weather was not expected! *R.E. Bowen*

An excursion using diesel railcars was run on 8th October, 1983 from Kidwelly to Coed Bach, where the passengers alighted to look around the site.   *R.E. Bowen*

Pairs of class '03' diesel-mechanical locomotives, sometimes aided by a third member of the class, became the motive power when steam ended in 1965. These two (Nos. 03119 + 03141) are seen crossing the Dock Road at the end of Glanmor Terrace in August 1982, looking towards Cwmmawr.   *Emlyn Davies*

Here No. 37268 has taken the train over from Nos. 03141 and 03145 in the exchange sidings at Burry Port on 17th June, 1983. The former GWR main line is in the background. *Tom Heavyside*

Larger locomotives were confined to the former BP&GV lines near the exchange sidings at Burry Port and, from 1983, the section from Tycoch Junction to Coed Bach. Here we see No. 37232 (which has lost her '7') in August 1982 in front of Silver Terrace of 1877 and the English Wesleyan Chapel of 1866, with the massive Carmarthen Bay power station as a backcloth.

Emlyn Davies

Work under way on 17th June, 1983 re-laying the track between Kidwelly and Coed Bach, viewed from Tycoch Junction. The two figures on the left are standing on the trackbed of the old line to Kymer's Quay; the former GWR main line can be seen running from left to right in the background. The line to Coed Bach re-opened on 19th September.   *Tom Heavyside*

A view of the Cwm Mawr Opencast Disposal Point looking north-east on 15th June, 1983. The locomotives from the left are Nos. 03141, 03145 and (in the centre) 03152 with one of the site's own shunters on the right.   *Tom Heavyside*

Specially cut-down class '08' diesel-electric locomotives took over in 1985. Here we see No. 08995 *Kidwelly* setting off from Pontyates with a loaded train for Coed Bach on 25th June, 1990.

M.R.C. Price

This is what happens when a class '08' which has not been cut down is sent up the line by mistake. Caught under the Glyn Abbey bridge on 9th November, 1988 is No. 08898, whilst the rescue mission is performed by No. 08994 *Ashburnham*. Note the difference in height of the two locomotives.

Llanelli Star

over the maintainance of the locomotives so they were stabled overnight at Cwmmawr with the train crews travelling by road (by taxicab if necessary) the nine miles from and to Pantyffynnon, the signing-on point. This was preferred to working the engine light all the way between Coed Bach and Llanelli.

On the short section from Coed Bach to Kidwelly (now spelt Cydweli) it was main line diesel-electric locomotives that were used from 19th September, 1983 as the track had been relaid to modern standards. Apart from the occasional class '56' and previously class '33', the trains were invariably hauled by one of the numerous class '37' locomotives, of which in October 1973 no less than 43 built in 1963-65 were then maintained at Landore, and they practically monopolised the freight services through Llanelli to Burry Port and Kidwelly. This class was originally numbered D6700 to D6999 plus D6600-08, but had been altered to 37000 to 37308 in the same order; they ran on two six-wheel bogies with all axles available for traction, a type popularly referred to as 'Co-Cos', and had been built by the English Electric Co. with engines rated at 1,750 hp. The class '56' could produce 3,250 hp even though only having the same number of axles; 30 had been built in Romania, the others at Crewe or Doncaster. Both classes, but mostly the '37s', continued to work the line until the final closure took place.

The very last train from and to Cwmmawr ran on Friday 29th March, 1996 so the closure of this remaining section of the BP&GV main line took effect from Monday 1st April, 1996. The closure of the disposal point at Cwmmawr meant the redundancy of nine workers. Coed Bach continued to be fed by road so there was still rail traffic over the short distance between there and Cydweli yard, worked by main line trains and locomotives. This remaining stub of the BP&GV, and also of the GVR, finally closed for the last time on 23rd March, 1998 and trains were no more to be seen in the valley of the Gwendraeth Fach. The Coed Bach disposal point also closed, with the loss of 40 jobs, and much of the equipment was transferred to Onllwyn in the Dulais valley.

An announcement was made by the developers Walters Group on 11th July, 2007 that a £20 million proposal to turn the 608 acre derelict Ffos Las former opencast site at Trimsaran into a National Hunt racecourse complete with hotel, housing and other facilities had been given the go-ahead. The first race meeting is scheduled to take place in 2009; a second phase in the development would include an equestrian centre. The Cwmmawr site had by this time been successfully landscaped and become the Mynydd Mawr Woodland Park. All trace of the old Cwm-y-Glo reservoir had disappeared due to the opencast mining.

The trains may have ceased but the track (except for a short section) remained *in situ*, just in case the possibility of carrying freight returned. There had been several attempts to start new opencast sites for the extraction of anthracite, all refused on planning grounds (one in 1994 at Tir Dafydd after a public enquiry) to date, but the situation could always change. The short section of track that has disappeared is at 50 chains (1 km) south-west of the level crossing at Pontyberem where the lane to Railway Terrace has, because of subsidence, been diverted onto the former trackbed for a length of about 80 yards.

There have also been schemes to re-open the line for tourist passengers. The Llanelli & District Railway Society obtained a three-coach diesel train which

Rather superior accommodation in the form of two modern corridor carriages attached to a train of air-braked Speedlink hopper wagons was provided for the official re-opening of the Coed Bach to Kidwelly section on 27th October, 1983. No. 37180 *Sir Dyfed/County of Dyfed'* is at Coed Bach ready to break the tape on the return to Kidwelly.   *NCB Y283/5*

Type 'HEA' air-braked hoppers are being used to convey anthracite from Cwmmawr to Coed Bach on 25th June, 1990. The locomotive is No. 08995 *Kidwelly* in the 'Coal Section' two-tone grey livery and the location is Pontyates.   *M.R.C. Price*

The new Pont-y-Plough of 1993 at Pontyberem, looking towards Burry Port on 24th October, 2004. The original Plough bridge was slightly nearer the camera. *Author*

was actually stored at Coed Bach until 1996, after which it was sent to the Swansea Vale Railway. The society published its draft proposals for the future use of the route in March 1998. Then in 2002 the Gwendraeth Railway Society announced its plan to form a trust to acquire the route from Network Rail and lay down metre gauge track, with locomotives and rolling stock imported from Portugal. Later in the year the Burry Port & Gwendraeth Valley Railway Company Limited was registered with the same agenda. Since then the intension to convert the line to metre gauge has been abandoned due to Network Rail's insistence that their option to carry any future freight must be retained.

Accordingly one of the reduced-height class '03' locomotives (No. 03141) has been saved and in June 2007 was under restoration on the Swansea Valley Railway. The last remaining BP&GV steam locomotive *Pontyberem* was purchased from the Great Western Society in the Spring of 2008 and taken to Blaenavon for restoration. At the same time negotiations were progressing towards obtaining a lease from Network Rail of the line from Coed Bach to Cwmmawr (New Dynant), the aim being to re-open a section to celebrate in 2009 the centenary of the Light Railway, and permission to clear the line of all the undergrowth was granted in July. As there are plans to develop an industrial plant on the site of the former opencast distribution point, the section of line from Coed Bach to Cydweli is being retained by Network Rail.

Of course leaving the track down but unused was a temptation to some, and a section was stolen at Cwmmawr in 2004. Then a year later, on 5th April at Pontyberem, an audacious attempt was made at a further theft. A gang of men posing as contractors, and wearing orange jackets bearing the name of a well-known contractor, marked out sections of the track, brought in lifting gear, and cut the rails into six foot sections. The thieves chatted to neighbours and passers-by to allay suspicions but they did not fool one lady council worker

The former BP&GV locomotive No. 2 *Pontyberem* working at Mountain Ash for the NCB in 1952.
Author's Collection

By 21st June, 1969 the former *Pontyberem* was at Penrikyber Colliery and was missing her brass
dome cover, but note the smokebox door was now conventionally hung.   *F.K. Davies*

On 2nd January, 1990 at the Great Western Society's headquarters at Didcot and looking rather sorry for herself, old No. 2 was now the only surviving BP&GV steam locomotive and in need of some t.l.c. In the Spring of 2008 she was taken away for restoration. *M.R.C. Price*

who, having earlier been speaking to the wife of one of the Gwendraeth Railway Society members, knew the position and alerted the British Transport Police who were able to foil the raid and make an arrest.

Remarkably, five of the other cut-down class '03' diesels have been safely preserved, No. 03119 on the West Somerset Railway, No. 03120 on the Fawley Hill Railway, No. 03144 on the Wensleydale line, No. 03145 at a site in Moreton-on-Lugg, and No. 03152 on the Swindon & Cricklade Railway. Another cut-down locomotive, No. 07012, is under restoration at Barrow Hill, having worked for Powell Dyffryn at both Cwmmawr and Coed Bach from 1977 to 1992.

After finishing their work on the BP&GV the three remaining class '08/9' locomotives went to perform other duties on the railway network, all subsequently receiving the English, Welsh & Scottish Railway red and gold livery. No. 08993 was at St Blazey in August 2005 and at Washwood Heath in October 2006; No. 08994 went to Margam, Toton and Tinsley in turn, being at Peak Forest (without nameplates) in December 2006; No. 08995 left the BP&GV in March 1994 for Cardiff Canton, moved to Thornaby in June 1998, then came back to Cardiff in 1999, and was in November 2006 waiting at Margam to undergo repairs. Early in 2007 it was proposed to transfer all three to Bury to be accommodated on East Lancashire Railway property. There they were for use by the contractor Carillion Rail on permanent way trains during the relaying of the overhead-wire Manchester tramway system ('Metrolink') between Bury and Victoria from 29th May to 12th September, 2007, their reduced height being an advantage through the Whitefield and Heaton Park tunnels. Accordingly all three were sent to Doncaster works during March and April 2007 for thorough overhauls, and had arrived at Bury by the first week in May freshly repainted and looking very smart except that they had now lost their distinctive nameplates.

Appendix One

Half-Yearly Dividends, 1899-1922

Note that these dividends are for the six-monthly periods ending on the dates shown. For an annual figure the average of the two half-year dividends should be taken. For example, the annual rate paid to the ordinary shareholders for 1900 works out at 3¾ per cent, being the average of the two payments of 5 and 2½ per cent in the year. No dividends were awarded before 1899.

½ year ending	preference shares (%)	ordinary shares (%)	½ year ending	preference shares (%)	ordinary shares (%)
30/6/1899	2½	-	30/6/1911	5	10
31/12/1899	5	-	31/12/1911	5	10
30/6/1900	5	5	30/6/1912	5	3
31/12/1900	5	2½	31/12/1912	5	10
30/6/1901	3½*	-	30/6/1913	5	7½
31/12/1901	3½*	-	31/12/1913	5	12½
30/6/1902	5	-	30/6/1914	5	7½
31/12/1902	5	5	31/12/1914	5	6½
30/6/1903	5	5	30/6/1915	5	6
31/12/1903	5	5	31/12/1915	5	14
30/6/1904	5	5	30/6/1916	5	6
31/12/1904	5	5	31/12/1916	5	14
30/6/1905	5	5	30/6/1917	5	6
31/12/1905	5	7	31/12/1917	5	14
30/6/1906	5	10	30/6/1918	5	6
31/12/1906	5	10	31/12/1918	5	14
30/6/1907	5	10	30/6/1919	5	6
31/12/1907	5	5	31/12/1919	5	14
30/6/1908	5	5	30/6/1920	5	6
31/12/1908	5	10	31/12/1920	5	14
30/6/1909	5	10	30/6/1921	5	6
31/12/1909	5	10	31/12/1921	5	14
30/6/1910	5	10	30/6/1922	2½	3
31/12/1910	5	10			

* Just a single dividend of 3½ per cent announced for the whole year ending 31st December, 1901 which equates to 3½ per cent for each half year.

Principal Shareholdings,
1st July, 1922

	No. of 5% Preference £10 shares	No. of Ordinary £10 shares	No. of 4% Debentures	No. of 4% Debenture stocks
Allen, F.L.	140	-	-	220
Bathhurst, S.L.	230	121	-	78
Bischoffsheim, Exors. of Mrs C.	-	368	26,500	14,300
Bischoffsheim, others of family	496	-	-	-
Bowlby, C.N.	185	-	-	-
Cancellor, Miss Emily	66	-	-	620
Harcourt, Hon. Rachel	152	17	-	-
Morgan, Arthur	5	30	-	500
Peel, Hon. Sidney	50	-	5,000	-
Pemberton, Mrs Patience	93	12	-	815
Pemberton, others of family	187	83	-	-
Pilkington, Sir Thomas	300	250	-	-
Public Trustee (in probate) mostly Exors of Bischoffsheim	446	75	10,500	14,477
Taylor, Seaton F.	204	351	-	-
Wateley, H.A.	152	50	-	-
Woolnough, C.W.	115	61	-	39

All holders of 100 or more BP&GV shares on this date are listed above.

Source: Carmarthenshire Archive Service ref. DB/103 *BP&GV Stock & Share Register 1922.*

Chairmen, Directors and Officers, 1866-1922

Chairmen

Charles Cancellor	1866-1872
Lt Gen. George Alexander Malcolm CB	1872-1888
Francis Cancellor	1888-1889
Bertram, 5th Earl of Ashburnham	1889-1905
George Herring	1905-1906
Lt Col Sir Thomas M.S. Pilkington Bt	1906-1922

Directors

Maj. Christopher Robert Pemberton	1866-1871
Charles Cancellor	1866-1872
Wadham Locke Sutton	1866-1874
George F. Prince Sutton	1866-1874
Lt Gen. George A. Malcolm CB	1866-1888
Francis Alexander Pemberton	1871-1888
Sir Harcourt Johnstone Bt MP	1872-1884
Francis Cancellor	1884-1892
John Clarke Crossthwaite McCaul	1888-1891
Francis Ommanney	1888-1896
Bertram, 5th Earl of Ashburnham	1889-1905
Charles Henry Ommanney CMG	1891-1896
William Armine Bevan	1892-1896
William Joseph Buckley	1894-1895 and 1896-1905
William Sproston Caine MP	1895-1898
George Herring	1896-1906
Thomas M.S. Pilkington (became 12th Baronet in 1901)	1898-1922
Henri Louis Bischoffsheim	1902-1908
John Leonard Matthews	1905-1912
Hon. Sidney Peel DSO, MP	1907-1922
William Herring	1908-1916
Alexander, 8th Earl of Dunmore VC, DSO, MVO	1913-1922
Col Atherton Edward Jenkins	1917-1922

Secretaries

John James Russell	1866-1898
Seaton Frank Taylor	1899-1919
Walter John Wenham	1920-1922

Engineers

Capt. John Paisley Luckraft	1866-1887
Henry Court	1889-1899
Fred R. Willcocks	1899
Robert A. Carr	1899-1901
John Eager	1901-1922

Harbour Masters

William McKiernon (& *Superintendent*)	*by* 1842-1854
Thomas Briggs (& *Superintendent*)	1854-1863
Capt. John Paisley Luckraft	1864-1887
John James Russell	1887-1898
Arthur Morgan	1899-1922

General Managers

Capt. Luckraft (*Superintendent*)	1869-1881
John J. Russell (*Receiver and Manager*)	1881-1898
Arthur Morgan (*General Manager*)	1899-1922

Accountants

Edward Evans	*by* 1881-1912
John George Hancock	1912-1922

Solicitors

Sutton & Ommmanney	1866-1874
Johnston & Stead	1874-1895
Sutton, Ommanney & Rendall	1895-1897
Seaton F. Taylor	1897-1922

Dock Masters

David Lloyd	1871-1899
David Rees	1899-1900
Capt. Davies	1900-1905
Capt. Morgan	1906-1920
Capt. Hughes	1920-1922

Traffic Managers

George Redford	1869-1873
John Mitchell	1873-1892
Edward J.H. Russell	1892-1899

Appendix Four

Log of Journey 1951

By 1.45 pm passenger train from Burry Port on Monday 16th July, 1951.
(Supplied by Richard J. Doran.)

Locomotives Nos. 1633 + 1607. Carriages Nos. 2796, 1323, 180, 1324.

Load: 76 tons tare, 80 tons gross.

Schedule			Duration of stop		Arrive			Actual times Depart		
h.	*m.*		*h.*	*m.*	*s.*	*h.*	*m.*	*s.*	*h.*	*m.*	*s.*
1	45	Burry Port	-	-	-	-	-	-	1	50	00
1	50	Pembrey	0	57		1	54	42	1	55	39
1	53	Craiglon Bridge	0	07		1	58	42	1	58	49
1	58	Pinged	0	05		2	02	17	2	02	22
-		*Trimsaran Junction*				*pass*		2	05	00
2	05	Trimsaran Road	1	26		2	06	33	2	07	59
2	10	Glyn Abbey	1	13		2	11	24	2	12	37
2	18	Pontyates	2	36		2	18	53	2	21	29
2	21	Ponthenry	0	37		2	24	22	2	24	59
-		Pentremawr Colliery	0	32		2	28	37	2	29	09
2	30	Pontyberem	1	15		2	32	52	2	34	07
2	38	Cwmmawr	--			2	39	16	-		

All speed limits were strictly observed. Most of the passengers who boarded at Burry Port and the intermediate stops were colliers who alighted at Pentremawr Colliery (although the stop lasted for only 32 seconds). At Cwmmawr the train was divided, with locomotive No. 1633 and carriages Nos. 1324 and 180 forming the 3.20 pm departure; the others comprising the 4.15 pm train. All carriages except No. 2796 carried a 'W' prefix.

In later years two locomotives headed the 1.45 pm departure with a mixture of workmen's four-wheelers and third class bogie stock. On 16th July, 1951 the engines were Nos. 1633 and 1607.
R.J. Doran

Appendix Five

Trials with Locomotive *Mountaineer*, 20th June, 1870

1st trial. 16 wagons, tare 61 t. 19 c., gross load 130 t. 1 c. including an allowance of 2 tons for the 'passengers'. 160 lb. pressure at start on level track; train brought to a halt after 6¼ miles with 80 lb. pressure. Resuming with a pressure of 157 lb. the 11½ mile trip was completed with 85 lb. pressure, total running time was 28½ minutes.

2nd trial. Same load, starting on level track 100 yards before an incline of 1 in 32.18 with a pressure of 155 lb. Pressure after passing the top of the incline was 143 lb. The length of the incline was not stated but was very short, only about 75 yards (believed up to the broad gauge loading bank at Burry Port).

3rd trial. Load increased to 17 wagons, gross 140 t. 15 c., starting on level track 50 yards before the same incline with 157 lb. pressure, reduced to 137 lb. after passing the top.

4th trial. With the increased load, pressure of 160 lb. and starting at the foot of the incline. The locomotive slipped to a stand with 150 lb. pressure a little more than half way up the incline, despite sand being freely used.

5th trial. Again with the increased load and starting at the foot of the incline with a pressure of 157 lb. The trial was brought to an abrupt termination when the last wagon became derailed at the points at the incline foot.

In response to an enquiry by Robert Fairlie, the reply sent by Captain Luckraft on 1st June, 1870 was that, for the same work, the *Mountaineer* would consume *about* 2 tons of coal compared with the 3 tons consumed by the *Gwendreath* [sic] and he was able to give actual figures for the consumption of oil and tallow during an 11 day period:

	Oil	Tallow
Mountaineer (Fairlie engine)	11 quarts	7 lb.
Gwendreath (Ordinary engine)	7 quarts	11 lb.

The party of Engineers included Henry J. Wylie (Resident Engineer, Northern Punjab State Railway), F.S. Gilbert CE, Fred. Chas. Danvers CE (India Office), Geo. Allan CE (of Smith, Fleming & Co.), Thomas C. Glover (of Glover & Co. Railway Engineers and Contractors, Bombay), T.J. Dewar CE (of the same Bombay firm), Thomas Cargil CE, and Robert F. Fairlie.

Source: Fairlie, R.F., *Second Series of Experiments with Fairlie Engines*, 1870, pp.13-16, 22. The British Library reference is TJ 605 FAI.

Appendix Six

Working Collieries in
1884, 1896, 1909 and 1923

December 1884, *Gwendraeth Valley (anthracite):*
Carway, Closyryn, Dynant, Pentremawr, Plasbach, Pontyberem Pit and New Slant, Pumpquart, Trimsaran Slant.

December 1884, *Burry Port area (bituminous):*
Cwm Capel, New Lodge, New Pool.

December 1896, *Gwendraeth Valley (anthracite):*
Cwm Mawr 20 (18), Glynhebog 74 (51), Llandyry 38 (27), New Carway 13 (6), Pont Henry 192 (160), Pontyberem Slants 355 (270), Trimsaran 144 (106), Waunhir 15 (12). In addition Danybanc and Lambert's are both listed as 'discontinued'.

December 1896, *Burry Port area (bituminous):*
Cwm Capel 107 (91), Frood (Ffrwd) 11 (10), New Lodge 15 (3), New Pool 18 (16), Pemberton 20 (17), Pwll Level 2 (2).

July 1909, *Gwendraeth Valley (anthracite):*
Caepontbren, Carway, Closucha, Closyryn, Gwendraeth, New Cwmmawr, New Dynant, Pentremawr, Pontyberem, Trimsaran.

July 1909, *Burry Port area (bituminous):*
Achddu, Cwm Capel, Crown, Gwscwm, New Pool, Rhiwlas.

July 1923, *Gwendraeth Valley (anthracite):*
Carway, Closyryn, Glynhebog, Gwendraeth, New Cwmmawr, New Dynant, Pentremawr, Plasbach, Ponthenry, Pontyberem, Trimsaran.

July 1923, *Burry Port area (bituminous):*
Crown, Cwm Capel (Ashburnham), Gwscwm (Pembrey), New Lodge, Panthowell, Pwll.

Note: The figures given in the 1896 listings are for the total number of workers at each colliery, with those underground shown in parenthesis.

Sources: Mining & Mineral Statistics for 1884 (Home Office, 1885); Ditto for 1896 (Home Office, 1897); *Llanelly and County Guardian*, 29th July, 1909; *Collieries on the Great Western Railway* (GWR Paddington, July 1923).

Sources and Bibliography

Abbott, Rowland A.S.,*The Fairlie Locomotive*, (David & Charles, 1970).

Baker, Allan C., *Black, Hawthorn & Co (with Chapman & Furneaux) Works List*, (Industrial Locomotive Society, 1988).

Bradshaw's Railway Manual, Shareholders Guide and Official Directory (Henry Blacklock & Co.), various years including 1869, 1891, 1892, 1893, 1910.

Board of Trade *Railway Returns for 1913* and *for 1920* (HMSO, 1914 and 1921).

Bourne, John, *Railway Magazine*, November 1953.

Bowen, Raymond, *My First Voyage with my Father*, Wrth Ddwr a Thân, Vol. 1, No. 6, 1987.

Bowen, Raymond E., *The Carmarthenshire Antiquary Vol XII*, 1976.

Bowtell, Harold D. & Hill, Geoffrey *Reservoir Builders of South Wales* (Industrial Locomotive Society, 2006).

The Cambrian January 1836, February 1838, October 1842, January 1843.

Carmarthen Journal September 1868, June 1869, February 1887.

Carmarthenshire Archives, Carmarthen, *BPGV Cash Book 1866-70* ref. M44; *BPGV Rly Letter Book 1 - 1866-70* ref. M45; *Book 9 - 1880-82* ref. M46; *Book 12 - 1886-88*; *Book 13 - 1888-89* ref. M47; *Book 14 - 1889-91* ref. M48; *BPGV Stock & Share Register* ref. DB/103; *Cawdor Papers* ref. 1/235; *Trimsaran Coal Co. Agreement* ref. DB121/1.

Cole, David *Contractors' Locomotives Part I, Part II, (Union Publications, 1965)*.

Colliery Guardian, 29/8/1868, 8/7/1870, 28/11/1873, 2/4/1875, 27/1/1876, 1/2/1878, 16/8/1878, 10/9/1880, 28/1/1881, 23/6/1905, 4/5/1923.

Contract Journal, The, 5th April, 1905 (advertisement by A.T. & E.A. Crow).

Cooke, R.A., *Coal Mines of South Wales 1850-2003* (unpublished when seen).

Craig, R.S., *The Industrial & Maritime History of Llanelli & Burry Port* (Carmarthenshire Council, 2002).

Croughton G. & ors, *Private & Untimetabled Railway Stations*, (Oakwood Press 1982).

Cummings, John, *Rly Motor Buses & Bus Services 1902-1933*, Vol. 2, (OPC 1980).

Cummings, John, *Great Western Roadmotors*, Old Motor Magazine Vol. 5, 1967).

Daly, Steve, *Welsh Railways Archive* Vol. II. No. 4.

Davies, W.J.K., *Light Railways*, (Ian Allen 1964).

De Haviland, John, *Industrial Locomotives of Dyfed & Powis*, (Industrial Railway Society, 1994).

Down, C.G. & Warrington, A.J., *History of the Somerset Coalfield*, (David & Charles, 1971).

Fairlie, R.S., *Second Series of Experiments with Fairlie Engines*, 1870.

Gentry, W.C., *The Railway Magazine* Vol. 31, September 1912.

Great Western Railway Magazine Vol. 34, 1922.

Great Western Railway Wagon Registers, National Railway Museum Library, York.

Hadfield, Charles, *Canals of South Wales & the Border*, (David & Charles, 1967).

Harris, Michael, *Great Western Coaches: 1890-1954*, (David & Charles, 1966).

Hughes, D.G. Lloyd, *The Burry Port Reading Room & Club, A History*, 1981.

Iron & Coal Trades Review, 10th April, 1908.

Hunt, R., *Mineral Statistics of the United Kingdom*, (HMSO, 1984).

Joby, R.S., *The Railway Builders*, (David & Charles, 1983).

Kidner, R.W., *Carriage Stock of Minor Standard Gauge Railways*, (Oakwood Press, 1978).

Light Railways (Investigation) Committee, *Report*, 1921.

Llanelli Star, 10th November, 1988, 30th November, 1995.

Llanelly & County Guardian, 20/1/1876, 14/12/1876, 29/9/1881, 5/7/1883, 11/12/1884, 21/2/1889, 6/10/1892, 29/7/1909, 11/2/1915.

Llanelly Mercury, 6/3/1893, 14/6/1894, 20/8/1903, 17/9/1903, 13/6/1935, 18/4/1947.

Locomotive, The, Vol. XV 1909, Vol. XVI, 1910.

MacDermot, E.T., *History of the Great Western Railway Vols. I, II* (GWR, 1927/31).

Maggs, Colin C., *The Weston, Clevedon & Portishead Light Railway*, (Oakwood Press, 1990).

Miller, Bob, *The Burry Port Fairlies* - Historical Model Railway Soc. *Journal* Vol. 19, 2008.

Miller, Bob & Wear, R., *George & Frederick Furniss*, The Industrial Loco Nos. 121/2 (2006).

Mining Journal, 6th July, 1872, 3rd May, 1873.

Morgan, Harold, *Historical Model Railway Society Journal* Vol. 12, April 1985.

Morris, John, *The Gwendraeth*, Signalling Record Society.

Morris, W. H., *The Port of Kidwelly*, The Carmarthenshire Antiquary Vol. XXVI, 1990.

Musgrave, G.A., *Piston & Valve Rod Gland Packing*, LNER Magazine, 1936.

National Archives, Kew, British Transport Historical Records *RAIL 89/1, 89/2, 89/3, 89/4, 89/7, 253/744, 254/244 , 282/1143-4, 282/1146-9, 282/1151-2, 282/1154, 1057/422, 1057/433,1057/435, 1057/437, 1057/451, 1057/MPR70/3, 1110/45-46, MT6/1820/1, 1834/2, 2016/3, 2109/3, 2298/5, 2370/7, 2528/12, 2429/5, 2430/3, 2436/22, 2439/13, 2538, MT 58/370.*

Nicholson, John A., *Pembrey & Burry Port: - 1 Aspects of their History, 2 A Historical Miscellany (* Llanelli Borough 1993/4); *3 Some Historical Events & Recolections, 4 Further Historical Glimpses,*(Carmarthen County Council, 1994/6).

Oliver, Henry and Airey, John, *Hand-book of all the Stations, Junctions, Sidings, Collieries, &c on the Railways in the United Kingdom*, 5th Edit. (RCH, 1877).

Parliamentary reply, WM 20th April, 1928.

Penney, Brian, *Welsh Railways Archive Vol. IV*, (May 2005).

Jenkins, W.D. Hall, *History of Burry Port*, unpublished manuscript, pre-1976.

Powell, T., *Staith to Conveyor, An Illustrated History of Coal Shipment Machinery*, p. 57 (2000).

Price, M.R.C. *The Gwendraeth Valleys Railway Kidwelly to Mynydd-y-Garreg*, (Oakwood Press, 1997).

Price, M.R.C., *The Llanelly and Mynydd Mawr Railway*, (Oakwood Press, 1992).

Reed, M.C., *The London & North Western Railway*, (Atlantic 1996).

Richards, S., *The Gwendraeth Valley Railway*, (Author, Norwich, 1977).

Scott-Morgan, John, *Railways of Arcadia*, (P.E. Waters & Assoc., 1989).

Smith, Martin, *Steam Days No. 58*, June 1994.

South Wales Daily News 15/1/1876, 12/2/1876, 8/12/1879, 5/11/1883, 22/7/1885, 14/7/1887, 12/3/1889, 10/2/1925.

South Wales Press 4th December, 1879, 21st October, 1886.

Stephens Museum, The H.F., Tenterden, Kent.

Tickets examined from the collections of T. David, the author and others.

Transactions of the Carmarthen Antiquarian Society & Field Club, Vol. 20, 1926-27

Western Mail, 6th and 12th July, 1905, 29th October, 1991, 14th March. 1996.

Wright, Ian L., *Last of the Great Western Four-Wheelers, Back Track*, Vol. 4, No. 4, July 1990.

Index

Amalgamated Society of Rly. Servants, 91
Ashburnham, Lord, 31, 39, 51, 52, 61, 71, 87, 118, 119, 123, 127, 129, 217, 336
Ashbury Rly. Carr. & Iron Co., 57, 285, 291
Avonside Engine Co., 66, 72, 207, 226, 230, 232, 238, 241, 245, 247, 249

Bevan, William, 53, 217, 336
Bischoffsheim, Henri, 71, 73, 335, 336
Bowen, David, 64
Bowen, Owen, 13, 41
Bowser, Capt. G., 119, 123, 125
Brawn, Thomas & Co., 89
Briggs, Thomas, 20, 111, 126, 337
Buckley, William J., 53, 54, 61, 71, 336
Bus sevices, motor, 311, 312, 314, 315, 317

Caine, William S., 53, 61, 336
Cancellor, Charles, 14, 27, 39, 336
Cancellor, Francis, 39, 53, 335, 336
Capital authorized, 14, 15, 37, 52, 61, 64
Carr, Robert A., 68, 69, 129, 131, 229, 230, 235, 238, 239, 337
Carway branch, 13, 17, 33, 35, 41, 44, 143, 157, 158, 192, 319
Chapman & Furneaux, 230, 235, 238, 239, 247
Coedbach, 180, 209, 319, 321, 323, 329, 331
Collins, Robert, 91
Court, Henry, 29, 39, 43, 46, 59, 64, 225, 337
Crompton & Co., 131
Cross & Co., 227
Cwm Capel branch, 11, 14, 20, 35, 40, 42, 109, 126, 141, 143, 181 et seq., 189, 213, 219, 223, 297, 313
Cwmmawr, 11, 23, 29, 30, 71, 78, 92, 93 et seq., 99, 143, 172 et seq., 211, 280, 290, 298, 319, 321, 323, 329, 331

Davies & Co., D.M., 115
Davies, Capt. W., 64, 71, 124, 131, 337
Davies, George, (ganger), 89, 153
Defries of Holborn, 118
Dring, William, 69
Druitt, Col. E, 94, 99, 103, 151, 154, 165, 173
Dunkin, Robert, 21
Dunmore, Earl of, 87, 101, 309, 336
Dynevor, Lord, 13, 31, 181

Eager, John, 68, 69, 71, 77, 79, 80, 87, 92, 94, 101, 105, 124, 131, 218, 307, 309, 310, 337, 343
Earhart, Amelia, 138, 139
Evans, Edward, 44, 47 et seq., 64, 71, 87, 123, 127, 146, 337
Evans, F. John, 87, 135, 218

Fairlie, Robert, 35, 37, 226, 227, 339
Finch & Co., Edward, 131
Furniss, Frederick, 17, 18, 20, 21, 25, 27, 29, 31, 33, 35, 225, 226

Glascodine, Richard, 16
Green & Burrows, 79
Griffiths, D., 123
Guest, Keen & Co., 77
Gwendraeth Valleys Rly, 13, 39, 69, 70, 73, 180, 190, 191, 217, 223, 229, 230, 273, 297, 309
Gwynne, William, 20

Hancock, J. George, 47, 49, 87, 92, 101, 105, 108, 123, 127, 307, 309, 337
Harries, W.R., 64, 307, 309
Henderson (ship canvasser), 87, 131, 135
Herring, George, 45, 57, 59, 61, 68, 70-1, 73, 197, 203, 217, 229, 336
Herring, William, 73, 101, 336
Holden, Howard, 16
Hudswell, Clarke & Co., 85, 88-90, 101, 103, 193, 205, 207, 213, 251, 255, 259, 261, 265, 268, 269, 271
Hughes & Co., Henry, 23, 225, 226
Hughes, Capt., 131, 337
Hurst, Nelson & Co., 303

Jenkins, Col A.E., 101, 104, 309, 336
Jennett Walker & Co., 73
Johnston & Stead, 39, 51, 52, 54, 117, 337
Johnstone, Sir Harcourt, 39, 336

Kidwelly & Burry Port Railway, 13, 14
Kidwelly (Cydweli), 37, 65, 79, 85, 86, 131, 143, 155, 177 et seq., 297, 319, 321, 329, 331

Lawson, Revd R., 15
Lear, John, 47, 64, 117
Lewis, Mansel, 16, 49
Light Railway Act, 76
Llewellyn, W.D., 15
Lloyd, David, 64, 131
Luckraft, Capt. John, 14, 16 et seq., 21, 25, 27, 46, 49, 111, 225, 337

Mackay, Roderick, 39
Malcolm, General G.A., 14, 18, 19, 27, 39, 48, 54, 55, 114, 225, 299, 336
Manning, Wardle & Co., 205, 206, 218, 221, 224, 230, 233, 238
Martin, Anne, 63
Mason & Elkington, 35, 42, 112, 131, 197, 213, 215, 216, 218, 219
Matthews, J.L., 71, 87, 92, 336
McCaul, John, 39, 53, 336
McKiernon, William, 20, 111, 137, 215, 337
Mitchell, John, 41, 46 *et seq.*, 51 *et seq.*, 63, 64, 114, 118, 224, 231, 337
Morgan, Arthur, 62, 63, 67, 68, 70, 71, 75, 77 *et seq.*, 83, 86, 87, 89, 92, 99, 101, 104, 105, 108, 124, 129, 131, 218, 224, 281, 283, 285 *et seq.*, 301, 307, 309, 335, 337
Morgan, Capt., 71, 131, 337
Morris, William, 64

Neptune Hotel, 20, 27, 111, 126, 131, 146, 147

Ommanney, Charles, 53, 54, 59, 336, 337
Ommanney, Francis, 39, 51, 54, 59, 336, 337
Onslow, Col Douglas, 20, 203, 222
Owen, Charles H., 64, 104, 138, 307, 309

Pearne, Fanny, 46, 47
Pearson & Co., 92
Peat, W. Barclay, 39, 54, 87
Peckett & Sons, 53, 204, 205, 207, 218, 229, 231 *et seq.*
Peel, Hon. Sidney, 73, 75, 76, 101, 105, 309, 335, 336
Pemberton, Christopher, 14, 27, 29, 31, 39, 335, 336
Pemberton, Francis, 39, 335, 336
Petre, R.B., 69, 108
Pilkington, Sir Thomas., 61, 71, 73, 75, 92, 197, 203, 283, 309, 335-6
Ponthenry (-henri), 11, 23, 86, 164, 165, 321
Pontyates, 86, 159 *et seq.*, 296, 298, 317, 321
Pontyberem, 27, 86, 92, 94, 143, 166 *et seq.*, 296, 317, 321, 329
Populations, 9, 113, 219, 317
Pwll (Pool), 11, 14, 16, 35, 41, 50, 64, 109, 111, 143, 183 *et seq.*, 189, 215, 216, 219, 296, 313, 319

Railway Signal Co., 78, 85, 95
Reading Room & Club, 127, 131, 147

Rees, David, 131, 337
Reynolds, Lewis, 42
Robinson, Henry, 14, 15, 18, 23, 25, 27, 71, 225
Roderick, Capt. Thomas, 20, 27
Rothwell & Co., 78, 85
Russell, Edward, 53, 63, 337
Russell, John, 14 *et seq.*, 20, 21, 41, 44 *et seq.*, 51 *et seq.*, 63, 70, 114, 117, 118, 123, 127, 129, 231, 335, 336

Sandy branch, *see Pwll (Pool)*
Seal of the BP&GVR, 1, 78, 83
Sefton Praed & Co., 87
Shelford, Sir William, 14, 27
Smith & Sons of Derby, 92
Smith, H.J., 105
South Wales Rly (GWR), 9, 58, 111, 112
Stephens, H.F., 76 *et seq.*, 83, 85, 92 *et seq.*, 255, 281, 283
Stepney, Col., 20, 31
Stilwell, W.J., 54, 69
Sutton, George, 14, 19, 29, 39, 54, 59, 336, 337
Sutton, Wadham L., 14, 18, 39, 336

Taylor, Raymond, 87
Taylor, Seaton, 59, 63, 71, 73, 76, 77, 101, 103, 105, 108, 129, 335, 336
Taylor, William, 14, 39
Thomas, A.G., 51
Thomas, Revd D.P., 27, 30, 45, 193
Thompson, Astley (& Wise), 20, 29, 31, 43, 54, 113, 127, 158, 193, 195, 203, 215, 222
Trimsaran branch, 33, 35, 143, 176, 177, 189, 205, 223
Tub-boats (canal), 10, 11, 19
Tyer & Co., 77, 78, 83 *et seq.*, 99

Vaughan, John, 14

Waddell, John & Sons, 49, 51, 188, 189
Waddle, John Robert, 21
Waterlow & Sons, 97
Watney, D., 23, 193, 195, 203
Welsh speakers, 9, 119
Wenham, Walter J., 105, 108, 307, 336
Willcocks, Fred, 64, 67, 127, 129, 229, 337
Williams, A.D., 20, 21, 29
Williams, Thomas, 87, 307
Williamson & Co., 79, 95, 97

Yorke, Col. H.A., 70